Interfaces in economic and social analysis

Interfaces in economic and social analysis

Edited by Ulf Himmelstrand

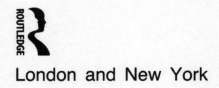

London and New York

First published 1992
by Routledge
11 New Fetter Lane, London EC4P 4EE

Simultaneously published in the USA and Canada
by Routledge
a division of Routledge, Chapman and Hall, Inc.
29 West 35th Street, New York, NY 10001

© 1992 Ulf Himmelstrand

British Library Cataloguing in Publication Data
Interfaces in economic and social analysis.
 I. Himmelstrand, Ulf
 306.3
 ISBN 0-415-06872-X

Library of Congress Cataloging in Publication Data
Interfaces in economic and social analysis / edited by Ulf Himmelstrand.
 p. cm.
 Includes bibliographical references and index.
 ISBN 0-415-06872-X
 1. Economics-Methodology. 2. Social sciences-Methodology.
I. Himmelstrand, Ulf.
HB131.I57 1992
300'.72-dc20
91-20580
CIP

Typeset in Palatino by
Input Typesetting Ltd, London
Printed and bound in Great Britain by
Mackays of Chatham PLC, Chatham, Kent

To Clemens Heller

Contents

Contributors

Britt-Mari Blegvad was educated in law and sociology at the universities of Copenhagen and Uppsala. In 1965 she obtained the degree of jur.lic. (Ph.D.) at the latter institution. Since then she has taught at the economic faculty of the Copenhagen Business School where she now holds the position of Docent (Reader). Her research has been in criminology, organizational theory and legal sociology. She has been particularly interested in interdisciplinary studies and has contributed to and edited a number of collective works, including *Virksomheden mellem økonomi og jura – om retsøkonomi og styring* (*The Firm between Economics and Law – On Law and Economics and Government*) Samfundslitteratur, Copenhagen 1987 (edited together with Finn Collin). From 1974 to 1990 she served as chairman of the board of the *Institute of Sociology of Law for Europe*.

Samuel Bowles is Professor of Economics at the University of Massachusetts at Amherst, and works at the Center for Popular Economics. He has been engaged in research on economic and political theory, and in an econometric study of the accumulation process in the post second world war era. Among publications beyond those mentioned in the references to his chapter in this book could be mentioned *Beyond the Wasteland: A Democratic Alternative to Economic Decline* (1983) (with T. Weisskopf and D. Gordon), and numerous journal articles in journals of economics.

Finn Collin is a Lecturer in Philosophy at the University of Copenhagen and life member of Clare Hall, Cambridge. He holds a D.Phil. in philosophy from the University of Copenhagen and a Ph.D. in philosophy from the University of California at Berkeley. He has published on the philosophy of the social sciences and the philosophy of language, including *Theory and Understanding. A Critique of Interpretive Science*, Basil Blackwell, 1985.

Keith Hartley is Director of the Institute for Research in the Social Sciences and the Centre of Defence Economics, University of York. He is engaged in research on defence policy, public choice and industrial organization. He is co-editor of *Defence Economics* and recent publications include *The Economics of Defence Policy*, Brasseys, 1991 and (with N. Hooper) *The Economics of Defence, Disarmament and Peace*: an annotated bibliography, Elgar, 1990.

Ulf Himmelstrand: Professor Emeritus of Sociology at the University of Uppsala, Sweden, and Visiting Professor of Sociology, University of Nairobi, Kenya. He has been a President of the International Sociological Association, and a Vice-President of the International Social Science Council, Paris; and in the latter capacity he launched the so-called IDEA Project which resulted in this book. He has published numerous articles in political sociology, sociological theory, mass communications and the sociology of development. A book in Swedish about the background to the Nigeria-Biafra civil war was published 1969. Recent books are *Beyond Welfare Capitalism* (1981) (with G. Ahrne and L. Lundberg), and *Sweden – Social Structure and Everyday Life* (1988), in Swedish, of which he was an editor and co-author.

Geoffrey Hodgson is Professor of Economics and Government, Newcastle-upon Tyne Polytechnic. He has published extensively in journals such as the *Cambridge Journal of Economics*, *New Left Review*, the *Journal of Post Keynesian Economics*, and the *Review of Radical Political Economics*. Among his books are *Capitalism, Value and Exploitation* (1982), *The Democratic Economy* (1984), and *Economics and Institutions* (1989). He is the General Secretary of EAEPE, The European Association of Evolutionary Political Economy.

Samuel Hollander is University Professor and Professor of Economics at the University of Toronto, Canada. He has published *The Sources of Increased Efficiency* (1965), *The Economics of Adam Smith* (1973), *The Economics of David Ricardo* (1979), *The Economics of John Stuart Mill* (1985) and *Classical Economics* (1987) as well as articles in the *Economic Journal*, *American Economic Review* and *Oxford Economic Papers*.

Arjo Klamer is currently Associate Professor of Economics at George Washington University. He is the author of *Conversations with Economists* (1983, published in England under the title *New Classical Macro-economics*), co-editor (with Donald McCloskey and Robert Solow) of *The Consequences of Economic Rhetoric* (1989), and co-author (with David Colander) of *The Making of an Economist* (1990).

Don Lamberton is Deputy Director, CIRCIT (Centre for International Research on Communication and Information Technologies), Melbourne, Australia and formerly Professor of Economics, University of Queensland and Case Western Reserve University. He is author of *The Theory of Profit* (Blackwell); editor of *Economics of Information and Knowledge*

(Penguin) and *The Information Revolution* (The Annals of the American Academy of Political and Social Science); and co-editor of *Communication Economics and Development* (Praeger), *The Trouble with Technology* (Frances Pinter), and *The Cost of Thinking* (Ablex).

Alan Lewis is Director of the Bath University Centre for Economic Psychology, UK. His main publications include *The Psychology of Taxation* (1982), and, with Adrian Furnham, *The Economic Mind* (1986). He has published numerous articles on economic psychology which have appeared in such journals as *Kyklos, Human Relations, Journal of Economic Psychology, Public Finance*, and *Journal of Behavioural Economics*. His current research interests are in ethical investing and savings behaviour.

Leon Lindberg is Professor of Political Science at the University of Wisconsin, Madison, USA. He has published extensively on problems of government economic policy, the limitations of markets, the production and selection of economic knowledge, and economists as policy intellectuals – for instance *The Politics of Inflation and Economic Stagnation*, edited with Charles S. Maier (1985), and *Governance of the American Economy*, co-author and co-editor (1991).

Ernest Mandel is Professor in the Faculty of Economic, Social and Political Science of the Vrije Universiteit, Brussels, Belgium, and Director of the Centre for Political Studies there. His major works are: *Marxist Economic Theory* (1962), *Formation of the Economic Thought of Karl Marx* (1967), *Late Capitalism* (1972), *The Second Slump* (1976, 1985 3rd revised edition), and *Long Waves of Capitalist Development* (1980), *Beyond Perestroika* (1989, 1991 2nd revised edition), and *Power and Money, the Marxist Theory of Bureaucracy* (1991).

Alberto Martinelli is Professor of Sociology and Political Science at the University of Milan, Italy, and Dean of the Faculty of Political Science there. He has published *Università e società negli Stati Uniti* (1978), several articles in the field of economic sociology, and edited collections of articles on this topic, for instance *The New International Economy*, with H. Makler and N. Smelser (1982), and *Economy and Society*, with N. Smelser (1990), and *International Markets and Global Firms* (1991).

Samuel Preston is Professor at the Department of Sociology, and the Population Studies Center, University of Pennsylvania, USA. His main publications are in the field of social and historical demography. Apart from numerous journal articles he published *Mortality Patterns in National Populations* (1976).

Neil Smelser is Professor of Sociology at University of California, Berkeley. Among his numerous publications are *Economy and Society*, with Talcott Parsons (1956), *Social Change in the Industrial Revolution* (1959), and *The Sociology of Economic Life* (1962, 1974). He has published several editions of widely used textbooks in Sociology. He edited and co-authored *Handbook of Sociology* (1988). He has served as Vice President of the American Sociological Association, and is a Fellow of the American Academy of Arts and Sciences, and presently a Vice-President of the International Sociological Association.

Lars Udéhn is a Research Associate at the Department of Sociology, University of Uppsala, Sweden. He is the author of *Methodological Individualism. A Critical Appraisal* (1987), and of articles regarding the possibilities of economic planning, on methodological aspects of Weber's rationalization thesis, and on sociological theory and social practice. He is currently working on a book with the tentative title *Economic Imperialism and the Province of Sociology. A Critique of Economic Reason.*

Preface

THE IMPORTANCE OF SOCIO-ECONOMICS

The question of how best to combine the perspectives, insights and findings of economics with those of other social sciences is of far greater import than one may at first perceive. A casual observer might feel that all that is at issue in this effort at synthesis is some intra-social science arrangement of a highly academic or theoretical nature. However, there is much more to it than that.

This is not to deny that an intra-social science arrangement is a key component of the subject matter before us. There is a serious difference of opinion among social scientists with regard to how best to study economic behaviour and the more general area of choice behaviour.

Some economists believe that the best way to go about this is to use the neoclassical paradigm to study all choices. Thus, Gay Becker studies prejudice, addiction and marriage in these terms. And there are some sociologists and anthropologists who take the opposite extreme viewpoint, that all choices are to be studied strictly in terms of culture, values and institutions.

Between these two poles are those who try to expand the reach of the neoclassical paradigm by adding ideas, concepts and theorems from other social sciences, using terms such as dissonance (in the work of George Akerlof) and affect (in the work of Robert Frank). And finally there are those who see a new paradigm that stresses values, power and institutions while placing market forces and rational conduct as a sub-system within that paradigm. (This is a position championed by many members of the Society for the Advancement of Socio-Economics, including myself).

Most of the papers in this volume, illuminate the subject matter from these various perspectives. But before one can form a judgment as to which approach to adopt, one must determine the evaluation criteria of the respective approaches. One would rank the merit of the various approaches quite differently according to how much merit one puts, for example, into mathematization *per se* (much higher in the neoclassical approach than for any of the others, although they are not without mathematization potential) as opposed to the capacity to predict, to explain, and moral appropriateness. While the various approaches are frequently ranked informally, there has not yet been, to the best of my knowledge, a systematic comparative evaluation, using all relevant criteria.

Through all of this, one should not lose sight of the great import of the larger issue at hand – it reaches well beyond any intra-social science arrangements or squabbles. For it is an indisputable fact that social science perspectives deeply affect how public policy makers form and implement policies and, indeed, the way society views itself.

The neoclassical paradigm, for example, sustains those who view society and historical processes as a rational unfolding of human choices and designs. The other paradigms, however, make far greater allowance for values, affect, unanticipated consequences, and institutions that reflect past commitments and powers and cannot readily be redone. The neoclassical approach is highly optimistic, the others much less so; which is more realistic and which leads either to naïve squandering of resources or to undue passivity, I leave to each reader to sort out.

In addition to framing and colouring general perspectives and acting as mirrors which societies use to view and analyse themselves, the various social science paradigms deeply affect actual choices and conduct. Theories in our minds make a difference. Thus, in the United States these days, under the influence of the neoclassical paradigm and libertarian and *laissez-faire* conservative ideologies that accompany it, the government is trying to use cash incentives to affect anti-social behaviour. For example, welfare payments to families are cut if one of the children truants; and it is suggested that one should pay teenage females if they refrain from becoming pregnant while unmarried or at least while in high school. Furthermore, many states are experimenting with a 'choice' programme that urges public schools to compete with one another, as corporations do in the market-place.

However, advocates of the other, non-neoclassical, paradigms argue that without attention to impulses and values internalized and enforced by the various sub-cultures whose members are the targets of these policies, the role and impact of incentives are likely to be limited. Moreover they argue that even in 'normal' work-place behaviour, we are finding that non-economic rewards and relations play a key role.

The final evidence on these matters is not in. And, as I suggested above, the criteria for evaluation are not agreed upon. One thing, however, is clear beyond any reasonable doubt: the questions at hand matter a great deal not only for the betterment of social sciences but also for improvements in public policies and – through them and through social philosophies – for the way societies view and treat themselves.

The essays before us extensively explore these matters from the viewpoint of a variety of the paradigms and to the careful exclusion of others, as such volumes often do. The essays within also go a long way to satisfy our need for programmatic platforms and pronouncements as to what needs to be done; in other words, how we ought to proceed. We must then make our way to the next crucial step – to follow these or other recipes and attend to the actual cooking and nourishing of social sciences and society.

Amitai Etzioni
(Author of *The Moral Dimension: Toward a New Economics*)

Acknowledgements

There are projects which take off to full realization whatever the attendant circumstances. A philosopher who conceives a problem, and its possible solution, is likely to pursue the matter until he has solved the problem. Other projects remain in the head of a scientist without ever getting realized – unless favourable circumstances emerge, or are created after considerable efforts. This is particularly true, I think, of hybrid, interdisciplinary projects which require the co-operation of scholars from many different fields of study. This book is the result of such a project. This project, the IDEA Project (Interdisciplinary Dimensions of Economic Analysis), is the child of some very fortunate and, at the time quite unexpected, lucky circumstances.

The problem itself, and the so-called 'method of dissection' (see chapter 1 in this book) with which the problem might be approached, were planted in my head in a conversation with Professor Ojetunji Aboyade, an economist at the University of Ibadan, Nigeria, in the mid-sixties. It remained there in my head until the early '80s when I happened to become a vice-president of the *International Social Science Council* (ISSC) in Paris, a truly multi-disciplinary body of social scientists. This may have been a necessary condition for the actual launching of the project, but it was not a sufficient condition. The man who made the project possible was Clemens Heller, the Director of *Maison des Sciences de l'Homme*, in Paris.

My dear friend Elina Almasy at MSH introduced me to Clemens Heller, busy and overburdened with responsibilities as usual, a day after I had been made a vice-president of ISSC. Clemens Heller was teasing me jokingly, as I recall, for having joined the jet-set of social scientists meeting at ISSC. Could there possibly be any use in the social sciences coming together at the ISSC from time to time? This provocation could not remain unanswered. I assured Clemens that I would do my best to launch some multi-disciplinary project within the framework of the ISSC which, after all, had a network of social-science scholars all over the world. Quite frankly, I did not at that very moment have any notion of what kind of multi-disciplinary project we might pursue. . . . But suddenly I recalled that old, and nearly forgotten idea of the IDEA project from my conversation with Tunji Aboyade fifteen years earlier. I described the idea, the methods and the strategy of the project to Clemens Heller. Clemens immediately responded by inviting me to submit a project proposal to him in the near future. He would then provide office space, and financial support at the MSH for a month so that I could meet with a number of interested social scientists there, to build a launching pad for the realization of the project. The immediacy and generosity of this offer were impelling. Without this offer I am pretty sure that the IDEA Project, and this book would have remained unrealized ideas, and successively forgotten in the mind of the present writer.

Once the IDEA Project had been initiated with the support of Clemens Heller and the MSH, and the backing of the ISSC, I must acknowledge the intellectual support of many scholars, and the further financial aid from ISSC through its President Candido Mendes de Almeida, from UNESCO, and most substantially from the Bank of Sweden Tercentenary Foundation. At the first meeting of the IDEA Project at MSH, in March 1982, I wish to mention in particular Professor Jerzy Kostrowicki who was then another vice-president of the ISSC, Professor David Apter, Professor Chavdar Kiuranov, Professor Christian Schmidt, Professor Dudley Seers, and Professor Victor Urquidi. In later meetings at MSH where most of the co-authors in this book participated there were a few who are not co-authors but contributed most significantly to our discussions – Professors Cyril Belshaw, F. Gregory Hayden, and Michael Intriligator to whom I wish to express particular gratitude. Mrs Elina Almasy was of considerable help in arranging several of these meetings, and in publishing the first versions of several of the chapters in this book in her journal *Social Science Information*. A special word of thanks should also go to Professor Ragnar Bentzel who was an excellent chairman at one of our last meetings, and to Ali Kazancigil, UNESCO, who published several policy-oriented papers originating in our project, but falling outside the framework of this book, in a special issue of the *International Social Science Journal* (August 1987, no. 113).

Luis Ramallo, Secretary General of the ISSC, helped me a lot to establish contacts with interested economists at a World Congress of Economists in Madrid in the early 1980s. I am particularly grateful for the advice I received from Professor Amartya Sen at that congress.

A project like this requires excellent and committed assistants. At a time when my work-load was particularly forbidding, an 'angel' (in the sense of T. S. Eliot) appeared on the scene, Dr Richard Swedberg, who helped me immensely in solving some of the most time-consuming intellectual and administrative problems of the project. Mrs Lola Billås was a Project Secretary, and helped to keep track of our world-wide correspondence, our accounts, travel arrangements, and minutes from our meetings. Both of them deserve praise and gratitude in great measure.

A word of thanks must go to the co-authors of our book for their cooperation in allowing further editing, and in some cases shortening of their chapters, and particularly to the few authors who joined us rather late without having taken part in our MSH meetings. As an editor of this book I had to look for new co-authors in a few cases when the chapters intended were not delivered, or had to be rejected, not because of a lack of excellence in most cases, but simply because they did not quite fit into the overall framework of the book. These time-consuming efforts at late recruitment of new co-authors did of course considerably delay the conclusion of our project.

In particular I wish to thank one of our co-authors, Neil Smelser, for his encouragement, and his advice at some critical passages in making this book ready for publication.

The copy-editors at Routledge, finally, did a marvellous work in helping me to find and fill lacunae in the references of most chapters, and in improving the language of our authors.

Ulf Himmelstrand
Nairobi

Part I

Exogenous factors in economic theory

Chapter 1

Project IDEA

An introduction

Ulf Himmelstrand

ORIGIN AND SCOPE OF THE PROJECT

Those who emphasize the need for an interdisciplinary approach in the social sciences today often derive their concern from the fact that the 'real world', unlike the social sciences, is not divided into disciplines. Therefore, it is said, no realistic analysis of any social, economic, cultural or political processes, and no reasonably reliable predictions of future events in this domain, can be achieved without taking into account the factors which are exogenous to whatever social science discipline is being pursued or applied otherwise. Only if an assumed set of exogenous factors are uncorrelated with what is going on in a given domain, can they be disregarded. But this would be rather rare in contemporary societies with their high degree of interdependence between the parts of the whole.

Unfortunately those who expound the need for interdisciplinarity often fall prey to holistic mysticism which, however, on closer inspection, often turns out to be no more than a blown-up and overgeneralized version of tenets derived from some more specific discipline. 'Disciplinary imperialism' in the form of 'economic imperialism' (Tullock 1972; Stigler 1984) is one instance of this tendency, as indicated by the vast expansion of economics, under the name of public choice theory, into territory previously occupied exclusively by political scientists, sociologists, anthropologists and legal scientists.

For reasons which have been explained by Lars Udéhn in his chapter on the limits of economic imperialism we have found this 'imperialistic' solution to the quest for interdisciplinarity quite unsatisfactory. But how could interdisciplinarity be attained, then, without the formalistic imperialism of some highly-advanced discipline like economics? One answer to this question is provided by the institutionalist school of economics. The holistic approach suggested by this school of thought implies that the boundaries of analysis should be defined, not by whatever predetermined set of concepts that are available in given formalized models of economic processes, but should be 'designed to encompass the analysis necessary to understand the problem' (Hayden 1985: 874f). The 'partitioning tools' to be used to decide the boundaries of the 'whole' to be analysed therefore must be applied by making an initial inventory of all the relevant components that seem necessary to include in order to understand a given problem. Different arrays of components may be necessary for the understanding of different problems. This approach would seem highly adequate for the kind of policy-relevant analysis and implementation which has attracted the attention of many institutionalist economists.

However, the *ad hoc* character of this approach would seem to make it difficult to arrive at a more generalized and precise theoretical solution to the problem of interdisciplinary analysis of the economy, and therefore it is unlikely to enhance a fruitful dialogue with scholars who are committed to a less amorphous and more universalistic and stringent theory-building.[1] Since such a dialogue has been one of the main strategies of the present project, the question remains how a broadly interdisciplinary or at least multidisciplinary analysis of the economy can be achieved without relying either on the formalistic imperialism of neo-classical public choice theory, or on the pragmatic *ad hoc* approach of Veblen-type institutionalist economics.

This kind of question regarding interdisciplinarity – at least among the social sciences – attracted a great deal of attention in the Programme Committee of the *International Social Science Council* (ISSC) at its meetings in 1983–4. It was decided to use the international crossdisciplinary network existing within the ISSC to launch a fresh and more systematic attack on this problem. Two alternative but not mutually exclusive approaches were contemplated by myself and Professor Jerzy Kostrowicki when we were co-chairmen of the ISSC Program Committee.

One approach would be to select a topical area of common concern to many social sciences – for instance, urbanization and urban problems – and then to organize a multipronged multidisciplinary attack on these problems. The collected essays of such a multidisciplinary study would then be examined for common and contrasting elements which could be used as a foundation for a more interdisciplinary approach.

For several reasons, both personal and methodological, a theoretical rather than topical approach was chosen. I, for one, felt that the two approaches should be combined, but that a more theoretical and methodological approach should be launched first in order to build conceptual bridgeheads between disciplines and to establish 'conversational' habits of addressing each other across disciplinary boundaries before a joint attack was made on concrete topics of common concern. We assumed that the building of such conceptual bridgeheads could start most successfully on the territory of a discipline which already was rather advanced in terms of formal-theoretical and conceptual development.

We selected economics as our first 'bridgehead' because it is the most highly developed of the social sciences, in terms of formal theory, and consequently very well suited for a concerted interdisciplinary effort of the kind we had in mind. However, as Richard Swedberg (1985: 916) has remarked in a very thoughtful commentary to our project, we are running the risk of becoming too 'economistic' even in our attempts at being interdisciplinary by allowing economists to provide the first and quite dominant 'bridgehead' for contacts with other disciplines which have contributed to the understanding of the economy. This is a calculated risk, however; and awareness of that risk, hopefully, may have helped us to avoid becoming too 'economistic'. To my mind there were several reasons for taking this risk in launching our project.

It is a fact – for good or bad – that economics, and more precisely the various brands of neo-classical economic theory and its close relatives, occupy a virtually hegemonic position in the analysis of economic processes and events, not only at some of the most influential western universities, but also in advisory bodies in various fields of economic policy. It has proved rather futile to try opening up this hegemonic set of doctrines to a dialogue with other social sciences by aggressively criticizing its hegemony from outside. In drawing up the strategy of this project I favoured a less aggressive approach by looking for potential but less commonly used openings within 'endogenous' economic theory itself – openings prompting economists to open their windows to the outside world, and allowing non-economic social scientists to penetrate deep into economic territory through these openings in order to find out how non-economic factors may have an impact on the economy in terms potentially acceptable and understandable by economists themselves. As Donald McCloskey (1986: 179 ff) has suggested in his provocative and penetrating study of the 'rhetoric of economics', such rhetoric does have some advantages. Certainly it can antagonize proponents of other social science disciplines; but the rhetoric of economics can also improve relations with other disciplines, under certain conditions. Our project was launched several years before McCloskey's book was published, but intuitively I felt that it was important for the success of our project to take off from the most well-developed and established social-science language or 'rhetoric' existing – the language of neo-classical economic theory – both in order to get economists involved in the project, and to make non-economists understand the more or less hidden challenges, potentials and limitations of economic theory.

More recently, Mattei Dogan and Robert Pahre (1990: 222) have criticized the kind of 'interdisciplinarity' which attempts to tackle 'gigantic topics by throwing every causal factor they can think of into the heap', without a sound basis in specialized, well-established disciplines. I share this kind of criticism; and therefore economics as a highly-specialized discipline would seem to provide an excellent launching pad in a search for a fruitful hybrid social science. However, unlike Dogan and Pahre, I do not consider 'interdisciplinarity' as a word which is 'virtually devoid of meaning', and which therefore should be 'banished' (ibid.: 65). Hopefully this will become more obvious toward the end of this book. But let us now return to the beginning of our project.

For our project to succeed, two conditions had to be fulfilled. First, the work had to grow out of a truly collaborative effort between economists and scholars from the other social sciences, and second, certain theoretical guidelines for the debate had to be established to make the contributions truly compatible. A concrete topic had to be chosen, and it was decided that the focus should be on the notion of 'exogenous factors' in economic theory. It was felt that being an accepted and potentially interdisciplinary concept, whose promising possibilities have remained uncharted, it would provide a fine starting-point for the effort to create a theoretical bridge between economic theory and the other social sciences.

The Macmillan Dictionary of Modern Economics (Pearce 1983: 144) defines 'exogenous variable' in the following manner:

> A variable whose value is not determined within an economic model, but which plays a role in the determination of endogenous variables. Thus an exogenous variable is an explanatory variable (i.e. appears on the right hand side of an equation), but never appears as a dependent variable in the model.

This sense of 'exogenous variable' should be distinguished from those factors which are external to a particular analysis by virtue of the fact that they have no empirical or conceivable theoretical bearings at all on the endogenous variables of that analysis. In the following we do not use the term 'exogenous' in that sense of an 'external' and irrelevant variable. However, the standard dictionary definition of 'exogenous variable' quoted above also neglects outside variables which affect the magnitude and sign of shift and slope parameters on the right side of an econometric equation; but such exogenous variables are extremely significant in pursuing our analysis of exogenous effects on economic processes. The dictionary definition quoted above also excludes so-called externalities, that is, external effects such as air-pollution which are caused by economic activities, but which are not usually priced on a market. However, these will be included in our attempt at formulating an interdisciplinary approach to economics.

The name chosen for the project was IDEA, the acronym for 'Interdisciplinary Dimensions of Economic Analysis'. In order to secure an effective collaboration between economists and representatives from the other social sciences, it was decided to execute the project in four phases. First, the economists should be asked to write papers outlining in detail how the concept of exogenous factors has been used in different schools of economic thought. Second, in brief review papers, scholars from the other social sciences should analyse and comment upon the economists' contributions from the vantage-point of their own disciplines. Much of what is considered exogenous in, say, neo-classical economic theory, is endogenous in other social science disciplines. Third, the original papers by the economists and the working papers by the non-economists should be used as a basis for a theoretical attempt at integrating the various contributions, or at least to lay the foundations for an integrating social science methodology. And lastly, a series of concrete case studies should be commissioned, applying the methodology developed in the project to concrete topics of common concern. A collective volume including these various contributions would then be one outcome of Project IDEA.

The present volume is one outcome of the IDEA Project and covers contributions from the first three phases of the project. The concrete case studies commissioned for the fourth and final stage of the project have been published separately in a special issue of *International Social Science Journal*, no. 113, 1987. They cover a broad spectrum of economic events: inflation and distributional struggles (Burns, de Ville and Flam); the economics of famine (Desai); consequences of technical change for employment and work (Gershuny); workers' self-management (Himmelstrand and Horvat); problems of so-called market socialism (Köbli); management in a planned economy (Petrakov); and the origin of the debt crisis (Swedberg).

THE THEORETICAL GUIDELINES OF THE 'IDEA' PROJECT

Two complementary attitudes characterize Project IDEA's theoretical framework. First, there is the need for theoretical stringency in carrying out the task. The 'fuzziness' which often characterizes attempts at interdisciplinarity should be avoided by delineating a systematic method of analysis which *could* be used by all participants. As a theoretical basis for the project a method of 'successive dissection' was formulated. Second, it was realized that the project would also be of an exploratory character. This meant that our attitude to the more holistic versions of economic theory (Marxism, institutionalism and Latin American structuralism) should be characterized by open-mindedness and flexibility in spite of the fact that the distinction between exogenous and endogenous factors is most adequate for the neo-classical, marginalist school of economics (see, for instance, the chapters by Ernest Mandel and Samuel Bowles on classical Marxist and post-Marxist analysis in this book). This open-mindedness also implied a realization of the fact that the method of dissection itself probably would undergo certain modifications during the research process, and that it might turn out to be unpalatable to some non-economic social scientists participating in the project. This has proved to be true; but the 'method of dissection' is still presented in this introductory chapter as one of the seven methods one might pursue in attempting to arrive at a more interdisciplinary method, and theoretical framework.

THE METHOD OF SUCCESSIVE DISSECTION

I have called this approach the method of successive dissection because it is built on the premise that several successive steps have to be taken in order for the analysis to be satisfactory. This is true both from a practical and a theoretical point of view. It proved to be most practical to organize our work in four different steps, as indicated earlier. From a more theoretical perspective, the method is 'successive' in that it first locates the exogenous factors of economics and then gradually explores different ways of building these into the original economic theory. I am using the expression of 'building' the exogenous factors into economic theory rather than the expression 'endogenizing' exogenous factors for a very important reason. What the IDEA Project has been aiming at is not the endogenization of exogenous factors in formalist economic models. Quite the contrary. To endogenize an exogenous variable – for instance, the behaviour of politicians and of legislative and administrative bodies – implies that such exogenous variables are made subject to explanations in terms of economic theory, as indeed is the case in public choice theory (compare Keith Hartley's chapter in this book). Rather our first aim is to identify economically relevant exogenous variables, and to find ways of 'building' or 'plugging' them into economic theory without sacrificing the substance and form of non-economic theories which cover the exogenous domain.

The 'dissection' part of the method starts from the realization that the economy is not a closed system. In order to find out what kind of inputs other disciplines can contribute to the analysis of economic processes, and what kind of outputs of economics can be made useful in these other disciplines, one must first try to locate the openings of the economy seen as a system. It is as if you were dissecting and following the vessels and nerves in an anatomically unknown body to find out where they are leading.

The simplest, or at least the most manageable, way in which we can conceive a system is to represent it as a system of equations. Economic 'laws' are frequently formulated in the form of equations. Such equations can take many forms, for example, differential equations at various levels, equations including stochastic processes or ordinary functional equations. It turns out that already a close look at a simple linear functional equation can help us to identify at least the main types of links between economic and other social science disciplines, in very abstract terms, of course:

$$y = a + b \cdot x$$

Conditions and processes covered by other disciplines can be seen as plug-

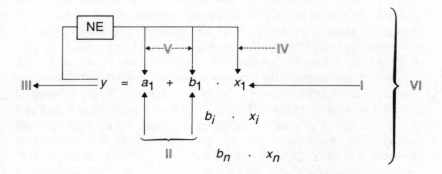

Figure 1.1 Various types of 'plug-ins' in economic processes

ins and spill-overs and mediated feedbacks in relationship to the ordinary functional equation of economics, such as equation (1). These relationships have been represented in Figure 1.1 in the form of numbered arrows which indicate two types of plug-ins (I and II), one main type of spill-over (III), and two types of feedbacks mediated through non-economic processes (IV and V). In addition we have indicated the existence of more profound exogenous structural impacts (VI).

Let us now examine Figure 1.1 in more detail.

  I Social processes, psychological processes, political decisions, geographical openings or constraints, legal rules, and so on, may influence the magnitude or possible range of independent variables, and in that sense plug into the economic system. Since these processes and conditions are exogenous, let us call this type of relationship between economic and other social science disciplines *exogenous independent variable plug-in*. From the examples mentioned above, it is obvious that these plug-ins may originate from several different disciplines: sociology, psychology, political science, and law, for instance.

 II Similarly, various conditions and processes specified and explained in different disciplines may plug into economic systems by influencing the magnitude and sign of parameters in equations of type (1). Parameters are usually seen as constants, but over time, and as results or precursors of changes in the overall system, parameters and not only variables may change. The kind of relationship between economics and other disciplines envisaged in this case could be called *exogenous parameter plug-in*. Price elasticities, for instance, while usually being considered as constants, may change as a result of changes in the socio-cultural definition of relevant commodities.

III On the side of dependent variables in economic equations we may discern more or less direct or indirect psychological, social, political or legal, and even geographic or environmental effects of economic changes. If there is no feedback on the economy we simply speak of *spill-overs*. So-called 'externalities' may be considered a kind of spill-over, as long as they do not entail any financial costs or do not furnish inputs without costs to the economy in a strict financial sense.

IV Feedbacks are quite common in economic systems. Many of them – so-called multiplying effects, forward and backward linkages, and certain processes of growth including the growth of oligopolistic and monopolistic structures – can be accounted for purely in terms of economic variables. Other feedback loops are mediated through non-economic processes (NE) which can be accounted for only within other disciplines than economics. Here we will consider only the *NE-mediated feedbacks*. However, purely economic feedbacks may also become interesting in the present context if the *parameters* which characterize such feedback processes are affected by non-economic processes or conditions. But the focus will then be on parameter plug-ins.

As indicated in Figure 1.1 there are several types of feedback. Type IV is a feedback affecting the 'independent' variable input. In contrast to type I – exogenous variable plug-in – we are here dealing with NE-mediated variable feedback. Feedbacks are by definition endogenous, but can be mediated exogenously.

V It is also conceivable that NE-mediated feedbacks affect the parameters of our equation(s). For this we suggest the label *NE-mediated parameter feedback*.

VI Wherever a dependent variable is affected by a number of independent variables, it may be necessary to introduce a clause of *ceteris paribus*, when studying the effects of one particular independent variable, endogenous or exogenous. However, even though such a clause is easy to apply in numerical experiments or in laboratory experimentation, it may be quite difficult to apply it in a real-life situation. As a result of the given social structure and other non-economic conditions, certain combinations of economic variables may be virtually ruled out in reality. The given social structure may similarly force certain combinations of economic variables to occur as more or less permanent fixtures, whereas such combinations in idealized models of rational economic behaviour would occur only as transient disturbances of equilibrium. Market imperfections in market economies or administrative imperfections in planned economies may be due to such exogenous structural impacts. Structural contradictions such as those described by Marxist analysts could quite possibly be subsumed under the same label.

As Gudmund Hernes (1976), a Norwegian sociologist, has shown, it is possible to characterize social structures and various types of structural change or constancy by looking at profiles or change or constancy in those equations, parameters, and variables which characterize a given system. For instance, if all the equations (processes) needed to describe a system, and the parameters of these equations remain unchanged over time whereas the output (the dependent variables) exhibits incremental change, then we can speak of an extended reproduction of the social system thus described. If the parameters change as well, then we have a transition, and if both output and parameters and processes change, then the system is involved in a transformation. For instance, if a process of industrialization is introduced in a less developed rural society at the same time as parameters of wage determination are changing, and output increases, this is a case of transformation. It might be possible to make use of this typology of structural change and impact as a method of assessing some of the structural qualities and attributes of societal wholes which must be brought into the picture in the last stage of our exercise in successive dissections.

The description given above constitutes the original version of the method of successive dissection. At a workshop held in Paris at Maison des Sciences de l'Homme in 1984, however, it became obvious that the exogenous/endogenous process analysis must be combined with an analysis at the actor level (see Udéhn 1986).

THE SIGNIFICANCE OF ACTORS

In economic analysis we often find that the actors involved somehow disappear as a result of the fact that they are treated only as 'bearers' of the variables or processes involved (wage demands and profit-making, for instance). Wage-earners are the kind of actors who make wage demands and shareholders are profit-making; but these actors can be excluded in economic analysis and represented by variables such as wages and profits which then are entered into a system of co-ordinates with curves representing the relationship between these variables.

But in the real world the relationship involving wage-earners on the one side and shareholders and company management on the other is a game situation where psychological factors of trust and distrust have a great impact; and these psychological factors certainly belong to the actor level of analysis. But the emergence and the significance of these psychological factors in their turn depend on exogenous structural factors such as those discussed in an article by Himmelstrand and Horvat (1987), or in the social relations of production, as a Marxist would put it.

Suppose that a stable and trustworthy 'historical compromise' has been formed between labour and capital in a particular country. Then the game of distrust mentioned above would not be present to the same extent. On

closer scrutiny of this particular 'historical compromise' it may turn out
that a certain sharing of responsibilities between capital and labour is
involved which destroys the clear-cut picture of capital and labour as
exclusive 'bearers' of distinctly different and contradictory processes. The
usual dimensions of conflict may be overlaid with a certain amount of
'criss-cross' relationships, to borrow a term from Lewis Coser's sociological theory of conflict.

Here is thus a case where the actors cannot be left out of the picture
and be represented by variables and processes – and this because the
actors no longer unambiguously 'belong' to one particular process but are
involved on both sides in several contradictory processes. This means that
the conflicts implied no longer take place exclusively *between* categories
of actors but *within* these actors as well. The actors involved are to some
extent straddling the underlying contradiction between wage-earning and
profit-making.

To return to the method of successive dissection, it would seem useful
to supplement its basic ideas with actor-process matrices where the cells
in the matrix would contain parameters indicating the extent to which
actors are the bearers of particular processes, and the extent to which they
are beneficiaries or 'victims' of these processes, or occupy some kind of
neutral position in this regard (Himmelstrand 1986).

If the kind of straddling relationship indicated above is completely
absent, then all the parameters of the matrix could be arranged along
the diagonal, and the matrix would be virtually superfluous. Straddling
relationships are indicated by the occurrences of significant parameter
values beside the diagonal in the actor-process matrix, as is the case when
a given category of actors are bearers of several processes. Particularly
interesting is the case when an actor is straddling processes which counteract each other, as indeed is the case in many aspects of the capital/labour
relationships.

The elaboration of the exogenous/endogenous distinction which is so
crucial to the IDEA Project could in my opinion, probably become more
fruitful if endogenous domains could be seen as consisting of actor-process
matrices, and if exogenous impacts could be depicted, for instance, in the
following ways:

- the entry or exit of a particular actor, or category of actors, in a given
  endogenous actor-process matrix, as a result of exogenous impacts;
- the addition or exclusion of processes in the endogenous actor-process
  matrix as a result of exogenous impacts;
- changes in single variable, or parameter values in the endogenous actor-
  process matrix as a result of exogenous factors;
- changes in actor-process straddling or non-straddling relationships in
  endogenous matrices as a result of exogenous impacts.

Exactly how the actor analysis is to be incorporated in a formal way into the original version of the method of dissection cannot be discussed in this context. In my chapter on a lexicographic preference-actor-structure approach in this book I have in an informal manner used some hints derived from the method of actor-process matrix analysis.

CONCLUDING REMARKS

While these were the guidelines originally laid out for the project, and somewhat amended in the course of our several meetings and workshops, I cannot claim that the actual implementation of these guidelines has been perfect, perhaps because they were felt to be too constraining and alien in the view of some of our project participants. However, it is worth noting that the participating economists turned out to be the most disciplined in adopting the 'method of dissection' suggested for the project. In view of the fact that this method makes use of a distinction exogenous/ endogenous which is quite familiar to neo-classical economists, and which classifies exogenous impacts and externalities in mathematical terms which are part and parcel of the formalist 'rhetoric of economics', this is not so surprising.

The utility of the 'method of dissection' in building bridges between economic and non-economic theory in the social sciences can and should be questioned toward the end of a project like this. In my final chapter in this book such questions are dealt with in some detail. However, it is only fair to address this question also in this introduction. I will do this by briefly referring to some remarks we have obtained from some readers of our manuscript. Some of them did not like the 'strait-jacket' that we imposed on the project by making neo-classical theory our point of departure, and by asking participants to use our so-called methods of dissection. Some of these critical remarks were probably made by institutionalist economists of somewhat fundamentalist leanings who consider any attempt to reform, revise and supplement neo-classical theory as a completely futile exercise. It would be easy to discount such remarks simply as a matter of opinion and ideology. But perhaps there is a more fundamental issue buried here which is a matter of basic methodology in theory building rather than a purely ideological matter.

According to my personal experience, and with some insight into the history of ideas in the social sciences, it would seem that ideas and theoretical frameworks lacking relatively formal 'strait-jackets' have their own in-built sources of longevity and conservatism which are quite comparable with the rigidity and conservatism of 'strait-jacketed' formal theory. After all, a formalized theory can be more easily challenged and modified, first, because it is making rather precise assertions and predictions in contrast to the more fuzzy and less easily falsifiable statements

of a less precisely formalized theory, and second, because the vagueness
and lack of precision which is found even in parts of formalized theory
can be criticized in the spirit of formalism while such vagueness is an
intrinsic and accepted feature of somewhat feature-less theory which is
not equipped with a 'strait-jacket' – so how could you then criticize it?!
At an early stage of our project Dudley Seers, the structuralist economist
who unfortunately died much too early, encouraged me to pursue the use
of our 'strait-jacket' by saying: 'When you as a sociologist speak to
economists, don't tell them that they are too rigorous and mathematical.
Tell them that they are not rigorous enough – particularly in dealing with
exogenous factors. Then they will listen to you!'

There is no better way to get out of a theoretical and methodological
strait-jacket than to take it on as your daily dress, and to invite yourself
and others to a dance at the interfaces of exogenous and endogenous
factors. Then ruptures in the strait-jacket will appear, and eventually make
it possible to break out of it. The problem of extreme rigidity and conservatism in strait-jacketed theory lies not in the strait-jacket itself, but in
the fact that some of those who have taken it on feel too much at home
in it, and restrict their movements to what is possible within it, avoiding
movements stretching out toward exogenous and empirical domains that
could produce ruptures requiring a thorough retailoring of their outfit.

However, in rounding off the project in my own concluding and integrating chapter to this book, I found it particularly difficult to deal with
the formal aspect of building or plugging exogenous variables into economic analysis. What I have done, however, is to summarize and list the
kind of exogenous variables mentioned in the papers by our economists,
and the kind of impact suggested for these exogenous factors. Furthermore,
I have indicated how exogenous factors in some cases can be introduced
as dummy variables in econometric equations.

In view of the formalism of economic theory, and the pervasive and
perhaps rhetorical character of formalism among economic scholars, as
pointed out by Arjo Klamer in one of our workshops, and later by Donald
McCloskey (1986), the lack of a full-fledged formalization of exogenous-
endogenous relationships in my concluding chapter may, of course, prevent some economists from seriously considering my conclusion. However, what may seem inconclusive in the eyes of some economists may
hopefully be considered a challenge by others. The building of more
formal links between exogenous and endogenous variables so as to make
it possible to take account of exogenous variable and parameter plug-ins
in a formally more satisfactory manner is a challenging task for economists
and econometricians who master the art of formalism. For a social scientist
like myself lacking such mastery but convinced that a formalization of the
kind of exogenous-endogenous relationships covered in the IDEA Project
could pave the way for a more fruitful dialogue between economists and

non-economic social scientists, and for a more realistic approach among economists, that is quite enough. At least it is 'satisficing', to borrow a term from Herbert Simon.

Finally, it should be mentioned that the 'experiment in conversation' between economists and non-economists pursued within the framework of the IDEA Project was a success in a social-intellectual sense, as emphatically agreed by everybody participating – not the least by our participating economists. Formalistic and disciplinary rhetoric in the bad sense was indeed avoided. The group of scholars who participated are now scattered, but hopefully an interdisciplinary 'conversational habit' was formed among them which will bear fruits in the future. I also hope that this volume, in spite of not incorporating the detailed substance of the dialogical conversations at our workshops, will provide a basis for further dialogue and continued scholarly work at the boundaries between social science disciplines, academic and applied.

An explication of varieties of the exogenous in economic analysis, and various types of 'plug-ins' and 'spill-overs', can serve to suggest interfaces in socio-economic analysis through which neo-classical economists can grasp the outside world, and through which other social scientists can view the inside of the workshops of economists. The title of this book refers to this possibility.

NOTES

1 Geoff Hodgson (1989: 265f), a co-author of this book, and himself an institutionalist with an interest in theory-building, has pointed out that the post-Veblen generations of 'old' institutionalists have had an inclination for descriptive empirical case studies rather than for theory-building.

Bibliography

Dogan, Mattei and Pahre, Robert (1990) *Creative Marginality. Innovation at the Intersections of Social Sciences*, Boulder, San Francisco and Oxford, Westview Press.

Hayden, F. Gregory (1985) 'A transdisciplinary matrix for economics and policy analysis', *Social Science Information* 24, no. 4, 869–904.

Hernes, Gudmund (1976) 'Structural change in social processes', *American Journal of Sociology* 82, 513–47.

Himmelstrand, Ulf (1986) 'Formalized historical materialism as a research tool', *International Sociology* 1(2), 113–36.

Himmelstrand, Ulf and Horvat, B. (1987) 'The socio-economics of workers' self-management', *International Social Science Journal*, 113, 353–64.

Hodgson, Geoff (1989) 'Institutional economic theory: the old versus the new', *Review of Political Economy* 1(3), 249–69.

McCloskey, Donald (1986) *The Rhetoric of Economics*, Brighton, Wheatsheaf Books.

Pearce, David W., (ed.) (1983) *The Dictionary of Modern Economics*, (revised edn) London, Macmillan.
Stigler, G. J. (1984) 'Economics – the imperial science?', *Scandinavian Journal of Economics* 86, 301–13.
Swedberg, Richard (1985) 'Economic sociology and exogenous factors', *Social Science Information* 24(4), 905–20.
Tullock, G. (1972) 'Economic imperialism', in J. M. Buchanan and R. D. Tollison (eds) *Theory of Public Choice. Political Applications of Economics*, Ann Arbor, The University of Michigan Press, pp. 317–29.
Udéhn, Lars (1986) 'Economics, exogenous factors and interdisciplinary research', *Social Science Information* 24(1), 259–76.

Chapter 2

Exogenous factors and classical economics[1]

Samuel Hollander

INTRODUCTION

In this paper John Stuart Mill (1806–73) is taken as our primary representative 'classic'. Not only did he bring the classical line of thought (the economics of Adam Smith and David Ricardo) to fruition, but no other nineteenth-century economist did more to define the scope and method of economics. Indeed, it is Mill who argued a case of the kind made out by the present project.

We proceed in the second section to a statement of the case argued by Mill for a specialist science of economics. Economics, largely based upon rational calculation of costs and returns, was not envisaged as the 'science of wealth', but as one branch of such an investigation. The decision to proceed by way of quasi-independent disciplines turned upon a strategic evaluation of a higher likelihood of insightful results relating to casual process by an 'analytical' (as distinct from a 'synthetical') treatment, with an eye to the problem of 'disturbing causes'. The synthesis of causal influences in their entirety was, however, the ideal, while in the interval the very greatest care had to be taken to avoid causal application to policy of the conclusions drawn from necessarily incomprehensive models.

The treatment of exogenous factors from the perspectives of pricing and growth is taken up in the third section. The fourth section elaborates further on exogenous factors in the growth context.

THE CASE FOR SPECIALIZATION AND THE PROBLEM OF 'DISTURBING CAUSES'

The outstanding characteristic of natural and of social phenomena was, in Mill's account, that of 'Composition of Causes' where 'the effects of different causes are . . . not dissimilar, but homogeneous, and marked out by no assignable boundaries from one another; A and B may produce not *a* and *b*, but different portions of *a* . . .' (Mill, *Collected Works* (CW), VII: 434). The composition of causes was responsible for an optical

illusion. While each (separate) cause-effect relationship continued to operate, it might not, at first sight, appear to be in operation at all. To
underscore the continuous operation of the individual 'causes', Mill supported use of the term 'tendency' (ibid.: 443–4).

The primary tasks of science were to determine the effect that will
follow a certain *combination* of causes, and conversely the *combination* of
causes that would produce a given effect (ibid.: 458, 460). Inductive procedures – even when based on well-established experimental methods of
empirical enquiry – could not deal with this kind of problem. In the
presence of 'mutual interference of causes, where each cause continues to
produce its own proper effect according to the same laws to which it
conforms in its separate state', deduction alone was 'adequate to unravel
the complexities', and the empirical methods had the task of supplying
premises for, and verification of, deductions (ibid.: 439).

The social sciences dealt with a subject matter characterized more than
any other (with the exception of physiology) by plurality and composition
of causes. Social phenomena are pre-eminently of a nature requiring
deductive treatment, based upon an axiomatic foundation. But there existed
practical limits to the complexity of deductive models. The solution was
to limit the range of applicability of the methods to classes of social
phenomena 'which, though influenced . . . by all sociological agents, are
under the *immediate* influence, principally at least, of a few only' (*CW*,
VII: 900). This practical objective dictated the location of disciplinary
boundaries, the basic presumption being that different classes of social fact
depended 'immediately and in the first resort . . . on different kinds of
causes', allowing therefore for 'distinct and separate, though not independent, branches of sociological speculation'. As far as it concerned economics, the class of relevant social phenomena was that

> in which the immediately determining causes are *principally* those which
> act through the desire of wealth; and in which the psychological law
> *mainly* concerned is the familiar one, that a greater gain is preferred to
> a smaller. I mean, of course, that portion of the phenomena of society
> which emanates from the industrial, or productive operations of man-
> kind; and from those of their acts through which the distribution of
> the products of those industrial operations takes place in so far as not
> effected by force, or modified by voluntary gift.

The separate science of political economy, with its basis in wealth maximization, was conceived as part of the first stage of construction of a general
theory of wealth. A *general* theory would, ideally, combine a variety of
specialist scientific treatments each based on alternative motivation – those
behavioural assumptions involving motives other than wealth maximization, which constitute 'disturbing causes' from the perspective of political
economy, belonged 'to some other science' (*CW*, IV: 331) – and would

thus incorporate into its axiomatic base a wide range of behavioural patterns.

For the specialist procedures of economics to be legitimate, it must be the case empirically that the range of specialist study encompasses a sufficiently *homogeneous* pattern of behaviour:

> Those portions alone of the social phenomena can with advantage be made the subjects, even provisionally, of distinct branches of science, into which the diversities of character between different nations or different times enter as influencing causes only in a secondary degree.

The specialist exercises are 'liable to (*CW*, VIII: 906) fail in all cases in which the progressive movement of society is one of the influencing elements', 'for this movement is implicitly frozen within *ceteris paribus* conditions' (ibid.: 916).

'Causes' formally incorporated in the economic model are distinguished from those excluded (as 'disturbing' or 'modifying') by their predominating influence in the sense that the class of phenomena under investigation (the production and distribution of wealth in our case) depends largely upon them, and by their ubiquity – that they are causes 'common to the whole class of cases under consideration' (*CW*, IV: 326). Allowance for modifying circumstances at a subsequent stage of investigation was particularly desirable 'as certain fixed, combinations' of the influences common to all cases were 'apt to recur often, in conjunction with ever-varying circumstances' of the class of the less important or less ubiquitous influences (*CW*, VIII: 901).

The formal demarcation line between those 'causes' to be incorporated within economics and those which are to be treated as 'disturbances' and the subject matter of other sciences was, for Mill, far from rigid. In fact, a disturbing cause 'which operates through the same law of human nature out of which the general principles of the science arise . . . might always be brought within the pale of the abstract science, if it were worthwhile' thereby adding a 'supplementary theorem' thereto (*CW*, IV: 331). The axiomatic foundation of contemporary economics even included behavioural assumptions in conflict with wealth maximization:

> in a few of the most striking cases (such as the important one of the principle of population) [these corrections] are . . . interpolated into the expositions of Political Economy itself; the strictness of purely scientific arrangement being thereby somewhat departed from, for the sake of practical utility.

Similarly, the science allowed (ibid. 323) for 'two perpetually antagonizing principles' to the desire for wealth – namely 'aversion to labour' and 'the desire for the present enjoyment of costly indulgences' (ibid: 321).

Mill failed to specify the particular specializations which would (in principle) complement economics. But it is probable that when he distinguished between 'competition' and 'custom' and argued that 'only through the principle of competition has political economy any pretension to the character of a science' (*CW*, II: 239) he had in mind the character of an *independent* science, custom being the subject of complementary sciences based upon alternative axiomatic bases. An investigation of wealth founded on altruistic behaviour might provide a second example.

It is sometimes suggested that J. S. Mill introduced the notion of 'disturbing causes'. But in fact it was a view central to both Smith and Ricardo. It reflects a belief that economics is not a predictive science (such as astronomy) amenable to test by the measure of accuracy of prediction, and this because of the almost inevitable intervention of disturbing causes. For example, Ricardo adopted an analytical framework incorporating the principle of diminishing agricultural returns, although he was conscious of the historical and prospective intervention of technological change. This was because technological progress takes the form of random shocks and so might be accorded secondary status compared to diminishing returns – a force in 'constant operation':

> The causes, which render the acquisition of an additional quantity of corn more difficult are, in progressive countries, in constant operation, whilst marked improvements in agriculture, or in the implements of husbandry are of less frequent occurrence. If these opposite causes acted with equal effect, corn would be subject only to accidental variation of price, arising from bad seasons, from greater or less real wages of labour, or from an alteration in the value of the precious metals, proceeding from their abundance or scarcity.
>
> (Ricardo, 1951, IV: 19n)

A similar notion is implied in the monetary context where Ricardo explained his insistence that note reduction would tend to lower the value of gold despite apparent refutations: 'Because, in commerce, it appears to me that a cause may operate for a certain time without our being warranted to expect that it should continue to operate for a much greater length of time' (1951, V: 377). Again the disturbance to a clear-cut relation between note contraction and the value of gold is envisaged to be of a random nature.

As noted, a principal outcome of the classical perspective is the rejection of the notion of economics as a *predictive* science. It had, rather, an *explanatory* function, and in this exercise, theorists were duty bound to fight against the natural reluctance 'to admit the reality or relevancy of any facts which they have not previously either taken into account, or left a place open for, in their system' (*CW*, IV: 336). Paul Samuelson (1972: 780) was struck by Charles Darwin's advice to 'always study your residuals' – in his case by writing down arguments *against* the theory of evolution. For us, J. S. Mill is closer to home. (The same recommendation was made by Sir John Herschel.) The ultimate function, however, is *prescriptive*:

> The aim of practical politics is to surround any given society with the greatest possible number of circumstances of which the tendencies are beneficial and to remove or counteract, as far as possible, those of which the tendencies are injurious. A knowledge of the tendencies only, though without the power of accurately predicting their conjunct result, gives us, to a considerable extent, this power.
>
> (*CW*, VIII: 898)

EXOGENOUS FACTORS: PRICING AND GROWTH

In the sphere of microeconomics, *exogenous structural impacts* predominate. The analysis of pricing turns on the rule that 'only through the principle of competition, has political economy any pretension to the character of a science' (*CW*, II: 239), for only so far as prices are competitively determined 'can they be reduced to any assignable law' (*CW*, III: 460). On these grounds the analysis – based on 'the axiom . . . that there cannot be for the same article, of the same quality, two prices in the same market' – is limited to the wholesale sector, for Mill represents individual consumers as typically failing to act in maximizing fashion, the 'axiom' actually constituting a second stage deduction from more basic behaviour postulates which do not apply in the retail sector:

> the feelings which come into play in the operation of getting, and in that of spending . . . income, are often extremely different . . . Either from indolence, or carelessness, or because people think it fine to pay and ask no questions, three-fourths of those who can afford it give much higher prices than necessary for the things they consume; while the poor often do the same from ignorance and defect of judgement, want of time for searching and making inquiry, and not unfrequently, from coercion, open and disguised.
>
> (*CW*)

Considering this position on consumer behaviour one might be justified in supposing that the negative slope of the market demand curve based on individual maximization principles is inapplicable in the retail sector. But this is not so; the rationale in question (income effects) refers to final consumers. Mill evidently uses the methodological distinction between 'scientific' economics – based on the standard maximization axiom – and 'applied' economics which allows for qualifications, the subject matter of '*other* sciences'. At all events, the outcome, in practice, is a failure of competitive market pricing at the retail level.

Search costs can (logically) be incorporated within maximization econ-omics but this is less true of 'ignorance', 'defective judgment', and 'coercion'. As for the wealthy, the issue here is that of conspicuous consumption resulting in an upward-sloping demand curve (*CW*, III: 869). In effect, in the case of low-income earners sociological factors prevent the attainment of positions on the utility frontier; in that of high-income earners, they 'distort' the frontier.

In some cases 'custom' – again an *exogenous structural impact* – encourages forms of price discrimination. In others the impact manifests itself as a fixing of (retail) prices with free entry resulting in reduced markets for individual sellers who operate at less than full capacity – the 'monopolistic competition' model (*CW*, II: 243). The monopolistic competition model emerges also in the discussion of professional remuner-ation and banking.

Technological considerations also are recognized as influencing market structure. In the context of increasing returns Mill observed that 'where competitors are so few, they always end up agreeing not to compete. They may run a race of cheapness to ruin a new candidate, but as soon as he has established his footing they come to terms with him' (ibid.: 142). The implication is that (*ceteris paribus*) price will be higher the smaller the number of independent firms in the industry (*CW*, III: 927–8).

'Strict' or 'absolute' monopoly – a single seller – was easily dealt with as the limiting case. Mill (following Smith) provided a statement of the total revenue function, which implies revenue rather than profit maximiz-ation as the objective (ibid.: 468); cost of production determines the minimum. The formal restriction of the 'scientific' treatment of pricing to the competitive case was thus qualified: monopoly, whether natural or artificial, is designated as a 'disturbing cause', but it was one which had 'always been allowed for by political economists' and (as in the case of monopolistic competition) Mill applies to it the tools of economic analysis. It is in markets characterized by 'small numbers' that problems arise which were not perceived to be subject to 'assignable law'.

Further *exogenous structural impacts*, reflecting social and financial obstacles to upward mobility, are conspicuous in the analysis of the wage structure. Thus the recognition that the costs even of a minimal education and of maintenance during the training period 'exclude the greater body of the labouring people from the possibility of any such competition' as would reduce the 'monopoly' return of the skilled (ibid.: 372). Even within the basic Smithian framework, a wide variety of social attitudes will govern labour and capital supplies to particular industries and thus the pattern of wage and profit rates.

The key feature of classical growth economics is the technological principle of diminishing agricultural returns which formally relates the labour force as an independent variable to marginal productivity as dependent variable. Here arise openings for *exogenous independent-variable plug-ins* in the guise of manpower quality: 'A day's labour of a Hindoo or a South American ... cannot be compared with that of an Englishman' (Ricardo, 1951, II: 272). This in turn limits the range of applicability of the theory of profits; in relating the profit rate to the proportion of the workday devoted to the production of wage goods, we take for granted a specific social, productive, and geographic context defining the 'quality' of labour: 'I should not estimate profits in England by the labour of a Hindoo ... unless I had the means of reducing them to a common standard'.

Mill gave precedence to manpower quality over natural advantages (including location); areas with the 'best climate and soil' had 'few incentives' for sustained labour and little concern for 'remote objects' (*CW*, II: 102–3). (In these terms he even explained backwardness in the creation of good political institutions including those for the protection of property.) British industrial predominance is attributed partly to the energy of its work-force – a consequence rather of climatic conditions than original temperament – intending by 'energy' not the efforts people are 'able and willing to make under strong immediate incentives', for in this there was comparatively little distinction between nations, but rather 'the capacity of present exertion for a distant object; and ... the thoroughness of ... application to work on ordinary occasions' (ibid.: 103–4).

The impact of *exogenous independent-variable plug-ins* is extensive. Thus regarding the general level of intelligence: '... there is hardly any source from which a more indefinite amount of improvement may be looked for in productive power than by endowing with brains those who now have hands' – an observation covering superintendence and non-routine as well as routine tasks (ibid.: 105f). Trustworthiness of labour, and friendly industrial relations – which themselves have sociological sources – are weighed on a par with intelligence as affecting labour quality. And much weight is placed upon 'security' – 'no improvements operate more directly upon the productiveness of labour, than those in the tenure of farms, and in the laws relating to landed property' (ibid.: 183). The French Revolution is described as having been 'equivalent to many industrial inventions' – a Ricardian proposition which Mill illustrates in terms of the strengthening of redress against injury to person and property by people of rank (ibid.: 183).

There is also an *exogenous impact* on the quality of manpower peculiarly pertinent to underdeveloped economies – the potential stimulus to effort provided by 'new wants and desires' (ibid.: 104) – in contrast to advanced societies where 'indulgence tends to impoverish'. The opening of foreign trade, by:

> making a [people] acquainted with new objects, or tempting them by

the easier acquisition of things which they had not previously thought attainable, sometimes works a sort of industrial revolution in a country whose resources were previously underdeveloped for want of energy and ambition in the people: inducing those who were satisfied with scanty comforts and little work to work harder for the gratification of their new tastes.

(*CW*, III: 593–4).

In the absence of such stimuli, Mill suggests that the pressure of numbers (in semibarbarous countries) helps break the habit of indolence (*CW*, II: 102f).

The issue is crucial to the scope of the model in a further sense. The assumption of 'insatiability of human wants' was used to support the view that there can be no long-run deficiency of aggregated demand – the law of markets – which is taken for granted in construction of the growth model. But the assumption was not universally valid: Only in developed countries such as England was it 'not necessary that . . . new tastes and new wants should be generated – the old tastes are sufficient for the purpose. Tastes and wants exist already in a sufficient degree, give but the means of satisfying them and demand follows' (Ricardo, 1951, IV: 344). Even in developed economies 'satiation' might in principle pose a problem for the future, although workers would then choose to enjoy higher real incomes in the form of increased leisure, so that 'overproduction . . . could not . . . then take place in fact, for want of labourers' (Mill, *CW*, III: 574). The classical growth model presupposes a particular 'character'.

It is desirable to distinguish *exogenous independent-variable plug-ins* from *exogenous parameter plug-ins* – in the present instance changes in the 'quality' of labour from changes in the technology (possibly embodied in fixed capital) with which it operates, and which affect productivity of labour of given 'quality'. The 'laws of production' – which include the principle of diminishing agricultural returns but also increasing returns in manufacturing, the constraint imposed on industry by capital, and the differential impact of productive and unproductive consumption (*CW*, II: 199) – are formally said by Mill to be 'immutable' in contrast with the 'malleable' laws of distribution. But this holds good with the state of knowledge given; and knowledge indeed is sometimes placed on a par with 'the properties of nature', as a *datum* from the perspective of economics (ibid: 3, 20–21).

We turn to the labour–supply function where the scope for exogenous intervention is particularly extensive. It is fair to say that the *raison d'être* of classicism resides just here, namely in a concern with the inculcation of 'prudential' demographic behaviour patterns.

'Prudence' can be purely exogenous acting to reduce population growth rates by on-going educational–propaganda programmes. It is conceivable that steady, even rising real wages might be generated in this manner, notwithstanding increasing land scarcity and decelerating accumulation and, therefore, labour demand. Here we have a prime instance of a *'Type II' or exogenous parameter plug-in* affecting the magnitude of the parameters of the equation.

Alternatively, workers (as a class) might constrain the population growth rate to prevent the wage from falling below some designated 'conventional' level, as capital accumulation decelerates. This process ascribes to labour prescience of the steady decline in net investment.

Since the classical growth model was designed to portray the effect of an instillation of responsible habits, this assumption makes considerable sense. There will, however, be problems of the 'free-riding' type. It is important to note the role of organization in this regard; free-riding will be a lesser problem under peasant-proprietorship than under a wage system since the impact of excess numbers will be much clearer.

Reference is also made to societies where the exercise of foresight is imposed by the state, particularly control of the minimum age of and the material conditions to be satisfied prior to, marriage. Eighteenth-century Britain provided an instance of prudential behaviour imposed by 'accidental habit', the customary need for private cottages by married couples and the unwillingness of landowners to provide them, circumstances transformed by the Revolutionary Wars and the encouragement given on 'patriotic grounds' to a large population.

In some versions experience of high wages (due say to a short-run spurt in demand for labour), if extensive enough, may serve to alter *long-run* supply conditions by influencing the conception of a minimum standard on the part of the new generation of workers. This is a case of *non-economic mediated feed-back* acting on the parameter of the supply equation.

Exogenous impacts upon the magnitude of the parameter and possibly the elasticity are equally conspicuous in the case of the capital growth rate function. For savings out of surplus depends not only on the return to capital but also on a variety of personal, sociological and institutional considerations including the state of national security and life expectation, intellectual development and consciousness of the future, and the strength of other, as distinct from self-regarding, interests.

The import of the sociological conditions that lie behind the savings schedule is enhanced by recognition of divergencies between the paths taken by the interest and the profit rates. Thus Mill (*CW*, XIV:91; IV:305) recognized a decline in the interest rate since 1840 unrelated to deteriorating agricultural productivity, having in mind features of the social structure pertinent to the relationship between the lending and borrowing classes of the community – a perspective reminiscent of that of Turgot (1770).

A striking instance of a *spill-over effect* occurs in the growth context, namely the psychological implications of secular expansion, the consequences of the falling profit rate:

> By the time a few years have passed over without a crisis, so much additional capital has been accumulated, that it is no longer possible to invest it at the accustomed profit... But the diminished scale of all safe gains, inclines people to give a ready ear to any projects which hold out, though at the risk of loss, the hope of a higher rate of profit; and speculations ensue... [with cyclical implications].
>
> (*CW*, III: 742)

These implications include 'capital loss' and thus a corrective to the falling profit rate – providing an instance of *NE (non-economic)-mediated variable feedback*.

The impact of biological constraints – the differential demand elasticities for food and other goods – is the source of our earlier observation that the downward wage path cannot involve full microeconomic equilibrium even in the absence of technological progress. For *per capita* demand for food remains constant upon real wage reductions, but that for other goods declines; accordingly increases in market demands with population growth necessarily diverge for the different products. In the preclusion of full microeconomic equilibrium patterns arises an instance of *exogenous structural impact*.

Various purely technological characteristics imply that the rate of productivity change is partly governed by the distribution of activity (itself to some degree a matter of exogenously-given taste patterns) between manufacturing, agriculture and mining. Again these impose constraints of a structural order on the values economic variables can attain. For there is a particular amenability of manufacturing to 'improvement' whereas agricultural skill and knowledge are of slow growth, and still slower diffusion (*CW*, III: 729). Mining shares with agriculture the characteristic that it 'yields an increase of produce at a more than proportional increase of expense'. There is the further problem of exhaustibility. But conversely,

> the antagonizing agency, that of improvements in production, also applies in a still greater degree. Mining operations are more susceptible of mechanical improvements than agricultural: the first great application of the steam-engine was to mining; and there are unlimited possibilities of improvement in the chemical processes by which the metals are extracted.
>
> (*CW*, II: 184–5)

One of the *ceteris paribus* conditions in the analysis of the declining profit-rate trend is the distribution of the work-force between the unproductive

and productive classes – any transfer from the former to the latter counter-
acting the decline. Again, there is scope for an exogenous impact upon a
key economic variable by way of the distribution of activity.

CLASSICAL GROWTH THEORY: SOME FURTHER CONSIDERATIONS

It is sometimes claimed that the productive–unproductive dichotomy
reflects a concern for the liquidation of the primitive sector of the economy
in which menial servants are maintained on a feudal basis, and for the
development of the advanced industrial sector where well-managed and
well-disciplined workers would be employed at higher wages (Bladen,
1965: xlii). But concern with 'development' in this sense cannot alone or
even primarily explain the classification. Physical commodities are distinguished from services because of an insistence that satisfaction as such be
divorced from its source. As earlier explained, the annual product measures
sales of producer and consumer goods envisaged as the *source* of utilities
and not utilities as such, while final services are excluded since in their
case the source and the utilities cannot be separated.

The growth model outlined above appears highly constrained at first
sight by its preoccupation with the agricultural sector. But the purpose
must be kept in mind – namely to trace out the implications for the
distributive returns in an advanced capitalist-exchange system, of land
scarcity *specifically* taking account of the high profile of food in the wage
basket. In underdeveloped economies the problem was seen primarily to
be one of motivation. The policy implications were totally different. In
the one case the key to satisfactory living standards for the masses – the
main object of the classicists – lay (broadly speaking) in new technology
and/or higher savings propensities and/or population control; in the other,
overcoming 'indolence' was the first order of business. The formal model
served its purpose well.

Sir John Hicks (1985) has argued that Mill's notions on the stationary
state influenced the whole structure of his work in that the investigation
of 'equilibrium positions', for which static theory is appropriate, takes
precedence over the 'path to equilibrium', a weighting reflected in his
concern for a desirable pattern of distribution as an end in itself. Mill's
concern with equilibrium positions and desirable distribution is not in
question; but it is going much too far to conclude that he 'disposed of
the old growth economics'. The stationary state was, of course, closer
with population control than without – a fact that comes out very clearly
in terms of our prudential wage path. Yet Mill was fully aware that both
technological progress and increases in the 'effective desire for accumulation' were in practice proceeding apace, so that stationarity was not in
sight; indeed, in the Britain of his day steady-state wages (in fact a constant

return on capital) were possible even without population control because of the extremely high rate of capital accumulation permitted by new technology. We must here emphasize Mill's recognition that new industrial and transport technology was responsible for sustaining ongoing aggregate expansion without pressure on wage and profit rates partly by way of its impact on agriculture. He feared for living standards in the event that the sources of new technology should dry up before adequate population control had been achieved – an unlikely possibility.

Criticisms of Mill for having played down labour productivity and the rate of technical progress, and for underestimating the importance of applied knowledge and modern technical education (for example, Spengler 1960) are invalid. These matters were of the essence. In our account above, technology was treated purely as a shift parameter, neglecting the *economic* determinants of invention and innovation. Invention, however, is said to be sometimes 'undergone . . . in the prospect of a remuneration from the produce' (Mill, *CW*, II: 42). Market structure is pertinent (*CW*, III: 928), and size of establishment and organization play a role (*CW*, II: 147; III: 902–3). While Mill was unprepared to designate as a 'law' increased manufacturing productivity due simply to scale economies, he did so describe an observed upward secular trend allowance made for new technology (*CW*, III: 713). This positive relation between manufacturing productivity and scale (allowing for innovation) turns partly on the Smithian linkage of invention to specialization (*CW*, II: 182) but also on the observation that experiments 'can seldom be made with advantage except by rich proprietors or capitalists' (ibid.: 147). What Mill has to say regarding joint-stock organization is also relevant; such firms are in a position to attract management of a quality particularly suitable for the undertaking of projects 'out of the ordinary routine' (ibid.: 139).

Most important in the growth context, a falling profit rate is said to act as a stimulus both to investment and innovation: 'The curtailment of profit, and the consequent increased difficulty in making a fortune or obtaining a subsistence by the employment of capital, may act as a stimulus to inventions, and to the use of them when made' (ibid.: 827). Mill in fact wrote of the profit-technology relation as a 'tendency', thus according it the same methodological status as the pressure on profits of scarce land. The treatment of technical progress entirely as a non-economic exogenous factor is clearly inappropriate.

Theoretical science, however, is said to be a purely exogenous matter: the

> material fruits [of] speculative thought are seldom the direct purpose of the pursuit of savants, nor is their remuneration in general derived from the increased production which may be caused, incidentally, and mostly after a long interval, by their discoveries.

Science, therefore, 'does not, for most of the purposes of political economy require to be taken into consideration'. It is allowed only that:

> when (as in political economy one should always be prepared to do) we shift our point of view, and consider not individual acts, and the motives by which they are determined, but national and universal results, intellectual speculation must be looked upon as a most influential part of the productive labour of society, and the portion of its resources employed in carrying on and remunerating such labour, is a highly productive part of its expenditures.
>
> (CW, II: 42–3)

Accordingly:

> In a national or universal point of view, the labour of the savant, or speculative thinker, is as much a part of production in the very narrowest sense, as that of the inventor of a practical art; many such inventions having been the direct consequences of theoretic discoveries, and every extension of knowledge of the powers of nature being fruitful of application to the purposes of outward life.

The same distinction between the 'individual' and the 'national' points of view is made regarding elementary education and health expenditures (ibid.: 41). From the former perspective such outlays are said not, in the main, to reflect economic decision making, whereas:

> to the community at large the labour and expense of rearing its infant population form part of the outlay which is a condition of production, and which is to be replaced with increase from the future produce of their labour. By the individuals, this labour and expense are usually incurred from other motives than to obtain such ultimate return, and, for most purposes of political economy, need not to be taken into account as expenses of production.

The assertion that wealth-maximizing motivation is generally not at play in matters pertaining to theoretical science, elementary education and health, is of crucial import. It is all the more regrettable that Mill – who was so keenly conscious of the significance to the growth process of the fraction of the community's resources devoted to technological advance, health and education – failed to carry out an investigation of the topic as a whole. Clearly, the incorporation within economics of the determinants of pure science was a mere 'proposal', albeit flowing from a realization that (even though maximization motivation might be irrelevant) the topic could safely be delegated to 'some other science'. Yet the allowance is crucial; for it indicates strikingly that economics, narrowly defined as based on purely economic rationality, was not a predictive science. This characteristic is particularly noticeable in the context of the

'Influence of the Progress of Society on Production and Distribution, a context where the *spill-over effects* from the economic domain, with probable *feedbacks*, are most conspicuous.

Mill takes for granted as characteristic of 'civilized' countries, the 'progress of wealth' in the sense of 'growing material prosperity' – an allusion to aggregate wealth and population (*CW*, III: 705–6) – and spells out three 'tendencies' which characterize this 'progressive economical movement': Advances in technology, in security and in 'co-operation'. These are treated as causal phenomena responsible (directly or indirectly) for expanding aggregate output, but in turn played upon by economic growth. In each case the range of determinants governing the force in question is unstated, except for the impact of economic progress itself.

Thus allusion is made to 'the changes which the progress of industry causes or presupposes in the circumstances of society . . .' (ibid.: 710) with reference to technological advance, implying a mutual cause-effect relation. Mill is very explicit about the multicausal character of knowledge creation including the state of wealth:

> These remarkable differences in the state of different portions of the human race, with regard to the production and distribution of wealth, must, like all other phenomena, depend on causes. And it is not a sufficient explanation to ascribe them exclusively to the degrees of knowledge, possessed at different times and places, of the laws of nature and the physical arts of life. Many other causes co-operate; and *that very progress and unequal distribution of physical knowledge are partly the effects*, as well as partly the causes, of the *state of the production and distribution of wealth*
>
> (CW, II: 20; emphasis added).

We know that, for example, size of productive unit has an impact on knowledge creation; but 'the other causes' are left unexplained.

The second change, 'which has always hitherto characterized, and will assuredly continue to characterize the progress of civilized society', namely 'a continual increase of the security of person and property' is also not explained; we have merely a panagyric to the phenomenon with optimistic observations regarding the future (*CW*, III: 706). And again, a mutual relation is asserted: 'progress' – in this case social progress in the large as well as economic progress – is encouraged by increased security (ibid.: 706) but is also itself responsible for improvements in that regard: '. . . one of the acknowledged effects of that progress is an increase of general security. Destruction by wars, and spoliation by private or public violence, are less and less to be apprehended . . .' (ibid.: 737).

The third tendency refers to 'co-operation'. Here the mutual linkage is better justified. The impact of specialization characterizing civilized society is said to have 'a debilitating effect upon intelligence and efficiency of the individual' – his ability to adapt means to ends – but not upon collective intelligence and efficiency: 'What is lost in the separate efficiency of each, is far more than made up by the greater capacity of united action', an increased capacity for co-operation reflected in better industrial discipline, adherence to plan, subordination of individual caprice, and so forth (ibid.: 708). (This same set of issues had been raised by Adam Smith in the context of invention.) Such capacity reinforces itself for 'this, like other faculties, tends to improve by practice, and becomes capable of assuming a constantly wider sphere of action'.

The reverse linkage from wealth may be illustrated from the discussion of joint-stock organization. Despite a negative evaluation of hired workers in general, Mill rejected Adam Smith's low evaluation of joint-stock organization; Smith had overplayed

> the superior energy and more unremitting attention brought to a business in which the whole stake and the whole gain belong to the persons conducting it; and he overlooked various countervailing considerations which go a great way towards neutralizing even that great point in superiority.
>
> (CW, II: 138)

The disadvantages might be reduced by resort to some form of profit-sharing relating the 'interest of the employees with the pecuniary success of the concern', but also, where size permits it, by attraction of 'a class of candidates superior to the common average in intelligence' thereby raising 'the quality of the service much above that which the generality of masters are capable of rendering to themselves' (ibid.: 140).

The pervasive impact of general 'progress' in the sense of advances in technology can be illustrated from our discussion of retailing. A major source of market imperfection, in addition to the rigidities imposed by 'custom', was seen to lie in the ability to practise price differentiation – by location if not by product. This ability, Mill argues, was increasingly weakened by the development of 'great emporia of trade' where retail business could be conducted on a large scale – a consequence in part of the transport revolution which breaks down dependency on local dealers (ibid.: 141, 243, 410).

When we extend the scope of progress to incorporate 'opinion' the impact on pricing widens considerably to the correction by appropriate education of such 'deformities' as conspicuous consumption. The phenomenon of non-competing industrial groups was considered by Mill to be in the course of disintegration in consequence of broader educational opportunities and changes 'so rapidly taking place in usages and ideas' (ibid.: 3861f).

NOTES

1 This paper is an abbreviated version of a longer paper published in *Social Science Information (SSI)* 24(3)(1985), 423–56. For a full statement of classical micro- and macro-economics, see that issue of *SSI*, sections IV and V.

BIBLIOGRAPHY

Bladen, V. W. (1965) 'Introduction', in *Collected Works of J. S. Mill*, II, III Toronto, Toronto University Press.

Hicks, Sir John (1985) 'Sraffa and Ricardo: a critical view', in G. Caravale (ed.) *The Legacy of Ricardo*, Oxford, Blackwell.

Hollander, S. (1979) *The Economics of David Ricardo*, Toronto, Toronto University Press.

Hollander, S. (1982) 'On the substantive identity of the classical and neoclassical conceptions of economic organization. The French connection in British classicism', *Canadian Journal of Economics* 15 (November), 586–612.

Hollander, S. (1984a) 'Marx and Malthusianism: Marx's secular path of wages', *American Economic Review* 74 (March), 139–51.

Hollander, S. (1984b) 'The wage path in classical growth models: Ricardo, Malthus and Mill', *Oxford Economic Papers* 36, 200–12.

Mill, J. S. (1965–73) *Collected Works of J. S. Mill* (see under Bladen), II, III (1965), IV, V (1967), VII, VIII (1973), X (1969), XIV (1972), XVII (1972), Toronto, Toronto University Press.

Ricardo, D. (1951) *Works and Correspondence*, II, IV, V Cambridge, Cambridge University Press.

Samuelson, P. A. (1972) 'Economic forecasting and science', *Collected Scientific Papers*, 3:774–80, Cambridge, Mass., MIT Press.

Smith, A. (1937) *An Inquiry into the Nature and Causes of the Wealth of Nations*, New York, The Modern Library (originally published 1776).

Spengler, J. J. (1960) 'John Stuart Mill on economic development', in B. F. Hoselitz, *et al*. Theories of Economic Growth, New York, Free Press, pp. 113–54.

Turgot, A. R. J. (1770) *Reflections on the Foundation and Distribution of Riches*, New York, Kelley, 1963.

Chapter 3

Partially independent variables and internal logic in classical Marxist economic analysis

Ernest Mandel

THE THEORETICAL FRAMEWORK

The main propositions of Marxist economic theory, as applied to the capitalist mode of production, can be summarized as follows:

1 Capitalist production is generalized commodity production. Commodity production is impossible without the parallel circulation of commodities and money (a special commodity serving as a general equivalent for all other commodities). Commodities therefore always have prices and can only be acquired through their exchange against money. These prices might fluctuate in the short run under the pressure of market laws (the law of supply and demand). But these fluctuations are around an axis in the last analysis determined by the value of these commodities, that is by the costs of production measurable in abstract human labour (hours of labour). Production in the long run determines circulation and consumption, and not the other way around.

2 Under capitalism, production is organized by private owners of the means of production (capitalist firms) who, with their money capital, purchase means of production (buildings, equipment, raw material, energy, and so on) and labour power, in order to produce goods and services to be sold as commodities on the market. Their initiative is decisive for determining the level and dynamic of productive activity, and therefore the state of the economy as a whole. Private property implies competition, That is, decisions taken by firms independently from each other. Under the spur of competition, these independent firms are forced to operate with the purpose of realizing profits (maximizing profits) for themselves, because without enough profit they cannot expand (accumulate capital), and without enough expansion they lose ground in the competitive struggle and eventually disappear.

3 The only ultimate source of profit (and therefore of capital accumulation) is surplus-value, the amount of value produced by living human labour over and above its own costs of maintenance and reproduction. Capital's drive to maximize profits and capital accumulation is therefore

a drive to extort the maximum amount of surplus-value from the wage-labour force, either in the form of wage cuts, longer working hours or more intensive labour expenditure, or through an increase in labour productivity not compensated by an equivalent increase in real wages (that is, cheapening and diversification of wage goods).

4 Under capitalism, commodities are not simply products of labour; they are products of labour acquired and dominated by capital. They therefore do not exchange proportionally to the amount of labour directly spent in their production; they do not lead to profits proportional to the direct input in their production. They exchange proportionally to the total amount of capital spent on their production. Given the different structure of capital in different branches of production, for a given commodity, this might lead to profits considerably different from surplus-value directly created through their production. But for the economy as a whole, over a certain time-span, the sum total of the prices of production – production costs plus the average rate of profit – will equal the sum total of value produced in the course of the process of production.

5 As a result of capitalist competition, large firms emerge more and more in industry, transportation, banking and credit, foreign trade, wholesale trade, and so on. The number of decisive competitors decreases in each particular branch, after an initial period of experimental and chaotic expansion. From a certain threshold, this concentration and centralization of capital leads to a restriction of price competition and the appearance of various market control techniques (oligopolies, monopolies). But given private property, no absolute long-term control of markets is possible by monopolies. The law of value continues to assert itself, be it only in the long run. Monopolies do not eliminate the trend towards the equalization of the rate of profit. They can only assure, for certain periods, the emergence of two 'average rates', a lower one in the non-monopolized sectors of the economy, a higher one in the monopolized sectors (incorporating an 'average rate of surplus profits', that is of rents). In the very long run, these two rates will also tend to equalize.

6 Competition and capital accumulation take essentially the form of constant changes in technology, with the purpose of cutting production costs. Technology progress and technological revolutions are basically labour-saving under capitalism, although they cheapen equipment and raw material as well as wage goods. Labour-saving biased technological progress implies substitution of dead labour for living labour, that is not only mechanization but, as a secular trend, semi-automatization and automatization. High rates of capital accumulation (capitalist growth) can momentarily neutralize or overturn this tendency to reduce the rate of growth of living labour spent in the productive

process. But in the long run, this tendency will assert itself and even lead to stagnation or an absolute decline of living labour spent in production.

7 The division of the new value produced, for example, during a year – that is, the net product or national income in a given country – between capital and labour (surplus-value and the productive workers' wages and salaries) is not exclusively determined by market forces. The value of the commodity labour power is a peculiar one, for the costs of reproduction of human labour power are not purely physiological but include a moral-historical element, that is, the satisfaction of needs which are socially recognized as indispensable for workers hired at any specific moment. This incorporation or expulsion of a given set of commodities and services into or from the socially recognized mini-mum (average) wage results from the ups and downs of the class struggle. These are in turn influenced by the fluctuations of employ-ment and unemployment (the fluctuations of the 'reserve army of labour'). Hence labour-saving biased capital accumulation also serves the key function for capitalism to guarantee that the rise of wages induced in periods of relative scarcity of labour power will not go beyond a threshold where it would seriously threaten to wipe out profits.

8 The rise in the 'organic composition of capital' leads to a tendency for the average rate of profit to decline. This can be partially compensated by various counter-forces, the most important of which is the tendency for the rate of surplus-value (the rate of exploitation of the working class) to increase, independently from the level of real wages (which can rise under the same circumstances, given a sufficient rate of increase in productivity or labour). However, in the long run, the rate of surplus-value cannot rise proportionally to the rate of increase in the organic composition of capital, and most of the 'countervailing forces' tend to be superseded in their turn, at least periodically (and also in the very long run).

9 The very nature of private property, decision-making by private firms, and the tendency to make investments depend upon profit (both *ex ante* and *ex post*), give economic life under capitalism the form of spasmodic development, that is, make the levels of output, employ-ment, income and consumption fluctuate, passing through successive stages of the business cycle and making periodic crises unavoidable. The objective overall results of decisions taken by independent firms can be completely different from their intended goals. Measures taken by all firms for individual profit maximization can lead to an overall decline of profits in the economy. Together with the decline in the average rate of profit, the tendency of production (productive capacity) to outgrow effective demand (consumption) determined by the

bourgeois laws (norms) of income distribution is the basic cause of capitalist crises. These are simultaneously crises of over-production of capital (over-accumulation) and crises of underconsumption (over-production of commodities). The business cycle (of an average duration of seven years in the last 160 years) is the normal time-frame in which the value of commodities asserts itself as the basic axis for market prices, in which the average rate of profit is equalized and in which the less efficient (in the capitalist sense of less profitable) firms are eliminated.

10 While there is no necessary linear trend of crises becoming ever more grave with each business cycle, the combination of the secular trend of a tendency of the average rate of profit to decline, the secular trend of the mass (number of hours) of living labour in production first to stagnate and then to decline, the secular trend of the geographical expansion of the system (and hence the world market) to stop and the secular trend of the class struggle to become more intensive and to have more and more radical goals (undermining the inner logic of the system), leads to the growing possibility of the system degenerating towards more and more violent upheavals (wars, revolutions, counter-revolutions) and finally breaking down either into a big decline or overall collapse of human civilization, or into a higher form of social organization: socialism.

We could call these ten propositions:

1 the law of value;
2 the law of capital accumulation;
3 the law of surplus-value;
4 the law of equalization of the rate of profit;
5 the law of concentration and centralization of capital;
6 the law of the tendency of the organic composition of capital to rise;
7 the law of class struggle determination of wages;
8 the law of tendency for the average rate of profit to decline;
9 the law of the cyclical nature of capitalist production and of the inevitability of crises of over-production;
10 the law of the unavoidable collapse of the system (*Zusammenbruchstheorie*).

Most of these laws would be accepted by all those claiming to be Marxists, with the possible exception of proposition (10). My own contribution to Marxist economic theory contains an additional time-frame for proposition (9): the 'long waves of capitalist development', in which, among other things, basic technological revolutions are realized, and the equalization of the rate of profit between non-monopolized and monopolized sectors asserts itself.

PARTIALLY INDEPENDENT VARIABLES

The above-mentioned ten propositions have a logical coherence and are essentially endogenous from an economic point of view. Given the general initial framework and 'push' (private ownership of the means of production, plus primitive accumulation of money capital, plus creation of a class of wage-earners, plus expanding commodity production, that is, market economy) they flow automatically from the structure of the system itself, independently from the operation of other forces or the influence of outside factors. These can determine the speed, direction, degree of homogeneity/heterogeneity of the development. They cannot alter the nature of the system or overturn its general historical trends. Even when large-scale semi-feudal landowners are still around, or when there is still a large number of small producers, the number of capitalist factories will not decline secularly but increase, capital accumulation will not disappear but grow, the number of wage-earners will not go towards zero, money economy will not be throttled, growth will not be smooth and evenly distributed throughout time, wages will not explode upwards, and so on.

But if we look more carefully at the ten propositions, we shall notice that many of them imply a certain number of partially undetermined conclusions (outcomes). Besides the inner logic of the system, exogenous factors are at work, which partially co-determine the system's development, at least at short- and medium-term ranges (one can even add: long-term, as long as one doesn't identify the 'long-term' with 'secular', but situates it between the duration of a single business cycle and the secular trend).

Why is this so? Because the concrete historical process of capitalist development is always the result of an interaction between the system and the environment in which it develops; this environment is never 100 per cent capitalist. In other words, the laws of motion of capitalism (its inner logic) would be the *exclusive* determinants of history under the prevailing capitalist mode of production only if that mode of production would be a 'pure' one on a world scale. But this has never been the case until now, and it does not look like ever becoming so, be it only for the fact that long before capitalism has thoroughly 'capitalized', that is, industrialized, the whole world, it has itself, since 1914–17, started to decline and slowly disintegrate.

Hence what really happens in economic history since the beginning of capitalism is the product of the contradictory combination of capitalist, semi-capitalist and non-capitalist (first pre-capitalist ones, and later also post-capitalist) relations of production and circulation interacting with each other.

Does that mean that the laws of motion of the capitalist mode of production, as laid bare by Marx, are either 'false' or 'inoperative'? Of course not. First of all they assert themselves – they can be verified empirically – in the long run; after all, there *have* been twenty-one crises of over-production since 1825, and they can *all* be explained in terms of the Marxist theory of crises. Second, to say that they do not assert themselves in a 'pure' way, that they are combined with exogenous factors reacting upon them, is not identical with stating that they do not operate.

The theory of rent is a good example in that respect. Grain prices, oil prices, can deviate for some time – and even deviate strongly – from the value of the 'price of production' of these commodities, under the influence of several extra-economic 'institutional' factors (that is, social and political forces). But as both the American farmers and the governments of the OPEC countries are presently finding out at their expense, they cannot violate the law of value for ever, or even for a long time. The law of value ends by asserting itself, US government policies, US political parties' electoral calculations, oil sheikhs' greed, anti-imperialist mass mobilizations, military relationship of forces, and so on, notwithstanding.

On the other hand, the impact of exogenous forces upon the development of the capitalist economy during the last 200 years has been very real. The present structure of the world economy, the geographical distribution of agriculture and industry, the size and composition of the world market, would be impossible to understand if the influence of these extra-economic factors were not taken into account. One cannot explain the emergence of the USSR – to give just that example – and its later impact on the politics and economy of the twentieth century exclusively as a result of the ten propositions spelled out above, through the inner logic of capitalism, either in Russia or on a world scale.

But before we pass on to a more detailed examination of these exogenous factors, their relation to, and their reaction upon the system's intricate laws of motion (inner logic), two methodological difficulties which arise precisely out of the specific nature of the Marxist method of analysis in social science should be underlined.

Marxism views society as an organic structured totality, moved by the weight of its inner contradictions. This dialectical approach cannot be reduced to the operation of feedback mechanisms or similar devices. An organic whole reproduces itself, that is, has precise parameters which limit its possibilities of change. One of the key differences between Marxists and non-Marxists when analysing history (including economic history) relates precisely to that nature of a social system.

It is not that Marxists underestimate the capacity of capitalism to change, to adjust itself, and so on (although, of course, some Marxist analyses were guilty of such underestimations). It is that they understand the limits of such changes, the constraints springing from the very nature of the system. Capitalist states and governments can do many things, and so can capitalist entrepreneurs and firms. But they cannot abolish money capital and profit as the starting-point and final point of the system's operations, nor can they abolish the operation of market forces, or eliminate the law of value. Neither Hitler nor the Pentagon could realize such qualitative 'changes' in capitalism's *modus operandi*. The only way this could be achieved is by abolishing capitalism, by eliminating the system. *Inside* the system you can boost or undermine profits, deliberately or inadvertently. But you cannot suppress profits.

Hence any interaction between endogenous and exogenous forces is always limited by these parameters, by these constraints, it reaches its limit when it threatens to eliminate basic mechanisms of the system (the role of the class struggle as a source of 'social wages' or different labour-protecting social policies is a good example of the kind). This interaction is in its turn 'over-determined; by the nature of the system itself. This means that the influence of exogenous factors upon the capitalist economy cannot go beyond a certain point. Or, to say it otherwise, politics, the class struggle, cultural traditions, national peculiarities, and so on, from a given degree of impact on the economy, all become themselves 'economic', and cease to be 'exogenous' altogether.

Furthermore, these exogenous forces are never *totally* independent. In order to be completely autonomous from a given economic structure, they would have to be completely outside a given social framework; and if they would be completely outside that framework, they would obviously be outside any action upon that framework as well. The capitalist system and the environment in which it operates can in its turn be viewed as a higher 'unity' (less pure, less homogeneous than 'pure capitalism', but nevertheless a unity), in which both sides – the system and the environment – cannot be mechanically separated from each other.

For that reason we prefer the formula: 'partially autonomous variables' to 'independent variables'. Not only does the latter correspond better to a scientific analysis of what really occurred in history during the last 200 years, it also enables us to avoid the pitfalls of vulgar eclecticism.

Nothing is further from Marxism, that is, the scientific method applied to the study of social phenomena, than a crude juxtaposition of 'factors' based upon analysis abundant with formulae like: 'on the one hand . . . but on the other hand', giving each of these 'factors' more or less equal weight in explaining reality. 'On the one hand' capitalism is crisis-torn; 'on the other hand', it produces mechanisms of self-preservation, that is, of avoiding crises. 'On the one hand', capital accumulation leads to unemployment; 'on the other hand', economic growth, spurned by capital accumulation, leads to full employment. And so on and so forth, *ad nauseam*. That type of 'analysis' does not lead to any understanding of what is happening, nor allow any prediction of what is going to happen.

Reality is always concrete. In spite of all its mechanisms of self-preservation, capitalism *does* necessarily lead to crises. In spite of all mechanisms of economic growth, even long-term booms end by producing massive unemployment. In spite of all its eagerness to maintain socio-political consensus through full employment policies, capitalism ends by producing situations in which it is forced to accept structural long-term unemployment (with the very real risk of a decline of the socio-political consensus between capital and labour around a certain number of fundamental policy assumptions).

Analytical eclecticism can only be avoided if the impact of the extra-economic variables upon the economic process is seen in turn as being at least partially determined by the logic of the economic system itself. And this implies that these variables are only partially independent variables, that they are themselves connected, through an umbilical cord so to speak, with the inner logic of the system, even if they are not its direct products (in which case they would not be autonomous at all).

HISTORICAL SPECIFICITIES

The impact of the past upon the present, more precisely of pre-capitalist and semi-capitalist past relations on the concrete shape of capitalism in each specific social-economic formation (each specific country in a specific epoch), is the most obvious of extra-economic influences upon the capitalist economy. It includes a great variety of variables, of which we shall enumerate only the most important ones:

1 **The relative weight of petty-commodity producers** in society, and the degree to which subsistence farming limits the scope of the internal market. This has led to quite different dynamics of capitalism, say, in China and in Japan, between 1870 and 1920.
2 **The degree to which the native capitalist class** can use the state as an instrument of 'primitive capital accumulation', that is, the specific historically-grown nature of the state apparatus, its relation with pre-capitalist ruling classes (and their specific nature), with foreign powers, and so on. This led, for example, to quite different dynamics of capitalism in Italy and France between 1780 and 1830, or in India and Japan between 1850 and 1900.
3 **The precise historical roots and specificities of each 'national' bourgeoisie**, its relations with other social classes, and its particular 'specialization' in each historical epoch. The special relationship of the English commercial and banking bourgeoisie with the landowning class (which was in no way 'endogenous' to capitalism) of the eighteenth and early nineteenth centuries exercised a precise influence upon the level of food prices and hence upon the level of wages in Britain. Likewise, the 'overspecialization' of the Dutch bourgeoisie in the carrying trade and in banking in the seventeenth to eighteenth century made it unable to

carry through the industrial revolution, in spite of a relative abundance of capital and relatively high wages in Holland. Dutch capital rather participated in financing the industrial revolution in Britain.

4 **The specific political tradition of each country's bourgeoisie, petty-bourgeoisie and working class,** which can have roots as far back as 1,000 years. The relative weakness of central power under Western European feudalism led to a rapid relative autonomy of the towns, therefore to a long historical tradition of class politics and class consciousness of the Belgian, Dutch, English, French bourgeoisies, quite different from, for example, that of the Prussian, Austrian, Polish, Spanish bourgeoisies, not to speak of the Turkish, Russian or Chinese ones. This difference in historical tradition expressed itself throughout the second half of the nineteenth century and the beginning of the twentieth century in terms of quite different abilities to manoeuvre with regard to the working class, which even led to different levels of wages unrelated to fundamental differences in industrial and/or financial strength of various bourgeoisies.

5 **The difference in modern revolutionary tradition,** closely related to the date and specific forms of the bourgeois revolutions, and their impact on the traditions of the labour movement. The fact that the development of the American labour movement has been so strikingly different from that of the Western European, is at least influenced by that 'exogenous' factor, which has had profound repercussions upon the American economy throughout the twentieth century. Likewise, the tradition of the French Revolution has had a much greater impact on the French labour movement (and on French politics in general) than any revolutionary tradition in Germany has had. This situation has had a deep influence upon the march of German capitalism in the twentieth century, and upon the German economy, especially in 1918–19 and in 1923, but also in 1930–4 and later.

More generally, Karl Marx (in vol. 3 of *Das Kapital*) pointed to this key influence of historical specificity upon each concrete socio-economic formation, a proposition which, according to him, does not only apply to the capitalist mode of production but to all modes of production:

> The specific economic form in which unpaid surplus labour is pumped out of the direct producer determines the relationship of domination and servitude, as this grows directly out of production itself and reacts back on it in turn as a determinant. On this is based the entire configuration of the economic community arising from the actual relations of production, and hence also its specific political form. It is in each case the direct relationship of the owners of the conditions of production to the immediate producers – a relationship whose particular form naturally corresponds always to a certain level of development of the type and

manner of labour, and hence to its social productive power – in which we find the innermost secret, the hidden basis of the entire social edifice, and hence also the political form of the relationship of sovereignty and dependence, in short, the specific form of state in each case. *This does not prevent the same economic basis – the same in its major conditions – from displaying endless variations and gradations in its appearance, as the result of innumerable different empirical circumstances, natural conditions, racial relations, historical influences acting from outside, etc., and these can only be understood by analysing these empirically given conditions* (my italics).

(*Das Capital*, 3, 927–8, Penguin, 1981)

DE-SYNCHRONIZATION OF THE CLASS STRUGGLE CYCLE AND OF THE BUSINESS CYCLE

Proposition (7) stresses the importance of the class struggle on the level of wages and therefore on the level of profits. It is not the only determinant and not even the most important determinant of wages, as the neo-Ricardian proponents of the 'profit squeeze' theory, as well as most of the neo-liberal economists, wrongly assume. But it is certainly one of the determinants of the relative wage levels of different industrialized capitalist countries.

Classical and neo-classical economists alike – including Ricardo and not a few socialists influenced by Ricardo, even among self-styled Marxists – assumed that the relative level of the class struggle and the way it could influence wages, depended itself in the last analysis upon market forces, that is basically on the level of employment and unemployment. Mrs Thatcher's and Mr Reagan's economic and social strategies were to a large degree determined by that conviction.

However, experience confirms what theoretical analysis suggests: the level and intensity of the class struggle in a given country in a given period is much more a function of the relative militancy of the working class accumulated as a result of the effects of the *previous* phases of the business cycle, than a straight function of current levels of employment. It is sufficient to compare the strike curves say in Italy and Belgium on the one hand between 1978 and 1983 and those of France and Britain on the other hand, to see that there is absolutely no mechanical correlation between the level of the class struggle and the level of unemployment. Likewise, if one compares the dynamic of real wages in the countries during the present depression, one will find a much greater correlation with relative levels of workers' militancy than with relative levels of unemployment. The same is even more true if one brings countries like Sweden or Japan into the picture. Likewise, there is no mechanical correlation between the level of unemployment and the rate of decline of union strength. An example of this is Britain, if one compares the most recent years with the 1930–9 period.

Another striking confirmation of this role of workers' militancy as a partially independent variable is offered by the labour history of the United States and its impact on the level of wages (both direct wages and – later – socialized wages) in different periods of its history. There was a general upsurge of workers' militancy in the periods of 1890–1914 and 1934–46 in the USA, linked both to increasing levels of unionization, important progress of political mass activity, and massive strikes. The weight of 'radicals' inside the organized labour movements also increased significantly in these periods. In reverse, in the 1914–24 period, and even more in that since the vote of the Taft-Hartley Law and the surge of McCarthyism, there has been a significant decline of unionization, of mass strikes and of mass political activity. It is impossible to establish any direct correlation between these ups and downs of class struggle intensity on the one hand, and the business cycle, or 'long waves', or the level of employment/unemployment on the other hand.

The conclusion is obvious: there is a definite de-synchronization between the business cycle and the cycle of the class struggle. The level of class militancy of the workers at a given moment is much more a function of what happened during the previous fifteen to twenty years in the class struggle than of the economic situation (including the degree of unemployment) *hic et nunc*. For sure, a high level of unionization will *in the long run* be eroded by massive, structural lasting unemployment. Likewise, near full employment lasting for several decades will certainly strengthen the workers *vis-à-vis* the employers in the labour market. Such modifications in the relationship of forces between capital and labour will have a certain impact on workers' militancy too. But what precisely that impact will be, how it will manifest itself, how long it will take for it to lead to a radical modification (increase or decline) in workers' militancy, how and in what rhythm it will 'radicalize' either the employers, or the workers or both, that will depend also on a variety of other circumstances, and must therefore be considered at least partially as 'exogenous' to the current economic process itself.

What is true for the class struggle in general is even more true for the class struggle in its highest form, that is, revolutions and counter-revolutions. If one studies the curve of such revolutions and counter-revolutions in Europe in the twentieth century (leaving aside the problem of revolutions and counter-revolutions in so-called Third World countries), one will be unable to establish any correlation with ups and downs of the business cycle or the general state of the economy. Marx's conclusion of the 1850s that a new revolution could only occur in relation with new economic crises, is certainly not true for twentieth-century Europe. The great dates which leap to one's mind – 1905 in Russia; 1917 in Russia;

1918–19 in Germany, Austria and Hungary; 1920 in Italy; 1923 in Germany; 1936 in France and Spain; 1946–8 in France and Italy; 1956 in Hungary; 1968–9 in France and Italy; 1974–5 in Portugal; 1980–1 in Poland – have absolutely no common denominator in the economic conjuncture. To understand why they occurred one has to take the sum total of the economic, social, political, military circumstances of the previous five to ten years (at least) into consideration, as well as a lot of structural-historical causes.

But the result of these revolutions – global victory, global defeat, partial victory, partial defeat – will have a profound impact on the economic development in the ensuing years. It must therefore be seen at least as a partially autonomous variable of the inner logic of capitalism properly speaking.

The same remark should apply to decisive victories of counter-revolution. To give the most striking example: the victory of Fascism in Germany, which has decisively influenced the march of the German capitalist economy, not only in the 1933–45 period, but up to the 1960s (among other things, through a decisive upward switch of the rate of surplus-value, making possible a strong increase in the rate of capital accumulation), can in no way be explained as a mechanical result of the economic situation, or the relationship of forces between capital and labour on the labour market between 1930 and 1933.

This relationship of forces certainly deteriorated at the expense of labour, while the gravity of economic crisis made the conservation of the bourgeois-democratic framework with free trade unions difficult for German capitalism. But from this it does not follow that Hitler's victory was inevitable, determined by the logic of the capitalist economy. This victory depended upon short-term shifts in the political and social relationship of forces, in which the levels of mass mobilization, the policies of social-democracy, the Communist Party and the trade unions, their analysis of the situation and of the perspectives, their understanding (or lack of understanding) of the nature of the Nazi Party and the dynamics of a Nazi government, were much more important than the level of wages and profits or the number of unemployed.

Hitler could have been stopped – not in the first place by a reduction of the unemployed by 500,000 or one million, but by a mobilization of millions of workers in the streets. Objectively, that was possible. If it did not happen it was for political and not for economic reasons. This historical fact – together with the victory of the Russian Revolution in 1917, the defeat of the German Revolution in 1918–19, the defeat of the Spanish Revolution in 1936–7 – is perhaps the best example of the impact on the world economy and on world history of forces, at least at a given moment, independent from the 'inner logic' of the capitalist economy in and by itself.

THE ROLE OF SCIENCE AND TECHNOLOGY

The cycle of technological revolution is to a large degree co-related to the 'long waves of capitalist development'. Generally, in a 'depressive long wave', the pressure to increase the rhythm of technological innovation is evident. We are witnessing such manifold pressures right now throughout the world. Simultaneously, however, during such a 'depressive long wave', the forces operating against *massive* implementation of technological innovations, and especially their generalization throughout the whole economy, are overwhelming. When the general level of profits is rather low, and there exists massive overcapacity, the incentives of a massive increase in the level of productive investment are limited.

On the other hand, during 'expansionist long waves', conditions favour 'extension', vulgarization, massive application and generalization of technological innovation. This is what happened with electricity in the period of 1893–1913 and with motorization and semi-automatization in the period of 1940(48)–70.

However, if this correlation is obvious, and if the 'feedback' effects between technological innovation, rise in the average rate of profit, rise in capital accumulation, expansion of the market, technological innovation turning into massive technical revolution, can be easily outlined, there remains one partially autonomous variable in the equation. The *precise* nature of one or several key technological innovations, and their dependence upon one or several key scientific discoveries, cannot be seen as a direct product of the business cycle, or of the 'long waves of capitalist development', or of any economic logic in and by itself.

The very most one could state here is that a certain economic climate (as well as a certain politico-cultural one, somehow correlated to it) either favours or hinders basic research, the increase of the number of scientists, their interchange of opinion, the equipment of research laboratories, and so on, all of which is somehow linked to economic needs and possibilities. But even that limited correlation is more complex than appears at first sight.

Nazi rule in Germany certainly hindered free research and free scientific debate, thereby causing growing delay in technological innovation in that country: massive emigration of German first-rank scientific scholars greatly increased the rhythm of scientific research and discoveries in the USA and Britain. But, on the other hand, limited, pragmatic war-economy-oriented state-funded research in Nazi Germany, with ruthlessly established priorities, did enable German science and technology to make significant breakthroughs, the jet plane and the rockets being outstanding examples.

Be that as it may, the character of scientific discovery and initial technological innovation in and by itself makes it at least partially independent from purely economic logic, and at least partially dependent on the inner logic of the development of a given science itself (whether one accepts Kuhn's theory about the nature of scientific revolutions or not). In a given economic situation, at a given turning-point of the 'long waves', a great number of already applied scientific discoveries may lie around, a sufficient number of technological innovations already being experimented with. But not all of them lend themselves to widespread generalization throughout the economy. Not all of them lead to genuine technological *revolutions*, yielding technological rents (surplus profits) by the billions of dollars during many years. For such revolutions to occur, specific discoveries and specific innovations are indispensable. And they depend at least in part upon factors 'exogenous' to the economy properly speaking.

QUALITATIVE CHANGES IN THE DOMINATION OF THE WORLD MARKET

Capitalist competition leads to competition between bourgeois nation-states, which leads to imperialist competition (as well as competition between imperialist and dependent bourgeoisies). The world market is structured by these states, each with a given impact upon the international division of labour, world trade, financing of industries and infrastructure in other countries, and so on. This competitive strife is not purely economic. States intervene through taxation, subsidies, custom systems, currency manipulations, trade restrictions, political pressure, corruption, economic-military alliances and outright wars, in order to modify economic relationship of forces to their advantage. The outcomes of these wars in their turn deeply influence the march of the international capitalist economy for years if not decades, and produce sharp shifts in the rhythm, orientation, structure of capital accumulation.

Again, the variable 'political-military weight upon the world market' is only partially independent from the 'purely' economic relationship of forces of different 'national' fractions of the international capitalist class. In the long run, no power which is weaker than others from the point of view of industrial productivity of labour or from the point of view of globally accumulated capital can maintain a position of political-military hegemony on the world market and in world politics. But for given periods, such an incongruity between military-political power on the one hand, and economic power on the other, can exist and has existed. Britain's naval-political supremacy in the 1900–20 period no longer corresponded to an industrial or even financial hegemony. France's military and political hegemony on the European continent in the period 1920–35 was likewise incongruous to the industrial and financial strength of that country. The same applies to Japanese military hegemony in East and South Asia in 1941–5. And since the mid–1960s there has been a growing incongruity between the USA's decisive weight in world politics and the military field, on the one side, and its relative decline as the technologically and industrially hegemonic power among the imperialist states on the other side.

This temporary incongruity makes situations of hegemony on the world market and in the field of world politics (generally linked to military hegemony), into partially independent variables of the world economy. For the impact of such hegemonies on the general march of the capitalist economy is obvious. It is sufficient in that respect to point to the fact that the hegemonic power's paper currency is able to play the role of reserve currency for the capitalist economy as a whole, to be a substitute or at least a partial 'relay' for gold, as a necessary motor for expanding the world economy.

Such hegemonic positions on the world market and in world politics are generally at least partially results of *previous wars* (there are few examples in world history of radical shifts in the international relationship of forces which are not the outcome of wars. Perhaps for the first time in centuries we are witnessing right now such a rare example in the change of the relationship of forces between the USA, Western Europe and Japan). Britain's hegemony in the nineteenth century was a product of the Napoleonic Wars. It was finally upset by the First World War. The USA's emergence as the hegemonic power of the capitalist world was an obvious result of the Second World War.

These shifts are clearly related to previous shifts in the economic relationship of forces. But once they have occurred, they have the tendency to be frozen for longer periods, as they are institutionally propped up, especially, through armed forces, above-average levels of military expenditures, international currency regulations which allow these expenditures, diplomatic alliances which extend them throughout time. The relative rigidity of these institutions makes it difficult to upset them thoroughly in a purely gradual way. New radical shifts need violent upheavals, that is, revolutions, counter-revolutions and wars.

The impact of these conditions of domination and/or subordination in the field of world politics on the economic development of nations, and of the world as a whole, goes far beyond these 'institutional' factors. The whole problem of imperialism and under-development of the Third World has, at least partially, to be studied under that heading. In order to avoid repeating trivialities, we shall not deal any further with these obvious aspects of nineteenth and twentieth century world history.

THE VALUE OF GOLD

We already indicated that the capacity of a given, hegemonic capitalist power to see its national paper currency used as 'world money' (a substitute for gold) does not depend exclusively upon the financial solidity and industrial advance of that power (although it cannot in the long run survive divorced from these conditions). But the existence of gold, or 'world money', independent from all 'partisan' manipulations by a particular sector of the international capitalist class, is indispensable for a smooth expansion of the world market, of the international capitalist economy. Hence the key importance of the value of gold for the dynamic of that economy.

We say *value* of gold, and not the amount of gold mined each year. Empirical studies have confirmed the correctness of Marx's theory about the fact that all gold currently mined and accumulated historically by no means needs to enter or remain in circulation. It can always be 'sterilized' in central bank stocks or private hoarding. The ups and downs of the trade cycle determine the ups and downs of gold (gold currencies, good-as-gold paper currencies) circulation, and not the other way around. It follows that gold production is generally counter-cyclical to the business cycle, a phenomenon the South African economy is just now experiencing at its expense.

However, what is true for the quantity of gold annually produced and its current 'price' (more correctly: the amount of gold a unit of leading paper currencies actually represents) is not true at all for the value of gold whenever that value is *radically* altered. Each of the great revolutions in gold production – that of the sixteenth century, the one after the discovery of the Californian gold fields, the one after the discovery of the rich South African Rand mines – meant a sharp decline in the value of gold, that is, in the amount of labour (time) necessary to produce one ounce of gold. This meant a steep increase in the general price level of all other commodities, as long as the strong sudden increase in the productivity of labour in gold-mining was not neutralized by an equivalent increase in the productivity of labour in industry and agriculture. A general increase in the price level, together with important surplus profits being gained out of gold-mining itself, favours a long boom throughout the international capitalist economy, as the one which occurred after 1848 and after 1893.

Again, while a climate favourable for frantic searches of new gold-fields throughout the world certainly depends upon current economic conditions (or can be hindered by a given phase of the 'long waves' or of the business cycle), the actual discovery of a large gold *bonanza* depends upon many accidental factors. It is therefore at least a partially independent variable of the march of the world economy. If such a new gold *bonanza* would, for example, be discovered today in Brazil (of the scope, say, of the South African gold-fields), this would certainly help international capitalism to overcome the present debt crisis and overcome the long depression of the 1970s and 1980s. If such a new gold *bonanza* is not discovered, it will be an additional obstacle for overcoming the depression.

Radical changes in the value of gold are not necessarily limited to increases in the productivity of labour in gold-mining. They can also take the form of sharp lasting increases in the production costs of an ounce of gold, either through the need to use less and less productive mines for keeping up at least a minimum of annual output, or through a sudden sharp increase in miners' average wages before mechanization can substantially reduce the relative weight of wages in total production costs.

From that point of view, the relative stability of the *apartheid* regime in South Africa, or alternatively the relative capacity of the black working class of South Africa to impose unionization and wages approaching white workers' wages in the South African mines, have an important impact upon the general price level throughout the world, and therefore an important impact on the world economy as a whole. This explains why, all hypocritical assertions to the contrary, the international bourgeois class has a vested interest in maintaining *apartheid*, far beyond the immediate profits which investments in *Anglo-American* or *De Beers* annually produce for the bourgeoisie.

Again, the vagaries of the discovery of new important gold-fields on our planet (and, who knows? At the bottom of the oceans? In outer space?), as well as the changes in the institutions and social relationship of forces inside South African society, are at least partially autonomous variables of world economic development, although their connections with the inner logic of the capitalist mode of production are manifold.

CONCLUSION

We have tried to indicate the operations of certain exogenous factors, as partially independent variables, on the development of the capitalist economy. We have tried to avoid the pitfalls of eclecticism arising out of a simple juxtaposition of 'endogenous logic' and 'exogenous forces'. Generally, the conclusion is that the former asserts itself in a decisive way in the long run (certainly at the level of 'secular' trends), while the latter have important weight in short- and medium-term time-ranges.

It is useful to consider this interaction – and its overall result – in the light of the key aspect of capitalist development: the weight of the *secular* trend of the 'reserve army of labour' (as distinct from its fluctuations as a function of the business cycle) upon the general level of wages and, hence, the rhythm of capital accumulation. Here, the impact of 'exogenous' forces and their gradual neutralization through the inner logic of capitalism, comes strikingly to the fore.

When the rate of demographic growth plus the rate of decline of employment in petty commodity production, outdistance the rate of capital accumulation, there will be a secular increase in unemployment, hence a secular tendency of stagnant real wages even with growing industrialization. This was the situation in Western Europe 1770–1870, in Eastern Europe 1870–1940, in the Third World 1900 (or earlier)–60.

According to whether this situation leads to a qualitatively growing access to foreign markets or not, it can reverse itself (as it did in Western Europe) or not (as is the case, for example, up till this day in India). The first move will be decisively assisted by massive emigration of surplus labour. An impossibility of such emigration of a substantial fraction of the 'reserve army of labour' is again a key factor in the stagnation of wages in India.

But massive emigration of labour needs massive reserves of free and/or available capital to which it can be attracted; this is the unavoidable logic of capitalism. The USA after the war of Secession, and Arabia after 1973, are examples of the kind (as was Western Europe after 1960). This means also that the thin population of the USA in the eighteenth and the beginning of the nineteenth century determined from the outset a high level of wages which prevented that country from being the centre of world capitalist industry in the nineteenth century, in spite of its huge mineral wealth. Only after 1870–80, after the disappearance of the Frontier, that is free land, did it start to achieve that supremacy.

Capitalist logic ends by asserting itself as a logic of surplus-value extraction; but only after a certain time and after the impacts of several 'exogenous' factors have been neutralized. The correlation between the distribution of masses of 'free land', 'excess capital' and 'excess labour' throughout the world – in different specific geographical zones – was not *predetermined* by the inner logic of capital. It became subordinated to that logic after a time – and in different time spaces in each geographical area. In other words, the *unevenness* of capitalist development had *both* precapitalist and capitalist origins, indissolubly combined and intertwined with each other.

Chapter 4

Exogenous factors in neo-classical microeconomics

Keith Hartley

INTRODUCTION

This paper outlines the central ideas of neo-classical economics which has been described as 'nothing but microeconomics' (Blaug 1978: 4) Macro-economics is the subject of other papers in this series. Initially, the major propositions of neo-classical economics are summarized. Some of the more recent developments in the neo-classical tradition are outlined, including extensions of the paradigm outside the conventional boundaries of econ-omics and into politics, sociology and social policy. The reasons for the continued dominance of the neo-classical paradigm and the role of exogen-ous factors within this framework are then considered. Three sets of exogenous factors are analysed, namely, preference functions, technology and government. These are amongst the major exogenous factors in stan-dard neo-classical economics. They also provide opportunities for applying neo-classical economics to other social science disciplines.

A consideration of exogenous factors provides the basis for looking out at the outside world. This outward look will be based on the neo-classical approach and will seek to identify opportunities for developing an inter-disciplinary social science framework. In this context, economics, politics and public choice are particularly suitable.

Public choice models apply economics to the political market – an area which economists have traditionally regarded as a 'black box', but which can be analysed using neo-classical microeconomics (that is, the study of markets). A public choice approach shows the impact of agents in the political market on policy formulation. For example, economists are fond of proposals to expand the opportunities for consumer choice, to introduce competition into monopoly situations and to promote mutually advan-tageous trade and exchange both with, and between, nations. Govern-ments, however, frequently seem to ignore obvious opportunities for making people better off. They introduce tariffs, subsidies and regulations which benefit producers rather than consumers. Changes which appear so attractive to economists often ignore the influence of actors in the political market-place and their impact on policy formulation.

THE MAJOR PROPOSITIONS OF NEO-CLASSICAL MICROECONOMICS

Choice

Choice is central to neo-classical microeconomics. Scarcity means that limited resources have to be allocated between different uses, so that choices have to be made about (a) What to produce? (b) How to produce it? (c) Who receives the resulting output (distribution)? (d) Who will choose? Choice involves sacrificing other things and the consequent loss of satisfaction which could have been obtained from alternative courses of action, hence the concept of opportunity cost which focuses on the subjective evaluation of alternatives. In neo-classical microeconomics, scarce resources are allocated between different uses and users by a system of market prices. *Markets* allow individual buyers and sellers to undertake voluntary trade and exchange, the basic premise being that there are gains from voluntary transactions. The analysis is applicable to markets for goods, services and factors of production (for example, labour, capital) both within and between nations.

Focus

Neo-classical economics focus on:

(a) The *concept of equilibrium* (a state of rest), where the *plans* of agents are satisfied. An equilibrium in product or factor markets is achieved when prices have adjusted to clear the market (that is, there are no surpluses nor shortages.)
(b) *General and partial equilibrium*. *General* equilibrium recognizes that capitalist economies are characterized by a large number of interdependent product and factor markets. Economists have devoted considerable efforts to determining the conditions required for the existence of a general equilibrium, its uniqueness and stability (Arrow and Debreu 1954; Arrow and Hahn 1971; Walras 1874). The task has been to determine whether there exists a set of relative prices which will simultaneously clear *all* markets in an economy (multi-market equilibrium). It has been shown that a general equilibrium is possible so long as returns to scale are constant or diminishing and there are no external effects in production or consumption. Also, the determination of a general equilibrium can result from an auctioneering process (*tâtonnement*) or from provisional contracting and recontracting, with the rules requiring that no trade and exchange occurs until the equilib-

rium prices for the whole system emerge. An economy with perfectly competitive product and factor markets results in a general equilibrium solution. Although highly abstract, mathematical and non-operational, general equilibrium analysis emphasizes the interdependence and complexity of economic systems.

   An alternative *partial* equilibrium approach simplifies the complexities of general equilibrium by concentrating on equilibrium in a single market (Marshall 1890). Partial equilibrium analyses behaviour, decisions and performance in one part of the economy (for example, the computer industry or the market for typists) under the *ceteris paribus* assumption – that is, other things being equal or everything else in the economy remaining unchanged so that a single market is analysed independently of all other markets and influences in the rest of the economy.

(c) Three sets of agents, namely *households*, *firms* and *governments* each with an objective function. Each agent is assumed to maximize an objective function subject to constraints, with *marginalism* being central to the maximizing process. Such analysis has provided extensive opportunities for the application of mathematics and the construction of logical and rigorous models yielding determinate solutions. Maximization requires equalization at the margin in an economy characterized by limited resources, by diminishing returns in production and diminishing utility in consumption. The principle applies to consumers spending a fixed income amongst a variety of goods and services (Hicks 1946; Samuelson 1948a); to firms spending a given sum on buildings, machinery and workers; and to governments dividing a budget between defence and state welfare services (Samuelson 1948b).

   Households and firms are assumed to be motivated by *self-interest*. Households are both consumers of final output and suppliers of factor services (for example, labour). In both capacities, they are assumed to be utility-maximizers (for example, as workers, they derive satisfaction from income and the non-monetary aspects of the job). Firms are assumed to be profit-maximizers, although there are alternative models of firm behaviour within the neo-classical maximizing tradition (for example, sales, growth, utility). Alternatively, firms can be regarded as more general utility-maximizers, with different arguments entering into the utility function. Finally, governments have traditionally been regarded as neutral and passive agencies, responding to the 'will of the electorate' and maximizing something called the 'welfare of the community' (that is, more formally, a social welfare function: Henderson and Quandt 1971).

(d) *Positive and normative economics.* The formulation of theories, derivation of predictions and empirical testing are central to positive economics (that is, the study of what is). Normative or welfare economics is concerned with the conditions under which individuals are made better or worse off as a result of changes in the economic system and/or public policy (for example, does economic growth represent a socially desirable change?). The conditions have been expressed in the Pareto criterion under which a socially desirable change occurs when one person is made better off without anyone else being made worse off. A Pareto optimum is reached when it is impossible to make anyone better off without making someone else worse off. Subsequent modifications have introduced the compensation principle to deal with changes which benefit some people and harm others (Hicks 1939; Kaldor 1939); the concept of a social welfare function for ordering alternative distributions of income and wealth (Bergson 1938); and second-best constraints which question the desirability of public policies to attain the Pareto conditions on a partial or piecemeal basis (Lipsey-Lancaster 1956).

(e) *Efficiency*. The central feature of neo-classical economics is its analysis of the allocation of limited and scarce resources between alternative and competing uses so as to maximize social welfare defined with respect to consumer satisfaction. Questions of efficiency dominate neo-classical economics leading to the analysis of general equilibrium and perfect competition under static conditions. As a result, the quantity and quality of scarce productive factors (population, national resources) are taken as given and determined outside the system (exogenous – cf. classical economics). In addition, efforts are made to separate efficiency from income distribution and equity issues. Given these qualifications, Paretian welfare economics shows that perfect competition results in an efficient allocation of resources. With private property rights and free enterprise, firms and consumers in pursuing their self-interest will be guided by the 'invisible hand' to maximize social welfare. However, capitalism and private ownership is not the only means of maximizing welfare. Market socialism with the decentralized decisions can also achieve a welfare maximum in a centrally directed and collectivist state (Lerner 1946).

Models of demand and supply in competitive markets

These are the starting point in neo-clasical microeconomics. The model can be applied to product and factor markets, both nationally and internationally. It can be summarized:

(1) $P = f(D, S)$.
(2) $D = f(P_x, P_s, Y, T, X_1)$.
(3) $S = f(P_x, P_f, F, A, X_2)$.
(4) Equilibrium condition: $D(p) - S(p) = 0$

where P = market price; D = demand; S = supply; P_x = price of the commodity; P_s = prices of all other commodities; Y = income of consumer; T = consumer tastes and preferences; X_1 = other influences on demand – for example, population characteristics, education, season, fashion; P_f = prices of all factors of production; F = objective function of firms – profit maximization is taken as the starting point, with the associated assumption of technical efficiency; A = state of technology; X_2 = other relevant influences on supply – for example, laws and regulations.

This simple but powerful model can be applied to price determination in markets for goods and services, foreign exchange, land, labour, money, capital and enterprise. Indeed, in neo-classical analysis, *distribution theory* is part of general price theory. Thus, rewards to factors of production are determined by supply and demand or marginal productivity (Koutsoyiannis 1979). On this basis, income distribution depends on the ownership of factors of production and their relative scarcities.

The basic demand and supply model results in a number of major predictions:

(a) More will be *bought* at a lower price.
(b) More will be *supplied* at a higher price.
(c) Controls on product and factor prices will result in shortages or surpluses. For example, where rent control sets the price below the market-clearing level, there will be excess demand in the housing market reflected in waiting lists and black markets. Similarly, if minimum wage or equal pay legislation increases wages above their equilibrium level, employment will decline and unemployment will emerge (Hartley and Tisdell 1981).

The production side of the model

This was expanded to allow for *non-competitive markets* embracing large and small numbers of firms. Modifications to the extremes of perfect competition and monopoly led to the development of models of profit-maximizing firms operating in intermediate situations of imperfect markets and monopolistic competition (Robinson 1933; Sraffa 1926). Profit-maximization requires the equality of marginal cost and marginal revenue. Firms' cost conditions were derived from a clearly specified production function showing how factor inputs can be combined to produce various outputs with a given technology (Cobb-Douglas 1928). With large numbers of firms and free entry, monopolistic competition predicted unexploited economies of scale and too many firms in an industry (the tangency solution: Chamberlin 1933). However, many of the industries which should conform to monopolistic competition and the tangency solution (for example, shops, garages, taxis) are often more appropriately analysed as oligopoly markets. Oligopoly is frequently regarded as the typical market structure in modern industrial economies. But economic models of oligopoly are far from satisfactory. The presence of only a few sellers means that interdependence, rivals' reactions and non-price competition (for example, advertising; R & D) are central features of oligopoly markets (Koutsoyiannis 1979; Chapters 9–10).

The development of the structure–conduct–performance paradigm

This paradigm (Bain 1972) can be summarized:

$$P_m = f(s)$$

where P_m = market performance in the form of allocative efficiency as reflected in the equality of price with marginal cost (Pareto optimum). Other performance indicators include profits, X–inefficiency and technical progress.

S = industry structure as measure by the number and size distribution of firms and entry conditions (for example, concentration ratios).

On this basis, perfectly competitive markets characterized by large numbers of relatively small buyers and sellers and no entry barriers will result in a Pareto optimum (price equals marginal cost) with no X–inefficiency and normal profits in the long-run. But not all markets are perfectly competitive, so that market failure is possible.

Market failure

If left to themselves, private markets might fail to work properly, in that they will fail to satisfy fully and accurately consumer preferences (assumed to be the end-purpose of economic activity). Market failure results from:

(a) Imperfections in the form of monopoly, oligopoly, entry barriers, and restrictive practices in product, factor and information markets. For instance, a single buyer or monopsony in the labour market results in exploitation with workers receiving less than the value of their marginal product. At the international level, tariff barriers can prevent nations from exploiting the gains from free trade based on each country's comparative advantage.

(b) Externalities, including public goods. Examples include pollution, defence and the collection and dissemination of information where private markets are likely to provide 'too much or too little' of these goods in relation to what is regarded as 'socially desirable'.

On this basis, neo-classical economics recognizes that there is a role for government in 'correcting' market failure. The standard options include competition policy for removing imperfections; taxes and subsidies for correcting externalities and a preference for marginal cost pricing with subsidies where there are decreasing cost industries. However, a distinction is made between the *technical issues* concerned with identifying the causes of any failure and the *policy issues* concerned with the choice of the most appropriate policy solutions.

MORE RECENT DEVELOPMENTS

There has been a variety of recent developments in the neo-classical tradition reflecting criticisms of some of its assumptions and the inevitable evolutionary search for further refinements. In addition, the paradigm has been applied to completely new areas, traditionally assumed to be the property of other disciplines, particularly politics and sociology. The application of neo-classical principles has led to the emergence of specialist disciplines in price theory, welfare economics, industrial organization, international trade, labour economics and mathematical economics. The assumption of perfect information and knowledge has been relaxed; alternatives to profit-maximizing models of firm behaviour have been formulated; and the microeconomic foundations of macroeconomics have been explored. Elsewhere, some economists have sought to expand the boundaries of conventional economics by applying the neo-classical paradigm to human investments such as education, training and health, to the family and to the political market-place. On this view, sometimes regarded as economic imperialism, there are no limits to the application of neo-classical economics as an explanation of all market and non-market activities.

Some of the more recent developments in the neo-classical tradition can be summarized:

(a) Market clearing analysis

It is now recognized that market activities involve search, information and transactions costs (Stigler 1961). For example, information and knowledge is an economic good whose acquisition is not costless. Consumers, workers and firms are all actively involved in searching for market opportunities (for example, R & D and job search) and seek to establish property rights in valuable ideas (for example, employment contracts, patents, copyright).

(b) Economic models of the firm

The existence of firms has been explained by efforts to economize on transactions costs where these include the costs of search, acquiring information, negotiating, bargaining, reaching contractual agreements and monitoring teamwork (Coase 1937). Alternative models of firm behaviour have been formulated to embrace sales, growth and utility maximization (that is, where managers have a preference for staff, managerial emoluments and discretionary expenditures: Williamson 1964). A comparative statics methodology has been used to derive alternative qualitative predictions from these different models. The methodology compares the output response of firms to changes in demand and cost conditions (for example, increases in lump sum taxes and taxes on profit rates). Finally, subject to the constraints of their employment contracts, and the costs of policing, managers and workers will seek opportunities to obtain utility from their working situation. This will be reflected in on-the-job leisure, a reluctance to work as hard and as effectively as possible and organizational slack: the result is X–inefficiency (Leibenstein 1966).

(c) Production functions and the sources of growth

Micro-production functions have been aggregated into economy production functions. There are, however, technical problems of aggregation, as well as difficulties of measuring and valuing capital (Robinson 1955). Nevertheless, neo-classical growth models based on an aggregate production function have been used for the empirical estimation of the sources of economic growth. Quantitative evidence has been obtained on the contribution to growth of labour and capital inputs and the residual factor representing technical advance and changes in the rate of application of new knowledge (Denison 1967). Critics have condemned this approach as measurement without theory (Walters 1963).

(d) The microeconomic foundations of macroeconomics

This focuses particularly on its theoretical and empirical analysis of the demand for money, expectations and the natural rate of unemployment. The quantity theory of money was reformulated as a theory of the demand for money, with the demand function based on the neo-classical theory of consumer choice (Friedman 1956). As a result, the quantity theory emerged as a theory of *nominal* income in which changes in the money supply led to changes in nominal income. Subsequently, the introduction of expectations about the behaviour of prices and the concept of the natural rate of unemployment provided a more complete model which explained the impact of a change in nominal income on prices and output.[1] On this view, the long-run Phillips curve is vertical and reductions in unemployment below its natural rate require microeconomic policies to reduce market imperfections. These theoretical developments have also been associated with a major empirical research programme. Indeed, it has been stated that there is perhaps no other empirical relation in economics that has been observed to recur so uniformly under so wide a variety of circumstances as the relation between substantial changes over short periods in the stock of money and in prices; the one is invariably linked with the other and is in the same direction; this uniformity is ... of the same order as many of the uniformities that form the basis of the physical sciences.

(Friedman 1956: 20–1)

Tests of the modern quantity theory based on monetary trends in the UK and the USA show high correlations between money and income (Friedman and Schwartz 1982). However, critics stress the problems of causation and question the division of changes in nominal income between prices and output. Moreover, on a basic methodological issue, worries arise since the monetarist models are rarely tested against alternative theories of prices, output and nominal income. Indeed, on the central issue of the demand for money, it has been suggested that

current theory provides few empirical hypotheses that are both sharply defined and *testable* with available data. The generalizations that are testable are typically so broad that the data have difficulty in distinguishing among them. Because of this, 'empirical' findings often reflect more the *a priori* beliefs of the researcher than they do any distinctions supported by the data.

(Judd and Scadding 1982: 1014–15)

(e) Human capital theory

This applies the standard economic theory of investment and capital to explain such human investments as education, health, industrial training, job search and mobility. These activities involve human beings in an investment decision leading to the creation of human capital (Becker 1964). People invest in themselves by sacrificing present consumption in return for an expected higher future income. They may undertake training which offers only low pay during the learning period but a higher lifetime income once the individual is skilled; or, they may incur costs searching for a higher paid job or in moving to an area offering better employment prospects. Human capital theory provides a number of distinctive explanations and predictions. It explains the demand for post-compulsory education and industrial training in terms of rates of return to such investments; it explains the distribution of training costs between workers and firms; whether skill shortages are due to poaching; and the effects of education and training on lifetime earnings, income differentials and inequality. Criticism has centred on the *ad hoc* nature of much of the empirical work, particularly earnings functions, and the emphasis on education to the relative neglect of industrial training. But the major criticism of human capital theory has come from advocates of the screening hypothesis. This rival hypothesis asserts that in selecting workers for jobs, firms lack information on a potential employee's productivity: hence, educational certificates and qualifications might be used as an initial screening device.

(f) The economics of the family

The Chicago school has applied neo-classical analysis to household behaviour, an area which is central to microeconomics but which traditionally has been viewed as a one-person unit and has been regarded as the territory of sociologists. The new economics of the family analyses the household as a two or more person unit maximizing a joint utility function from a production function whose inputs are market and non-market goods and services, together with the time, skills, information and knowledge of the family unit. The resulting analysis in terms of gains from two-person trade and exchange (contracts) offers explanations of marriage, divorce, the decision to have children and the allocation of household tasks between husband and wife. Other applications include crime and altruism (Becker, 1976). Crime can be explained in terms of whether criminal actions are expected to be worthwhile – that is, the expected costs and benefits of crime, including the probability of detection and the severity of punishment. Similarly, the economics of altruism analyses charity, caring and giving within and between households, both within and between nations (for example, foreign aid to developing nations). It is now recognized that individual efforts to raise utility can include the satisfaction from charitable acts – that is, an individual can derive satisfaction from both personal consumption and by contributing to improving the welfare of others. This research programme is still in its infancy. It seems to offer new insights into household behaviour but is often guilty of *ad hoc*ery and of failing to provide distinctive hypotheses capable of being refuted.

(g) Public choice

Public choice, where economists have applied neo-classical concepts to the political market-place of voters, political parties, governments, bureaucracies and interest groups (Mueller 1979). Voters are assumed to act like consumers and maximize their expected utility from the policies offered by rival political parties. Similarly, political parties resemble firms and aim to maximize votes, competing in market structures ranging from small to large numbers of rivals. Bureaucracies are analysed as monopoly suppliers of information and services, seeking to maximize their budgets. Interest or pressure groups pursue their own self-interest, trying to influence government policy in their favour (for example, via lobbying for tariff protection or government contracts). Public choice has both positive and normative aspects. Positive public choice explains the behaviour of agents in the political market under different voting rules and with two or more political parties. Normative public choice focuses on the features of different social welfare or social choice functions and the concept of a just social contract (Arrow 1951; Rawls 1971). In contrast to the traditional market failure paradigm, public choice analysis concludes that *governments can fail*.

(h) The revival of Austrian economics with its focus on choice under uncertainty

Austrians are critical of the concept of equilibrium, particularly general equilibrium and perfect competition. They stress ignorance, uncertainty and dynamic markets which are characterized by disequilibrium and continuous entrepreneurial adjustment to repeated change. On this view, price changes act as signals causing individuals to change their plans. Entrepreneurs will search for profitable opportunities before their rivals identify them. The result of rivalry and the competitive process will be *equilibrating tendencies* without implying that the process will lead to an equilibrium. To Austrians, competition means continuous rivalry, movement and change, none of which exists in a perfectly competitive equilibrium (Hayek 1983).

THE CONTRIBUTION OF NEO-CLASSICAL ECONOMICS

Neo-classical economics is attractive to economists wishing to emulate the methodology of the natural sciences. It comprises a set of rigorous and well-developed theories of economic agents and their exchange relationships. There are extensive opportunities for applying mathematics and parts are highly abstract, particularly general equilibrium theory. Often, the theories seem to offer clear, testable predictions, capable of being refuted. Moreover, neo-classical ideas have had a major influence on government economic policy and, during the 1970s and early 1980s, the subject experienced a revival at the expense of Keynesian macroeconomics. Examples include competition policy, the contracting out of public sector services to private contractors and deregulation (for example, US airlines; UK bus transport); the case for free trade and customs unions (for example, the EEC) and the use of cost-benefit analysis in the appraisal of public sector decisions (for example, railway closures; building new roads). Indeed, cost-benefit analysis as part of applied welfare economics, provides *one* basis for an interdisciplinary approach to policy problems. Its concern with identifying and measuring costs and benefits from society's viewpoint often requires the combined skills of different disciplines (for example, social scientists and engineers). For instance, the debate over the siting of London's third airport involved a major cost-benefit study, part of which estimated the effects of the proposed airport development on the local communities (for example, environmental effects, noise, cf. Roskill 1971).

The role of exogenous factors

In neo-classical economics, exogenous factors serve a variety of purposes including explanation, simplification and boundary determination. A useful distinction can be made between variables which are exogenous within the system and those which are external to the system. Thus, exogenous variables are the explanatory variables in a model: examples include prices and incomes in the theory of demand. But sometimes exogenous factors are used to simplify a complex world so that a model can be built to identify 'important' and relatively 'unimportant' factors, with the latter held constant through the *ceteris paribus* assumption. In neo-classical economics, exogenous factors which are often outside the system include population, technology, government and laws. Such exogenous factors determine the boundaries of economic modelling. This paper focuses on three sets of exogenous factors, namely tastes and preferences, technology and government. These have been chosen because they provide extensive opportunities for an interdisciplinary approach. Demographers, psychologists and sociologists are concerned with population and the impact of class, education, marital status, age and place of residence (rural or urban) on preference formation and household behaviour (for example, consumer demand). Both scientists and social scientists are interested in technology, whilst political scientists specialize in the study of government and constitutional arrangements (also of interest to lawyers). These exogenous factors are also areas which are increasingly subject to economic analysis based on the neo-classical paradigm. Economic analysis of the family, of R & D, and of the governments, bureaucracies and laws, represent efforts to extend the boundaries of economics to model factors which were traditionally regarded as outside the system.

Tastes and preferences

Utility or preference functions are central to neo-classical economics and are assumed to be given. They affect consumers, workers and firms. Consider the following examples:

Consumer tastes and preferences

These are likely to be influenced by the social class of parents, education, marriage (creating a joint utility function embracing a two or more person household), family size (*n* person households), age and sex, as well as by laws and social conventions. These factors influencing preference formation and changes in preferences correspond to Type I and II plug-ins which affect both independent variables (tastes) and parameters (see demand equation on p. 54). (These types of plug-in – I, II, III, etc. – refer to Himmelstrand's typology in Chapter 1. Type I and III plug-ins affect independent variables (tastes) and parameters respectively.) For instance, laws on, and social attitudes towards, alcohol, drugs and smoking will affect the consumption of these goods, some of which are addictive. However Type IV feedback effects are likely with firms responding to changing consumer tastes through advertising, promotion and new products (for example, alcohol-free lager; low-tar cigarettes). Of course, advertising raises doubts about consumer sovereignty and also means that tastes and preferences are no longer determined outside the system. Alternatively, laws banning the consumption of alcohol, cigarettes and drugs are also likely to create Type IV feedback effects through the creation of illegal or 'black' markets.

Workers and labour supply

The supply of labour depends on the size of population and the willingness of people to work which, in turn, depends on their preferences between income and leisure, and the rewards of working. Preferences or attitudes towards work will be influenced by such factors as social class, education and experience. Information about jobs and their characteristics is not freely available. Search and the acquisition of information can determine and change attitudes to different job offers, so affecting worker preferences (non-monetary variables).

Role of learning

Learning-by-doing and experience leads to the acquisition of information and knowledge and possible revisions of preference functions. For example, as a result of repeated purchases, consumers might decide to buy or not to buy certain products again leading to Type IV and V feedback effects (Hartley and Tisdell 1981).

Firms

Market structures might determine a firm's objective function (really its tastes and preferences or its subjective function). Imperfect markets, particularly imperfect capital markets, provide opportunities for firms and their managers to pursue non-profit aims which will be reflected in different utility functions (for example, sales, growth). In this context, performance is assumed to depend on industry structure; but performance which leads to the elimination of rivalry can *feedback* and affect structure, with implications for a firm's subjective function.

Technology

Traditionally, neo-classical economics assumed a given state of technology and concentrated on the effects of technical change on new production techniques. However, more recently, neo-classical economists have analysed technology markets by concentrating on demand and supply side influences on R & D, the costs of establishing property rights in new ideas and the role of industrial structure in the form of the number and size distribution of firms (monopoly v. oligopoly v. competition: Kamien and Schwartz 1982). In fact, technical change is a classic case study of an exogenous factor which embraces all types of plug-ins, spill-overs and feedback effects (Types I–VI). Take the example of information technology (IT) (cf. Hartley 1984a). European governments are supporting IT because they believe it will be the basis for the next industrial revolution, so affecting all aspects of economic and social activities and institutions. However, there is a real danger that technology will dominate public policy to the neglect of its wider implications for society. IT is expected to result in changes in:

The competitiveness of firms

The immediate impact is a Type I plug-in which will then feed through the economic system via changes in supply and hence changes in the market prices of both products and factors of production. For instance, Type III effects might be reflected in the environmental impact of new technology (for example, chemical plants and poisonous fumes; nuclear power and radiation; health hazards from word processors).

Employment and unemployment, and their implications for education, training and retraining

Which industries are likely to expand, which are likely to contract and where will the new jobs be located (for example, which communities will decline)? IT will affect employment directly through its impact on labour productivity: a Type II parameter plug-in through the production function. If IT is equivalent to a new industrial revolution, there will be wider effects on income distribution and ultimately on the whole of society (Type VI effects).

The home, family life and leisure

For instance, IT might allow more people to work at home (for example, teleworking) with implications for the organization of firms and for trade union membership. There will also be effects on the individual and family use of leisure – for example, cable TV and home videos might reduce the demand for cinemas, concerts, theatres and live sport.

Government

IT will affect the productivity of the public sector; it might have implications for political parties and social choices (for example, frequent referenda and instant opinion polls); it raises questions about the protection of individual rights and whether there is a role for government and public policy. Should the state intervene and, if so, should it seek to reduce barriers to change (how)? In principle, these issues embrace all types of effects (that is, I to VI).

Government

Government is a classic exogenous factor. Neo-classical economists assumed that government, the constitution, laws, regulations and public expenditure were given and that governing politicians and the bureaucracy will implement the 'will of the people'. Traditionally, they regarded government as a 'black box'. Only recently have neo-classical concepts been applied to the political market-place. Take the example of UK government policy towards cigarette smoking and alcohol consumption.[2] Assume that governments wish to reduce the consumption of these substances. Economists have responded by proposing such measures as higher taxes on the products, health warnings, advertising controls and prohibition. Such policy proposals have completely ignored the interest groups in the political market which will seek to influence and modify government policy in their favour. Figure 4.1 presents a framework for identifying, classifying and mapping the formal and informal linkages and relationships within the political market-place. The actors are:

(a) *The governing party* as reflected in the composition and behaviour of the Cabinet (a group of ministers) and whether the relevant ministers are experienced, qualified, thrusters or sleepers. It is assumed that the government will be concerned with re-election.

(b) *Elected politicians* who will be seeking votes. To explain behaviour, information is required on the declared interests of politicians. For example, are they major shareholders in alcohol and tobacco companies; do they raise questions and participate in Parliamentary debates on alcohol and smoking? Are there any educational, social (for example, clubs) and family links between politicians and the owners and managers of alcohol and tobacco companies?

(c) *Bureaucracies.* In the case of alcohol and tobacco, and within the UK, the Department of Health will be concerned with health care and the prevention of ill-health; the Departments of Industry and Employment will be concerned with the jobs, technology and balance-of-payments contributions of the industries; and the Treasury will be worried about the consequences for government revenue and hence for higher taxes elsewhere and/or cuts in public expenditure.

(d) *Pressure groups* will seek to influence government policy through advertising campaigns, consultancy reports, lobbying, public demonstrations, and approaches to elected politicians.

(e) *The alcohol and tobacco industries* and their suppliers will oppose policies likely to affect adversely their industrial performance, particularly their profitability.

(f) *Linkages* both *formal* and *informal* need to be identified. In this context, information is required on company directors, interlocking directorships, directorships for retired civil servants, and shareholdings by directors. Information is needed on the family background, education, hobbies and clubs of leading shareholders, company directors, civil servants and ministers. In other words, who is likely to gain and who is likely to lose from policy changes; and what are the relative costs and benefits to various actors of seeking to influence public policy? In terms of Figure 4.1, we need to know what happens within each box, how and why.

The public choice approach

The economics of politics and public choice applies neo-classical economics to the political market-place (Downs 1957). The maximizing postulate has been applied to voters, political parties, bureaucracies and interest groups, so providing a basis for explaining what happens within the various boxes shown in Figure 4.1. As a result, public choice analysis means that factors which were previously outside the system (for example, the constitution) have now been 'internalized'. Some of the predictions of the public choice approach are as follows:

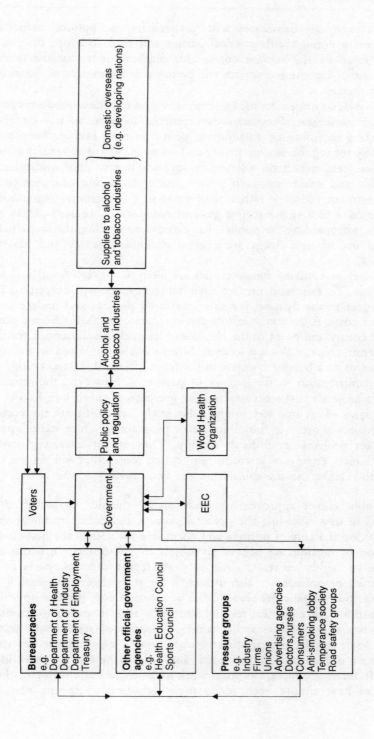

Figure 4.1 Linkages within the political market-place: the case of alcohol and tobacco

(a) In a two-party democracy with vote-maximizing political parties and majority voting, both political parties will tend to adopt the *policies favoured by the median voter*. One implication is that the redistribution of income and wealth will be towards the middle of the income distribution.

(b) The *policies* of democratic governments tend to *favour producers* rather than consumers. Producers can combine to form an interest group seeking to influence government policy in their favour. They might lobby for regulations on quality and safety standards to restrict competition from rival firms offering cheaper and hence, 'poor quality, unreliable and unsafe products'. As a result, regulation can protect and benefit an industry rather than society. Furthermore, regulation is attractive to a vote-sensitive government since it can demonstrate that it is 'safeguarding the public'. Regulations controlling the introduction and use of new drugs are a good example (Hartley and Maynard 1982).

(c) *Budget-maximizing bureaucracies* are likely to be *'too large'* and *inefficient*. To raise and protect their budgets, they will overestimate or exaggerate the demand for their preferred policies and underestimate their costs. A defence ministry can exaggerate the threat from a potential enemy and point to the number of its nuclear submarines, missiles, aircraft, ships, tanks and soldiers. Stress can also be placed on the social benefits of a bureau's project in the form of jobs, high technology and its contribution to the balance of payments. However, the reliability of a project's cost estimates and the presence of any external costs will be ignored. A ministry might deliberately underestimate the costs of a project in order to 'buy into' a new programme. Once started, public sector projects are difficult to stop. They attract interest groups of architects, engineers, scientists, surveyors, contractors and unions, each with relative income gains from the continuation of the work.

The public choice approach has made some valuable and useful contributions to understanding the political process and policy formulation. It has developed a core of positive and normative theories in the neo-classical tradition of maximizing behaviour subject to constraints. In addition to its use of highly abstract, rigorous and elegant theories, parts of the economics of politics are also attractive for their descriptive reality (for example, bureaucratic behaviour). But abstraction and intuitive appeal are no substitute for empirical testing. Problems arise in trying to formulate clear, testable hypotheses and obtaining appropriate data for their testing. What, for example, is a producer group; how is it possible to determine whether a bureaucracy is 'too large' and how is the median voter identified? In many instances, empirical work has been *ad hoc*, in which political variables have simply been added to an equation containing economic variables (Hartley and McLean 1981). Nevertheless, some predictions are capable of being tested. The hypothesis that bureaucracies are technically inefficient can be tested against the performance of private firms, supplying identical services, as in the UK's contracting-out policy (Hartley 1984b). Even so, to

> demonstrate that public choice has something useful to contribute to the existing empirical literature on public finance and public policy, its models must be tested against the existing models which ignore public choice considerations. Unless public choice derived models can out-perform the traditional *ad hoc* models against which it competes, the practical relevance of its theories must remain somewhat in doubt.
>
> (Mueller 1979: 111)

THE CONTRIBUTION TO DEVELOPMENT THEORY

In addition to neo-classical growth theory and empirical work on aggregate production functions, neo-classical economics has made three general contributions to development theory:

(a) Its emphasis on *markets* as a basis for mutually advantageous trade and exchange both within and between nations; and the recognition of market prices as an efficient signalling and allocative mechanism.
(b) The desire of all *agents* within any economic system to *satisfy their preferences*. A desire which leads workers in the public and private sectors to 'shirk' and consume on-the-job leisure unless there are strong incentives and rewards for good performance, and penalties for poor performance; and which also leads entrepreneurs in the private sector to respond to ignorance and uncertainty by seeking opportunities to make money before anyone else (they have private property rights over any resulting profits or losses).
(c) Whilst private markets can fail (for example, monopoly, externalities, pollution), developments in public choice analysis suggest that *governments can also fail*.

On the basis of these propositions, neo-classical economists are critical of massive state intervention in developing nations in the form of planning, protection and industrialization. They argue that state intervention can be harmful and that there is a role for private property, trading, prices and profits (cf. Hong Kong, Singapore) – a role which has been recognized in socialist states. To illustrate the problems of state intervention, consider the application of economic models of bureaucracy to technology policy with its implications for economic growth and development. Five propositions can be formulated to show how bureaucracies are likely to behave towards technology policy:

Proposition 1. Bureaucrats show an infinite capacity for ingenuity: they can adjust and play any games. Government officials will act in pursuit of their own interests subject to incentives, penalties and constraints on their behaviour. This self-interest might involve the pursuit of larger budgets, more staff, prestige projects and a quiet life. For instance efficiency-improving techniques such as cost-benefit analysis and programme budgeting will be used to support and reinforce the budget-maximizing aims of civil servants. Nor are actions restricted to national boundaries. It is often claimed that one of the 'benefits' of international collaborative projects involving governments is that they are much more difficult to cancel (for example, Concorde, Tornado)!

Proposition 2. Bureaucrats have every incentive to spend, since there are no rewards for not spending. Indeed, any savings might accrue to a rival division within a ministry or to another department, or, ultimately, to the national treasuries. And, of course, next time around a department which economizes will find that its budget will be cut!

Proposition 3. Bureaucracies will erect a set of myths around their preferred policies. References will be made to the technology gap – no one ever worries about a banana gap nor the cost of closing these gaps; and to the valuable, but difficult to quantify, technical spin-off benefits from government-supported R & D. The difficulties of measurement might reflect the fact that there is nothing there to be measured! Indeed, many of the arguments used by bureaucracies are long on emotion and short on economic analysis and supporting evidence.

Proposition 4. Bureaucrats prefer international collaboration and international organizations: there are more opportunities for discretionary action. No politician has an incentive nor opportunity to control an international bureaucracy: so international bureaucracies are characterised by major inefficiencies and massive 'red tape'. For instance, with international collaborative projects such as Concorde and Tornado, each partner nation required a 'fair' share in the R & D work for each sector of advanced technology (airframe, engine and electronics) so that the work tends to be allocated on equity rather than efficiency criteria (Hartley 1983).

Proposition 5. Bureaucrats have no incentive to co-operate in policies aimed at improving efficiency: they bear the costs (they're the losers) and they receive no benefits. Also, politicians need bureaucrats to implement their policies, so that politicians have only limited incentives to regulate bureaucratic behaviour and efficiency.

The total result is that bureaucrats have considerable discretionary power which they can use to pursue *their* preferred policies.

CONCLUSION

The standard criteria for assessing neo-classical economics (or any form of economics) must be its empirical performance against rival theories. But neo-classical economists often:

> preach the importance of submitting theories to empirical tests, but they rarely live up to their declared methodological canons. Analytical elegance, economy of theoretical means, and the widest possible scope obtained by ever more heroic simplification have been too often prized above predictability and significance for policy questions.
>
> (Blaug 1980: 259)

All of which raises the fundamental issue of why many economists continue to support neo-classical analysis and, within the neo-classical framework, allocate their efforts to some sections rather than others and to theory rather than to applied work? One answer would start from the utility-maximizing aims of economists and would explain their behaviour and allocation of effort in terms of the expected benefits and costs of alternative courses of action. They will select those research areas which are likely to be worthwhile, where the pattern of incentives, rewards and punishments will be determined by their terms and conditions of employment (employment contract). Of course, it does not follow that the research directions pursued by university economists will necessarily be those preferred by society. But this is very much a neo-classical explanation of the behaviour of economists!

NOTES

1 The quantity theory of nominal income was: $MV = Y$, where $Y = PQ$. $M =$ amount of money; $V =$ income velocity of circulation; $Y =$ nominal income; $P =$ general price level; $Q =$ national output.
2 This section is the result of work in the Education and Science Research Council (ESRC) Addiction Research Centre based at the Universities of Hull and York. Assistance and comments were provided by Roy Boakes, Research Fellow in the Centre.

BIBLIOGRAPHY

Arrow, K. J. (1951) *Social Choice and Individual Values*, New York, Wiley.
Arrow, K. J. and Debreu, G. (1954) 'Existence of an equilibrium for a competitive economy', *Econometrica* 22, 265–90.
Arrow, K. J. and Hahn, F. (1971) *General Competitive Analysis*, London, Oliver & Boyd.
Bain, J. (1972) *Essays on Price Theory and Industrial Organization*, Boston, Mass., Little and Brown.
Becker, G. (1964) *Human Capital*, New York, New York, Columbia University Press.

Becker G. (1976) *The Economic Approach to Human Behaviour*, Chicago, Ill., University of Chicago Press.

Bergson, A. (1938) 'A reformulation of certain aspects of welfare economics', *Quarterly Journal of Economics* 52 (February), 310–34.

Blaug, M. (1978) *Economic Theory in Retrospect*, Cambridge, Cambridge University Press (3rd edn).

Blaug, M. (1980) *The Methodology of Economics*, Cambridge, Cambridge University Press.

Chamberlin, E. H. (1933) *The Theory of Monopolistic Competition*, Cambridge, Mass., Harvard University Press.

Coase, R. H. (1937) 'The nature of the firm', *Economica* 4 (November), 386–405.

Cobb, C. W. and Douglas, P. H. (1928) 'A theory of production', *American Economic Review* (supplement) 139–65.

Denison, E. F. (1967) *Why Growth Rates Differ?* Washington, DC, Brookings Institution.

Downs, A. (1957) *An Economic Theory of Democracy*, New York, Harper & Row.

Downs, A. (1967) *Inside Bureaucracy*, Boston, Mass., Little and Brown.

Friedman, M. (ed.) (1956) *Studies in the Quantity Theory of Money*, Chicago, Ill. University of Chicago Press.

Friedman, M. and Schwartz, A. J. (1982) *Monetary Trends in the United States and the United Kingdom: Their Relation to Income, Prices and Interest Rates 1867–1975*, Chicago, Ill., University of Chicago Press.

Hartley, K. (1983) *NATO Arms Cooperation: A Study in Economics and Politics*, London, Allen & Unwin.

Hartley, K. (1984a) 'Information technology and society', 15–20 and 'IT and public policy', 164–71, in C. Lutz (ed.) *Western Europe on the Road to the Information Society*, Zurich, Gottlieb Duttweiler Institut.

Hartley, K. (1984b) 'Why contract out?' in *Contracting out in the Public Sector*. London, Royal Institute of Public Administration, 9–15.

Hartley, K. and McLean, P. (1981) 'UK defence expenditure', *Public Finance* 36, (2), 171–92.

Hartley, K. and Maynard A. (1982) *The Costs and Benefits of Regulating New Product Development in the UK Pharmaceutical Industry*, London, Office of Health Economics.

Hartley, K. and Tisdell, C. (1981) *Micro-economic Policy*, London, Wiley.

Hayek, F. A. (1983) *Knowledge, Evolution and Society*, London, Adam Smith Institute.

Henderson, J. M. and Quandt, R. E. (1971) *Microeconomic Theory: A Mathematical Approach*, London, McGraw-Hill.

Hicks, J. R. (1939) 'The foundations of welfare economics', *Economic Journal* 49 (December), 696–712.

Hicks, J. R. (1946) *Value and Capital*, Oxford, Clarendon Press (2nd edn).

Judd, J. P. and Scadding, J. L. (1982) 'The search for a stable money demand function', *Journal of Economic Literature* 20 (3), 993–1023.

Kaldor, N. (1939) 'Welfare propositions of economics and inter-personal comparisons of utility', *Economic Journal* 49 (September), 549–52.

Kamien, M. and Schwartz, N. (1982) *Market Structure and Innovation*, Cambridge, Cambridge University Press.

Koutsoyiannis, A. (1979) *Modern Microeconomics*, London, Macmillan.

Leibenstein, H. (1966) 'Allocative efficiency versus X-efficiency', *American Economic Review* 56 (June), 394.

Lerner, A. (1946) *The Economics of Control*, New York, Macmillan.

Lipsey, R. G. and Lancaster K. (1956) 'The general theory of second-best', *Review of Economic Studies* 24, 11–32.

Marshall, A. (1890) *Principles of Economics*, London, Macmillan.

Mueller, D. C. (1979) *Public Choice*, Cambridge, Cambridge University Press.

Rawls, J. (1971) *A Theory of Justice*, Cambridge, Mass., Harvard University Press.

Robinson, J. (1933) *The Economics of Imperfect Competition*, London, Macmillan.

Robinson J. (1955) 'The production function', *Economic Journal* 65 (March), 67–71.

Roskill, E. W. (1971) *Commission on the Third London Airport*, Report, London, HMSO.

Samuelson, P. A. (1948a) 'Consumption theory in terms of revealed preference', *Economica* 15 (November), 243–53.

Samuelson, P. A. (1948b) *Foundations of Economic Analysis*, Cambridge, Mass., Harvard University Press.

Sraffa, P. (1926) 'The laws of returns under competitive conditions', *Economic Journal* 36 (December), 535–50.

Stigler, G. J. (1961) 'The economics of information', *Journal of Political Economy* 69 (June), 213–25.

Walras, L. (1874) *Eléments d'économique politique pure*, Lausanne, L. Corbaz.

Walras, L. (1954) *Elements of Pure Economics*, (transl. by W. Jaffe), London, Allen & Unwin.

Walters, A. (1963) 'Production and cost functions: an econometric survey', *Econometrica* 31, 1–66.

Williamson, O. E. (1964) *The Economics of Discretionary Behavior: Managerial Objectives in a Theory of the Firm*, N. J., Englewood Cliffs, Prentice Hall (Ford Foundation doctoral dissertation series).

Chapter 5

Exogenous factors in neo-classical macroeconomics

Arjo Klamer

PRELUDE

There is an old joke about a drunk who loses his keys in the bushes late
one night. A passer-by finds him on his hands and knees, searching the
pavement directly under the street-light. 'What happened?' asks the stranger. 'I lost my keys in the bushes', replied the drunk. 'Then why are you
looking here?' the stranger asks in bewilderment. And the drunk responds,
'Because it is here that the light shines'.

Economists love this joke. It usually comes up when the discussion
turns to the truth value or realism of economic theories. The joke betrays
the strong ironic sense with which economists view their practice.
Although the economic establishment will defend its approach against any
undermining criticism and affirm its commitment to the pursuit of truth,
they laugh at someone who truly believes in the truth value of economic
theory. As Sartre notes: 'In irony a man nihilates what he posits within
one and the same act; he leads to believe in order not to believe; he
affirms to deny and denies to affirm' (Sartre 1956: 87).

A discussion of exogenous variables is pertinent for the exploration of
disciplinary boundaries. The exogenous variables show the limits and simultaneously, through their articulated presence, possibilities for extending
the boundaries. Those possibilities may include transgressions into other
disciplines.

A major objective of this essay is an exploration of the constraints that
the formalist discipline imposes on macroeconomics. I hope to show that
a discussion of exogenous variables is misguided if it is not combined with
a discussion of the formalist approach in economics. To that purpose I
will first define exogenous variables in the context of a general economic
model. After that I shall trace the emergence of the formalist approach in
macroeconomics and its consequences for the treatment of exogenous
variables. I have chosen business cycles theories as the back-drop for the
discussion as they are a major issue in macroeconomic debates nowadays.

I intend to show that divergent attitudes to the formalist approach account for at least part of the persistent disagreements among various schools of neo-classical macroeconomics, namely the neo-Keynesians, monetarists, new classical economists and new-Keynesians. The attention to exogenous variables in the models of each of these economists can further clarify the disagreements. In my concluding remarks I outline a possibly fruitful way of thinking about macroeconomic discourse and interdisciplinary possibilities.

EXOGENOUS VARIABLES IN ECONOMIC REASONING

As defined in the introduction to this volume, the exogenous variables in an economic analysis are the variables accounted for but not explained in the analysis. In economic lingo they are also called 'independent' or 'autonomous' variables. The exogenous variables are an implicit acknowledgement of limitation: the economist who introduces 'personal taste' as an exogenous variable in his model admits that, although relevant to the analysis, taste will be left undetermined.

The distinction between neo-classical and endogenous variables presumes a modelling strategy. Only in the context of a well-specified model does it become clear which variables are simply given, and hence external to the argument of the model. The most general articulation for a linear economic model is as follows

$$y = A \cdot y + B \cdot x + e$$

In this equation y is a vector of n variables, A an $n \times n$ matrix, x a vector of m variables, B an $m \times n$ matrix, and e a vector of n variables. The model defines n equations, of which equation j reads:

$$Y_j = \alpha_{j1} Y_1 + \alpha_{j2} Y_2 + \ldots + \alpha_{jn} Y_n + b_{j1} x + b_{j2} x_2 + \ldots + b_{jn} x_n + e_j$$

y is the vector of endogenous variables: each y is determined by the other endogenous variables, the exogenous variables x_i $(i=1, \ldots, m)$ and e_j, which e_j is a stochastic variable, that is, a variable subject to a certain probability distribution. The parameters are assumed constant.

The construction of a model – the preoccupation of economists today – involves the choosing of x's and y's. The economist has to decide which variables are to be explained by the model, that is, which variables will be the endogenous y's. Clearly, any variable that needs explanation has to be endogenous in the model. Thus if the recent increase in the inflation rate is to be explained, the inflation rate has to be endogenous. Very rarely is a model limited to one endogenous variable and one equation. Movements in variables that affect the inflation rate, such as the wage rate, import prices and, the money supply require an explanation as well, and hence need to be 'endogenized' with an equation for each one of them.

The endogenization could in principle go on till all relevant exogenous variables are moved from the right side of the equations to the left side. Even if that could be done, the model would soon become unmanageable. The analyst, therefore, has to make a decision. And so it happens that cumbersome variables such as preferences, exports, technology, and the money supply usually end up as exogenous variables in an economic model.

To repeat a point made in the introduction and the article by Hartley, exogenous variables are not all the same. By not writing down an equation for exports, for example, the analyst avoids the complications of modelling the economic conditions abroad and the international exchange markets. In this case exports are, in Hartley's terms, an exogenous variable within the economic model; they could be endogenized through an expansion of the model. No matter of principle is involved. It is different if a factor like 'the weather' were to be the exogenous variable (which might influence inflation through its impact of farm prices). Since economists are not in the business to explain the weather, they will consider the weather an exogenous variable external to the economic model. Here, too, no matter of principle is involved.

There are many other factors which could be taken into account in a model to explain inflation rates but are not because of procedural and disciplinary reasons. Historians, social psychologists and sociologists, to mention a few non-economists, might want to consider political circumstances, attitudes and beliefs, and cultural factors when they are asked to account for inflationary tendencies. Economists will generally not do so, committed as they are to a limited set of exogenous variables. They will identify, through the specification of a utility function, taste as an independent factor but assume it to be constant and leave it unexplored. Political, psychological, and cultural factors do not pertain to their domain, thus the argument goes. Of course, those are precisely the factors that the IDEA Project seeks to incorporate into the theory economic model – Himmelstrand captures them under the numerator of the *exogenous independent variable plug-in*.

The oversight of particular exogenous factors reminds one of the joke of the drunkard who is looking for the keys only where he can see. Economists have, however, also a technical excuse, namely that such factors are difficult to specify and to operationalize, and even where that were possible, their inclusion would make the model unnecessarily complicated. The implicit assumption is that these factors are subsumed in the constants and the error terms of the model. So a successful strike at a medium-sized company might have an impact on the national inflation rate but the effect is negligible and random. Accordingly, fluctuations in the error term have to allow for variations in factors that remain unspecified.

In principle economic theory determines the separation of the x's and y's in a model. But recently various economists have advocated a method that reduces the role of theoretical considerations. Sims (1980) introduces a method that entirely relies on time-series analysis; it is similar to the so-called exogeneity tests as applied in Sargent (1978). Such techniques, however, are still new and, more unfortunately, laborious, cumbersome, and not always feasible. They also have the disadvantage that the analyst lacks an understanding of why one variable is x and another y. In the language of the seminar: he does not have a good story. Hence it is unlikely that this purely technical approach will replace the method of model-specification by way of theoretical argument.

It should be furthermore pointed out that this discussion of the x's and y's presumes the model building approach. Ever since the nerve centre of economic analysis moved from Cambridge, England, to Cambridge, USA, economists have insisted on reasoning in terms of explicit models. Formalist rhetoric reigns in modern economic discourse. The implicit belief is that the only scientific way to represent economic reality is through a series of mathematical equations. Consequently, when a sociologist refers to social influence on economic behaviour the formalist approach dictates a question like 'That is interesting but how does that fit into a model?' The discipline that formalism imposes on economic discourse has been shown to be highly productive, but it also constrains the discourse as the following example clarifies.

Take the following consumption function:

$$C = a + b\ (Y-T)$$

Here C stands for consumption, Y for personal income and T for government taxes. Y and T are the identified exogenous variables. Neo-classical discipline requires a motivation of this function in terms of individual behaviour. The common way of proceeding is to postulate that each individual attempts to maximize her utility subject to specific constraints. Without simplification, further progress is impossible, so let us assume that each individual chooses between consuming now (C_1) and consuming in a next period (C_t+1). Her utility function will then be:

$$U = U\ (C_t,\ C_{t+1})\ \text{with}\ \delta U/\delta\ C_t > O\ \text{and}\ \delta U/\delta\ C_{t+1} > O$$

The problem is the construction of the constraints. We can make a beginning with the assumption that the income in both periods is equal to $Y-T$. The individual would then maximize her utility function with the following budget as her constraint:

$$2\ (Y-T)\ =\ C_t\ +\ C_{t+1}$$

This set-up constitutes a so-called constrained maximization problem which can be solved if we specify the utility function. After aggregation for all individual solutions of this problem (that is, ΣC) we may expect to achieve an equation like the original consumption function in which a and b will be composites of parameters in the utility function and the budget constraint.

Of course, this model is too simple to be persuasive. A severely truncated list of objections could read as follows: (1) the model fails to allow for a price difference between the two periods, (2) the individual may save part of her income and thus earn an interest that she can spend on C, (3) dollar amounts in the same period need to be 'discounted', and (4) income earned is part of the individual's choice (she may choose to consume more leisure) and therefore income should be treated as an endogenous variable. The neo-classical literature meets all these objections. The price is a significant complication of the consumption model as the entry for consumption in *The New Palgrave: A Dictionary of Economics* (MacMillan 1988) shows.

The formalist strategy that requires full specification of all variables, however, tends to bias the selection of objections that are met. A variable for advertisement, for instance, has been proved to resist satisfactory specification. It involves the elements of information and its interpretation by consumers, neither of which are easily captured in formal notations. Another strategy would be to include psychological factors to account for shifts in savings, and thus consumption behaviour. Maital and Maital (1990) argue, for example, that, during the 1970s and 1980s, forward-looking behaviour has receded in favour of myopic behaviour with a relative decline in national savings as a result. They furthermore argue the emergence of institutions that promote myopic behaviour, such as freely-available credit cards. Even though their appeal to psychological and institutional factors resolves the conundrum of declining saving rates, neo-classical economists are far from receptive. They maintain that analytical parsimony has priority over scope; hence the inclination is to ignore foreign arguments and to look for explanations within the confines of constrained maximization set-ups. This example goes to show that the fact of exogenous variables in economic analysis is tied up with the formal strategy of neo-classical economics.

THE FORMALIZATION OF ECONOMICS

The common justification for formalization refers to the clarity one achieves and the minimalization of disagreements. The latter result, however, does not materialize in macroeconomics. Whether the talk is about stabilization policies, long-term growth, inflation-unemployment trade-offs, or business cycle – all dominant topics in the field – macroeconomists tend to be divided and huddle together under different banners. Among those macroeconomists who are committed to formal reasoning we distin-

guish the neo-Keynesians, new-Keynesians, new-classicals, and monetarists. Disagreements among these schools of thought are significant and
persistent. Much of their disagreement can be reduced to different assessments of the formal strategy.[1]

It took a fair number of years before the formalist requirement got a grip
on conventional economic discourse. Adam Smith staked out a domain for
economic discourse with his non-formal *Wealth of Nations* in 1776. His
writing is literary and the dividing lines with history and philosophy and
what we now call sociology are hardly visible. For Adam Smith political
economy was a branch of moral philosophy with the specific objective to
establish the moral character of agents operating in a commercial society.
David Ricardo was the precursor of the formalist trend in economics. In
his *Principles of Political Economy and Taxation* (1815) he abstracts from
political, sociological, and historical factors and deduces conclusions from
a limited set of assumptions. Ricardo himself made minimal use of mathematics but later interpretations showed that his analysis could be captured
in the form of a mathematical model.

Ricardo's method of abstraction initially did not enchant the masses in
the way the informal, literary style of Adam Smith did. Economists
objected to what they called the Ricardian Vice. Malthus, in a direct
reference to Ricardo's method, opens his *Principles of Political Economy*
with the plea that 'The science of economy resembles more the sciences
of morals and politics than the science of mathematics'. W. Roscher and
other German economists prevailed with their empirical and historical
approach. During the latter part of the eighteenth century the pages of
the then new economic journals were filled with empirical studies; mathematical equations rarely made an appearance. American economists, too,
were taken by this empirical approach. Richard Ely, the founder of the
American Economic Association swore by it, and the so-called American
institutionalists were to carry the banner up till today.

Yet Richard Ely saw already in the late 1880s cause to defend his
approach. Formalism slowly but surely made its way into the profession.
The ascendancy of physics provided the impulse. A few rebellious minds
got captivated by the promises that the tightly argued physical metaphors
seem to hold for the analysis of economic phenomena.[2] Augustin Cournot,
Leon Walras, Hermann Gossen, and William Jevons, to mention a few of
them, were still a minority at their time and encountered strong opposition. During the first thirty years or so of the nineteenth century the
economic journals rarely included mathematical equations. Most economists paid not more than lip service to the idea of constructing mathematical
analogies of reality. Alfred Marshall put the mathematics of his argument
in appendices. But the mechanics of the physics metaphors proved to have
a strong attraction for economists.

An important factor was the move away from the discussion of moral character, as in Smith, to an analysis of economic choice. Taking their cues from Bentham's utilitarianism, Cournot, Gossen, and Jevons reduced economic life to moments of choice. They imagined individuals who seek to maximize a utility function while being constrained by various factors, such as their budget and the prices of the goods they desire. Another important move was the one by Leon Walras who envisaged the economy as an extended system of numerous interdependent markets. In this set-up the metaphor of a mechanism turned out to be fruitful as it inspired the idea of an equilibrium brought about by a mechanism of flexible prices. Thus the classical notions of classes, conflict, and social relations became history.

The writings of William Jevons, Leon Walras and followers such as Vilfredo Pareto and Francis Edgeworth continue to include sociological, psychological, and philosophical arguments. (There is still plenty of exogenous independent variable plug-in!) Their formal rhetoric was far from pure.

The same is true for the writings of John Maynard Keynes. In his *General Theory* (1936) he undertakes to expose the limitations of the mechanistic metaphor as he deems it unfit for a monetary economy. The theme that runs through the argument is that of uncertainty. It motivates the key elements, namely the liquidity preference, the marginal efficiency of capital, and, to a lesser extent, the marginal propensity to consume. This theme prevents him from casting the argument in a formal strait-jacket. There is no explicit model; the book contains only one diagram; and the equations are sparse. As a consequence Keynes does not clearly distinguish the endogenous and exogenous variables in his argument. Keynes does not even make an effort to motivate his behavioural functions in the neo-classical metaphor of constrained maximization. True to the heart of the IDEA Project he pulls in non-economic arguments and is not even self-conscious about them. A sociological argument portrays workers as caring about relative rather than absolute wages because the primary motive is the emulation of fellow workers. A psychological argument motivates consumption behaviour as follows:

> The fundamental psychological law, upon which we are entitled to depend with great confidence both *a priori* from our knowledge of human nature and from the detailed facts of experience, is that men are disposed, as a rule and on average, to increase their consumption as their income increases, but not by as much as the increase of their income.
>
> (Keynes 1936: 96)

In the discussion of investment behaviour Keynes alludes to the importance of confidence and animal spirits.

However, Keynes would fail to make a mark on the argumentative strategy of modern economics, the surge of Keynesian economics notwith-standing. With the move of the nerve centre of economics from Cambridge, England, to Cambridge, USA, the psychological and sociological arguments were left behind. The formal strategy took over. And as a consequence the range of exogenous variables in economic discourse got severely limited. Developments in the theory of business cycles tell the story.

BUSINESS CYCLE IN THE 1930s

The gyrations in economic aggregates are from time to time a major concern to macroeconomists. After the steady growth of the 1960s compelled them to focus on the theorizing of growth, the series of recessions in the 1970s and early 1980s made business cycle theory fashionable again. Not surprisingly, business cycles had also been a most popular topic during the 1930s. The fact that contemporary economists had to redo the work of the preceding generation is an indication that a good economic theory of the business cycle has been an elusive objective.

From the beginning the challenge has been to formulate an endogenous theory of business cycles in which the movements of the economy are explained by the interaction of endogenous variables in the articulated model. The easy way out is to let exogenous factors account for the recurrent cycles, as in Jevons's sunspot theory. But such explanations cannot hold the attention of economists for very long; after all, sunspots are beyond the control and comprehension of human beings, economists included.

One possible scenario for a business cycle reads as follows. After having restrained themselves during a recession, consumers return to the stores and consumption expenditures go up. That is the beginning. The extra spending stimulates investment; the demand for labour increases and so does total earnings with an additional boost to consumption and investment as a consequence. The increase in spending, however, is financed through an increase in credit; hence interest rates go up. More spending also implies higher prices. The combination of higher prices and interest rates slows down the increases in spending. Overcapacity becomes apparent; workers are being laid off, and the growth of personal income slows down. The economy enters the downswing till the decrease in interest rates and prices will be sufficient to stimulate a renewed surge in spending. At that point the economy starts a new cycle. This scenario relies exclusively on economic factors. No exogenous variables enter.

The scenario, however, leaves many questions unanswered. One wants to know, for instance, why an increase in spending (or demand) is not directly arrested by an increase in prices. The lag in the price adjustment needs an explanation. Furthermore, it is not clear what factors are responsible for the creation of overcapacity. The theorist wants to be more precise in the analysis of economic behaviour throughout the business cycle. The question is whether he can do so without seeking the aid outside the domain of economics.

One account of the business cycle is given by Keynes in chapter 22 of *The General Theory*. Keynes posits as the main cause of business cycles fluctuations in investment behaviour. To explain these fluctuations Keynes recognizes the influence of interest rates but attaches more importance to the role of 'expectations as to the future yield of capital goods'. With the introduction of expectations the analysis turns 'psychological': 'optimistic expectations' allegedly act up in the later stages of the boom (p. 315), 'market-sentiment' (p. 316) and the 'uncontrollable and disobedient psychology of the business world' produce speculative movements, and the loss of confidence, disillusion, 'doubts concerning the reliability of the prospective yield' (p. 317), and 'errors of pessimism' (p. 322) accelerate the downward trend. Keynes's argument for a sudden decline in investment reveals his strategy:

> It is of the nature of organised investment markets, under the influence of purchasers largely ignorant of what they are buying and of speculators who are more concerned with forecasting the next shift of market sentiment than with a reasonable estimate of the future yield of capital-assets, that, when disillusion falls upon an over-optimistic and over-bought market, it should fall with sudden and even catastrophic force.
>
> (Keynes 1936: 316)

Although this mode of reasoning is persuasive to many economists and most non-economists, the formalists among economists are troubled. The analysis fails their standard of rigour: the references to the psychology of the investor and the nature of investment markets are dragged in without being grounded in well-specified assumptions. Much of the analysis hinges, therefore, on factors that are extraneous to the conventional neo-classical discourse.

FROM NEO-CLASSICAL TO NEW CLASSICAL MACROECONOMICS

That Keynes continues to figure in contemporary economics, is due to the formal translations of his theory by John Hicks and Alvin Hansen. Their so-called IS/LM framework (Investment/Savings, Liquidity/Money Supply) became the standard equipment of the neo-Keynesian economists who were to dominate macroeconomics till the mid-1970s. Students of Keynes's ideas by-passed *The General Theory* to concentrate on this framework, usually taking the latter for what Keynes really meant. The IS/LM framework, however, ignored the major theme of *The General*

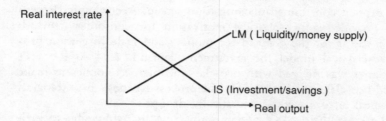

Figure 5.1 The IS/LM diagram: the Hicks-Hansen translation of Keynes's *General Theory*

Theory, namely, the uncertainty of a monetary economy and the psychological and sociological factors that act up as a consequence. Figure 5.1 shows the valiant reduction of a complex theory to a cross of two lines. The IS/LM diagram instructs to divide the economy in building blocks. The IS curve is the consolidation of the blocks for consumption, investment, international trade, and government spending. The LM curve stands for the financial block. The idea is to study each block separately and bring the results into the IS/LM diagram to see when and how the curves move with which result for real output and the interest rate.

The diagram is Keynesian because of the possibility that government spending moves the IS curve to change real output. In the neo-classical world of Keynes's predecessors such a real effect of government spending was not supposed to occur; if the government were to expand its spending, consumers and investors would be forced to reduce their spending and real output would remain unchanged. In the world of IS/LM real output effects are possible because of basically two assumptions: (1) prices are rigid, and (2) there is unemployment. Under these conditions, extra government spending can generate more production (there are people available to do the work) and prices will not immediately rise to discourage private spending.

The impression was given that all the government needed to do was to manipulate a few variables that were built into the equations for IS and LM, and the desired real output would be realized. Such variables, then, were the instruments of government policy. Presuming that the government would determine them, and since government behaviour is not endogenous in this set-up, these instruments are exogenous in the model. Think of tax rates, investment credits, military and other forms of government spending, and the money supply.

Neo-Keynesian economists considered as their main task the further formalization of the IS/LM framework. They aspired especially for a justification of the underlying behaviour relationships in neo-classical choice-theoretic terms. Consumers and investors had to act in accordance with some explicit constrained-maximization set-up. Accordingly, Franco Modigliani provided a neo-classical motivation for consumer demand; James Tobin did it for the demand for money; and Dale Jorgenson produced a neo-classical model for investment demand. And so Keynes's macroeconomics was merged with neo-classical microeconomics to make the so-called neo-classical synthesis. In the process Keynes's psychological and sociological factors were systematically dropped.

During the 1960s the neo-Keynesian rampart became vulnerable to various assaults. It began to show cracks. One attack came from the post-Keynesians, with Joan Robinson in England and Paul Davidson in the USA as leading figures. They claimed that the neo-Keynesians had misinterpreted Keynes by overlooking the effects of uncertainty and income distribution on macroeconomic outcomes. The radicals argued that the neo-Keynesians had lost sight of the fundamental problems of conflict, market power, and inequality. Both post-Keynesians and radicals questioned the neo-classical and formalist approach of neo-Keynesian economics. Their arguments made the profession waver but persuasive they ultimately were not.

The monetarists were more effective. Under the spirited leadership of Milton Friedman they succeeded to make big dents in the Keynesian rampart throughout the late 1960s and early 1970s. Aided by the accelerated inflation at the time, they were able to expose the constant-price assumption as an unwarranted simplification. The neo-Keynesians were forced to expand the IS/LM framework by adding on a block for the supply-side of the economy. One implication was that the labour market came into the picture. Friedman subsequently attacked the modelling of the labour market. Especially effective was his argument that expectations play a major role in that market (Friedman 1968). Till then expectations had not figured in the neo-Keynesian model. As a result every change had a diminished effectiveness on the government's instruments.

Friedman also cast doubt on the Keynesian treatment of the monetary block. He argued that the money supply has a much stronger effect on the economy than the Keynesian model allowed, and concluded that the money supply was too powerful an instrument with which to play. His proposal was, therefore, that the monetary authorities discipline themselves and maintain a constant growth in the money supply.

Although Friedman would neutralize the most extreme of the Keynesian policy claims, he was not to undo the Keynesian rampart. In hindsight we can say that his argumentation was too much like that of Keynes: loose, without a fully-specified model and without a formal statistical analysis. Ultimately more effective were Friedman's students, who pursued his basic insights through formal means. Robert Lucas, Thomas Sargent and others, going under the banner of new classical economists, exposed the formal inconsistencies and deficiencies of the neo-Keynesian framework. Especially devastating was their critique that neo-Keynesian analysis did not consistently apply neo-classical theorizing. They showed that if the formation of expectations was to be rational – a sensible presumption for neo-classicals with their belief in rational behaviour – the policy instruments would be ineffective.

The challenge that the new classicals posed to the neo-Keynesian framework was a formal one. How to articulate a model that is consistent with the neo-classical assumption of rational behaviour and shows real effects of economic policies? A new generation of Keynesians emerged. The new-Keynesians as they are called, have faced the challenge and have produced numerous models that are formal in accordance with the neo-classical prescriptions and suggest that the market economy is less perfect than the new classical models present it. Important for the IDEA Project has been the role of exogenous variables in these new-Keynesian models. Whereas new-classicals have been trying to reduce the relevant exogenous factors to preferences and the technological structure, new-Keynesians have been more willing to allow sociological considerations through the backdoor. Their efficiency-wage hypothesis, for instance, alludes to loyalty in employer-employee relationships. The sociological argument is, however, kept to its most rudimentary form as New-Keynesians subscribe to the neo-classical prescription that all economic behaviour be motivated by a constrained-maximization set-up. Furthermore, the rhetoric has to remain formal; a mathematical model is a prerequisite for participation in the debate.

Developments in the theorizing of business-cycle theory show first the trend towards formalization in macroeconomics, and the concurrent minimalization of the role of exogenous factors. The new-classical and new-Keynesian models constitute the culmination of this trend.

FORMALIZATION OF BUSINESS CYCLES

The impetus for the formalization of business cycle theory came early. Already in 1939 Paul Samuelson had constructed a tightly formulated model of a business cycle (Samuelson, 1939). The model consists of three equations, namely:

the consumption equation $C_t = \gamma\, Y_{t-1}$
an investment equation $I_t = \alpha\, (C_t - C_{t-1})$
a definition $Y_t = C_t + I_t + \bar{G}$

where C_t stands for consumption at time t, I_t for investment, $\bar{G}$ for autonomous government spending, and Y_t for real income. The solution of this simple model is a differential equation:

$$Y_t - (\gamma + \alpha\gamma)\, Y_{t-1} + \alpha\gamma Y_{t-1} \pm \bar{G}$$

Even this simple model is unmanageable without knowledge of differential equations. (Anyone interested in 'serious' economics be forewarned.) According to the theory of differential equations, Y can follow all kinds of patterns depending on the magnitude of the parameters γ and α If, for instance, $\gamma < \dfrac{4\,\alpha}{(1 + \alpha)^2}$ then Y will display cyclical fluctuation.

The immediate appeal of this model is that there are no references to bad weather or entrepreneurial psychology or an exogenous money supply; it is a formal, completely endogenous, account of the business cycle. Yet, as Samuelson was ready to acknowledge, the model is a gross simplification. The model does not specify a neo-classical justification of the consumption and investment equations; it does not include a price variable, nor an interest variable and lacks any reference to the financial block and the supply-side. It also does not describe reality very well as it cannot reproduce the irregular real cycles that we observe. Clearly, the model is only a first step. It was an important first step, though, because it showed the possibility for a formal representation of business cycles with a minimal reliance on exogenous factors.

Unfortunately for the Keynesian programme, more realistic formal models of business cycles proved to be hard to articulate. The model needed assumptions to account for slow adjustments to equilibrium in the goods and labour market, and the assumptions that neo-Keynesians came up with were not well grounded in neo-classical theoretic terms. Instances are the postulate of sticky prices or of a mismatch between skills asked and skills supplied due to a heterogeneous labour force. The latter assumption accounted for imperfections in the labour market. Why prices are sticky or why a mismatch occurs the models do not explain. Anyhow, the models explained business cycles as a disequilibrium phenomenon caused by slow adjustments after a shock to the system. That shock is usually some real shock such as a change in government spending, exports, or public confidence.

In monetarist models of the business cycles the real shocks play a subordinate role as they are quickly absorbed by means of changing prices. Instead, the (exogenous) money supply is cast as the prime mover in the market system, just as Irving Fisher had argued in the 1930s. The problems to be resolved are the slow adjustments of the system to the monetary shocks. Contrary to the Keynesians, the monetarists insist on the flexibility prices so the Keynesian option of sticky prices was not available to them. Friedman suggested as an explanation the time people use to learn about new developments. Expectations adapt but slowly. With adaptive expectations shocks in the money supply would last and, consequently, bring about business cycles.

The new classical economists agree with the monetarists on substantive issues. They, too, assign to monetary aggregates a critical role in the business cycle and generally advocate a hands-off policy. The difference is that the new classical economists take the neo-classical discipline and formalist standards far more seriously than the monetarists do or, for that matter, the neo-Keynesians. Lucas and Sargent began their revolution in the early 1970s by questioning the rationality of adaptive expectations. Why is it, they wondered, that rational agents in the monetarist model do not use all available information about the economy? If economists know what the long-term effects of a monetary shock are, a rational agent should know, so they argue. In other words rational agents have rational expectations.

John Muth (1961) provided a first formal formulation of rational expectations. Lucas showed how Muth's formulation could be integrated into a macroeconomic model (Lucas 1972, 1973, and 1976). The subsequent developments are relevant to the IDEA Project in so far as they show how one novel hypothesis can bring previously unidentified exogenous factors into the discussion. In this case those factors are information and the stochastic terms in the theoretical equations. Endowed with rational expectations, consumers, workers, and suppliers would know the long terms of a change in the money supply as soon as they learn about it, and they would act upon that knowledge. Adjustments to monetary shocks would be instantaneous and no fluctuation in real output occurs. Because we actually observe cyclical movements in real output, new classicals reason, agents must be constrained in their knowledge.

In the new classical models those constraints are limited information – the agents may not know, for instance, about the monetary shock – and the stochastic terms which will force rational agents to make guesses. The latter point can be clarified with the situation that workers face in the labour market. Since wages are paid out before they are spent, the suppliers of labour have to determine the real value of their wage in the future. To do so they have to know the prices of the goods they are planning to buy. That would be fine if the movement of prices is deterministic, but if prices are subject to random fluctuations, due to a stochastic term, workers have to guess future prices. Anyone who has to guess is bound to make mistakes. To speak with an analogy that Lucas offers, workers draw therefore a lot from the lottery. When they guess that prices go up and so bid for an increase in their nominal wage, bad luck may strike in the form of unemployment. Nobody and nothing are to be blamed but the stochastic nature of the market. The macroeconomic result of this stochastic feature, combined with rational expectations and imperfect information, is that monetary shocks generate cyclical movements in real output. And so models that are consistent with neo-classical prescriptions produce genuine business cycles.

A noteworthy feature of new classical models of business cycles is that they do not incorporate some kind of disequilibrium as the neo-Keynesian and monetarist models do. The latter models assume that either sticky prices or adaptive expectations prevent the markets from staying in equilibrium (with demand equal to supply) and place individuals in suboptimal positions (workers may be unemployed against their will). New classicals do not need such assumptions: in their models markets are always in equilibrium, a moving equilibrium, that is, and individuals are always doing what they rationally want to do given their constraints (the unemployed worker simply has drawn a bad lot from the lottery).

The new Keynesians, such as John Taylor and Stanley Fisher, pursue the new classical research programme. They accept the new classical hypothesis of rational expectations and the new classical commitment to rigorous model-specifications. Their disagreement concerns the new classical insistence that markets are always in equilibrium and that government policies are ineffective. They have taken as their task to justify market imperfections with arguments that are grounded in neo-classical microeconomics. In doing so they have introduced into the discussion phenomena that sociologists may recognize as theirs. (Psychological factors remain a taboo.) One of these phenomena is the different attitudes towards insiders in a firm and the outsiders. According to the insider-outsider hypothesis, nominal wages are sticky downwards as the insiders have the power to resist the competition of outsiders and hence are able to prevent wage cuts. Another phenomenon is that managers themselves are reluctant to cut wages as they fear a loss of motivation on the part of the workers and shirking. New Keynesians capture the latter phenomenon with their efficiency-wage hypothesis. The sociological content of the discussion is, however, kept to a minimum. The purpose of the insider-outsider and efficiency-wage hypothesis is to model rigidities and thus to account for persistent deviations from the macroeconomic equilibrium.

Lucas, Edward Prescott and other new classical economists have rejected these new-Keynesian hypotheses on grounds that their neo-classical justification is unpersuasive. To them it is not clear why rational agents would discriminate between outsiders and insiders or require efficiency-wages to prevent them from shirking. Even if they accept the plausibility of these phenomena, they insist that they need to be formalized before they are legitimate factors in a theoretical discussion.

The problems of articulating a fully-formalized model of business cycles, however, have also plagued the new classical camp. The latest generation of new classical models downplay the significance of monetary shocks and attribute most of the movements to shocks in technological variables. These real business-cycle models, as they are called, eliminate thereby remnants of the monetarist argument. Not all new classical economists subscribe to this intervention. The discussion continues.

COMMITMENTS TO FORMALISM

The preceding story of business-cycle theorizing has illustrated the commitment to formal reasoning and neo-classical microeconomic foundations in modern macroeconomics. The neo-Keynesian theories refrain from referring to Keynes's psychological factors, and Schumpeter's innovative entrepreneurs. No matter how significant those factors are, they do not fit in the model. For this very reason early neo-Keynesian models assumed constant expectations even though expectations figure prominently in *The General Theory*. Only after Muth's pioneering work did Lucas see a way to formalize expectations in a way that is consistent with neo-classical microeconomics. The consequence was the incorporation of 'information' and 'stochastic processes'.

The new classical modelling strategy is most extreme in its adherence to formalism and neo-classical microeconomics. They have the spirit of the time on their side. Monetarists, who resist the emphasis on formalization, have become minor players in the economic theatre. The same is true for the neo-Keynesians. The new Keynesians have taken over the Keynesian baton. They agree with the new classical modelling strategy but not with its extreme pro-market and anti-policy conclusions. Greg Mankiw, a self-proclaimed new Keynesian sums the situation up:

> Although some economists still doubt that expectations are rational, and despite the mixed evidence from surveys of expectations, the axiom of rational expectations is as firmly established in economic methodology as the axioms that firms maximize profit and households maximize utility. The debate over rules versus discretion continues, but time inconsistency is generally acknowledged to be a problem with discretionary policy. Most fundamentally, almost all macroeconomists agree that basing macroeconomics on firm microeconomic principles should be higher on the research agenda than it has been in the past.
>
> (Mankiw 1990: 1658)

EXOGENOUS FACTORS AND POSSIBILITIES FOR INTERDISCIPLINARY RESEARCH

Critics of neo-classical economics will often argue that neo-classical economics *necessarily* excludes possibilities for interdisciplinary research. The extraordinary inventiveness that neo-classical economists display in the applications of their choice analysis, however, challenges the notion of impossibility. Akerlof's tales, for instance, include 'asymmetric information, caste behaviour, obedience to work norms as motivated by the sociological literature, behaviour according to cognitive dissonance, and the acquisition of loyalty (and personality traits)' (Akerlof 1984: 4). Similarly, interest for a theorizing of government behaviour, usually an exogenous factor in models, is increasing (see Hartley's article in this volume.) And Mancur Olson (1982) impressed the macroeconomic profession with a neo-classical analysis of group interests and their impact on collective action.

In spite of these inventive extensions the constraints on neo-classical economics are severe. A major objective of the argument in this essay has been to show the constraints that formalist reasoning in macroeconomics imposes. Even the models of Akerlof and Olson appear to be too 'informal' to meet the 'scientific' norms of new classical economists. Their results still have to be absorbed in the mainstream.

The move towards a more disciplinary approach, therefore, involves a choice as to the mode of argument. If we want to engage the formalists among neo-classicals we face a series of tough tests which only the well-trained mathematician will survive. We could also develop a domain of discourse that is different from the neo-classical domain with, who knows what possibilities for overlap. Encouraging for the latter strategy is the irony, if not cynicism, with which many a neo-classical economist considers the formalist rhetoric. Maybe this is the time to look for the key where the light of formalism does not shine.

NOTES

1 See Klamer (1984).
2 See Mirowski (1990).

BIBLIOGRAPHY

Akerlof, George A., (1984) *An Economic Theorist's Book of Tales*, New York, Cambridge University Press.

Friedman, Milton (1968) 'The role of monetary policy', *American Economic Review* 58 (March), 1–17.

Keynes, John Maynard (1936) *The General Theory of Employment, Interest and Money*, London, Macmillan.

Klamer, Arjo (1984) *Conversations with Economists*, Rowman & Allenheld; published in the UK as *New Classical Macroeconomics. Conversations with New Classical Economists and their Opponents*, Wheatsheaf.

Klamer, Arjo and Colander, Dave, (1990) *The Making of an Economist*, Boulder, Westview Press.

Lucas, Robert E. Jr (1972) 'Expectations and the neutrality of money', *Journal of Economic Theory* 4 (April), 103–24.

Lucas, Robert E. Jr (1973) 'Some international evidence on output-inflation trade-offs', *American Economic Review* 63 (June), 326–34.

Lucas, Robert E. Jr (1976) 'An equilibrium model of the business cycle', *Journal of Political Economy* 83 (December), 1113–44.

Maital, Shlomo and Maital, Sharone (1990) 'Is the future what it used to be? A behavioral theory of the decline of saving in the west', in W. van Raaij (ed.) *The Consumption of Time and the Timing of Consumption*, Amsterdam, Elsevier.

Mankiw, N. Gregory (1990) 'A quick refresher course in macroeconomics', *Journal of Economic Literature* 28 (December), 1645–60.

Mirowski, Philip (1989) *More Heat than Light*, New York, Cambridge University Press.

Muth, John (1961) 'Rational expectations and the theory of price movements', *Econometrica* 29 (July), 315–35.

Olson, Mancur (1982) *The Rise and Decline of Nations. Economic Growth, Stagflation and Social Rigidities*, New Haven and London, Yale University Press.

Samuelson, Paul A., (1939) 'Interactions between the multiplier analysis and the principle of the accelerator', *Review of Economics and Statistics* (March) 75–8.

Sargent, Thomas J. (1978) 'Estimation of dynamic labor demand schedules under rational expectations', *Journal of Political Economy* 86 (December 1978) 1009–44.

Sartre, Jean-Paul (1956) *Being and Nothingness*, New York, Pocketbooks.

Sims, Christopher A. (1980), 'Macroeconomics and Reality', *Econometrica* 48 (January) 1–11.

Part II

Alternative approaches among economists

Chapter 6

Post-Marxian economics

Labour, learning and history

Samuel Bowles

Over the past two decades a strand of Marxian economic theory has diverged from classical Marxism. Because no precise formulation of what may be termed post-Marxian economics may be said to represent a consensus, any attempt at synthesis is bound to be idiosyncratic. Yet elements of a common model and methodological approach may be identified.[1] This approach may be distinguished from both the classical Marxist economic model and the neo-classical alternatives in its theoretical method, its conception of the economy, and its treatment of structural change. Given the methodological focus of this essay, I will not dwell on the substantial differences in the content of the analysis but will introduce just one sustained example – the analysis of labour – to illustrate the characteristic methods and approach of post-Marxian economics.

Post-Marxian economics shares with classical Marxism not only an emphasis on class relationships absent from other schools of economics, but a method in which the customary distinctions among exogenous and endogenous variables play a limited role. Amending Herodotus, Marxists often appear to proclaim: 'There is nothing exogenous under the sun!' As we will see, the distinctions – economic/non-economic – also play a limited role in post-Marxian theory in view of its political and cultural as well as economic modelling of the capitalist economy.

The distinctive character of the Marxian approach in this respect may be illustrated by means of a comparison with the paradigmatic treatment of exogenous and endogenous variables in neo-classical economic theory. The model of change in neo-classical economics (and by methodological imperialism in many strands of the adjacent disciplines as well) is generally termed comparative statics. A familiar example of this method is the standard model of supply and demand described by a system of $2n$ simultaneous equations in $2n$ unknowns (the prices and quantities exchanged of the n goods). The endogenous elements in the system – the prices and quantities exchanged – are termed economic variables, while some of the exogenous terms are considered to be non-economic, referring to such phenomena as consumer tastes, technologies, the supply of non-reproducible inputs such as land and the distribution of the ownership of initial property claims. Change is described as a displacement of equilibrium occasioned by the alteration of one or more of the exogenous terms in the equational system, for example, through a shift in consumer preferences or a change in one of the technologies of production. In general equilibrium systems the exogenous/endogenous distinction corresponds (in pedagogical and research practice if not in logic) almost exactly to the economic/non-economic distinction. Both the mathematics of displaced equilibria (for example, Cramer's rule), and the logic of the underlying models, bears the interesting implication that change is fully reversible: if the exogenous shock which initially perturbed the system is withdrawn, the system will return to the *status quo ante*.

The building blocks of the comparative static analysis of change are thus the exogenous/endogenous distinction, the privileged causal status of exogenous variables and the concept of logical, ahistorical, or reversible time. By contrast, post-Marxian analysis displaces the exogenous-endogenous distinction and causal ordering by an analysis of the mutually constitutive articulation of practice and structure, giving rise to a concept of learning, historical time and irreversible change.

I will first seek to distinguish the underlying methodological orientations of classical Marxian and post-Marxian economics. I will then illustrate the methodological presuppositions of the post-Marxian approach by means of its argument for the specificity of labour in economic theory, and turn in the concluding section to an analysis of the process of learning and change.

MARXIAN AND POST-MARXIAN ECONOMICS

The designation 'post-Marxian' refers to the rather considerable recent extensions and emendations of the basic economic model developed by Marx and presented in the outstanding modern works of the classical Marxian tradition such as Paul Sweezy's *Theory of Capitalist Development* and Ernest Mandel's *Marxian Economic Theory*.[2]

The innovations of the post-Marxian school – if it may be termed that – pertain both to the methods of analysis and to the substance. The main methodological developments reflect two important intellectual currents in post-Second World War intellectual life: the emergence of what Perry Anderson (1976) has termed Western Marxism, and the adoption of mathematical methods by economists and particularly the extensive use of linear economic models by economists working in the tradition of Piero Sraffa.

With respect to the first influence, post-Marxian economists have been greatly influenced by the critique of economist Marxism which emerged during the inter-war period in the works of Georg Lukacs, Antonio Gramsci, and Karl Korsch and which flowered after the war in the writings of Jean-Paul Sartre, Andre Gorz, Lucio Colletti, Jürgen Habermas, E. P. Thompson, Louis Althusser and others. Interestingly, none of these contributors to the Western Marxian tradition was an economist, while the outstanding classical Marxist economists of the post-Second World War period – Maurice Dobb, Ernest Mandel, and Paul Sweezy – remained unmoved by Western Marxism's primarily philosophical critiques of the structure of the classical model.

The result was a curious hiatus: the cultural and political analysis of the Western Marxist tradition and the economic theory in the classical Marxist tradition evolved in isolation. Because the innovations of the Western Marxist tradition did not extend to economic theory *per se*, the issues of contention between the two tendencies did not so much involve the structure of economic theory itself as the place of economics in Marxism. The critique of economism was therefore limited to a critique of economic determinism: the classical Marxian economic tradition was faulted only for placing too large an emphasis on the economic base as a determinant of the structure and dynamics of the society as a whole. The Western Marxist school thus did not achieve a rethinking of economic theory, but photo reduction of economics; not a transformation of its structure but a demotion of its importance.

By contrast, the post-Marxian economic approach affirms the centrality of class, surplus, and other economic categories in understanding the advanced capitalist world system. Its critique of the classical economic model focuses not so much on the problem of economic determinism – the relationship between the economy and the non-economic – as on the classical conception of the economy itself. Here, post-Marxian economists have identified another form of economism: by excising cultural and political practices from the constitution of the economic, the classical model reduces capitalist production to a restricted – indeed impoverished – subset of the variety of practices which jointly determine the dynamics of accumulation. Thus the economism of classical formulations is expressed at least as much in its economistic treatment of the economy as in its analysis of the articulation of the economy with other instances of the social formation.

The extensive use of mathematical methods also distinguishes post-Marxian economists from what C. Wright Mills termed (describing himself) the 'plain old Marxists'. The developments in mathematical economics associated with the names of Sraffa, Leontief and von Neumann have allowed a significant clarification of the underlying structure of Marxian economic models. Morishima, for example has strongly vindicated what he terms the fundamental theorem of Marxian economics, namely, that a necessary condition for profits is the exploitation of labour. Curiously, while the favoured target of critics of Marxian economics for a century – the transformation of labour values into prices – was shown to present no fundamental problems in the newly-developed linear economic models, the use of labour values to determine prices, wages, and profits was simultaneously shown to be unnecessary. From a purely formal standpoint inputs and outputs may be measured indifferently in labour hours, bushels of corn or tons of steel; no important mathematical result hinges on which unit of measurement is adopted.[3] Thus the labour theory of value was found innocent of the charge of illogic and mathematical contradiction only to be found guilty of redundancy.

Of perhaps greater importance, the infusion of mathematical methods has allowed a more searching analysis of the relationship between action and system or – in terms more congenial to the Marxian framework – practice and structure.[4] Much of the Marxian economic theory is based on an often implicit theory of the relationship between the self-interested actions of economic agents (capitalist firms, workers, others) and the processes of stability and change in the structures of prices, profits, wages, and economic relationships which induce and constrain these actions. A common example of this aspect of Marxian economic theory is the relationship between the profit-seeking competition of capitalist firms and the transformation of the system of competition through the centralization of capital.

While the analysis of self-interested action of non-colluding agents was central to Marx's analysis of capitalism as a competitive system, later Marxian economists have sometimes adopted a quite distinct approach, which may be termed the expressive theory of action. According to this view, we may derive the actions of individual agents from a knowledge of their class position or perhaps from the conditions necessary for the reproduction of their class position. Closely related is the functionalist view of action – also prevalent in classical Marxism – according to which the dynamics of a structure and the actions of agents may be inferred from some pre-given function attributed to the structure. Thus, to take a concrete example of the functionalist theory, the action of state managers in a liberal democracy might be explained by the pre-given function of the state to reproduce the capitalist relations of production. By contrast, a post-Marxian approach to this problem would be to enquire into the opportunities, objectives and constraints facing state managers – perhaps balancing the desire for greater tax revenues with the necessity of securing electoral success – the contingent result of which *may* be the reproduction of the capitalist relations of production.[5]

Within economic theory proper, a striking application of this careful attention to the opportunities and constraints facing individual actors is the celebrated Okishio theorem, which has prompted a reconsideration of Marx's theory of the tendency of the profit rate to fall due to the rise in the organic composition of capital.[6] Marx had asserted that there exists a class of innovations which will raise a single capitalist's profit rate but which, when adopted generally by all competing capitalists, will lower the average social profit rate. Okishio investigated this claim using a general equilibrium linear economic model to capture the effects of the general adoption of the initial innovation. According to Okishio's theorem, any innovation which at existing prices and money wages would yield super profits for an individual capitalist will, when it is emulated by other capitalists and a new set of prices and money wages emerges, result in a rise in the general competitive profit rate. While Marx had understood that a rise in the rate of exploitation *might* offset the possible increase in the organic composition of capital associated with the technical change, what Okishio demonstrated was that for the innovation to have been individually profitable in the first place, any resulting increase in the organic composition of capital *must* be offset by an increase in the rate of exploitation. Thus, whatever the effect on the organic composition of capital, individually profitable innovations will be generally profitable once they are generalized. The flaw of Marx's original reasoning was not that he assumed that individual and collective interests may diverge, but that he failed adequately to investigate the microeconomics of innovation which – according to the individual capitalist's profit criterion – would eliminate all innovations in which the rise in the organic composition of capital is not fully offset by a rise in the rate of exploitation.

The demise of the theory of the falling rate of profit due to a rise in the organic composition of capital, and the displacement of the labour theory of value from its privileged position in Marxian economics, cannot be attributed primarily to developments in mathematical economics, however. Both of these fundamental propositions of classical Marxian economics were subject to criticism, not only from the standpoint of formal logic, but also for their tendency to posit a structural determination of economic outcomes in which individual or collective human agency played little or no part. Thus the labour theory of value and the rising organic composition of capital theory of economic crisis were among the first casualties of the post-Marxian attempt to devise a non-economistic economic theory in which human action guided by culture and politics as well as economic considerations would play a major part.

The apparent results of the methodological orientations of post-Marxian economics appear at first blush to be almost entirely negative and perplexing; for they appear to deprive Marxian economics of two of its most fundamental structural and dynamic principles, and even to throw into question the *differentia specifica* of Marxian economic theory: the unique status it awards to labour as a theoretical category. But, as we shall see, this is not the case. Indeed, it is precisely the post-Marxist treatment of the uniqueness of labour which is the basis of its distinctive relationship among politics, culture and economics as well as its historical conception of time.

THE SPECIFICITY OF LABOUR

In analysing capitalist production, all Marxists regard labour as distinct from other inputs. Marxian economics argues that profits arise from the fact that the capitalist pays for the *labour power* of the worker, but gets the benefit of the *labour* of the worker. The difference between the two is the fulcrum on which the entire structure of Marxian economics turns. Few Marxian economists would disagree. Disagreements, however, surround the manner in which the distinction between labour and labour power is represented. In classical Marxian economics the specificity of labour is identified as its unique ability to produce a value greater than its own value, the results being surplus value or profit for the employer. Or, more formally, the value of labour power is less than the use value (to the capitalist) of labour. The post-Marxian model argues for the specificity of labour and the importance of the distinction between labour and labour power on grounds quite independent of the classical labour theory of value.[7]

The central analytical concept in the post-Marxian model of the production process is what may be termed a *substantive* rather than a *formal* distinction between labour and labour power, based on the treatment of labour as the initiator of practices rather than as an object.

Marx, of course, originally was attracted to Ricardo's labour theory of value because he thought that suitably amended it could combine the structural insights of the classical economists with his commitment to make human subjectivity central in economic theory. Labour – the intentional transformation of nature to meet human ends – was the linchpin which would unite structure and practice in his model.

Yet in the formal renditions of Marx's labour theory of value, the worker is represented by the wage bundle of commodities which reproduces the worker at his or her customary standard of living. Labour is represented, not as a practice, but as an output, or at best as a use value for the capitalist. Paradoxically, the worker as an actor disappears in this formalization of the labour theory of value. It is only a small step from this formulation to Sraffa's conception of *The production of commodities by means of commodities*.

The theoretical consequences of this representation are as debilitating to the Marxian analysis of the politics of production as they are to the analysis of the more familiar objects of economic analysis. For if labour is treated as an object, little different (except perhaps morally) from other inputs, the distinction between labour and labour power would hold no more theoretical interest than a simple translation of one metric (hours) into another (work); the amount of labour performed could be represented as a given multiple of the number of hours hired. In this case the following unfortunate theoretical results would obtain in a competitive model of the type Marx describes in volume 3 of *Das Kapital*.

First, capitalists would be forced by competitive pressures to utilize efficient technologies, and to adopt an efficient organization of production. It follows that neither technologies nor the organization of production would be altered by a change in the ownership or decision-making structure of the firm unless this change altered relative input or output prices. The clear implication is that a shift to democratic worker control could alter the distribution of income in the firm, but could change the social organization of production only at the cost of lower productivity. Ironically, this is just a restatement of Samuelson's dictum that in the competitive economic model it makes no difference whether capital hires labour or labour hires capital.

Second, just as the capitalist will avoid paying more for a ton of coal than the minimal supply price, so too will he seek the lowest price of an hour of labour power, preferring to hire women over men, or blacks over whites, should their wages (for equivalent levels of productive capacity) be lower. Those who, for racist, sexist, or whatever reasons, persist in hiring high-priced white male labour will be eliminated by competition.

Finally, if labour is 'just another input', then any unsold units of labour must be considered to be voluntarily withheld from the market. For, as with a glut of shirts on the clothing market, the excess supply can generally be eliminated if the seller is willing to lower the price. In this case, unemployment must be considered voluntary, based on a refusal to work for a lower wage – a form of speculation in one's own productive capacities. Involuntary unemployment could still occur as the result of frictions in the adjustment process, but we would have no more reason in the long run to expect excess supply than excess demand in the labour market.

The political import of these three consequences of treating labour as an object is clear enough. The first constitutes a wholesale denial of the critique of domination and fragmentation of work life. For if worker-run firms would organize production no differently from capitalist enterprises, the issue becomes a trivial choice of masters, neither of which exercises substantive options in the determination of technology and the structure of work life. The second implication of treating labour as an object is that racism, sexism and other forms of discrimination will wither away as a natural result of capital's competitive search for super-profits. Racism and sexism may exist, but only as cultural (or perhaps 'superstructural') attributes reproduced autonomously and despite the structure of the accumulation process of the capitalist economy. The third implies that unemployment is caused by workers' choices rather than by the structure of capitalism. Moreover, unemployment is neither the source of social waste, nor even a social problem – any more than is the fact that many workers do not choose to work full time.

The treatment of labour as an object thus achieves a radical partition in economic thought: politics and culture are banished from production. Because production is both efficient and apolitical, the socialist critique of capitalist production – that it is, undemocratic, unjust and wasteful – is narrowed to the problem of distribution of property. Socialism is thus reduced to a redistribution of property, with the cultural addition of the dissemination of 'new values'.

However, it can be easily shown that when labour is treated as a practice rather than an object, each of the above implications is sharply contradicted.

To do this I will adopt a simple model of the extraction of labour from labour power developed by post-Marxian economists in recent years. The production process may be represented by two relationships: first, the combination of labour with non-labour inputs to produce a given output; and second, the extraction of labour from labour-power through the combination of labour power with whatever inputs the owner allocates to induce a specific level of work intensity. I term the first the input-output relation and the second the labour extraction relation. The latter is precisely the missing relationship, whose absence from Sraffian, Keynesian and neo-classical models implies the treatment of labour as an object.

Labour must be *extracted* from labour power because workers will not willingly pursue the type and intensity of labour which maximises profits. This is not because labour is naturally unpleasant, as the theory of the 'disutility of labour' from Adam Smith to the present would have it. The way in which the worker experiences work, and the resulting motivations, resentments and resistances derive in important measure from the social organization of the production process itself. Indeed, the social structure of the capitalist production process – most particularly its authoritarian and exploitative form – induces a level of conflict over the organization and intensity of work above and beyond the conflicts induced by the simple free rider problem which would exist in any social organization.

But how is labour to be extracted? The power of capital over labour derives from the workers' need for employment as a means to livelihood, and from the scarcity of jobs.[8] Job scarcity simply means that jobs are hard to find, and that those who have them would like to hang on to them. The employer's only formal power over the worker – the right to hire and fire – depends on job scarcity and the worker's dependence on the job. Thus, the extraction of labour from labour power must be induced, in the last instance, by enhancing the threat of firing. Specifically the employer may raise the expected cost to the worker of pursuing a non-work strategy by any one of the following three counter-strategies: (a) raising the expected cost of losing one's job; (b) raising the expected probability of getting fired if detected pursuing a non-work strategy; and (c) increasing the probability of being detected if pursuing a non-work strategy. By investigating the application of these strategies, we may come to understand why the three above implications of labour as the object view of production – efficient production, no discrimination and no involuntary unemployment – are false. Let us consider each.

The probability that a non-work strategy will be detected by the employer will depend on the organization of work and the efficacy of the capitalist's surveillance system. The capitalist can organize the work process so that each worker's performance is more visible and measurable, for example, through the use of such production techniques as the assembly line. Even when such techniques are less efficient in the input-output sense, they may be profitable due to their ability to secure a high level of labour input (effort.) Similarly, the capitalist can divert resources from production into surveillance – in the form of careful accounting, electronic equipment, surveillance personnel, and the like. In either case, the claim that cost reduction pressures render capitalist production efficient must be rejected. Were it not for the problem of extraction of labour from labour power, additional resources could be allocated to increase output per worker, to shorten the work week, or to lower work intensity.

Next, consider the probability of being fired if a non-work strategy *is* detected. For simplicity I will represent this probability as a decreasing function of the unity of the work-force; if firing a worker will incite strike or slowdown of all workers, the capitalist will think twice about firing a worker whose non-work strategy has been detected. In general the degree of unity of the work-force will depend on its racial, sexual, age, credential-based and other divisions – including differences in wages and hierarchical status within the firm. Thus as John Roemer (1979), Michael Reich (1980) and others have demonstrated, the discriminating capitalist may facilitate the firing of a worker and otherwise weaken workers' bargaining power by promoting division, invidious distinction and hierarchy, even when such policies are costly from the standpoint of efficiency. Discrimination is thus consistent with rational profit maximization in a competitive environment.

Lastly, consider the third capitalist strategy, raising the cost to the worker of being fired. In view of the fact that the expected duration of the worker's spell of unemployment, and the level of unemployment benefits are both beyond the control of the firm, the only way the capitalist can raise the cost to the worker of getting fired is to pay the worker more than that wage which would make the worker indifferent to being fired or not. But if the profit-maximizing wage is thus higher than the worker's supply price, other workers who currently lack jobs would also prefer to have a job at that wage rather than remaining unemployed. And if this is the case, they are involuntarily unemployed according to any reasonable sense of the term. Job scarcity implies involuntary unemployment, and the converse.

Thus this simple model of labour extraction illustrates the fact that profit maximization and labour market equilibrium – even under the most stringent atomistic competitive assumptions – does not lead to market clearing. Unemployment, in the context of capitalist production, is thus involuntary and wasteful. The microeconomic basis of the 'reserve army' and its role, the subjugation of labour to capital, is thus vindicated by a model in which labour is represented as a practice rather than a commodity.

Given Marx's concept of labour as practice, and of exploitation as the domination of labour through a structure of power, it is ironic and regrettable that in the past half century at least, Marxian economics has been associated with what Helmut Fleischer (1969) termed a nomological and economistic conception of Marxism. Notable among the many consequences of this association has been the tendency of critics of economistic and of formalist structuralism to be critics of Marxian economics as well. Marxists who would save Marxism from economism have mistakenly attempted to save Marxism from economics.

But if the post-Marxian analysis is correct, the supposed opposition between culture and politics on the one hand and economics on the other is based on the false conception of the economy as apolitical and devoid of cultural content. Thus the crucial flaw in economistic Marxism is not the importance attributed to the economy, but the conception of the economy itself. Whence the misconceived notion of the photo reduction as a strategy to rid Marxism of economism.

Classical Marxian economics shares with its neo-classical adversary, and also with Cambridge and Keynesian economics, a conception of the capitalist economy as a property-based system of contractual exchange, or as Ernest Mandel puts it, a system of 'generalized commodity production'. As such, the political aspects of the economy are confined to the protection of property rights and the enforcement of contracts. Both of these political elements lie within the realm of the state rather than the economy. The economy is thus essentially apolitical.[9]

The labour extraction mechanism described above illustrates a major shortcoming of this conception. For it demonstrates that a fundamental capitalist relationship, that between employer and employee, cannot be treated as a contract enforced by means of the coercive apparatus of the state. The capitalist economy is political because the power to enforce the labour exchange must be embodied to a major extent in the structure of capitalist production itself.

The tendency to equate the endogenous with the economic and the exogenous with the non-economic is thus questioned: for the enforcement of the labour contract and determination of the intensity of labour is clearly endogenous to the economy, yet it exhibits aspects which would normally be termed political. This might be of little more than terminological importance, of course. But, as we shall see, a more fundamental issue is at stake: the status of the exogenous/endogenous distinction itself.

HISTORICAL TIME: LEARNING AND IRREVERSIBLE CHANGE

Expressing as he did so well the commonplaces of his day, the American sage Benjamin Franklin said, 'Time is money', a view most fully developed in the Hahn-Arrow general equilibrium model in which futures contracts in all goods are generally available. In his populist poem, 'The People, Yes', Carl Sandburg expressed a quite different view, one which resonates in post-Marxian analysis: 'Time is a great teacher'. Central to the writings of particularly the young Marx, and to the economics developed by post-Marxian theorists, is the view that the economy produces people as well as commodities. More generally, the preferences, desires, sentiments, capacities of workers and others are transformed in the production process as surely as are the raw materials converted into finished goods. As we shall see, the joint production of people and commodities by the capitalist economy ensures that the logical time of the comparative static approach will need to be jettisoned in favour of a concept of historical or irreversible time.

The endogeneity of people does not, of course, destroy the distinction between endogenous and exogenous. For most analytical tasks it is useful and not misleading to consider some aspects of a problem as exogenous, even when in some larger framework they are the result of the variables under consideration. And even the larger framework is likely to face its limits: genetically inherited traits (but not their social meaning), the geographic location of continents (but not the economic importance of the resulting distances), and other arguably exogenous phenomena readily come to mind even to the most cosmic of thinkers.

None the less, the peculiarity of the Marxian (both classical and post-) framework is that change is represented as substantially the result of an endogenous process. While exogenous developments may be of considerable importance, change or stasis is explained by the internally-generated erosion or consolidation of the conditions for the reproduction of the social relations which define the status quo. While classical Marxian models, following Marx, will endogenously generate change from the analysis of the mode of production itself, the post-Marxian model generates endogenous change from the practices of agents structured by the capitalist relations of production and its articulation with the family, the state and other sites. Thus the post-Marxian model is based on a considerably more complex conception of the reproduction of the social relations of production which define the capitalist system.

Two distinctive aspects of the theory of reproduction are particularly important; one dealing with the question of human agency and the other concerning the relationship among capitalist and non-capitalist structures. The reproduction of structures of domination – whether of class, state, race, gender or other – is not assured by the structure itself. Nor is the non-reproduction of these structures guaranteed by the logic of the structure. Rather, the reproduction of each structure is the contingent result of individual and collective practices taking place throughout the society and hence structured by the full variety of social relations.

The theory of economic crisis illustrates this difference. The classical Marxist model generates crisis from the internal logic of the capitalist mode of production itself – most often from the rising organic composition of capital or from the instability and insufficiency of aggregate demand. Political and other influences on crisis are regarded as modifying the outcomes of this process but not its logic. Thus political, ideological, and other influences are not theorized as part of the model itself, and thus remain exogenous empirical interventions into the otherwise self-contained working of the logic of the mode of production.

While not contesting the centrality of the profit rate in the theory of crisis, the post-Marxian theory roots the analysis of the profit rate in the variety of power relationships which mediate the relationship of capital to workers, to the state, and to external economic agents. Further, the relationship between the profit rate and the reproduction of the capitalist system is not represented as direct, but rather is mediated by political organization, ideology, family structure and other relationships. A low or declining profit rate only constitutes a crisis under conditions which cannot be fully specified except by reference to phenomena generally considered to be superstructural or 'external' to the capitalist mode of production itself.

Thus post-Marxian crisis theory, as developed in the Kaleckian tradition by Raford Boddy and James Crotty (1975), Thomas Weisskopf (1979), Andrew Glyn and Robert Sutcliffe (1972) and others consider the articulation of the capitalist economy with the state, and with other economies, as of central importance. Here a downward pressure on profits could possibly occur through the politically-induced movement towards full employment. The socialization of the reproduction of labour power could be achieved by the extension of the welfare state. On the other hand, a deterioration in the international terms of trade may occur reflecting shifting patterns of world-wide economic and military ascendancy.

The main theoretical orientations of this position may thus be summarized by four propositions: first, that change is the effect of the interaction of structure and practice (or in more common terms, system and action);

second, that neither may be either reduced to the other or taken as exogenous; third, that the reproduction or transformation of any given structure generally involves actions and discourses structured by other sites of social activity, and fourth, that because the actors are transformed by their own and others' practices, the process of change is irreversible in the same sense that learning is considered to be irreversible.

The view of change which emerges from the post-Marxian model obviously defies representation in terms of system adjustment to exogenous shocks. The couplet structure/practice has displaced the couplet exogenous/endogenous. Historical time has displaced logical time.

However, expressed in the highly abstract form above it may be considered to be so general as to be vacuous, for its main theoretical orientation is to broaden the theoretical terrain upon which the study of change is to take place. However, the impression of vacuous abstraction would be misplaced, for the post-Marxian theory of change (and of economic crisis) has been developed with respect to particular structured articulations of capitalist economies, states, families and other institutions. This articulation of structures, often termed the social structure of accumulation, is a conceptual framework for the analysis of reproduction and system transformation which occupies a theoretical terrain between the grand abstractions of Marxian theory – class, mode of production – and the empirical investigation of concrete societies. Thus, for example, David Gordon, Richard Edwards and Michael Reich (1982), and others have developed the concept of a social structure of accumulation of the advanced liberal democratic capitalist societies in the post-Second World War era, while Samir Amin (1976) and others have developed the quite distinct concept of a social structure of accumulation in the peripheral Third World capitalist societies. These and related contributions attempt a model of the political and cultural as well as economic structuring of the accumulation process and the manner in which the accumulation process gives rise to the potential for change, not only in its institutional framework, but in other social structures as well.

SCHOLARS, PRIESTS, ENGINEERS AND MILITANTS: THE POLITICS OF METHODOLOGY

Not surprisingly, in none of these contributions does the distinction between exogenous and endogenous or economic and non-economic variables play a prominent role. Why is a set of distinctions so essential to non-Marxian economic theory almost completely lacking in the Marxian approach? Some of the reasons have been suggested above: the functional analogues to these distinctions are to be found (in classical Marxian theory) in the base-superstructure couplet and (in post-Marxian theory) in the practice-structure couplet and the concept of society as an integrated totality of reproductive and contradictory structures none of which can claim a monopoly on economic affairs.

Let me offer a further speculation: the central role of the exogenous-endogenous distinction in neo-classical economics and its lesser importance in Marxian economics reflects not only the pecularities of each school's approach to scholarship, but their quite distinct social position in the advanced capitalist countries as well. If I am correct, the exogenous-endogenous distinction is congenial to neo-classical economists, not only for its utility as a simplifying device, but for its service in the justification or administration of the capitalist order.

Neo-classical economists are not only scholars, like other intellectuals they are – outside the universities – also social actors. Some are engaged in popular ideological defences of the capitalist economy; others – through government employment and other means – are engaged in managing the capitalist economy. Without insult to any of the professions involved, I term the first, the neo-classical priests and the second, the neo-classical engineers.

The priests invoke the exogenous-endogenous distinction to deflect the criticism of economic injustice, insecurity, the dictatorship of the work-place, and alienated labour away from the economy and to locate the origins of these social problems instead in the exogenous variables of the neo-classical model: individual preferences, technologies, natural endowments, and the distribution of titles to property. Their reasoning is impeccable. If one accepts the general equilibrium model (and imagines that its solutions are unique), one is thereby committed to tracing any unpleasant economic outcome to one of the above exogenous variables.

The import of this ideological *tour de force* is that the critique of capitalism is transformed into a lament against nature – be it the human nature underlying individual preferences or the natural world which limits and informs our level of technology. Among the permissible culprits, only the distribution of property titles is socially contrived, and even this determinant of economic outcomes may be attributed to the ostensibly sovereign liberal democratic state and hence – if indirectly – to the preferences of the voters. The critic is thus hustled away from what naïvely may have been thought to be the scene of the crime and urged to track down the nemesis of the good life instead in the far-flung theoretical suburbs of economics.

The neo-classical engineers pursue more practical concerns: they deploy Keynesian models, human capital theories, input output tables and the like to guide both government and corporate policy more intelligently. The engineers are often at odds with the priests, as might be expected. And their uses of the exogenous-endogenous distinctions are similarly at odds.

While priests use the distinction to displace responsibility for unpleasant outcomes, the engineers use the distinction to focus attention on the forms of state or corporate interventions which may be used to correct economic deficiencies. For the engineers the exogenous variables are the very policy instruments which they (or those whom they advise) control. Thus an archetypal engineer's model of the macro economy will include, as exogenously determined parameters, the tax rate on corporate profits and the level of government expenditure, both seen as policy instruments to be manipulated towards the end of stable economic growth or other desirable social objectives. The endogenous variables – the level of investment or consumption demand in this case, for example – measure those phenomena which escape the direct manipulation of the policy-maker.

Whatever their differences, the priests and the engineers alike draw inspiration in their use of the exogenous-endogenous distinction from the liberal theory of the state. In the first case the liberal democratic state is the means by which the critique of the distribution of property ownership is displaced to a critique of the voters' preferences. For the engineers, the exogeneity of the state – its autonomy from the economy – is essential to their conception of autonomous policy intervention through the manipulation of the exogenous variables of their models.

In the case of Marxian and post-Marxian scholars, moral inclination and social marginality conspire to produce a quite different social role: that of critic and militant. These are not quite the roles of anti-priest and anti-engineer. For the critic the exogenous-endogenous distinction has little value except as a scholarly simplification. For the militant, however, the matter is more complex. Political activists are interested in the effects of collective interventions, whether they be by unions, revolutionary cadres, feminist organizations or environmental groups. But the Marxist militant does not have the luxury enjoyed by the neo-classical engineer who, having the ear of the powerful, may devise models which presume the secure location of decision-making power. By contrast, the militant must seek to understand, not only the effects of an intervention within a given structure, but more importantly the ability of these interventions to enhance the possibilities for structural change. Thus the structural parameters often taken as datum in the neo-classical model are precisely the object of analysis and mobilization for the militant. Quite apart from the historical orientation of Marxism as a body of thought, it is hardly surprising that structural relations taken as exogenous by neo-classical theorists are more generally taken as endogenous by Marxists.

Rendering economic relations endogenous means understanding how they change and may be changed. The predilection to do so among Marxists is thus at once a political project and a scholarly practice.

APPENDIX

Mathematics and post-Marxian economics

Many of the propositions presented here have been rendered elsewhere in mathematical form, and often tested (or at least illustrated) econometrically. Herbert Gintis (1974), for example, developed an inter-temporal general equilibrium model with endogenous preferences. Other post-Marxian economists have developed mathematically precise, and econometrically robust models of the extraction of labour from labour power, the effects of racial discrimination on the distribution of income, and the determination of the profit rate by the social structure of accumulation.

Yet the mathematics used in these models – linear algebra and multivariate calculus – differ in no important respect from the methods employed in neo-classical economics. While much of the criticism of the use of mathematics in Marxian and post-Marxian economics is simply ill informed, it is certainly the case, as Frank Ackerman has claimed, that the mathematics of thermodynamic equilibrium – from which Samuelson borrowed the tools which revolutionized neo-classical economics – are inappropriate in the analysis of far-from-equilibrium structures with irreversible time, which seemingly would include much of what post-Marxian (and classical Marxian) economics is about. And it is equally the case that a coherent post-Marxian approach cannot make general use of the mathematical simplifications, made possible by rendering economic interactions in the subject-object form via the assumption that all actors in competitive equilibrium treat prices and wages, as parametric (that is, given). For in these models firms are active, interacting strategically with workers and other firms, and economic interactions generally take a subject-subject form.

The application of chaos theory and game theory to economic reasoning – as Roemer (1982), Ackerman (1984) and others have done – may provide a more appropriate methodological basis for post-Marxian economics. But the application of chaos theory to any of the social sciences is still in its infancy. And the correctness of the game theoretic attempt to model genuine interactions between two or more agents rather than the subject-object formulation which pervades most economic reasoning is matched by the difficulty of the task. Once one rejects the convenient assumption (the basis of neo-classical microeconomics) that each actor takes all prices as given (and hence treats all other agents as *not* reacting to the actor's decisions), the subject-object model of a decision-maker facing known and given parameters must be discarded in favour of a model of intersubjectivity, of strategy and counter-strategy, for the most part with indeterminate outcomes. The sparse result of the application of game theory to the problem of strategic interaction in economics thus lends credence to Abba Lerner's wise remark: neo-classical 'economics has gained the title Queen

of the Social Sciences by choosing solved political problems as its domain'
(Lerner 1972).

NOTES

1 As Thomas Kuhn has pointed out, the appearance of a textbook often marks
the consolidation of a paradigm and expresses its fundamental commitments and
methods. The basic structure of post-Marxian economics, as it has been taught
to undergraduates at the University of Massachusetts for the past decade, is
expressed in Bowles and Edwards (1985).
2 The relationship of post-Marxian to classical Marxian economics is thus similar
to that between post-Keynesian economics and the economics of Keynes. While
the term post-Marxian appears an apt description of the body of work I will
describe, it is not generally used by practitioners of the art, who are variously
termed 'radical economists', 'neo-Marxian economists' or simply 'Marxian economists'. Any attempt to demarcate a precise boundary between classical Marxian
and what I term post-Marxian economics would be highly arbitrary and point-
less, in part because the two viewpoints share a vast body of common theory
and outlook.
3 Marxian economists had long defended the labour theory of value as the only
method by which a set of prices and a profit rate could be derived from the
conditions of production (input-output relationships and the real wages bundle).
The system developed by Piero Sraffa, however, makes it transparent that the
derivation of prices and the profit rate need not make use of labour values and
can proceed directly from the conditions of production to profits and prices.
See Ian Steedman's insightful and polemical critique of the labour theory of
value (1977).
4 Though considerably less direct, the influence of modern linguistic theory has
also been felt in this respect: many post-Marxian analyses of the practice-
structure relationship correspond closely to the relationship of a speech act to
a discursive structure.
5 Jon Elster's influential critique of functionalism and advocacy of a game theoretic
foundation for Marxism (1979) expresses much of the underlying post-Marxian
orientation. But with the exception of the significant contributions of John
Roemer (1982) not much has come of the game theoretic approach (see Appendix
for a comment on why this might be the case).
6 See Okishio (1961) and Bowles (1981).
7 The arguments below, with citations to the relevant literature are developed in
Bowles and Gintis (1981 and 1986).
8 The model sketched below is presented formally in Bowles (1985).
9 The political nature of the capitalist economy is argued more formally against
counter claims based on neo-classical general equilibrium theory in Bowles and
Gintis (1982).

BIBLIOGRAPHY

Ackerman, F. (1984) 'Models of instability', mimeo.
Amin, S. (1976) *Unequal Development. An Essay on the Social Formations of
Peripheral Capitalism*, New York, Monthly Review Press.
Anderson, P. (1976) *Considerations on Western Marxism*, London, New Left
Books.

Boddy, R. and Crotty, J. (1975) 'Class conflict and macro policy: the political business cycle', *Review of Radical Political Economics* 7, 1–19.

Bowles, S. (1981) 'Technical change and the profit rate: a simple proof of the Okishio theorem', *Cambridge Journal of Economics* 5, 183–6.

Bowles, S. (1985) 'The production process in a competitive economy: Walrasian, Marxian, and neo-Hobbesian models, *American Economic Review* 75 (March), 16–36.

Bowles, S. and Edwards, R.C. (1985) *Understanding Capitalism: Competition, Command and Change in the United States Economy*, New York, Harper & Row.

Bowles, S. and Gintis, H. (1981) 'Structure and practice in the labor theory of value', *Review of Radical Political Economics* 12(4), 1–26.

Bowles, S. and Gintis, H. (1983) 'The power of capital: on the inadequacy of the conception of the capitalist economy as "Private",' *The Philosophical Forum* 14 (3–4), 225–45.

Bowles, S. and Gintis, (1986) *The Mosaic of Domination and the Future of Democracy*, New York, Basic Books (forthcoming).

Elster, J. (1979) *Ulysses and the Sirens: Studies in Rationality and Irrationality*, New York, Cambridge University Press.

Fleischer, H. (1969) *Marxism and History*, New York, Harper & Row.

Gintis, H. (1974) 'Welfare criteria with endogenous preferences', *International Economic Review* 14 (June), 415–30.

Glyn, A. and Sutcliffe, R. (1972) *British Capitalism, Workers, and the Profit Squeeze*, London, Penguin.

Gordon, D., Edwards, R.C. and Reich, M (1982) *Segmented Work, Divided Workers: The Historical Transformation of Labor in the United States*, Cambridge University Press.

Lerner, A. (1972) 'The economics and politics of consumer sovereignty', *American Economic Review, Papers and Proceedings* 62, 258–66.

Mandel, Ernest (1968) *Marxist Economic Theory*, 1 and 2, London, Merlin Press.

Okishio, N. (1961) 'Technical change and the profit rate', *Kobe University Economic Review* 7, 86–99.

Reich, M. (1980) *Racial Inequality and Class Conflict*, Princeton, Princeton University Press.

Roemer, J. (1979) 'Divide and conquer: microfoundations of a Marxian theory of wage discrimination', *Bell Journal of Economics* 10 (2), 695–705.

Roemer, J. (1982) *A General Theory of Exploitation and Class*, Cambridge, Mass., Harvard University Press.

Steedman, I. (1977) *Marx after Sraffa*, London, New Left Books.

Sweezy, Paul (1942) *The Theory of Capitalist Development*, New York and London, Monthly Review Press.

Weisskopf, T. (1979) 'Marxian crisis theory and the rate of profit in the postwar U.S. economy', *Cambridge Journal of Economics* 3 (4), 341–78.

Chapter 7

Information economics

'Threatened wreckage' or new paradigm?

Don Lamberton

He had to choose. But it was not a choice
Between excluding things. It was not a choice
Between, but of. He chose to include the things
That in each other are included, the whole,
The complicate, the amassing harmony.

Wallace Stevens, 'Canon Asprin', passage from
Notes Toward A Supreme Fiction

INTRODUCTION

New patterns of thought about rationality and information and their implications for economics find their place quite readily within the predictions of John von Neumann who long ago drew attention to the shift of science away from the concepts of energy, power, force and motion, to concern with problems of control, programming, information processing, communication, organization and systems (Burks 1970: 3).

This change of focus has brought to economics strong doubt about long-established maxims (Stiglitz 1985: 2). These can be reduced to three: nature abhorred both discontinuities and non-convexities, and the law of supply and demand. At the leading edge of this process of disillusionment has been the questioning of the role of information (Lamberton 1984: Braman 1989).

This chapter has three objectives: first, to introduce and thereby promote the diffusion of the new economics of information; second, to ask whether information economics threatens the wreckage of economic theory or is a creative new paradigm; and, third, to imply that the role of information is central to the conceptual difficulties that have led economists to treat diverse influences as exogenous.

What is exogenous has been sufficiently canvassed in other chapters to necessitate here no more than a gathering together of strands, the provision of a typology of the ways in which theorists have sought to curtail the plethora of equilibria. To this end they have made assumptions about time, space, sequentiality and knowledge. What has been overlooked is that those assumptions put out of bounds as it were, the informational and costly nature of what was being excluded. A catalogue of such exclusions could begin with tastes and technology and progress through the information needs of all decisions 'taken in the consciousness that they are part of a developing chain' (Hart 1958: 6).

Two comments serve to illustrate the interdisciplinary interactions taking place. In the course of what he calls his pursuit of the White Whale of excessively idealized models of the epistemic agent, Cherniak (1986: 3) writes:

> The most basic law of psychology is a rationality constraint on an agent's beliefs, desires, and actions: No rationality, no agent. How rational must a creature be to be an agent, that is, to qualify as having a cognitive system of beliefs, desires, perceptions? Until recently, philosophy has uncritically accepted highly idealized conceptions of rationality. But cognition, computation, and information have costs; they do not just subsist in some immaterial effluvium. We are, after all, only human.

Kenneth Arrow, who was receiving his Nobel Prize for his contribution to the understanding of the role of uncertainty and information about the same time (1973) as Cherniak was submitting his C. S. Peirce-inspired thesis on 'Pragmatism and Realism' at Oxford, states (1987a: 207) that 'All knowledge is costly, even the knowledge of prices'. He goes further (1987b: 242), drawing a contrast with a current emphasis in agency theory:

> Everybody is now into incentive compatibility and I want to say that the communication structure itself is a variable. In other words, everybody says, 'You have a given communication structure, the principal can see so much about his agent, but no more. What I want to do is make what is observed a variable . . . It is basically the question of information-gathering in private and collective spheres that I am concerned about.

Economics had created a fine theoretical structure that had breadth, systematization, elegance; it was both amenable to mathematical precision and well grounded in ideology. But there was a widening crack in the structure. Over thirty years ago Shackle (1957: 298) pointed to it:

> The prices of all goods could be decided if we knew with sufficient detail for each person in the market the answers to the questions 'What does he like?' and 'What does he possess?'. It did not occur to most of those who built the beautiful neoclassical structure of static value theory to put upon the same footing a third kind of question: 'What does he know?' or 'What does he believe?'

Traditional thought did not recognize that 'man's data processing capacity, his ability to understand complex or novel situations, and his ability to gain agreement' are bounded, with important consequences for administrative parsimony, responsiveness and capability, to innovate (Nelson 1981: 95).

INFORMATION ECONOMICS

Information economics has emphasized that knowing is costly. In its earlier phases, the focus was on the consequences of the availability of more information in a given market situation. Later, the theme became that information and organization, in their inextricably interwoven roles, demanded recognition of: (1) their fundamental character as economic resources; (2) their capacity – with limitations – for initiating, responding to and controlling change; and (3) associated, profound policy implications at all levels of decision-making. More recently, efforts have concentrated on information asymmetry.

Central ideas that have emerged and need to be taken into account in both economic analysis and the design of organizations are:

1 The division of information processing may well be the most fundamental form of the division of labour;
2 The cost of producing information is independent of the scale on which it is used;
3 The greater part of the cost of information is often the cost incurred by the recipient;
4 Learning takes time so there is a limit to the rate at which decision-makers can absorb information;
5 There are usually significant asymmetries in terms of possession of information, access to information, and capability of using information;
6 The stock of information and the organizations created to handle information have the economic characteristics of capital;
7 The output from information activities is used to a significant extent by business and government rather than consumers;
8 The demand for information equipment, for example, computers, is a derived demand;
9 The characteristics of information and organizations tend to leave organizations open to random influences, while the successful pursuit of efficiency tends to lead to unresponsiveness to change;
10 The complexity of information activities makes information as a resource difficult to deal with within the traditional production function mode of analysis;
11 The limitations on information as a commodity dictate resort to organizations as an alternative to markets;

12 The optimal design of organizations must take account of the costs of information; and

13 Too much time has been wasted in definitional debate.

Space does not permit development of each of these ideas but some illustrations can be provided. The division of labour, for example, leads quickly on to Arrow's extension of the inquiry to collective spheres, which is justified by the collective nature and use of information. The difficulties of keeping the individualistic and collective spheres apart are well illustrated in a context most economists are content to treat as outside their territory, that of social justice. Rawls (1971) invoked a hypothetical *original position* in which individuals have full general knowledge of the world, both physical and social, but do not know who they are or will be. This veil of ignorance generates tolerance, and justice is what is generally accepted.

In application, factual disagreement becomes a major problem (Arrow 1973: 254–5). Can the members of a society agree on what is knowledge? The difficulties of doing so are perhaps most readily appreciated if *knowledge* of the functioning of the market economic system, that is, *laissez-faire* doctrine, is the case in point; and one might go on to consider the right to hold opinions. There are further problems. Must an absence of disagreement on, for example, decisions about what information will be provided or the scope for altruistic behaviour, be assumed?

With respect to economies of scale, economic theorists have engaged in sleight-of-hand. For example, Samuelson could argue that the existence of increasing returns is the prime case of deviation from the model of the perfectly competitive economy and add that 'Universal constant returns to scale (in everything, including the effective acquisition and communication of knowledge) is practically certain to convert laissez-faire or free enterprise into perfect competition' (1967: 117), without feeling any obligation to explore the acquisition and communication of knowledge. The simple fact is that information creates pervasive economies of scale. With information activity now dominating resource use, this represents a very serious challenge to prevailing theoretical notions and to market ideology.

A further illustration could be information as a capital resource – including technology as one kind of information. If information is capital, it is important to look not only at the substitution effects that are often powerful forces leading to the adoption of new technologies, but also at the ways in which information capital complements other resources. Because information flows are the essence of economic dynamics, the notion of complementarity here must embrace co-evolving technologies, with applications spreading into many industries.

External effects in the accumulation of knowledge have a critical role in economic development (Schmitz, 1989). For example, communication and information technologies and new materials technologies have this co-evolving character in an informational city context.

The extent of the spillovers and interactions reflect the communication infrastructure. Great care must be taken, however, in interpreting 'infrastructure'. The most common error, with disastrous consequences, is to equate technology in the hardware sense with information and even with the use of information (Macdonald: forthcoming). This is done because it seems to permit the adoption of communication and information technology (CIT) equipment to be presented as a measure of how well the economy is handling information. In many economies in which there is heavy investment in CIT, the reality may well be 'Spending more; knowing less'.

To contribute to the overall perspective, the policy implications might be added. Shubik (1984: 615) points out the consequences of neglect of the costs of information with the story of the owl and the centipede:

> The owl was the wisest of animals. A centipede with 99 sore feet came to him seeking advice. 'Walk for two weeks one inch above the ground; the air under your feet and the lack of pressure will cure you', said the owl. 'How am I to do that?', asked the centipede. 'I have solved your conceptual problem, do not bother me with trivia concerning implementation', replied the owl.

This gap is the more significant if five features of the present state of affairs are taken into account:

1 The speed of the process

In contrast to the widely accepted impression of economic development as a slow process, the information aspects of the economy are changing with surprising rapidity. In the closing hours of 1989, the *New York Times* (*New York Times* 1989: 10) pondered the question of what characterized the 1980s. They decided against the *Age of Revolution* and the *Age of Greed* and settled for *When Information Accelerated*.

2 Pervasiveness

The pervasiveness of the new developments is such that no industries and few households are free from their impact. The projected demise (Branscombe 1987: 128) of the letter post service is a good reminder of just how pervasive these changes may prove to be.

3 Regional differences

Regional differences underlie conflicts and generate information flows, for example, technology transfer. Comparative regional study, regions being parts or the whole of a nation or groups of nations, is essential to the understanding of the role of information.

4 Interdisciplinary dimension

The role of information laps beyond the economic even when that is broadly interpreted. This calls for an interdisciplinary approach, more especially in terms of the sociological and political aspects (Hirschman 1971; Calvert 1986). Such interdisciplinary research is a highly skilled task, embracing joint efforts and interactive efforts and even a third form of co-operation that transcends these and can be viewed as steps, however faltering, in the evolution of new disciplines or subdisciplines (Streeten 1974).

5 The cost of information

All too frequently information is described as a commodity and its *commoditization* is seen as a dominant feature of the information society. From a technocratic point of view, the world now seems to have entered an age of information plenty, measured in terms of chips, fibres, information files, and so on. The reality is vastly different: information is a costly resource that must be managed and this calls for accounting, evaluation and conservation.

THEORETICAL DEVELOPMENTS

Any review of recent theoretical developments must note the following:

(a) A shift from considering the role of information simply as a means to improve the efficiency of markets to assigning a broader role that encompasses both the design and operation of other forms of organization and the production of information.
(b) An excessively sharp focus on the economics of asymmetric information; a focus so sharp that this is often equated with information economics, for example, different groups of buyers or sellers of foreign currencies; the doctor-patient relationship. This has yielded such a large literature on adverse selection and moral hazard that one writer (Shin 1989: 864–5) could deplore, not the earlier banishing of information to the world of footnotes, but the occupying of centre stage by information issues.
(c) Diffusion processes which have been subjected to detailed study. These studies have ranged widely through the adoption of new products by consumers and new technologies by producers, the spread of new ideas

(even amongst economists!) and the spread of price changes within markets.

(d) Rational expectations theory, which could well be called the economics of limited foresight. This approach permeates macroeconomics and has been exploited to resuscitate macromodelling. Some see this as virtually a return to the assumption of perfect knowledge. The central principle is that firms and consumers behave rationally, that is, they make the most of the information that is available to them.

These theoretical developments give rise to some interesting crosscurrents. For example, rational expectations play down the substantial and on-going nature of the costs of information and the extent to which information available now is a consequence of earlier investment decisions. Likewise, that approach ignores the capability to use the information which again is dependent upon the prior creation of individual human or organizational capital. At the aggregate level, the rational expectations approach fails to take into account asymmetric information – which is implicit in the diffusion studies.

Research agenda might well be directed to such aspects as the information-theoretic characteristics of currency and credit; national propensities for computer usage; changing forms of organization; the role of the state; the economics of language; and the effects on income distribution. Perhaps top priority might go to clarification of the current buzzword, global.

A NEW PARADIGM?

Many view information economics as a destructive development. Just as Hicks long ago was fearful of the consequences of 'general abandonment of the assumption of perfect competition' and 'the threatened wreckage' of 'the greater part of economic theory' unless it was assumed that 'the markets confronting most of the firms . . . do not differ very greatly from perfectly competitive markets' (Hicks 1939: 84), many now seek to evade the consequences of an explicit treatment of the role of information, arguing that the traditional concept of optimality cannot be employed in the analysis of the role of information. Yet others deny the difficulties, contending that information can be treated as just another commodity. While this latter course saves the formal theoretical structure, it does not satisfy those who consider information to be a commodity only to a limited extent (for two basic reasons: first, it is indivisible in use; and, second, it is difficult to appropriate (Arrow 1984: 142)).

An approach emerging from the research programme of the SPRU (Science Policy Research Unit), University of Sussex, proceeds as follows.

Uncertainty is seen to imply institutions that shape behaviour and co-ordinate the activities of agents working with limited information.

> Both the technological and institutional knowledge of *how and what people learn, what are their beliefs and how they change* occupy, in the approach suggested here, a role theoretically analogous to maximising rationality in neo-classical models; they are factors of *behavioural order* which contribute to explain co-ordination and consistency in uncertain, complex and changing environments.
>
> (Dosi and Orsenigo 1988: 19)

There is no clear point at which a new paradigm can be said to have emerged. The whole process of informatization is undermining the neo-classical paradigm in economics. Several aspects deserve emphasis: communication, computing and the costs and value of information. To merely substitute the new factors of behavioural order for the old maximizing rationality may seem to salvage the optimality notion that has been central to economics. However, the new paradigm calls for deeper probing and a return to definitional matters.

Braman (1989) surveys the bewildering abundance and diversity of definitions of information and distinguishes four approaches: information as a resource; information as a commodity; information as perception of pattern; and information as a constitutive force in society. Is there a broader view that interrelates or merges these separate approaches?

The commodity view is a useful starting point. This implies buying and selling and the concept of a production chain: information creation, generation, collection, processing, storage, transmission, distribution, depreciation, destruction, and seeking (Braman 1989: 237). Commoditized information passes through stages along the chain. However, a commodity can be also defined as an item 'that can be acquired at some resource cost' (Allen 1990: 268). This wider definition captures the Braman chain but extends to all the information activities interwoven with non-information production chains and to the creation of information handling capability (or organizational capital).

What is needed is an approach that extends the notion of optimality to the organization and its design. The theory must accommodate the process of organizational change, a process in which the costs of information and perceptions of its value are influential.

Having brought information issues to centre stage, it should have been an easy step to treat organization as a variable. However, the economics of organization has been slow in emerging and its component parts are in need of co-ordination. For example, information economics embraces transaction cost economics, principal/agent theory and the economics of organization. This may suggest imperialism. Such a reaction must be met at this juncture with a plea for a concerted effort to exploit the common

ground, that is, the role of information, in the search for greater understanding of social processes. Explicit treatment of information-theoretic
considerations and even the use of assumptions relating to information that
derive from other social sciences, have enriched the economist's analysis of
exogenous factors, contributed to the development of evolutionary modelling, and linked some elements of traditional theorizing with the new
institutional analysis.

A reconsideration of what is to be treated as exogenous and of the
notion of equilibrium itself, leads to the kind of analysis suggested in this
chapter. The major difficulty may prove to be that while the introduction
of informational considerations has opened the way for new theorizing
about change, growth and institutions, the forces of conservatism may yet
ensure that the new developments serve the purposes of traditional static
theory. This tendency is well illustrated by widespread efforts to treat
information as just another commodity, neglect of information and organization as capital, and, more recently, the heavy emphasis upon information asymmetry.

The heavy emphasis must shift to cognition, communication and computing processes if the new themes are to be heard and the full potential
of information economics realized. The development of that full potential
would seem timely in an information society facing major, continuing
problems of adjustment to new technologies, new industries, new trading
relationships, new forms of organization, and even new kinds of jobs.
Piecemeal much can be done with seeming precision. The precision and
determinateness of more aggregative models that are also more dynamic
will be found to be another matter – a price will have to be paid for the
enrichment. The structural changes implied by the term *Information Age*
require that the economist leave the shelter of his Ouspenskian 'perpetual
now'. The economics that survives will no doubt be less amenable to
mathematical precision and its policy counterpart will need to be more
tolerant of the role of judgement.

The diffusion of these new thoughts is a slow process because the
economics community itself amply demonstrates the thesis that the characteristics of information and organization lead to obsolescence. The very
success of that community's specializations ensures rigidity and unresponsiveness to further change. Perhaps this is the real meaning of 'paradigm'.
The informatization process with all its far-reaching consequences for
humanity is undermining that paradigm. It is difficult to detect how far
that process has gone, because the economics community still dreams of
the grand analytical system; dreams that seemed unlikely to be fulfilled
once the human dilemma of uncertainty, of incomplete information in the
evolutionary process of living that always imposes time constraints, had
assumed centre stage. Ears attuned to the Great Theory are reluctant 'to
go back to the miasmal swamp of reality' (Shubik 1970: 429) but that is

where the likes and possessions *and* the knowledge and beliefs are to be observed. Each finds its place in the information model of the economy which is needed to complete the traditional production/consumption model and for which the SPRU factors of behavioural order are an inadequate substitute. An information-theoretic approach that endogenizes information processes is not destructive of economic theory, although it will inevitably weaken and hopefully destroy some of the rigidities and associated vested interests. By pushing back the boundaries of the *economic*, the new approach permits a richer analysis that fuses together the continuing processes of resource allocation, learning, and development and yields insights into 'the amassing harmony'.

BIBLIOGRAPHY

Allen, Beth (1990) 'Information as an economic commodity', *American Economic Review* 80 (2), 268–73.

Arrow, K. J. (1973) 'Some ordinalist-utilitarian notes on Rawl's *Theory of Justice*', *Journal of Philosophy* LXX (9), 245–63.

Arrow, K. J. (1984) 'The Economics of Information' *Collected Papers*, vol. 4, p. 142, Oxford, Blackwell.

Arrow, K. J. (1987a) 'Rationality of self and others', in R. M. Hogarth and M. W. Reder (eds), *Rational Choice: The Contrast between Economics and Psychology*, Chicago, University of Chicago Press.

Arrow, K. J. (1987b) 'Oral history I: an interview', in G. F. Feiwel (ed.), *Arrow and the Ascent of Modern Economic Theory*, London, Macmillan.

Braman, Sandra (1989) 'Defining information: an approach for policymakers', *Telecommunications Policy* 13 (3), 233–42.

Branscomb, Lewis M. (1987) 'Information: the ultimate frontier', in A. E. Cawkell (ed.), *Evolution of an Information Society*, London, ASLIB.

Burks, Arthur W. (ed.) (1970) *Essays on Cellular Automata*, Urbana, University of Illinois Press.

Calvert, R. L. (1986) *Models of Imperfect Information in Politics*, London, Harwood.

Cherniak, Christopher (1986) *Minimal Rationality*, Cambridge, Mass., MIT Press.

Dosi, G. and Orsenigo, L. (1988) 'Coordination and transformation: an overview of structures, behaviours and change in evolutionary environments', in G. Dosi et al. (eds), *Technical Change and Economic Theory*, London, Pinter Publishers.

Hart, A. G. (1958) Discussion remark, reported in M. J. Bowman (ed.), *Expectations, Uncertainty, and Business Behaviour*, New York, Social Science Research Council.

Hicks, J. R. (1939) *Value and Capital*, Oxford, Oxford University Press.

Hirschman, A. O. (1971) *A Bias for Hope: Essays on Development and Latin America*, New Haven, Yale University Press.

Lamberton, D. M. (1984) 'The economics of information and organization', in M. E. Williams (ed.), *Annual Review of Information Science and Technology*, 19, 3–30. White Plains, New York, American Society for Information Science.

Macdonald, Stuart (forthcoming) 'Information and IT networks', in C. Antonelli, D. M. Lamberton, P. David, R. Mansell and G. Pogorel (eds), *The Economics of Information Networks*, Amsterdam, North Holland.

Nelson, R. R. (1981) 'Assessing private enterprise: an exegesis of tangled doctrine', *Bell Journal of Economics* 12 (1), 93–111.

New York Times, 31 December 1989.

Rawls, J. (1971) *A Theory of Justice*, Cambridge, Mass., Harvard University Press.

Samuelson, Paul A. (1967) 'The monopolistic competition revolution', in R. E. Kuenne (ed.), *Monopolistic Competition Theory: Studies in Impact*, New York, Wiley.

Schmitz, J. A. (1989) 'Imitation, entrepreneurship, and long-run Growth', *Journal of Political Economy* 97 (3), 721–39.

Shackle, G. L. S. (1957) 'The nature of the bargaining process', in J. T. Dunlop (ed.), *The Theory of Wage Determination*, Cambridge University Press, Cambridge.

Shin, Hyun Song (1989) 'Review of E. Rasmussen, *Games and Information: An Introduction to Games Theory*', *Economic Journal* 99, 864–5.

Shubik, Martin (1970) 'A curmudgeon's guide to microeconomics', *Journal of Economic Literature* 8 (2), 405–34.

Shubik, Martin (1984) *A Games-Theoretic Approach to Political Economy*, Cambridge Mass., MIT Press.

Stiglitz, J. E. (1985) 'Information and economic analysis: a perspective', *Economic Journal*, supplement to vol. 95.

Streeten, P. W. (1974) 'The limits of development research', *World Development*, 2 (10–12), 11–34.

Chapter 8

Institutional economics

Legacy and new directions[1]

Geoffrey Hodgson

Institutional economics has a strange history. The 'old' institutional school of Thorstein Veblen, John Commons, Wesley Mitchell and others was a prominent paradigm amongst US economists in the 1920s and 1930s. Subsequently, economics was affected, not simply by the 'Keynesian revolution' but arguably even more profoundly by the 'formalistic revolution' of the 1930s and 1940s, following the work of Sir John Hicks, Paul Samuelson and others (Ward 1972). It was largely this increasingly self-confident post-war tendency towards a mathematical formalism based on nineteenth-century physics (Mirowski 1988, 1989) that finally eclipsed American institutionalism and made it the pursuit of a small and relatively isolated minority.

By focusing on formalities, economics became less concerned about its basic assumptions, including the crucial underlying question of what was taken as endogenous or exogenous. It will be argued below that a consequence was to entrench the ideologically-related assumptions of individualism and classic liberalism at the core of the subject. To challenge this 'hard core' is now to risk being described as a 'non-economist', or worse still – the ultimate term of disapproval for economic orthodoxy – as a 'sociologist'.

Interdisciplinary work (including that which is well represented in this book) is thus discouraged by the economics mainstream. When orthodox economics ventures into other areas it does so in the manner of 'economic imperialism': to capture territory from sociologists, political scientists and others, in order to analyse their favourite topics with neo-classical theoretical tools. Typically, it does not enter this foreign territory to learn new ideas nor to understand its methods.

It this vein, and since the mid–1970s, there has been a remarkable growth in what has been dubbed the 'new institutional economics'. Notably, this has occurred, not via a re-emergence of traditional institutionalism, but mainly (although not wholly) through developments in orthodox economic theory itself. Notably, this 'new institutionalism' leaves many of the core orthodox assumptions unscathed. The irony, of course, is that the original institutionalism of Veblen and others emerged largely out of a critique of orthodox assumptions.

Although the label is not always used consistently or unambiguously, a list of contributors to the 'new institutionalism' could include Friedrich Hayek (1982, 1988), Douglass North and Robert Thomas (1973), Mancur Olson (1965, 1982), Richard Posner (1973), Andrew Schotter (1981) and Oliver Williamson (1975, 1985). Their work spans such diverse issues as economic history, economic growth and the economics of law. Furthermore, as discussed below, there is a variety of theoretical approaches represented here. However, they all share a prominent 'new institutionalist' theme: to explain the existence of political, legal, or more generally social institutions by reference to a model of individual behaviour, tracing out its consequences in terms of human interactions.

In addition, however, there are signs of a revival of the 'old' institutionalism as well. In addition to articles in the *Journal of Economic Issues* – published by the Association for Evolutionary Economics, the organization of American institutionalists – there have been a number of recent other publications with 'old' institutionalist themes. Furthermore, there are signs that 'old' institutionalism may be spreading to Europe and elsewhere, with several related publications by European writers and the formation in 1988 of the European Association for Evolutionary Political Economy. This 'European' variant has strong links with other schools of thought, including post-Keynesians, Schumpeterians, Marxists and the French régulation school.[2]

This present essay commences with a brief discussion of the 'new' institutionalism. On this basis a conceptual distinction between the 'old' and the 'new' institutionalism is proposed. This hinges in part on the choice of factors to be taken as exogenous, and in part on the questions deemed appropriate for study. Some related limitations of the approach of the 'new' institutionalists follow. The essay moves on to discuss the adoption of evolutionary ideas by institutionalists, and approaches to the theory of technological change. Finally, this paper provides arguments why the older version of institutionalism might, in a mutated form, be on the brink of a revival.

NEW INSTITUTIONALISM: TAKING INDIVIDUALS AS EXOGENOUS

New institutionalism has both neo-classical and Austrian wings, and includes a further subset which has utilized developments in game theory. Unless the term is stretched too wide, it would be misleading to describe all the 'new institutionalists' cited above as 'neo-classical'. For instance, being a member of the Austrian School, Hayek stresses problems of information and uncertainty which are ignored in the conventional paradigm. Furthermore, the Austrian School is famous for its critique of Walrasian general equilibrium analysis. Likewise, the work of a modern game theorist such as Schotter is different from neo-classical theory in several respects, including its treatments of the notions of time and rationality. In contrast, some of the other theorists cited above are closer to the neo-classical mainstream (Hodgson 1989b). Despite the differences, however, it is argued below that all these types of 'new' institutionalism share some common premises. But it is important to note that there are non-neoclassical as well as neo-classical members of the set of 'new institutionalist' writers, as defined here.

Despite the claim of its title, all elements of the 'new' institutionalism are based upon some long-established assumptions concerning the human agent, derived from the influence of classic liberalism. These assumptions are broader and deeper in scope than the defining presumptions of 'neo-classical' theory. Important and influential thinkers such as Jeremy Bentham, David Hume, John Locke, John Stuart Mill and Adam Smith could all be described as classic liberals, despite their individual differences. Since its inception, classic liberalism has overshadowed economics. Consequently, it is much easier to identify the few outcasts and exceptions to its rule – such as Karl Marx and Thorstein Veblen – than its many subjects. Classic liberalism has remained dominant in our discipline, despite its partial eclipse in other intellectual circles in the first two-thirds of the twentieth century. Nevertheless, with the rise of the New Right in the 1970s and 1980s, classic liberalism has re-emerged on a wide front.

Whilst many different ideas and approaches may be grouped under this title, including both neo-classical and non-neoclassical theories, a key common proposition of classic liberalism is the view that the individual can, in a sense, be 'taken for granted'. To put it another way, the individual, along with his or her assumed behavioural characteristics, is taken as the elemental building block in the theory of the social or economic system. The given individuals 'plug-in' to the analysis, to use the term employed by Ulf Himmelstrand in his introduction to this volume. It is this idea of the 'abstract individual' that is fundamental to classic liberalism as a whole. According to this conception, as Steven Lukes (1973: 73) puts it, 'individuals are pictured abstractly as given, with given interests, wants, purposes, needs, etc.'.

The notion of the abstract individual can be seen to relate to the doctrine of 'methodological individualism', although the latter term is rarely well defined. In classic and precise statements of methodological individualism, such as that of Ludwig von Mises (1949), the individual is regarded as the unit of explanation because the individual alone is the purposeful agent. It is seen as illegitimate to proceed further and attempt to explain the origin or moulding of those purposes themselves. Individual purposes are thus taken as exogenous (Hodgson 1988:   Ch. 3).

Strictly, it is not a question of whether or not a theorist is found to admit that individuals – or their wants and preferences – are changed by circumstances. Indeed, all intelligent economists, from Adam Smith to Friedrich Hayek inclusive, admit that individuals might so be changed. What is crucial is that the classic liberal economist may make such an admission but then go on to assume, *for the purposes of economic enquiry*, that individuals and their preferences must be taken as given. Thus the demarcating criterion is not the matter of individual malleability *per se*, but the willingness, or otherwise, to consider this issue as an important or legitimate matter for economic enquiry. The oft-repeated statement by orthodox economists that tastes and preferences are not the *explananda* of economics thus derives directly from the classic liberal tradition. It involves taking the individual 'for granted'.

As I have argued elsewhere (Hodgson 1989b), the assumption of the abstract individual which is fundamental to classic liberalism is basic to the 'new institutional economics' as well. It is thus possible to distinguish the 'new' institutionalism from the 'old' by means of this criterion. This distinction holds despite important theoretical and policy differences within the 'new institutionalist' camp.

Having taken the individual 'for granted' the new institutionalists are then set to attempt to explain the emergence, existence, and performance of social institutions on the basis of such assumptions. These explanations address the functioning of all kinds of social institutions in terms of the interactions between such given individuals. Of course, the existence of such institutions is seen to affect individual behaviour, but only in terms of the choices and constraints presented to the agents, not by the moulding of the preferences and indeed the very individuality of those agents themselves. In other words, institutions are first of all explained in terms of given individuals, and second, once institutions have been formed by individuals, such institutions are seen only as providing external constraints, conventions or openings to individuals who are taken as given. The possibility that individuals themselves may be shaped by social institutions is not considered.

These common features of the new institutionalism may be illustrated in a number of ways, and here we must confine ourselves to a few examples. Consider first the largely neo-classical work by North and Thomas (1973) on the rise of western capitalism. Although in their discussion of this transition from feudalism many factors are highlighted, the emergence of well-defined private property rights is given a central position. It is presumed that with the gradual emergence of private property in medieval England, rational, calculating individuals began to undertake profit-seeking activities, leading eventually to greater economic prosperity for the nation as a whole.

However, despite its value and sophistication, the North-Thomas analysis fails to explain the rational, deliberative and guileful individual which it assumes at the outset. Robert Holton (1985: 54) has made this point well in his comprehensive discussion of transition theories: 'As with so much economic theory, the calculative, rational individual is presumed rather than explained'. In this respect at least, the 'new institutionalist' approach of North and Thomas contrasts with the earlier, seminal work of Marx (1973: 84) and Weber (1930, 1947) who were both keen to explain the origin and development of a culture of self-interested maximizers, composed of individuals acting on the basis of rational calculation. They saw these as specific historical phenomena, rather than as elemental and universal features of human life. Thus Marx and Weber did not presume that such rational, calculating individuals have existed for all historical time. Their emergence had to be explained in terms of such factors as changes in culture and institutions.

Related points are central to Alexander Field's (1979, 1981, 1984) forceful critique of the North-Thomas approach and of associated developments in the game-theoretic approach to institutions. In attempting to explain the origin of social institutions, the 'new institutional' economic history has to presume given individuals acting in a certain context. What it forgets is that there is in the original 'state of nature' a number of weighty institutions, and cultural and social norms have already been presumed.

In particular, game theorists such as Schotter (1981) take the individual 'for granted', as an agent unambiguously maximizing his or her expected pay-off. Further, in attempting to explain the origin of institutions through game theory, Field points out that certain norms and rules must inevitably be presumed at the start. There can be no games without rules, and thus game theory can never explain the elemental rules themselves. Even in a sequence of repeated games, or of games about other (nested) games, at least one game or meta-game, with a structure and pay-offs, must be assumed at the outset. Any such attempt to deal with history in terms of sequential or nested games is thus involved in a problem of infinite regress: even with games about games about games to the nth degree there is still one preceding game left to be explained.

It seems, therefore, that all varieties of 'new institutionalism', despite big differences in analytical methods and even policy conclusions, are united by their treatment of the factors moulding individual preferences and purposes as exogenous. In all cases the processes governing their determination are disregarded. Furthermore, in game-theoretic explanations of institutions, some norms or meta-games must be taken as exogenous as well.

INSTITUTIONALIST CRITIQUES OF RATIONAL ECONOMIC MAN

In his famous critique of economic man as 'a lightning calculator of pleasures and pains', Veblen (1919; 73) foreshadows some of the later and more elaborate theoretical critiques of 'rational economic man'. The ironic 'lightning calculator' phrase suggests that the problems of global calculation of maximization opportunities are ignored by the neo-classical theorists. This reminds the modern reader of Herbert Simon's (1957) idea of limited computational capacity and 'bounded rationality'. In describing economic man as having 'neither antecedent nor consequent' Veblen identifies and criticizes the uncreative and mechanistic picture of the agent in neo-classical theory.

What is not widely recognized is that Veblen gave further grounds for rejecting orthodox assumptions, other than on the basis of their unrealism. As Thomas Sowell (1967) points out, Veblen (1919: 221) accepted that to be 'serviceable', a hypothesis need 'not be true to fact'. He understood that 'economic man' and similar conceptions were 'not intended as a competent expression of fact' but represented an 'expedient of abstract reasoning' (p. 142).

Veblen's crucial argument against orthodox theory was that it was inadequate for the theoretical purpose at hand. His intention was to analyse the processes of change and transformation in the modern economy. Neoclassical theory was defective in this respect because it indicated 'the conditions of survival to which any innovation is subject, supposing the innovation to have taken place, not the conditions of variational growth' (Veblen 1919: 176–7). But what Veblen was seeking was precisely a theory as to why such innovations take place, not a theory which muses over equilibrium conditions after technological possibilities are established. 'The question', he wrote, 'is not how things stabilize themselves in a "static state", but how they endlessly grow and change' (Veblen 1934: 8).

Thus, in his criticism of orthodox theory, Veblen put great stress both on the processes of economic evolution and technological transformation, and on the manner in which action is moulded by circumstances. He saw the individual's conduct as being influenced by relations of an institutional nature. He thus suggested an alternative to orthodox theory with its self-contained, rational individual, with autonomous preferences and beliefs, formed apart from the social and natural world: a 'globule of desire', to use Veblen's (1919: 73) famous and satiric phrase.

Veblen rejected the continuously-calculating, marginally-adjusting agent of neo-classical theory to place stress on inertia and habit instead:

The situation of today shapes the institutions of tomorrow through a selective, coercive process, by acting upon men's habitual view of things, and so altering or fortifying a point of view or a mental attitude handed down from the past.

(Veblen 1899: 190–1)

Veblen argues that neo-classical economics has a 'faulty conception of human nature' wrongly conceiving the individual 'in hedonistic terms; that is to say, in terms of a passive and substantially inert and immutably given human nature' (Veblen 1919: 73). Thus Veblen's critique goes even beyond neo-classical economics, to include all theorists who take the individual as given. Although it may be legitimate in the short run to treat wants as fundamental data, in the long run they are, as Frank Knight (1924: 262) put it, dependent variables, 'largely caused and formed by economic activity'. Thus it is particularly in regard to long-period analysis that tastes and preferences, as well as technology, must be seen to change.

The Veblenian theme of the endogeneity of preferences is persistent in the history of the old institutionalism, up to the present day. It can be seen graphically and dramatically, for instance, in the writings of John Kenneth Galbraith (1958, 1969) with his continuing insistence that tastes are malleable and that the idea of 'consumer sovereignty' is a myth.

Veblen's legacy was not entirely positive, however. He felt uneasy with intellectual 'symmetry and system-making' (1919: 68). This opened the door for an even more impressionistic approach to economics amongst his followers. After establishing the importance of institutions, routines and habits for the middle decades of this century, institutionalism largely underlined the value of mostly descriptive work on the nature and function of politico-economic institutions.

The mid-century impasse of the 'old' institutionalism did not mean, however, that its approach to economic theory had become irrelevant or outdated. Indeed, similar concerns have been expressed by many other theorists. For example, sociologists such as Anthony Giddens (1984: 220) have argued that the individual, as a fundamental unit, 'cannot be taken as obvious'. Likewise, the economist, Tony Lawson (1987: 969), expresses anti-reductionist sentiments when he remarks that 'individual agency and social structures and context are equally relevant for analysis – each presupposes each other. Thus any reductionist account stressing analytical primacy for either individual agents or for social "wholes" must be inadequate'.

Above all, the 'old' warnings about proceeding on classic liberal assumptions should not be ignored. In this respect at least the 'old' institutionalism retains some advantages over the 'new'.

INSTITUTIONALISM AND EVOLUTIONARY APPROACHES TO ECONOMICS

For Veblen, economic institutions are complexes of habits, roles and conventional behaviour. Habits are essentially non-deliberative, and even unconscious to some degree. This contrasts with the Austrian view that all action is purposeful, and with the neo-classical idea that all action is determined by single-valued preference functions (Hodgson 1988; Waller 1988). To some extent the idea of habits conflicts with the presuppositions of classic liberalism, in the sense that it undermines the idea of the general inviolability of individual judgement.

Veblen drew a number of implications from his conception of habit and routine. For instance, he saw production not primarily as a matter of 'inputs' into some mechanical function, but as an outcome of an institutional ensemble of habits and routines: 'the accumulated, habitual knowledge of the ways and means involved . . . the outcome of long experience and experimentation' (Veblen 1919: 185–6).

Importantly, these ideas connect with Veblen's view that economic development is best regarded as an evolutionary process. However, although he was influenced by Charles Darwin, he did not live to observe the modern synthesis of Darwinian natural selection with Mendelian genetics in biology. Nevertheless, Veblen was groping towards an understanding of mechanisms which play a similar evolutionary role to that of the gene in the natural world. Such mechanisms involve organizational structures, habits and routines. Whilst these are more malleable and do not mutate in the same way as their analogue in biology, structures and routines have a stable and inert quality, as Veblen observed, and tend to sustain and thus 'pass on' their important characteristics through time.

> The situation of today shapes the institutions of tomorrow through a selective, coercive process, by acting upon men's habitual view of things, and so altering or fortifying a point of view or a mental attitude handed down from the past.
>
> (Veblen 1899: 190–1)

> A habitual line of action constitutes a habitual line of thought, and gives the point of view from which facts and events are apprehended and reduced to a body of knowledge.
>
> (Veblen 1934: 88)

The power and durability of institutions and routines are manifest in a number of ways. With the benefit of modern developments in modern anthropology and psychology, it can be seen that institutions play an essential role in providing a cognitive framework for interpreting sense data and in providing intellectual habits or routines for transforming information into useful knowledge (Hodgson 1988). These cultural and cognitive functions have been investigated by anthropologists such as Mary Douglas (1973, 1987) and Barbara Lloyd (1972).

Given that it is impossible to deal with and understand the entire amount of sense-data which reaches the brain, we rely on concepts and cognitive frames to select aspects of the data and to make sense of these stimuli. These procedures of perception and cognition are learned and acquired through our upbringing and from our social surroundings. As cultural anthropologists argue, social institutions, culture and routines give rise to certain ways of selecting and understanding data. It is in this manner that there is a link between culture and institutions, on the one hand, and cognition on the other.

Reference to the cognitive functions of institutions and routines is clearly important in understanding their relative stability and capacity to replicate. Habits and routines are both durable, and present in a variety of forms in any complex economy. As in the case of Darwin's theory, this combination of variety with durability provides a basis for evolutionary selection to work. Often unwittingly and without human design, certain institutions and patterns of behaviour become more effective in the given environmental context. Even without changes in the environment, the evolutionary process is unceasing. But environment changes can accelerate, hinder or disrupt the processes of selection, often in dramatic ways.

The idea that routines within the firm act as 'genes' to pass on skills and information is adopted by Nelson and Winter (1982: 134–6) and forms a crucial part of their theoretical model of the modern corporation. Despite making no reference to the earlier work of Veblen, their work is much closer to the 'old' institutionalism than to the 'new'.

The 'selective, coercive process' of institutional replication is not, however, confined to a fixed groove. Institutions change, and even gradual change can eventually put such a strain on a system that there can be outbreaks of conflict or crisis, leading to a change in actions and attitudes. Thus there is always the possibility of the breakdown of regularity: 'there will be moments of crisis situations or structural breaks when existing conventions or social practices are disrupted' (Lawson 1985: 920). In any social system there is an interplay between routinized behaviour and the variable or volatile decisions of other agents.

Such a tension between regularity and crisis is shown in the following quotation from Veblen:

Not only is the individual's conduct hedged about and directed by his habitual relations to his fellows in the group, but these relations, being of an institutional character, vary as the institutional scene varies. The wants and desires, the end and the aim, the ways and the means, the amplitude and drift of the individual's conduct are functions of an institutional variable that is of a highly complex and wholly unstable character.

(Veblen 1919: 242–3)

With these ingredients it is possible to envisage processes whereby for long periods the reigning habits of thought and action are cumulatively reinforced. But this very process can lead to sudden and rapid change. Veblen's conception of evolution is thus more like the idea of 'punctuated equilibria' advanced by biologists Niles Eldredge and Stephen Jay Gould (1972) than orthodox Darwinian gradualism. Crucially, the Eldredge-Gould idea of punctuated equilibria relies on the notion of a hierarchy of both processes and units of replication. Whilst relative stability may arise from sufficient compatibility between the different levels for some time, cumulative disturbances at one or more levels, or exogenous shocks, can lead to a breakdown in the former 'equilibrium' and herald developments along a different path.

In Veblen's view the economic system is not a 'self-balancing mechanism' but a 'cumulatively unfolding process'. It is not well known, but Veblen's idea of cumulative causation was an important precursor of other developments of the very same concept by Allyn Young (1928), Gunnar Myrdal (1939, 1944, 1957), Nicholas Kaldor (1972) and K. William Kapp (1976). Because of the momentum of technological and social change in modern industrial society, and the clashing new conceptions and traditions thrown up with each innovation in management and technique, the cumulative character of economic development can mean crisis on occasions rather than continuous change or advance.

As I have shown elsewhere (Hodgson 1989a, 1991 forthcoming), such a 'punctuated equilibria' model of economic growth is capable of empirical applications. The main hypothesis is that for years or sometimes even decades, socio-economic systems become locked-in to a fixed overall pattern of dynamic development. Whilst there will be *parametric* change in economic variables such as output and employment, there may be years or decades of overall and relative *structural* stability, punctuated by rapid transitions from one structural regime to another. Most of the major structural shifts are associated with socio-political disruptions such as wars or revolutions. With strict criteria, it is possible to develop a crude index of the degree of disruption in each country. Econometric tests with data from sixteen major OECD countries have given good results, explaining much of the productivity growth over the chosen periods.[3]

EVOLUTIONARY THEORIES OF TECHNOLOGICAL CHANGE

The aforementioned works by Veblen, Nelson, Winter and others have prepared the ground for modern developments in the theory of technological change, linking crucially with the earlier theories of Joseph Schumpeter (1934, 1976). Important examples of this genre are found in the works of Norman Clark and Calestous Juma (1987), Giovanni Dosi (1988) and Giovanni Dosi *et al.* (1988).

However, the links with the institutionalist tradition are not always explicit, and some are worth spelling out here. First, in attempting to explain technological change, these writers are breaking away from the neo-classical and Austrian traditions which have taken technology as exogenous. In doing so they have firmly aligned themselves with the work of Veblen and some of his followers. Although the deterministic modelling or prediction of future technological advance is, in principle, ruled out (Popper 1960: v-vii), this recent work has shown that technology and innovations can be analysed in terms of a multi-levelled taxonomy of 'paradigms', 'systems', 'paths' or 'trajectories' which are useful both analytically and as a guide to business and government policy.

Second, in using the biological metaphor of evolution, links have again been created with Veblen and the institutionalists, as well as with Schumpeter and other writers. In particular, however, some writers have borrowed ideas from the evolutionary theory found in modern biology to illuminate the processes of change. A good example is Clark and Juma's (1987) use of Conrad Waddington's (1957) biological concept of the 'chreod' to describe a constrained path of technological development.

A chreod is a relatively stable trajectory of development for a species or technology. Although changes and perturbations may occur, past developments ensure that development is channelled along a certain route. A biological example is the survival of the same basic configuration of the skeletal frame amongst mammals, reptiles and birds. Evolution cannot provide a more optimal configuration in every case, as the basic skeletal frame is determined by the history of the species. A technological example is the adoption of the internal combustion engine for the motor car around 1900. Despite its supremacy, with sufficient research and development there still may be other superior alternatives, such as steam or electrical power.

Third, Nelson and Winter (1982) and Dosi (1988) in particular have stressed the tacit nature of much technical knowledge, and its connection with routinized behaviour within the firm. This connects with Veblen's conception of habit, and the use of habits and routines as the analogue for the gene in economic evolution. The tacitness of knowledge is also tied up with the importance of cognitive frames. Given that the acquisition of the latter is often subtle and lasting, and critical introspection is difficult at such a basic level, such durable habits of thought are tricky to alter or replace.

This work on technological change has been linked by institutionalists to other, related issues, particularly information and systems theory (Clark

1988; Hodgson 1987, 1988; Neale 1984; Weinel and Crossland 1989). Here there is further evidence of the 'old' institutionalist aversion to reductionism and single levels of explanation.

CONCLUSION: TOWARDS A NEW BEGINNING?

A number of developments suggest that after decades of isolation the institutionalists may be moving once again into the limelight. First, despite the qualifications voiced above, the 'new' institutionalism has put the analysis of the origins and functions of institutions right back near the top of the orthodox theorist's agenda. It is no longer valid to repeat the criticism made by radicals in the 1960s and 1970s that orthodox economists take institutions, such as the state, for granted.

Second, neo-classical economic theory has not overcome its inability to analyse the processes of structural development and long-run economic change. Instead it has become locked into the static irrelevancies of general equilibrium theorizing. As rapid and dramatic politico-economic change is occurring on the world scale, much of the economics profession is unfortunately engaged in a formalistic binge of dubious utility, and is often intolerant of alternative approaches and methods. But just as the convulsions of the 1930s helped to bring about the Keynesian revolution in economic theory, institutionalists and others will be aided by the limitations of the reigning orthodoxy. Particular questions such as that of the nature of technological change, as well as the general question of which variables are to be taken as exogenous, will come to the fore.

Third, formal progress in economics is not only being confounded by the limitations of orthodox assumptions, new results in mathematics have led to questions about the predictive methods that are prominent in economic science. Developments in chaos theory have drawn attention to the limitations of the models involving linear equations which are widely-used in economic theory. Chaos theory shows that apparently random or chaotic behaviour can flow from simple, non-linear models. Furthermore, such models are often so sensitive to initial parameter values that precise prediction is impossible (Gleick 1988).

Institutionalists have been quick to point out some of the implications of chaos theory for economics (Coricelli and Dosi 1988; Dopfer 1988; Radzicki 1990). The results for science as a whole are likely to be profound. Not only is the common obsession with precise prediction confounded. In addition, the whole atomistic tradition in science of attempting to reduce each phenomenon to its component parts is placed into question. Here the institutionalists can again make a comeback. By embracing non-reductionist methods they have prepared the ground for an approach to economic theory that is more in line with the implications of recent developments in the theory of chaos.

Finally, the institutionalist adherence to the evolutionary metaphor has a number of advantages. Evolutionary theory, for instance, emphasizes the concept of irreversibility or the 'arrow of time'.[4] It instates a concept of process rather than comparative statics. It includes disequilibrium as well as equilibrium situations. It embraces diversity in reality and qualitative as well as quantitative change. It involves error-making, and not simply optimizing, behaviour. With increasing awareness of the limitations of the mechanistic paradigm in economics (Mirowski, 1988, 1989) it has been argued that the biological analogy, as used by many institutionalists, has a great deal to offer (Georgescu-Roegen 1971, 1979; Dragan and Demetrescu 1986).

Given the proven resilience of orthodoxy, Myrdal's (1976: 86) prediction that 'within the next ten or twenty years the now fashionable highly abstract analysis of conventional economists will lose out' and a 'more institutional approach will win ground' already seems over-optimistic. Indeed, institutionalism is not yet sufficiently developed to replace orthodoxy. On the other hand, however, the pressures for change are now so strong that orthodox economics is unlikely to emerge unaltered.

NOTES

1 The author is very grateful to Ulf Himmelstrand for critical and helpful remarks on an earlier version of this chapter.
2 See Clark and Juma (1987), Dosi et al. (1988), Foster (1987), Hanusch (1988) and Hodgson (1988, 1989c, forthcoming) for implicit and explicit discussions of some of these links.
3 In some respects this work is similar to that of Olson (1982), but there are many differences. Especially in my latter work (Hodgson, 1991 forthcoming), Olson's idea that institutions automatically become more schlerotic with age is countered by the proposition that, short of major disruptions, economic systems tend to be confined to the margins of a fixed growth track – be it a low, medium or high rate of growth – depending on the circumstances when the last major structural changes occurred.
4 The irreversibility of economic processes has been investigated by a number of writers, notably Nicholas Georgescu-Roegen (1971) and Joan Robinson (1974), but see also the chapter by Samuel Bowles in the present volume.

BIBLIOGRAPHY

Clark, N. G. (1988) 'Some new approaches to evolutionary economics', *Journal of Economic Issues* 22(2), 511–31.
Clark, N. G. and Juma, C. (1987) *Long-Run Economics: An Evolutionary Approach to Economic Growth*, London, Pinter.
Coricelli, F. and Dosi, G. (1988) 'Coordination and order in economic change and the interpretative power of economic theory', in Dosi, Freeman, Nelson, Silverberg and Soete (eds), (124–47).

Dopfer, K. (1988) 'Classical mechanics with an ethical dimension: Professor Tinbergen's economics', *Journal of Economic Issues* 22(3), 675–706.

Dosi, G. (1988) 'The sources, procedures, and microeconomic effects of innovation', *Journal of Economic Literature* 26(3), 1120–71.

Dosi, G., Freeman, C., Nelson, R., Silverberg, G. and Soete, L. (eds) (1988) *Technical Change and Economic Theory*, London, Pinter.

Douglas, M. (ed.) (1973) *Rules and Meanings*, Harmondsworth, Penguin.

Douglas, M. (1987) *How Institutions Think*, London, Routledge & Kegan Paul.

Dragan, J. C. and Demetrescu, M. C. (1986) *Entropy and Bioeconomics: The New Paradigm of Nicholas Georgescu-Roegen*, Milan, Nagard.

Eldredge, N. and Gould, S. J. (1972) 'Punctuated equilibria: an alternative to phyletic gradualism', in T. J. M. Schopf (ed.) (1972) *Models in Paleobiology*, San Francisco, Freeman, Cooper & Co., 82–115.

Field, A. J. (1979) 'On the explanation of rules using rational choice models', *Journal of Economic Issues* 13(1), 49–72.

Field, A. J. (1981) 'The problem with neoclassical institutional economics: a critique with special reference to the North/Thomas model of pre–1500 Europe', *Explorations in Economic History* 18(2), 174–98.

Field, A. J. (1984) 'Microeconomics, norms and rationality', *Economic Development and Cultural Change* 32(4), 683–711.

Foster, J. (1987) *Evolutionary Macroeconomics*, London, Allen & Unwin.

Galbraith, J. K. (1958) *The Affluent Society*, London, Hamilton.

Galbriath, J. K. (1969) *The New Industrial State*, Harmondsworth, Penguin.

Georgescu-Roegen, N. (1971) *The Entropy Law and the Economic Process*, Cambridge, Mass., Harvard University Press.

Georgescu-Roegen, N. (1979) 'Methods in economic science', *Journal of Economic Issues* 13(2), 317–28.

Giddens, A. (1984) *The Constitution of Society: Outline of the Theory of Structuration*, Cambridge, Polity Press.

Gleick, J. (1988) *Chaos: Making a New Science*, London, Heinemann.

Hanusch, H. (ed.) (1988) *Evolutionary Economics: Applications of Schumpeter's Ideas*, Cambridge, Cambridge University Press.

Hayek, F. A. (1982) *Law, Legislation and Liberty*, 3-volume combined edn, London, Routledge & Kegan Paul.

Hayek, F. A. (1988) *The Fatal Conceit: The Errors of Socialism, the Collected Works of Friedrich August Hayek*, I, W. W. Bartley III (ed.), London, Routledge.

Hodgson, G. M. (1987) 'Economics and systems theory', *Journal of Economic Studies* 14(4), 65–86, reprinted in Hodgson (in press).

Hodgson, G. M. (1988) *Economics and Institutions: A Manifesto for a Modern Institutional Economics*, Cambridge, Polity Press.

Hodgson, G. M. (1989a) 'Institutional rigidities and economic growth', *Cambridge Journal of Economics* 13(1), 79–101, reprinted in A. Lawson, J. G. Palma and J. Sender, (eds) (1989) *Kaldor's Political Economy*, London, Academic Press, and in Hodgson (in press).

Hodgson, G. M. (1989b) 'Institutional economic theory: the old versus the new', *Review of Political Economy* 1(3), 249–69, reprinted in Hodgson (in press).

Hodgson, G. M. (1989c) 'Post-Keynesianism and institutionalism: the missing link', in J. Pheby (ed.) *New Directions in Post-Keynesian Economics*, Aldershot, Edward Elgar, 94–123, reprinted in Hodgson (in press).

Hodgson, G. M. (1991 forthcoming) 'Socio-political disruption and economic growth', in G. M. Hodgson and E. Screpanti (eds), *Rethinking*

Economics: Markets, Technology and Economic Evolution, Aldershot, Edward Elgar.

Hodgson, G. M. (forthcoming) *Economics and Evolution*, Cambridge, Polity Press.

Hodgson, G. M. (in press) *After Marx and Sraffa*, Basingstoke, Macmillan.

Holton, R. J. (1985) *The Transition from Feudalism to Capitalism*, Basingstoke, Macmillan.

Kaldor, N. (1972) 'The irrelevance of equilibrium economics', *Economic Journal* 82(4), 1237–55, reprinted in N. Kaldor (1978) *Further Essays on Economic Theory: (Collected Economic Essays*, 5), London, Duckworth.

Kapp, K. W. (1976) 'The nature and significance of institutional economics', *Kyklos* 29 (fasc. 2), 209–32.

Knight, F. H. (1924) 'The limitations of scientific method in economics', in R. G. Tugwell (ed.) *The Trend of Economics*, New York, Alfred Knopf, 229–67.

Lawson, A. (1985) 'Uncertainty and economic analysis', *Economic Journal* 95(4), 909–27.

Lawson, A. (1987) 'The relative/absolute nature of knowledge and economic analysis', *Economic Journal* 97(4), 951–70.

Lloyd, B. B. (1972) *Perception and Cognition: A Cross-Cultural Perspective*, Harmondsworth, Penguin.

Lukes, S. (1973) *Individualism*, Oxford, Basil Blackwell.

Marx, K. (1973) *Grundrisse: Foundations of the Critique of Political Economy*, trans. M. Nicolaus, Harmondsworth, Penguin.

Mirowski, P. (1988) *Against Mechanism: Protecting Economics from Science*, Totowa, NJ, Rowman & Littlefield.

Mirowski, P. (1989) *More Heat Than Light: Economics as Social Physics, Physics as Nature's Economics*, Cambridge, Cambridge University Press.

Mises, L. von (1949) *Human Action: A Treatise on Economics*, London, William Hodge.

Myrdal, G. (1939) *Monetary Equilibrium*, London, Hodge.

Myrdal, G. (1944) *An American Dilemma: The Negro Problem and Modern Democracy*, New York, Harper & Row.

Myrdal, G. (1957) *Economic Theory and Underdeveloped Regions*, London, Duckworth.

Myrdal, G. (1976) 'The meaning and validity of institutional economics', in K. Dopfer (ed.) *Economics in the Future*, London, Macmillan, 82–9.

Neale, W. C. (1984) 'Technology as social process: a commentary on knowledge and human capital', *Journal of Economic Issues* 18(2), 573–80.

Nelson, R. R. and Winter, S. G. (1982) *An Evolutionary Theory of Economic Change*, Cambridge, Mass., Harvard University Press.

North, D. C. and Thomas, R. P. (1973) *The Rise of the Western World*, London, Cambridge University Press.

Olson, M. (1965) *The Logic of Collective Action. Public Goods and the Theory of Groups*, Cambridge, Mass., Harvard University Press.

Olson, M. (1982) *The Rise and Decline of Nations. Economic Growth, Stagflation, and Social Rigidities*, New Haven and London, Yale University Press.

Popper. K. R. (1960) *The Poverty of Historicism*, London, Routledge & Kegan Paul.

Posner, R. (1973) *Economic Analysis of Law*, Boston, Little, Brown.

Radzicki, M. J. (1990) 'Institutional dynamics, deterministic chaos, and self-organizing systems', *Journal of Economic Issues* 24(1), 57–102.

Robinson, J. (1974) *History versus Equilibrium*, London, Thames Papers in Political Economy.

Schotter, A. (1981) *The Economic Theory of Social Institutions*, Cambridge, Cambridge University Press.

Schumpeter, J. A. (1934) *The Theory of Economic Development*, Cambridge, Mass., Harvard University Press.

Schumpeter, J. A. (1976) *Capitalism, Socialism and Democracy*, 5th edn, London, Allen & Unwin.

Simon, H. A. (1957) *Models of Man: Social and Rational*, New York, Wiley.

Sowell, T. (1967) 'The "evolutionary" economics of Thorstein Veblen', *Oxford Economic Papers* 19(2), 177–98.

Veblen, T. B. (1899) *The Theory of the Leisure Class: An Economic Study of Institutions*, New York, Macmillan.

Veblen, T. B. (1919) *The Place of Science in Modern Civilisation and Other Essays*, New York, Huebsch, reprinted 1990 with a new introduction by W. J. Samuels, New Brunswick, NJ, Transaction Publishers.

Veblen, T. B. (1934) *Essays on Our Changing Order*, L. Ardzrooni (ed.), New York, The Viking Press.

Waddington, C. H. (1957) *The Strategy of the Genes*, London, Allen & Unwin.

Waller, Jr, W. J. (1988) 'Habit in economic analysis', *Journal of Economic Issues* 22(1), 113–26.

Ward, B. (1972) *What's Wrong With Economics?*, London, Macmillan.

Weber, M. (1930) *The Protestant Ethic and the Spirit of Capitalism*, London, Allen & Unwin.

Weber, M. (1947) *The Theory of Social and Economic Organization*, New York, The Free Press.

Weinel, I. and Crossland, P. D. (1989) 'The scientific foundations of technical progress', *Journal of Economic Issues* 23(3), 795–808.

Williamson, O. E. (1975) *Markets and Hierarchies: Analysis and Anti-Trust Implications*, New York, The Free Press.

Williamson, O. E. (1985) *The Economic Institutions of Capitalism: Firms, Markets, Relational Contracting*, London, Macmillan.

Young. A. A. (1928) 'Increasing returns and economic progress', *Economic Journal* 38(4), 527–42.

Part III

Voices from the exogenous domain

Chapter 9

Political science and the study of the economy

Leon Lindberg

INTRODUCTION

The polity–economy relationship has elicited growing interest and a very substantial literature in political science, especially in the last decade. By far the greater part of this literature has been concerned with the macro-economy, that is, with short-to-medium term employment and price stabil-ization performance and policy-making, and more recently with economic growth and the performance of industrial sectors (Goldthorpe 1984; Hol-lingsworth 1982; Lindberg and Maier 1985; Dyson and Wilks 1983).

Political scientists have increasingly addressed themselves to the econ-omy *per se*, that is, to the impact of power, ideology, and institutional factors on economic policy and economic performance, as well as to the patterned interactions among economic actors, collective interests and state agencies in determining prices and profits and in processes of production, distribution and the co-ordination of economic activities (Katzenstein 1978; Lindberg and Maier 1985; Peretz 1983; Zysman 1983). This work is probably best understood as 'exogenous structural impacts'. This is so because so much of it argues for the importance of understanding complex institutions and actors as bearers of economic processes, and especially, on the extent to which cross-national and historical differences systematically condition or override the behaviours postulated by stylized models of rational and constrained economic choice. In these domains political scien-tists have incorporated elements of Marxian economics and state theory, organizational theory and the 'new economic sociology', to such a degree that it seems artificial to claim a distinctive political science analytical tradition. In other words, the most interesting and important work is already very interdisciplinary.

Nevertheless, the earliest and still perhaps most widespread preoccu-pation among political scientists interested in the economy has been with the impact of macroeconomic conditions on the electorate, voting patterns and electoral outcomes, and 'mediated feedbacks' from elections to econ-omic policy and performance (Tufte 1978; Hibbs 1987). This literature has converged with rich economic traditions in 'the theory of economic policy' on political–economic cycles, policy optimization and reaction function modelling (Borooah and van der Ploeg 1983; Alt and Chrystal 1983). The emphasis in recent political science contributions seems increasingly to be to point to the lack of empirical evidence for the existence of systematic electorally motivated political business cycles implying suboptimal economic outcomes (Hibbs 1987; Lindberg and Maier 1985; Grant and Nath 1984; Alt and Chrystal 1983). Other themes have included: the importance of class-based interests and partisan alignments in determining voter reactions to economic conditions *and* in determining economic policies and performance outcomes; and the importance in reaction function modelling of describing dominant coalitions and the institutional arrangements that determine or constrain the goals chosen by policy-makers and the instruments that are available to them.

EXOGENOUS VARIABLES IN NEO-CLASSICAL ECONOMICS FROM A POLITICAL SCIENCE PERSPECTIVE

Hartley identifies three sets of variables that economists in the neo-classical tradition have typically treated as exogenous: tastes and preferences, technology and government (see chapter 4 in this volume). The public choice approach to 'endogenizing' the latter is, of course, most directly pertinent to an evaluation from the perspective of political science, but some brief comments and suggested relationships will also be provided with respect to preference functions and technology.

Government

Hartley embraces public choice theory as the most promising approach to understanding the behaviour of voters, political parties, governments, bureaucracies and interest groups in the making and implementation of economic policies (or policies affecting the economy). Many political scientists would agree, for public choice theorizing (that is, the application of neo-classical concepts and economic reasoning to 'the political marketplace') has many adherents. Political science work in the public choice tradition largely converges with the form and substance of the deductions/predictions, and with the individualistic and anti-statist normative stance illustrated in Hartley's Chapter. On the other hand, most political scientists still analyse economic policy-making in terms of differences in the power of groups and classes, the role of dominant elites or coalitions, and unequal access to material, informational and skill resources. Economic policy-making involves periodic struggles over the distribution of power and income in electoral and *in multiple other* arenas, implying positional and structural inequalities of power and influence among business, labour, and other organized interests, including the state. Besides attending to the inequalities of power in diverse arenas through which economic policy objectives of states and dominant elites are determined, a second characteristic element in political science analysis is on the importance of institutions as contexts determining or constraining the ways in which preferences are articulated and transformed into selected targets and chosen instruments of economic policy (Lindberg and Maier 1985; Zysman 1983).

From this 'neo-institutional' perspective, much of the public choice literature seeking to establish the influence of political factors upon economic policy seems 'superficial and tendentious' (Alt and Chrystal 1983: 242), and broadly ignorant of the extent to which the applicability of the maximizing postulate, and the metaphor of a 'political market-place', in which voters and politicians exchange votes for policies, is subject to cross-nationally and historically contingent conditions of political mobilization, or domination and institutional structures in the state and the economy. I will illustrate with respect to the literatures on voting and economic policy, vote-maximizing politicians and the political business cycle, and bureaucrats and the 'excessive' scale and size of government.

Voting and economic policy

The economic theory of voting assumes that voters make rational cost-benefit calculations on the basis of available information and expectations of utility. Choice theoretic models of voting assume electoral arenas are decisive in determining government policies and provide stylized answers to such questions as: do voters evaluate candidates promises or past performance of the economy when deciding to vote? How large a role is played by economic and by non-economic conditions in this evaluation? However, empirical results show that economic variables generally explain a relatively minor share of variations in popular support for candidates, but that this proportion varies substantially and systematically from country to country (for example, it is much higher in the UK and the US than in most other countries). Furthermore, there is great instability (that is, the coefficients change from sample to sample) in empirical results across and even within countries and over even short periods of time (Alt and Chrystal 1983).

Voters may evaluate different parties according to different criteria; mass opinion tends to respond to the structure of the agenda set by the media or by competing politicians, the availability of information about economic conditions and their distributional implications, and about policy options and trade-offs, and varies according to degrees of party organization or weakness, the relative mobilization of business and labour, occupational and class positions, and ideological hegemony and the boundaries of acceptable policy ideas that prevail in a society at a particular time.

In short, we must go well beyond economic reasoning if we are to develop a theory of the public's demand for economic outcomes, a theory of information usage by mass publics or a theory of power in economic policy-making. Preferences, economic policy demands and information, and their importance in determining policies or economic outcomes, clearly vary in decisive ways from one country to another in accordance with the kinds of variables and factors enumerated above.

Vote-maximizing politicians and political business cycles

One of the most popular and durable choice theoretic arguments about politics and the economy sees a built-in tendency for vote-maximizing politicians and political parties in a democracy to produce suboptimal economic outcomes by virtue of their interest in re-election or election. Either an incumbent party manufactures boom conditions to win re-election, implying subsequent bursts of inflation, or competing parties escalate unrealistic expectations on the part of voters which subsequently impose unrealizable employment targets. The assumptions here are that policy-makers can successfully manipulate the economy when needed, that voters are myopic and amnesiac, and that parties and politicians are only interested in re-election, with no regard for the long-term interests of the economy *or* the party. There are many variations on such political business cycle models but empirical research by political scientists does not suggest that any of them is a good description of what has happened in any country over any substantial period of time. There *are* cases where politicians have successfully undertaken electorally-motivated economic interventions (for example, the US in 1972 and 1984) but these seem to be exceptions and not the rule and must apparently be understood in their own terms. There is also evidence that electorates in some countries or circumstances are able to behave 'strategically', and that politicians and political parties may act 'responsibly' as to maximize the chances of an uninterrupted term in office. Clearly, available trade-offs as well as the goals of politicians and administrations vary considerably, and understanding this requires systematic analysis of how policy-makers respond to their economic and political environments.

Some advances have been made in the reaction function approach in which observed outcomes are treated as the result of optimal decisions, inferring from this what the preferences and weights attached to different objectives and targets appear to have been. But, as Alt and Chrystal (1983) point out, it remains unclear where these preferences and weights have come from, and how we are to separate the effects of policy-makers' objectives from structural constraints. Familiarity with the specific workings of economic and policy-making institutions is a necessary basis for the effective application of reaction functions to the study of economic policy.

Bureaucrats and the excessive scale and size of government

The 'myth' of the budget-maximizing bureaucrat seems as durable among public choice theorists as the myth of the vote-maximizing politician. Either separately or in tandem, these narrowly self-interested state actors tend to be blamed: for 'excessive' spending and inflationary deficits that force out private sector investment, and for overly intrusive government regulation that imposes unrealistic compliance costs that deter investment and innovation. Bureaucrats seek to maximize their budgets for reasons of public reputation, patronage or salary. Bureaucracies tend to perpetrate themselves because they are spending other people's money and are never subject to market tests. They 'advertise' to drum up business for services to justify ever-increasing budgets and staff size. Bureaucratic myopia prevents overall budgetary controls; state bureaucracies persistently make uninformed decisions and spend exorbitant sums for goods they purchase. Bureaucratic policies favour short-term and concentrated benefits, deferred and diffused costs, new and expanded programmes, conspicuous projects, and place unnecessary constraints on producers that amount to taxation of market efficiency. The interaction of vote-maximizing politicians and budget-maximizing bureaucrats leads to an endemic tendency of democracies to 'oversupply' bureaucratic goods and services.

That such arguments do not do very well as explanations of the growth of public expenditures or of variations across countries in spending, or of trends in the scale or goals of state intervention should not come as a surprise. Nor do they succeed as descriptions of the behaviour of bureaucrats or state managers in economic policy-making. With respect to public expenditures, we have a rich empirical literature, dating at least as far back as the work of Adolf Wagner in 1883, that demonstrates the uselessness of monocausal or 'all pervasive' or universally-valid theories in explaining secular and cross-national variations and trends in state spending. The general pattern of growth in expenditures closely tracks industrialization and the growth of national income, many expenditures arise as an unintended by-product of other policies or as a function of demographic trends. Wars and 'accumulation and legitimation crises' have periodic powerful effects on trends in spending and taxing. Among factors associated with differences in spending and taxing levels are: working-class mobilization, control of government by Left parties and Catholic parties, but the relationships are not uniform. Different institutional structures in which expenditure decisions are made are perhaps most important of all, especially degrees of fragmentation and decentralization in fiscal policy processes, weakness in policy co-ordination mechanisms such as parties, bureaucratic structures and corporatist networks linking the public sector to a highly organized 'and concerted' private sector. High spending and taxing have not been associated with deficits and a poor stabilization or growth performance. Indeed, the empirical evidence provides a stronger case for the opposite (Lindberg and Maier 1985).

If the goal is to explain *when* governments intervene in the economy and with what effect, the public choice paradigm again provides a very restrictive view. Political scientists on the basis of extensive cross-national research have demonstrated that economic policy-making involves continuous conflicts among business, labour and other organized interests, party politicians, and state officials over the selection of targets or goals. Policy implementation involves the selection and effective exercise of policy instruments, but policy-makers do not have a free choice of instruments. Some can choose only among direct and global instruments that influence aggregate demand and the money supply, whereas others may also choose instruments that influence manpower skills, prices and wages, and industrial structures. In some countries the development and implementation of regulatory policies are deeply constrained by adversarial relationships between business and government or between business and labour, whereas elsewhere co-operative relationships predominate and identical regulatory goals and rules have completely different economic effects. Political authorities in some countries are able to use a co-ordinated set of policy instruments, whereas in others a fragmented government structure prevents adoption of a sustained and coherent policy. Variations in the scope and effectiveness of government economic policies must then be sought in terms of historically and nationally contingent variations in: the political and labour market mobilization of the working class, and the mobilization and associational capacities of business (Katzenstein 1976; Lindberg and Maier 1985); the structures and behaviourial rules of the financial system that governs the flows of capital in the economy and that mediates relationship among savings, investment and the state (Zysman 1983); the organizational skills, managerial ideologies and political capacities of state executives and bureaucratic actors (Evans *et al.* 1985); the ways in which intellectual innovations (ideas about economic policy and those that produce them) relate to policy-making (Weir and Skocpol, 1985; Odell 1983); the constitutionally and politically-determined power relationships among and within various state institutions; the goals and internal dynamics of political parties as institutions; electoral systems, campaign and financing practices and voter turnout patterns that constrain the roles of voters in economic outcomes; and 'industrial cultures' that establish generally-accepted norms about the proper spheres of the autonomous firm, institutions that provide industrial finance and agencies of the state (Dyson and Wilks 1983).

International interdependencies, power relationships, and institutional arrangements in the trade and monetary realms are systematic and crucial contexts for, and constraints upon, economic policies and economic outcomes. They have been extensively studied by political scientists. It has been observed that the most appropriate generalization about the world economy during the past 200 years is that it displays a pattern of liberalization when a dominant or hegemonic power emerges, followed by a phase of fragmentation as the economic and military power of nations evens out. Rapid growth and extended periods of economic stability tend to be associated with periods of hegemony, especially in the 'lead country' but also spreading to 'follower' economies. But such hegemonic relationships are inherently unstable. They may give way to mercantilism and growth restraining protectionisms or to the collapse of trade and monetary flows, or they may be followed by mutually-managed trade and monetary relationships if national policy-makers display adaptive and co-operative capacities.

Extensive international economic interdependence creates endemic problems of 'adjustment' that are not adequately handled in conventional theories of free trade. Comparative advantage is not static but dynamic, and government policies inevitably alter the pattern of comparative advantages. Policy prescriptions of international trade theory are 'no longer obvious', and new theoretical and policy approaches are required to address problems of industrial and innovation policy and the 'collective management' of international trade and monetary regimes' (Zysman and Tyson 1983).

Preference functions

With respect to the exogenously given preference functions of consumers, labour and firms assumed by neo-classical economics, most political scientists would probably take the same critical stance as the 'new economic sociology' (see Swedberg, *et al.* 1987; see also Bowles's paper in the IDEA Project chapter 6 in this volume). Actors should be conceptualized as social agents; the behaviour of these agents is complex, and agents should be modelled as having internal processes and politics; agents are 'procedurally rational', that is, their behaviour involves 'appropriate deliberation' and search routines; agents are strategically rational, one must model strategy and counterstrategy; power relations, class conflict, institutional inheritance and ideology shape preferences and the internal processes of economic agents. One of the most important implications for neo-classical theories is in the area of *expectations*. An active debate rages over whether expectations are 'rational' or 'adaptive'. A political science analysis would surely stress as potential determinants (or intervening variables) of the expectations of labour, consumers and firms: conceptions of fairness, labour power, norms of 'class compromise', corporatist arrangements, and so on.

Technology

We know that the growth potential of an interlinked system of national economies depends, in any given historical period, on the rate at which the lead country (or hegemon) pushes out the frontiers of technology, that is, that the pace of technological progress is a function of the vitality of the lead country. Follower countries are able to optimize growth rates within this 'stock' of technical knowledge to the extent that governments maintain aggregate demand and develop effective science and R & D policies, and to the extent that government-business relationships are co-operative and business rivalry does not frustrate government politics seeking to maximize 'public returns' from technological advances. Research by political scientists and other investigators suggests that industrial and R & D policies can also facilitate technological advance *at the frontiers* (Dyson and Wilks 1983; Pinder 1982) where the relationships between industry structure and technological innovation on the one hand, and government policy on the other, are mediated by capital requirements, barriers to entry, infrastructure and legitimation requirements of technologies, and by non-market collaborative/collusive relationships among firms in a sector (associations, 'clans') and between firms, finance, and labour. Market-induced R & D suffers from serious failures in optimizing the rate of technical change, especially where industrial structures are highly competitive and where there is an uncertain regulatory environment.

The sources of technological change and processes of innovation must be central to any research agenda in political economy; technological choice, industrial maturation, and learning curves must be incorporated in a framework that recognizes that the structure of markets and the distribution of political and economic power may outweigh efficiency improvements as determinants of technological change (for example, Piore and Sabel 1984).

OTHER EXOGENOUS FACTORS

Industrial change and adjustment

The role of government and institutional contexts in processes of industrial adjustment to saturated markets, excess capacity, changes in technology and tastes or terms of international trade, have been extensively studied by political scientists. Major findings suggesting variables that must be 'endogenized' would include the following:

- the level of adjustment is a function of the structure of firms *and* the internal strategies of firms *in interaction with* government policies and the general institutional environment;

- government intervention is an important intervening variable in explaining the performance of industries;
- government policy must be seen within the context of the institutional environment of labour relations, financial systems, power coalitions, centralization and decentralization of the economic system and of state structures, the capacities of business and labour to concert their behaviours internally and with each other (that is, strength of associations, corporatist linkages);
- macro- and microeconomic regulation and economic performance have more to do with the evolution of institutional control structures at the level of the corporation and the shop floor among labour, firms, finance and the state that can be recognized by neo-classical theory (Piore and Sabel 1984);
- structural differences in national financial systems is a critical determinant of the strategies of firms and the state and helps establish a general capacity on the part of political groups or governments to develop coherent strategies for aiding processes of industrial adjustment. Different financial structures conduce to different solutions to the political, technological and economic problems posed by industrial adjustment (Zysman 1983).
- non-interventionist strategies without compensation tend to create continuous political conflicts that disrupt the functioning of the marketplace. A stable settlement of the distributional gains and pains of economic change is a political prerequisite for a smoothly running economy.

Problematics of the co-ordination of economic activities

Political scientists (together with organizational sociologists, economic historians and institutional economists) are increasingly interested in some classic problems of the co-ordination of economic activities. How do the diverse activities engaged in by the numerous agents in a capitalist market economy (that is, firms, state agencies, unions, finance providers, innovators and technology providers) come to, are made, or fail to mesh? How do economic agents adapt their internal structures and strategies to environmental conditions of information complexity and resource scarcity in making macro and micro economically-appropriate decisions about production, pricing, allocation of resources, new investment relations with labour, the securing of finance, product innovation and the development and dissemination of new technologies? It may be useful to conceptualize the co-ordination of economic activities in terms of a typology of 'economic governance mechanisms' that describe distinctive modes of inter-organizational co-ordination among actors or organizations in the production process (Hollingsworth and Lindberg 1985). These would represent discrete solutions to economic choice problems of information exchange, collective decision, and ethical or normative bases of action. Auction markets, long-term contracts, corporate hierarchies, regulation or subsidy by clientelistic state agencies, 'clans' or networks and formal trade associations are examples of such 'governance' mechanisms. All depend on state action for their 'social space' and societal legitimation. As technology changes or profitability accumulation problems arise, pressures for changes in existing modes of governance mount up giving rise to political struggles and the intervention of the state to sanction new governance arrangements (Lindberg 1986). Industries and sectors seem to vary substantially in their 'governance structure', and the same industries or sectors are often 'governed' differently in different countries. There is no uniform 'statist drift' or market-seeking logic. How shall we explain these variations? How shall we understand transformations in governance arrangements? One important political and theoretical implication of analysis in these terms is that the governance structure of a sector or an industry not only helps shape its economic performance, but also defines both the need for, and the constraints on, government policies designed to improve industrial performance.

The production and selection of ideas about economic policy

The structure of economics as a profession, the social processes of knowledge production and the roles of economists and economic ideas in economic policy-making have only recently begun to receive the attention they merit. Economic ideas, that is, intellectual understandings about how the economy works and how (and whether) governments might intervene are important constraints on economic policy-making. Innovations in economic ideas, for example, the emergence of Keynesian fiscal theory in the 1930s and its widespread adoption (in different forms in different countries!) in the 1950s and 1960s, or the rise of monetarism and new classical economics in the 1970s and 1980s, seem as important as changes in market distribution of power in explaining changes in economic policies (Weir and Skocpol 1985; Odell 1983; Lindberg 1983). Yet we know very little about why the content of economic ideas varies significantly among economists in different countries, or how the organization and structure of scientific professions influences theoretical and policy developments, or why idea innovations are readily adopted in some countries and not in others, or how the structure of the advisory process affects the way the state uses economic ideas.

CONCLUSIONS

It has not seemed necessary in this all-too-brief survey of political science and the study of the economy to specifically comment on the treatment accorded exogenous variables in Hollander's paper on 'classical economics' (see Chapter 2 in this volume). In my view, the classical tradition leads to a symmetrical position on the need for, and opportunities to be found in, a broadly interdisciplinary approach to the economy.

The thrust of my comments has not only been to challenge, from the perspective of a 'neo-institutionalist' political scientist, the *specific claims* of neo-classical economics to adequately handle *acknowledged* exogenous variables (especially government) in economic processes, but also to contest the more *general claims* neo-classical economics make (but classical economics does not make) to be a broadly self-sufficient epistemological basis for a general science of the micro- and macroeconomics. Of course, my comments might well have implications that go beyond what Hollander or classical, or other economist would find acceptable. It would be very interesting to probe deeply into the question of the extent to which my emphasis on factors that are historically and nationally contingent necessarily calls into question the homogeneity of behaviour assumptions that underlie the legitimacy of 'the specialist procedures of economics'. Do 'diversities of character between different nations or different times enter as influencing causes only in a secondary degree'?

BIBLIOGRAPHY

Alford, Robert and Friedland, Roger (1985) *Powers of Theory: The State, Capitalism and Democracy*, Cambridge, Cambridge University Press.

Alt, James E. (1985) 'Political parties, world demand to unemployment: domestic and international sources of economic activity', *APSR* 79, 1016–40.

Alt, J. and Chrystal, K. (1983) *Political Economics*, Berkeley, University of California Press.

Borooah, Vani K. and van der Ploeg, F. (1983) *Political Aspects of the Economy*, Cambridge, Cambridge University Press.

Cameron, David, (1978) 'The expansion of the public economy: a comparative analysis', *American Political Science Review*, 72, December, 1,243–61.

Coats, A. W. (ed.) (1981) *Economists in Government: An International Comparative Study*, Durham, N.C., Duke University Press.

Dyson, Kenneth and Wilks, Stephen (eds) (1983) *Industrial Crisis*, Oxford, Martin Robertson.

Evans, Peter E. and Rueschmeyer, D. and Skocpol, Theda (1985) *Bringing the State Back In*, New York, Cambridge University Press.

Goldthorpe, J. (1984) *Order and Conflict in Contemporary Capitalism*, New York, Oxford University Press.

Grant, Wyn and Nath, Shiv (1984) *The Politics of Economic Policymaking*, Oxford, Basil Blackwell.

Hibbs, Douglas A. Jr (1987) *The American Political Economy: Macroeconomics and Electoral Politics in the U.S.*, Cambridge, Mass. Harvard University Press.

Hibbs, Douglas A. Jr and Fassbender, H. (eds) (1981) *Contemporary Political Economy*, Amsterdam, North Holland.

Hollinsworth, J. Rogers (ed.) (1982) *Government and Economic Performance*, Beverly Hills, Sage.

Hollingsworth, J. Rogers and Lindberg, Leon N. (1985) 'The governance of the American economy: the role of markets, clans, hierarchies, and associative Behavior', in Wolfgang Streeck and Philippe C. Schmitter (eds) *Private Interest Government and Public Policy*, London, Sage.

Katzenstein, Peter (ed.) (1978) *Between Power and Plenty*, Madison, University of Wisconsin Press.

Katzenstein, Peter (1985) *Small States in World Markets: Industrial Policies in Europe*, Ithaca, New York, Cornell University Press.

Krasner, S. (1984) 'Review article: approaches to the state: alternative conceptions and historical dynamics', *Comparative Politics* 16 (January), 223–46.

Lindberg, Leon N. (1983) 'Wirtschaftswissenschaftler als politikberater: der rückzug aus Keynesianismus und staats-interventionismus in der U.S.A. nach 1970, *Journal für Sozialforschung* 1, 3–25; 2, 185–204.

Lindberg, Leon, N. (1986) 'Political economy, economic governance, and the coordination of economic activities', *Jahrbuch 1984/85*, Wissenschaftskolleg 2u Berlin.

Lindberg, Leon N. and Charles S. Maier (eds) (1985) *The Politics of Inflation and Economic Stagnation*, Washington, DC, The Brookings Institution.

Martin, Andrew (1978) 'The dynamics of change in a Keynesian political economy: the Swedish case and its implications', in Colin Crouch (ed.) *British Political Sociology Yearbook* 4.

Meehan, Eugene, J. (1982) *Economics and Policymaking: The Tragic Illusion*, Westport, Conn., Greenwood Press.

Meier, Kenneth, J. (1985) *Regulation: Politics, Bureaucracy and Economics*, London, St. Martin's Press.

Monroe, K. (1984) *Presidential Popularity and the Economy* New York, Praeger Press. N.

Odell, John S. (1983) *U.S. International Monetary Policy: Markets, Power, and Ideas as Sources of Change*, Princeton, Princeton University Press.

Peretz, Paul (1983) *The Political Economy of Inflation in the U.S.*, Chicago, University of Chicago Press.

Piore, Michael and Sabel, Charles (1984) *The Second Industrial Divide: Possibilities for Prosperity*, New York, Basic Books.

Schmidt, M. (1982) 'The role of parties in shaping macroeconomic policy', in F. Castles (ed.) *The Impact of Parties*, Beverly Hills, Sage.

Shepherd, Geoffrey, Duchene, Francois and Saunders, Christopher (eds) (1983) *Europe's Industries: Public and Private Strategies for Change*, Ithaca, New York, Cornell University Press.

Swedberg, Richard, Himmelstrand, Ulf, and Brulin, Göran (1987) 'The paradigm of economic sociology. Premises and promises', *Theory and Society*, 16, 169–213.

Tsoukalis, Loukas (ed.) (1985) *The Political Economy of International Money*, London, Sage Publications.

Tufte, Edward, R. (1978) *Political Control of the Economy*, Princeton, NJ, Princeton University Press.

Vogel, David (1978) 'Why businessmen mistrust their state: the political consciousness of American corporate executives', *British Journal of Political Science* 8, 45–78.

Weir, Margaret and Skocpol, Theda (1985) 'State structures and the possibilities for "Keynesian" responses to the Great Depression in Sweden, Britain, and the U.S.', in Evans *et al.*

Whiteley, P. (1983) 'The political economy of growth', *European Journal of Political Research* 11, 197–213.

Whiteley, P. (1984) *Models of Political Economy*, Beverly Hills, Sage Publications.
Woolley, John T. (1984) *Monetary Politics: The Federal Reserve and the Politics of Monetary Policy*, New York, Cambridge University Press.
Zysman, John (1983) *Governments, Markets, and Growth*, Ithaca, New York, Cornell University Press.
Zysman, John and Tyson, Laura (eds) (1983) *American Industry in International Competition: Government Policies and Corporate Strategies*, Ithaca, New York, Cornell University Press.

Chapter 10

Endogenous and exogenous factors in the analysis of linkages between economics and demography

Samuel Preston

In its most basic representation, an economy consists of a stock of productive factors – labour, capital, material resources, technological possibilities, and institutional structures – and price-directed flows of goods and services among individuals and firms. Certain of the flows are diverted from immediate consumption to augment the stock of productive factors. These diversions include research and development expenditures, investment in physical capital, and investment in human capital.

A population also consists of stocks and flows. At a moment in time, a population consists of counts of individuals arrayed by a vast number of characteristics. These arrays change continuously as individuals are born into, die out of, and migrate among the various states.

The points of contact between populations and economies are extensive. To state the most obvious:

1 The labour force is drawn from the populations. Population size sets a strict upper limit on the size of the labour force. In the long run, the growth rate of the labour force must be, to a close approximation, equal to the growth rate of the population.
2 The level of economic performance (for example, per capita income levels) influences the rate of population growth. At present, high income countries have uniformly low mortality, low fertility, and low (and even negative) growth rates. Poor countries have high fertility and high rates of population growth.
3 The rate of population growth affects the rate of income growth. In densely-populated agrarian countries where natural resource/population ratios are important determinants of per capita income, more rapid growth of population often means slower growth of per capita income. Where populations are sparse, as in parts of Africa, faster growth can bring advantages in the form of economies in the provision of infrastructure and public goods (National Academy of Sciences 1986).

One is tempted to say that populations and economies are locked into a complex system of reciprocal causation and that no analysis of one could be complete or satisfying without analysis of the other. But surely there are many issues in economics and demography where these linkages can be safely ignored. In the short run (say, fifteen years), the relations just mentioned cannot be very powerful: the size of the labour force over this period is essentially fixed by the number of people already born; economic growth could not be so abrupt as to move a country into a very different development context that would dramatically affect its vital rates; and altering population growth rates by 1 or 2 per cent a year (huge changes by historical standards) could not, in this space of time, have massive effects on per capita income.

Since fifteen years represents a fairly distant planning horizon, especially for elected governments, it is not surprising that many macroeconomic analyses ignore population matters. It is in long-run growth models, or in timeless comparative static analyses where nearly all parameters remain fixed, that population has received its most detailed treatment in economic analysis. For Malthus's long-run model, of course, population size was completely endogenous. The tendency for populations to grow as long as wages remained above the subsistence level assured that, short of demographic innovations of which he (at least initially) imagined the masses incapable, living standards would remain abysmally low. In a fundamental sense, the size of population and its living conditions were jointly determined. While it is common to fault Malthus for his failure to predict what was to come, recent work by economic historians suggests that his model had substantial validity for the 500-year period that was ending as he wrote (Lee 1980; Gould 1972).

In order to organize this discussion, it is convenient to discuss separately the effects of economic variables on population variables and the effect of population variables on economic ones. Here we will emphasize the role of neo-classical theory, as concisely summarized in the excellent paper by Hartley (1985).

ECONOMIC VARIABLES AND THEIR INFLUENCE ON POPULATION VARIABLES

In the past two decades economists have invaded what was previously a privileged domain of sociologists and demographers. Armed with the powerful apparatus of neo-classical theory, economists, starting with Gary Becker, analysed many forms of behaviour occurring in families and households. Chief among these behaviours were labour force participation, fertility, educational attainment, marriage and child mortality. Since levels of fertility and mortality in populations are simply the aggregate of levels within households, economists began to play a major role in attempts to explain population change.

In the neo-classical imperialist view, households are little factories, producing goods and services for their members by allocating labour to the market-place and investing and consuming the fruits thereof. They are seen as maximizing a 'household utility function', subject to the constraints posed by factor endowments (especially educational attainment among working age members) and market conditions for labour. Initially, children were valued as items of consumption for the parent, and different 'qualities' of children connoted different utilities. In subsequent models, children's utility (over their life cycle) entered parents' own utility functions, allowing for various forms of apparently altruistic behaviour.

This paradigm has proven exceptionally valuable in clarifying the distinctions between endogenous and exogenous variables. Indeed, I would argue that this has been the single most important contribution of this approach (for an example of the dominance of this issue among adherents of the model, see Schultz 1985). Sociologists had been, and still are to an unfortunate extent, inclined to choose arbitrarily one household variable as 'dependent' (that is, endogenous) while all or some set of other household variables are 'independent' (that is, exogenous). So, for example, some were studying household fertility as a function of female labour force participation, while others were studying female labour force participation as a function of household fertility. The new neo-classical approach viewed both as, to an important extent, simultaneously chosen. Households were seen as being aware of their time constraints and recognizing that childbearing and wives working were competitive activities. They set the level of both activities accordingly. Likewise, there were trade-offs between quantities and qualities of children, where quality comprised both educational attainment and health/mortality risks. For the neo-classical economists, the true exogenous variables were market conditions for labour and prices of various commodities. Especially important among the prices affecting mortality and fertility were the technology of contraception and disease control and the availability of this technology to the household.

Once viewed in this light, the household never again looks quite the same. Especially in the analysis of fertility, there have been protests from other disciplines that people are not behaving 'rationally', that is, purposively in pursuit of defined objectives. But these fly in the face of evidence that even peasants in poor countries are able to enumerate many perceived benefits and costs of an additional child (Bulatao 1979), and that in cross-section, at least, they appear to vary their fertility levels in accordance with economists' notions of what would be in their self-interest (for example, fertility is nearly always lower in urban areas).

There are many inadequacies in the neo-classical approach. In regard to the distinction between endogenous and exogenous factors, the inclination in empirical work has been to treat the economic environment in which a household is located as exogenously determined. But it is obvious that households can migrate from one environment to another. A full-blown model that integrates the choice of environment into the choice of outcomes within a particular environment is missing.

The neo-classical model is static and almost always assumes that lifetime decisions (for example, on the number of offspring) are made in a one-shot fashion. Obviously, this view is inconsistent with the more or less continuous nature of most household decision-making. The outcome of decisions made at time t are reasonably treated as exogenous factors in the decision that must be made at the time $t+1$. (They may also reflect enduring traits about which there is no information, raising statistical problems of 'unobserved heterogeneity'.) But no coherent model of sequential household decision-making has yet emerged. Furthermore, the possibilities of conflict between spouses and among other household members, and the role of bargaining in resolving those conflicts, is rather cavalierly assumed away by folding all distributional and interpersonal issues into a single household utility function (Arthur 1982). This disadvantage is partially overcome by allowing bargaining to take place before marriage, but the world is as uncertain at the time of marriage as at any other time and analytic tractability is a poor substitute for realism.

More generally, the question needs to be asked about whether the exogenous variables on which the neo-classical models focus are where the action is. For explaining cross-sectional variation in demographic behaviour within a particular cultural context, I believe that there is no more powerful analytic framework available, nor one that promises any higher payoffs in 'explained variance'. The virtues of the model in regard to fertility have been enhanced by the introduction of more realistic biological constraints and of more explicit modelling of the role of tastes (see especially Easterlin, Pollak and Wachter 1980).

In regard to *trends* in fertility and mortality, however, it seems that much of the action lies outside the core of the neo-classical framework. The case is most readily made with regard to mortality. Between 1940 and 1970, the curve relating life expectancy at birth (on the Y-axis) to national income per capita in constant dollars (on the X-axis) shifted upwards by about 8 to 10 years (Preston 1980). This shift represents more than half of the world-wide advance in mortality during the period. The shift remains about the same when literacy and caloric consumption are added to the statistical model. In other words, changes in mortality were largely exogenous to the economic circumstances of households and even governments. The shift probably represents the implementation of technical improvements in methods of disease control: anti-malarial programmes, immunization campaigns, and the spread of modern medical practices to households in developing countries on the wings of the revolutionary notion that disease is caused by germs. The result is that the poorest classes in developing countries today have the same level of child mortality as the professional/technical classes in the US in 1900. By this time the

US had already achieved a level of per capita income (roughly $2,500 in 1983 dollars) that is very high by contemporary standards in developing countries (Preston 1985).

While such technical changes can be incorporated into the neo-classical model by viewing them as changes in the relative 'price' of health, such an assignment assumes away most of the interesting issues. A nuclear holocaust would also represent a change in the 'price' of good health, but the neo-classical framework would shed no light on the factors that produced it. Neo-classical economists have avoided studying the central questions of how government health programmes have been formulated and implemented, the role of international assistance and technical breakthroughs, and the manner in which the germ theory and its corollary sanitary practices have diffused among households. At best, it inserts a variable representing distance from clinics into cross-sectional, micro-level analyses. The larger questions have been left to the occasional economic historian or demographer.

A similar situation exists with respect to fertility change. The neo-classical framework, in less rigorous form, was a key element in the reasoning of demographic transition theorists writing in the 1950s. Fertility was expected to fall when mortality fell (so that fewer births would be needed to produce a particular desired family size) and when the desired family size fell as result of a rise in the cost of children (especially as a product of urbanization). Becker (1981 and earlier) added a positive income effect to this mix, assuming that children were 'normal' goods; the pervasive decline in fertility observed as countries moved from poor to rich was explained by asserting that parents also had a 'taste' for child quality. This notion became less arbitrary when altruism was added to the model; but the manner in which such tastes were formed remained essentially outside the model.

In the last several years, the neo-classical assumptions that had been adopted by economists, sociologists and demographers alike have come under increasing attack. Two of the largest comparative social science projects ever undertaken – the European Fertility Project and the World Fertility Survey – both seem to suggest that principal factors in the process of fertility decline lie outside of the neo-classical framework. The European Fertility Project (Coale and Watkins 1986) highlights the importance of 'culture', represented by linguistic group and religious and political practice, in conditioning the decline of European fertility in the past century. Language barriers appear to represent 'firebreaks' in the process of fertility decline. Once begun, the decline invariably spreads quickly from social group to social group within a particular cultural setting, irrespective of levels and changes in economic conditions among the different groups. Some sort of innovation/diffusion process seems to be at work, with interhousehold and interpersonal features that are poorly captured in the neo-classical model.

In an article reviewing what has been learned from the forty-two national surveys in developing countries that were conducted under the auspices of the World Fertility Survey, a similar conclusion was reached:

> Taken *en masse*, the results [of WFS] are more consistent with an ideational theory of change based on the spread of new aspirations or new attitudes towards family formation or birth control, than with a structural theory, which emphasized changes in the economic roles of family units or of children.

> (Cleland 1985: 243)

It should be noted that no other discipline has done better at explaining fertility change than economics; the other disciplines have to date functioned mainly as critics, pointing out the inadequacies, or partial nature of the successes, of a purely economic approach. It seems likely that over the next decade more satisfactory explanatory schema will be developed that integrate the neo-classical approach with the conventional sociological concerns over norms and values. It is possible, for example, that innovative behaviour by certain members of society, perhaps as a straightforward neo-classical response to changes in endowments and prices (including family planning programmes), can alter the salience of the social constructions that have traditionally governed childbearing. As the social context changes, the innovative behaviour spreads. In any event, it seems unlikely that fully satisfying explanations of observed fertility changes will emerge from the neo-classical framework alone. The interpersonal and dynamic nature of 'tastes', assumed fixed in the neo-classical framework, needs far more scrutiny.

POPULATION VARIABLES AND THEIR INFLUENCE ON ECONOMIC VARIABLES

The distinction between exogenous and endogenous variables is also key to understanding the impact of demographic variables on the economy. Since the Second World War and until the last decade or so, the fundamental question in economic demography was 'What is the effect of a change in the rate of population growth (or level of fertility) on the growth rate of per capita income'? This was the principal question asked in Coale and Hoover (1958), the touchstone of economic demography for several decades, and of an influential volume of the National Academy of Sciences (1971). It was a question that could be addressed exclusively through macro-level models.

The increasing dominance of neo-classical economics in development studies in the past decade has led to a redefinition of the question. If couples are *choosing* to have an extra child, then they can be assured to be better off if they achieve it, even though it may reduce per capita income in the family and nation. The welfare implications of lower fertility thus depend on how it's achieved; if through family planning programmes that enable couples better to achieve childbearing targets, then the first-order advantages are clear. If through imposition of a strict quantity limit, as in China, then the first-order effects are negative rather than positive. One must demonstrate positive externalities for other families from one family's reduced childbearing in order to justify programmes that go 'beyond family planning'. To date this justification is altogether missing, despite many commonsense (and sometimes wrong) views on the matter.

So neo-classical economics has had the salutary effect, in my view, of directing attention to the *welfare* implications of *particular* government programmes, and away from the use of crude indicators of welfare, such as per capita income, as they are related to an undifferentiated rate of population growth or level of fertility. The success of this effort depended entirely on the recognition that couples were *endogenously* choosing their fertility levels and that government programmes were a form of *exogenous* shock to the couple's childbearing calculus.

The distinction between endogenous and exogenous variables has also been central to a more precise understanding of some of the distinct mechanisms that relate population patterns to economic performance. In particular, a central relationship for many of those advocating slower growth is that children from smaller families typically enjoyed higher levels of health and education (for example, see World Bank 1984). But if couples are simultaneously *choosing* numbers of children and child quality, it is no longer obvious that reductions in numbers would lead to an improvement in quality; those with large numbers could be expected, *ceteris paribus*, to have below-average 'tastes' for child quality. This recognition led researchers to investigate the specific impact of the birth of unwanted or unanticipated children on child quality. Such studies also demonstrated a negative impact (for example, Rosenzweig and Wolpin 1980; Rodgers 1984), thus providing additional support for the advocates of voluntaristic family planning programmes.

Some of the conceptual clarity of the neo-classical distinction between endogenous and exogenous variables is lost when the interpersonal features of fertility decline alluded to above are added to the explanatory framework. If, for example, couples can be induced to reduce their desired family size simply by a demonstration that other couples are doing so (a change in 'tastes'), then neo-classical economics loses some of its moorings as a guide to public policy decisions. Neo-classical economics has nothing to say about the relative attractiveness of two different outcomes that reflect different sets of 'tastes'. As theories and models of fertility determinants develop, we can expect corresponding alteration in the framework for public policy discussions, perhaps even a movement back toward models that function exclusively at the macro-level. But neo-classical economics has been of enormous value over the past decade by clarifying the distinctions between endogenous and exogenous variables.

BIBLIOGRAPHY

Arthur, Brian (1982) 'The family as firm', *Population and Development Review* 8, 393–7.

Becker, Gary (1981) *A Treatise on the Family*, Cambridge, Mass., Harvard University Press.

Bulatao, R. (1979) 'On the nature of the transition in the value of children', paper no. 60-A, The East-West Policy Institute, Honolulu, Hawaii.

Cleland, John (1985) 'Marital fertility decline in developing countries: theories and the evidence', in John Cleland and John Hobcraft (eds) *Reproductive Change in Developing Countries: Insights from the World Fertility Survey*, Cambridge, Mass., Oxford University Press, 223–52.

Coale, A. J. and Hoover, E. M. (1958) *Population Growth and Economic Development in Low-Income Countries*, Princeton, N.J., Princeton University Press.

Coale, A. J. and Watkins, Susan C. (1986) (eds) *The Decline of Fertility in Europe*, Princeton N.J., Princeton University Press.

Easterlin, Richard A., Pollak, Robert and Wachter, Michael (1980) 'Toward a more general economic model of fertility determination: endogenous preferences and natural fertility', in R. A. Easterlin (ed.) *Population and Economic Change in Developing Countries*, Chicago, University of Chicago Press, 81–150.

Gould, J. (1972) *Economic Growth in History: Survey and Analysis*, London, Methuen.

Hartley, Keith (1985) 'Exogenous factors in economic theory: neo-classical economics', prepared for Interdisciplinary Dimensions of Economic Analysis, Paris.

Lee, R. (1980) 'An historical perspective on economic aspects of the population explosion: the case of pre-industrial England', in R. A. Easterlin (ed.) *Population and Economic Change in Developing Countries*, Chicago, University of Chicago Press, 517–56.

National Academy of Sciences (1971) *Rapid Population Growth: Consequences and Policy Implications*, 2 vols, Baltimore, Johns Hopkins University Press.

National Academy of Sciences (1986) *Population Growth and Economic Development: Policy Questions*, Washington, DC, National Academy Press.

Preston, Samuel H. (1980) 'Causes and consequences of mortality declines in less developed countries during the twentieth century', in R. A. Easterlin (ed.) *Population and Economic Change in Developing Countries*, Chicago, University of Chicago Press, 289–315.

Preston, Samuel H. (1985) 'Resources, knowledge, and child mortality: comparison of the U.S. in the late nineteenth century and developing countries today', *Proceedings* 4, 373–88, IUSSP International Population Conference, Florence, Italy.

Rodgers, G. (1984) *Poverty and Population: Approaches and Evidence*, Geneva, International Labour Organization.

Rosenzweig, M. and Wolpin, K. I. (1980) 'Testing the quantity-quality fertility model: the use of twins as a natural experiment', *Econometrica* 48(1), 227–40.

Schultz, T. Paul (1985) 'Household economic and community variables as

determinants of mortality', *Proceedings* 4, 225–36, IUSSP International Population Conference, Florence, Italy.
World Bank (1984) *World Development Report*, Washington, DC, World Bank.

Chapter 11

The psychologist's view of the exogenous domain

Alan Lewis

INTRODUCTION

Psychologists have shown an increased interest in economics in the last ten years: the *Journal of Economic Psychology* publishes its thirteenth volume in 1992 and there are now at least three recognized texts in economic psychology, namely, *The Economic Mind* (Furnham and Lewis 1986a), *The Individual in the Economy* (Lea, Tarpy and Webley 1987), and *The Handbook of Economic Psychology* (van Raaij *et al.* 1988). These texts are concerned with learning and socialization in an attempt to explain where economic preferences come from and how they are maintained. Knowledge of internal states (people's economic minds) is then used to examine such diverse topics as tax evasion, spending and saving patterns, charitable giving and gambling behaviours. Many economic psychologists feel that the expansion of the study of psychology into the economic realm is a legitimate advancement of psychological science because, for example, the study of how children are encouraged to use their pocket money, may not only tell us about spending and saving patterns that persist into adulthood, but more importantly to these psychologists, something about the socialization process itself (Webley, Levine and Lewis 1991).

As more and more researchers have piled in, distinctions have arisen between them. Devotees of behavioural economics and psychological economics (for example, Earl 1988; Gilad and Kaish 1986), as distinct from economic psychology, have dedicated their time to illuminating the black box between economic antecedents and economic consequences; they have employed findings from psychology (and sociology) with the aim of improving economic predictions: they tend to be economists with an interest in psychology and related social sciences, rather than the other way around. But even they have not been left to their own devices: the Kuhnian world of competing paradigms and explanations is an apt one; a fight for dominance is going on, albeit a gentle one. The *Journal of Behavioural Economics* became the *Journal of Socio-Economics* in 1991 as the sociologists, led by Amitai Etzioni, shifted the emphasis toward macro-analytic considerations.

In Kuhnian terms the disciplines of economics and psychology (sociology) may be incommensurable. Economic psychologists and behavioural economists appear to share the idea that a productive dialogue is possible, although a little bit of this and a little of that may not do – one player playing chess and another draughts/checkers can use the same board but cannot play the same game – what we may need is a whole lot of something else. This appears to be the view of socio-economists (Etzioni 1988) who envisage a new 'moral' economics – the sociologists are the revolutionaries; the psychologists the revisionists.

Things are not even simple within economic psychology, some authors placing emphasis on social psychology and others on experimental psychology, on social surveys and interviews or experimental simulations, even animal experiments (cf. Furnham and Lewis 1986a; Lea, Tarpy and Webley 1987). The importance of experimental psychology cannot be denied; a large literature in its own right now exists on how people make decisions based on evidence gathered in this way (Rachlin 1989).

CHOICE, DECISIONS AND EXPERIMENTAL SIMULATIONS

Psychologists, because of their preference for inductive, behavioural methods, are less concerned with axiomatic assumption (and mathematical modelling) of decisions, and more with the examination of how choosers choose.[1] The psychologist and Nobel prize winner in economics, Herbert Simon has persuasively written how decision options are limited by cognitive capacity, rather than by information and search costs (Simon 1976). His other major and now familiar contribution being the concept of 'satisficing' where economic actors settle, not for the optimal solution, but for the one that will do: people do not constantly strive for more wages, or for continued expansion of their firms; more is not always better.[2]

Psychologists also are concerned with the vagaries of memory and of perception: when choosing between alternatives, the alternatives themselves have to be recalled from memory and the merits of these are a function of how they are perceived. This 'subjective' approach is also favoured by, among others, Edwards (1961) who, in his theory of expected utility, is concerned not with the probability of the outcomes of choice maximizing utility, but in the subjective probability of such occurrences. Various other models combine objective and subjective utilities and probabilities, even the preferences of other people (Fishbein and Ajzen 1975).

Motivation is also a vital component in some analyses, for example, in the work of the economist Peter Earl (Earl 1983) who, using Kelly's construct theory (Kelly 1963), presents as his thesis that people choose from sets which reflect their views and interpretations of the world, because of their motivation to make sense of it.

Cognitive psychologists in the field generally agree that people do not make choices as a machine would, nor are there numerous individual differences which simply cancel out when aggregated: they believe instead that there are systematic behavioural, essentially 'human' choice patterns and methods of processing information.

Probably the most quoted pertinent contemporary writings are those by Kahneman and Tversky (and other co-authors) based on experimental choice studies (Kahneman *et al.* 1982). Following on from Simon, Kahneman and Tversky believe that decision heuristics are a common way of reducing cognitive loading (or the processing costs of optimal decision rules). Three principal heuristics have been identified, namely, 'availability', 'representativeness' and 'anchoring'. In processing information when making uncertain decisions, say betting on a horse race, assessment of which horses have won and how often is based not on a systematic search but by how readily particular occurrences can be brought to mind (availability). The heuristic of representativeness is the use of irrelevant criteria over statistical probability such as stereotypic judgements and punters' theories' where unwarranted meaningfulness is attached to particular events. Finally, anchoring refers to the tendency to make judgements depending on from where you are starting; people fail to move very much from such a point in the light of new information. Kahneman and Tversky are famous too for their 'prospect' theory: people reveal a tendency to underweigh outcomes that merely are probable, in comparison with outcomes that are obtained with certainty, contributing to risk aversion in choices involving sure gains over probable ones, and risk-seeking for sure losses over probable ones.

Economists have found a place for this cross-fertilization and have called it experimental economics; a useful review is that of Roth (1988). There is now a body of experimental evidence dealing with two-person bargaining, the prisoner's dilemma (and the 'free-rider' problem), auction behaviour and individual choice behaviour. We have already mentioned Kahneman and Tversky, researchers dealings with, from the economists' point of view, anomalies in expected utility theory in individual choice behaviour. Another exemplar, this time concerning auction behaviour, is the 'winner's curse'. In an experiment by Bazerman and Samuelson (1983), subjects were asked to guess the number of coins in a jar (there was a prize for the best guess). Subjects then bid for (among other things) the contents of the jar with the understanding that the highest bidder would receive the value of the coins in the jar. In this and other experiments the finding of the winner's curse appears to be a robust one, in the specific case of the Bazerman and Samuelson (1983) experiment the average winning bids were $10, a full two dollars more than the value of objects auctioned.

ALTERNATIVE MODELS OF CHOICE

Several specific models have been put forward as alternatives to neo-classical economics. These are cleverly and entertainingly discussed by the economist (a psychological economist), Peter Earl (1983). Marketing psychologists favour compensatory models of choice which are not far removed from the 'characteristics' approach championed by the economist Lancaster (1966). These behavioural models assume that consumers simul-taneously weigh up a limited number of attributes (or characteristics) that goods have, trading-off characteristics, one for another. In choosing a car one might want good acceleration, safety features and economy, but be prepared to buy a car not as fast as its competitors, because it scores highly on the other two attributes. Furthermore, in compensatory models (for example, Fishbein and Ajzen 1975; Rosenberg 1956) choosers consider whether particular goods are *likely* to have the attributes they want; they multiply (in some way) this probability (expectancy) with the value they place on each attribute, add the 'expectancy values' for the good up across attributes and choose the good with the highest expectancy value.

The Fishbein and Ajzen approach has been heavily used in the marketing of literature in the last fifteen years; a recent review by Grunert (1989) implies that this is surprising as the explanatory power of the model is rather weak, yet it is an improvement on 'psychological' models used hitherto. Experimental studies have been undertaken using, for example, conjoint measurement techniques, but these have too often been concerned with marketing particular products, from shaving-brushes to airlines, rather than furthering our knowledge of how choosers choose (Lewis 1988). In addition, some of the models used in the popular marketing texts are comprehensive and descriptive covering exposure, information processing, search, memory, beliefs, attitudes, life-styles, cultural norms, reference groups, the interaction between marketing and buyers behaviour and so on (Engel and Blackwell 1982), yet they fail in the sense that they cannot be tested in a way that an economist or experimental psychologist might want to do.

Peter Earl (1983) has shown a penchant instead for non-compensatory, or lexicographic choice modelling where people choose a good because it passes a particular test, or set of tests in an appropriate sequence: the scores are not added together. Goods (or schemes) are then assessed with regard to a single attribute at a time, taking the most important attribute first. Among other reasons this model is attractive as it does not require the complex mental arithmetic that compensatory models do; it may be more 'realistic', more plausible.

SOCIAL PSYCHOLOGY

Social psychologists (broadly defined) interested in economics have chosen social surveys and questionnaire studies as the tools of their trade. The pioneering work of George Katona and his colleagues of the 'Michigan' school (Katona 1977) have produced a series of impressive results in the form of predicting the aggregate demand for motor cars using his measure of 'consumer sentiment', a series of questions enquiring about consumer economic optimism or pessimism. The results persuade one that economic changes are led by consumer preferences, and that they can be effectively measured using questionnaires. Katona has done much, perhaps more than anyone, in developing modern-day interest in economic psychology, but it is not always easy to appraise his work critically. However, in a review by Vanden Abeele (1983) he concludes that it cannot be convincingly shown that the index of consumer sentiment is superior to objective economic indicators such as consumer price and stock exchange indexes. 'One pays your money and takes your choice': economic and psychological predictions (and explanations) may be equally good in some cases, but what is the incentive then to change one's academic trade? This is a point that will be discussed again later.

Social surveys have been widely used in studies of perceptions and preferences for the public sector (Coughlin 1982; Lewis 1982) and the development of fiscal psychology (Schmolders 1970; Lewis 1989). These continue the familiar theme that consumers' subjective perceptions and preferences matter and that they can be adequately recorded and represented. The 'traditional' approach in economics has been to assume that the tax evasion decision is just another decision made in uncertainty: rational economic man will attempt to minimize his tax bill and will only be restrained from doing so by the probability of detection and the size of fine imposed. Alternative behavioural models employ *perceptions* of tax rates, opportunity to evade, probability of detection, which may be systematically different from 'objective' rates. If radical economic man were a reality the tax system would break down very quickly as it depends, to a significant degree, on voluntary compliance. This has been captured in the behavioural models by measures of 'tax mentality' or 'tax ethics' – people's willingness and sense of moral obligation to pay (these models have been appraised by Kinsey 1986, for the American Bar Foundation). The behavioural approach has different policy implications to the economic one – in the latter if tax evasion increased then the probability of detection and perhaps the size of fine should be increased to combat it – in the former it could be argued that such a move might increase tax resistance and alienation as taxpayer attitudes towards the state deteriorates.

Both the Internal Revenue Service (IRS) in the USA and Inland Revenue in the UK run regular 'consumer' attitude surveys. The IRS even attempt to assess the level of tax evasion by asking questions about personal evasion where individual answers cannot be traced (the randomized response technique).

The behavioural examination of public expenditure has included questions on how much is perceived being spent on particular items such as health and defence, and where the money comes from to pay for it. This has been followed by questions about public expenditure preferences, that is, whether the government should spend more, less or the same on education, housing and the like. Results show that voters exhibit consistent preferences, which in turn can frequently be predicted from voting preferences and not just self-interest assumptions (Lewis and Cullis 1988). Perceptual information is of importance too as it provides empirical evidence about the visibility of taxes and the perceived costs of public expenditure – there are grounds to believe from the UK data that people underestimate their tax burdens, making public goods appear 'cheaper'. This said, the 'fiscal connection' is rarely uppermost in people's minds when relaying their preferences, which has implications for question wording as questions about public expenditure alone encourages fiscal expansionism as the 'tax price' is not mentioned; on the other side of the coin people are more antipathetic towards taxation when the public expenditure 'benefits' are not apparent.

SOCIAL LEARNING (SOCIALIZATION)

Economists have no story of how preferences change or how they come about.[3] The study of fiscal preferences is informative in this regard, as between 1975 and 1982 fiscal referenda results in the USA showed a change which economic self-interest, or rational ignorance hypotheses alone, could not predict. More voters appear to have learnt the 'fiscal connection' during this period, become more fiscally conscious due to their voting experience; and during an initial period of highly-visible taxes they moved from a position of fiscal conservatism to a more supportive view of state expenditure, as the relationship between tax reductions and the loss of services became apparent (Lewis 1982).

The quest to understand the socialization process is a central interest of social and developmental psychology: there is now a respectable body of work looking specifically at economic socialization, for example, Berti and Bombi 1981; Emler and Dickinson 1985; Furnham and Thomas 1984; Stacey 1982; Webley et al. 1991. Some of the research traces how children develop economic concepts in the Kinder economy of the playground and the classroom, passing through the cognitive stages described by Piaget, while others study functional and cultural influences on development. Underlining much of both sets of investigation is an idea largely taken for granted by psychologists, that what is learnt during 'critical' periods is not continually modified throughout life; children's learning about the fairness of income distribution or the moral superiority of saving over spending, for example, are likely to persist into adulthood and have economic consequences.

Another way of looking at this is in terms of 'vintage preferences': a willingness to save and an unwillingness to spend may persist even when inflation rates are running higher than interest rates; it is well known that there have been periods when aggregate savings have increased under these economic circumstances stretching the credulity of purely economic explanations.

FAIRNESS AND ETHICS

One of the things children learn are the social rules about 'give and take', of 'fairness' and of reasonable behaviour. If we were continually striving to put ourselves in economically superior positions to our fellows, life would be intolerable, there would be no such thing as society. Daniel Kahneman has the distinction of appearing in both the sections on experimental psychology and social psychology of this current chapter because of his contribution to a survey on the perceived fairness of profit-seeking (Kahneman et al. 1986). Questions were asked, for example, employing economic vignettes, where employees' wages were reduced because unemployment had risen and comparable employees were being paid less. Eighty-three per cent of the sample judged these and other similar moves to be unfair. The authors conclude that the commonly-observed 'stickiness' of wage adaptation to changes in macroeconomic circumstances is due in part to participants' shared notions about what is fair and acceptable.[4]

In the behavioural view people are driven by moral considerations as well as narrow self-interest. A natural field of study is in the explanation of the growth of 'green' and 'ethical' investments – an example where individuals have the opportunity to put their money where their morals are (Lewis and Cullis 1990). The results are far from straightforward as ethical investments do not necessarily perform any worse than 'unethical' investments in 'weaponry', or in firms with poor pollution records: ethical investors seem to be able to have 'their cake and eat it'.

LAY EXPLANATION AND ATTRIBUTION THEORY

Attribution theory deals with people's explanations of what causes what – did she fall or was she pushed? Many of the influential early studies were conducted in the laboratory where 'subjects' were provided with systematically-designed vignettes and asked to choose between, say in the case of a car accident, whether the car driver was to blame, or some aspect of the environment – a slippery road, a defaced traffic hazard sign. More recently research has turned to 'lay explanations' – the explanations that people use *in situ*, unrestricted by experiments or laboratories. While this is the ideal case, more common has been the examination of lay explanations using interviews and questionnaires.

In an economic context it becomes of interest to know what people think causes inflation, unemployment, poverty and why some people are wealthy and others are not. This is of obvious importance to psychologists: it also matters to economists. The reasons it matters to economists, especially political economists, is that if, say, economic reason is in accord with government policy, it offers legitimacy. More radically it can make what is after all just a theory or hypothesis about causality 'real'; it can become common coinage, a belief in its legitimacy can make it happen.[5]

In his questionnaire investigations of lay explanations Adrian Furnham, employing factor analytic techniques, had divided lay explanations, based on replies, into three categories, namely, societal, individualistic and fatalistic. For the case of unemployment societal explanations entail blaming structural inequalities; individual explanations: personal weaknesses on the part of the unemployed, for example, the inability to ride a bicycle in order to find work; fatalistic explanations: the inevitability of the phenomenon (Furnham 1982a, 1982b, 1983). The majority of respondents favour societal explanations for economic ills, but there are systematic differences among those voting Conservative compared to Labour, the former favouring individualistic explanations over the latter: the poor and the unemployed only have themselves to blame, the rich are rich because they have worked harder, taken bigger risks, and made better use of their opportunities. If the blame is shifted to the individual then the government can hardly be held responsible in quite the same way; explanations for causes are related to preferences for legitimate cures (Furnham and Lewis 1986b).

CONCLUSIONS

Psychology is a behavioural discipline. Psychologists are uneasy about making axiomatic assumptions about choice, for instance, whatever the favourable implications for modelling and mathematical elegance may be. The results that are produced from behavioural analyses are often messy but economists need not totally despair, some of the literature on choice and experimental economics are directly relevant to their concerns. Much else is relevant but requires more of an economic imagination.

There has been much talk in this current chapter about 'preferences'. These preferences have included perceptions (what people see is selective and dependent upon their prejudices), beliefs (including causal beliefs), attitudes, values, ethics and morals – far from being exogenous, psychologists consider preferences to be of central explanatory value.

Psychologists use a variety of methods, in particular we have concentrated on experiments and field studies employing social surveys and questionnaires. Psychologists disagree among themselves but, compared to economists, they share an interest in the 'subjective' world, in people's 'economic minds'.

The level of the analysis is that of the individual and of small groups. There are exceptions in contemporary social psychology, but it is this which primarily distinguishes economic psychology from economic sociology. The overlap between social psychology, sociology and political science is, however, apparent in the discussion of lay explanations where social class, ideological and functional explanations come into play.

Psychologists have a large research history (over a hundred years), which grapples with the learning (and socialization) process; findings on how people learn about economic concepts and economic relationships is a crop in a growing field, waiting to be reaped by enterprising economic farmers.

Psychologists differ among themselves as to their relative allegiance to normative as opposed to positive science: with the exception of the strictest experimentalists, psychologists, like other social scientists, agree that research cannot be value-free. The choice by economists to exclude ethics, and preferences, from their models is in itself a value judgement which has, among other things, reductionist policy implications (for example, in the case of tax evasion). Economics is now the only social science (if indeed it is 'social' at all) which has not embraced the ideas of 'post-positivism': It still worships prediction at the expense of competing claims of comprehension and description.

It is far from all doom and gloom; there are many economists who have been unable to ignore what has been going on around them. In economic terms, it has to be worth their while to make the investment to learn something new – having a go at learning some psychology is a risky business – and while there are now journal outlets for their work, there is still the very real fear that their colleagues will feel that such an enterprise is not quite 'kosher'. Those from other disciplines must do more than simply criticize; they must offer a legitimate alternative way forward for those who wish to take it.

From the work I have done with my colleagues it appears to make little sense to set up a contest with economic explanations in the blue corner and psychological explanations in the red: there is no final test; each discipline can take the same findings and interpret them convincingly in their own way (Lewis and Cullis 1990). For there to be progress, economists have to want to make their discipline more empirical, more realistic, less abstract; conversely, psychologists perhaps will need to concentrate more on theory and engage less in 'mindless' empiricism for its own sake; there is a need to make clear statements about what psychologists know about human nature, which economists ignore at their peril. This would provide an admirable discipline for psychology and psychologists.

Economic psychology, psychological economics, socio-economics, behavioural economics, experimental economics all have a future, but there is a good deal of 'in-fighting' to come. It is to be hoped that these are not just skirmishes on the fringes of economics.

NOTES

1 Hartley, in the current volume, argues that economic hypotheses may be too broad to test with data making a distinction between 'analytic' and 'synthetic' science. Using these terms psychologists are engaged in 'synthetic' science in a way that economists are not. Yet some economists still seem to believe that rational behaviour theory is an empirically falsifiable theory (Hollis and Nell 1975; Sen 1977).
2 Hollander, chapter 2 in the present volume, calls for 'independent variable plug-ins' when considering labour force motivation. There is a large literature in occupational psychology dealing with these issues, showing that other motivations besides the attainment of wages become prominent as wealth increases (Lawler 1971; Maslow 1954), for example, the need for self-esteem, and 'self-actualization' (see chapter 2 of current volume).
3 Hollander uses Mill's distinction that such an examination would constitute research in 'applied economics' and not 'scientific economics'.
4 These may be 'spill-over effects with probable feedbacks' (see Hollander and Himmelstrand). Maital has alluded to the 'economic games people play' and has developed non-zero sum games between the competing interests of capital and labour which provide insights into how co-operation and competitive behaviour come about (Maital and Maital 1984). There is also a literature dealing with how people decide whether the pay they receive is fair or not; through social comparisons with similar groups (Delafield 1979) and subjective notions of equity (Adams 1965) and exchange (Homans 1961).
5 Hartley (chapter 4) remarks that neo-classical ideas have a major influence on government policy. Once those in a position of power and influence accept particular economic doctrines, their application and subsequent evaluation becomes part of a self-fulfilling prophecy. As governments will not evaluate these theories 'objectively', it is tempting to suggest that the relative ascendency of economic theories depends on their ideological acceptability. Bowles (chapter 6) makes similar points.

BIBLIOGRAPHY

Adams, J. (1965) 'Inequity in social exchange', in L. Berkowitz (ed.) *Advances in Experimental Social Psychology* 2, 267–99.
Bazerman, M. and Samuelson, W. (1983) 'I won the auction but don't want the prize', *Journal of Conflict Resolution* 27, 618–34.
Berti, A. and Bombi, A. (1981) 'The development of the concept of money and its value. A longitudinal study', *Child Development* 52, 1179–82.
Coughlin, R. (1982) *Ideology, Public Opinion and Welfare Policy*, Berkeley, Calif., Institute of International Studies, University of California.
Delafield, G. (1979) 'Social comparisons and pay', in G. Stephenson and C.

Brotherton (eds) *Industrial Relations: A Social Psychological Approach* London, Wiley.

Earl, P. (1983) *The Economic Imagination Towards a Behavioral Analysis of Choice*, New York, Wheatsheaf-Sharpe.

Earl, P. (1988) (ed.) *Psychological Economics*, Boston, Kluwer.

Edwards, W. (1961) 'Behavioural decision theory', *Annual Review of Psychology* 12, 473–98.

Emler, N. and Dickinson, J. (1985) 'Children's representation of economic inequalities', *British Journal of Developmental Psychology* 3, 191–8.

Engel, J. and Blackwell, R. (1982) *Consumer Behaviour*, Chicago, Dryden Press.

Etzioni, A. (1988) *The Moral Dimension: Toward a New Economics*, New York, The Free Press.

Fishbein, M. and Ajzen, I. (1975) *Belief, Attitude, Intention and Behavior*, Reading, Mass., Addison-Wesley.

Furnham, A. (1982a) 'Explanations for unemployment in Britain', *European Journal of Social Psychology* 12, 335–52.

Furnham, A. (1982b) 'Why are the poor always with us? Explanations for poverty in Britain', *British Journal of Social Psychology* 20, 311–22.

Furnham, A. (1983) 'Attributions for affluence', *Personality and Individual Differences* 4, 31–40.

Furnham, A. and Lewis, A. (1986a) *The Economic Mind*, New York, St Martin's.

Furnham, A. and Lewis, A. (1986b) 'Reducing unemployment: lay beliefs about how to reduce current unemployment', *Journal of Economic Psychology* 7, 75–85.

Furnham, A, and Thomas, P. (1984) 'Pocket-money: a study of economic education', *British Journal of Developmental Psychology* 2, 205–12.

Gilad, B. and Kaish, S. (1986) *Handbook of Behavioral Economics*, vols I, II, Greenwich, Conn., JAI Press.

Grunert, K. (1989) 'Another attitude towards multi-attribute attitude theories', in K. Grunert and F. Olander (eds) *Understanding Economic Behaviour*, Dordrecht, Kluwer.

Hollis, M. and Nell, E. (1975) *Rational Economic Man*, Cambridge, Cambridge University Press.

Homans, G. (1961) *Social Behavior: Its Elementary Forms*, New York, Harcourt Brace Jovanovich.

Kahneman, D. Slovic, P. and Tversky, A. (eds) (1982) *Judgement Under Uncertainty: Heuristics and Biases*, Cambridge, Mass., Cambridge University Press.

Kahneman, D., Knetsch, J. and Thaler, R. (1986) 'Fairness as a constraint on profit seeking: entitlements in the market', *American Economic Review* 76, 728–41.

Katona, G. (1977) *Psychological Analysis of Economic Behavior*, Westport, Greenwood Press.

Kelly, G. (1963) *A Theory of Personality*, New York, Norton.

Kinsey, K. (1986) 'Theories and models of tax cheating', *Criminal Justice Abstracts* 18 (3), 403–25.

Lancaster, K. (1966) 'A new approach to consumer theory', *Journal of Political Economy* 74, 132–57.

Lawler, E. (1971) *Pay and Organization Effectiveness*, New York, McGraw-Hill.

Lea, S. Tarpy, R. and Webley, P. (1987) *The Individual in the Economy*, Cambridge, Cambridge University Press.

Lewis, A. (1982) *The Psychology of Taxation*, New York, St. Martin's Press.

Lewis, A. (1988) 'Some methods in psychological economics', in P. Earl (ed.) *Psychological Economics*, Boston, Kluwer.

Lewis, A. (1989) 'Fiscal psychology', in D. Collard (ed.) *Fiscal Policy*, Aldershot, Avebury.

Lewis, A. and Cullis, J. (1988) 'Preferences, economics and psychology and the psychology of economic preferences', *Journal of Behavioural Economics* 17, 19–33.

Lewis, A. and Cullis, J. (1990) 'Ethical investments: preferences and morality', *Journal of Behavioural Economics* 19 (4) 395–411.

Maital, S. and Maital, S. (1984) *Economic Games People Play*, New York, Basic Books.

Maslow, A. (1954) *Motivation and Personality*, New York, Harper & Son.

Rachlin, H. (1989) *Judgement, Decision and Choice: A Cognitive/Behavioral Synthesis* New York, Freeman.

van Raiij, W. van Veldhoven, G. and Warneryd, K. E. (1988) *The Handbook of Economic Psychology*, Dordrecht, Kluwer.

Rosenberg, M. (1956) 'Cognitive structure and attitudinal effect', *Journal of Abnormal and Social Psychology* 53, 367–72.

Roth, A. (1988) 'Laboratory experimentation in economics: a methodological overview', *Economic Journal* 98, 974–1031.

Schmolders, G. (1970) 'Survey research in public finance: a behavioural approach to fiscal policy', *Public Finance* 25, 300–6.

Sen, A. (1977) 'Rational fools: a critique of the behavioural foundations of economic theory', *Philosophy and Public Affairs* 6, 317–44.

Simon, H. (1976) *Administrative Behavior*, New York, The Free Press.

Stacey, B. (1982) 'Economic socialization in the pre-adult years', *British Journal of Social Psychology* 21, 159–73.

Vanden Abeele, P. (1983) 'The index consumer sentiment: predictability and predictive power in the EEC', *Journal of Economic Psychology*, 3, 1–17.

Webley, P. Levine, R. M. and Lewis, A. (1991) 'A study in economic psychology', *Human Relations* 44, 2, 127–46.

Chapter 12

A sociological perspective on strategies of dealing with exogenous complexity in economic analysis

Alberto Martinelli and Neil Smelser

Upon reading the papers of Professors Hartley (see chapter 4 this volume) and Hollander (see chapter 2 this volume), we decided that our best strategy in this commentary would be to develop a few reflections based on their articles, rather than a standard critique of them. This decision was stimulated partly by the fact that their summaries and analyses are so thorough and penetrating that criticism in a conventional way becomes a difficult road to travel. We decided to take a somewhat less arduous, but at the same time it is hoped more productive, road of offering a few points in overview.

A FEW POINTS ON THE GENERAL SOCIOLOGY OF ECONOMIC KNOWLEDGE

Both authors take cognizance from time to time of certain historical conditions under which classical and neo-classical economic theory has been developed, but both do so only occasionally and illustratively. A more thorough understanding of the rise of classical economics and its evolution into different strands of neo-classical economics would, of course, have to take both general and detailed account of the cultural, institutional and political contexts in which these traditions evolved.

More particularly, an argument of the following sort might be put forth as one general possibility: if the late eighteenth and early nineteenth century history of Great Britain – and in varying degree the histories of other capitalist nations – is examined, many historical trends may be regarded as working toward establishing those institutional and political conditions that were picked up and taken as the general parameters (conditions, general assumptions, exogenous factors) within which classical and later neo-classical analyses were constructed. Some of these trends were the following:

- A multi-sided assault on conditions inhibiting the development of contract wage labour and labour mobility in the market. Among the important developments were the disintegration, brought about by the enclosure movement, of ascriptive (including hereditary) landholding arrangements; an assault on relief and poor-law arrangements that appeared to root the poor in their localities; less relevant to Britain itself, an assault on slavery (a coercive, non-market appropriation of workers); the insistence on the 'independence' of the worker to make his own work arrangements with masters without regulation; the decline of the apprenticeship system, and its hereditary aspects in particular; and the assault on combinations or unions of labourers which were regarded as restrictive influences on wages and employment in a free market. All these developments worked toward the institutionalization of free labour; labour unconstrained in its contractual freedom and its freedom of movement. And classical economics built the perfect mobility of resources, including labour, into its assumptions.

- The improvement of communication and transportation systems, enhancing both market information and the movement of resources and products through the market. These developments also pushed institutionally toward what were to be the general assumptions of complete information and perfect mobility of resources.
- The development of the state as an order-keeping agency. Mill noted that an essential condition for the analysis of economic phenomena was that they be 'not effected by force'. To insure that, is the primary business of a state, which would guarantee, for example, that the price of bread not be affected by bread riots and that production for the market not be affected by the destruction of machinery. This kind of effect is accomplished only by the existence of the state; it is reminiscent of one of Weber's conditions for maximum formal rationality: 'complete calculability of the functioning of public administration and the legal order' (Weber 1968 (I): 1962).
- The rationalization of money and credit, through the development of a banking system, and the assurance of the legitimacy of the monetary system by the state. These developments surely contributed to the mobility of capital, another resource.
- On the cultural level, the development of a philosophical system of utilitarianism, stressing maximization of pleasure, minimization of pain, and the principle of calculation; this philosophical tradition was among many assaults on the traditional 'paternalistic-deference' model of society, and one of the main intellectual forces in the general transition from 'status' to 'contract' society.
- Also on the cultural side, the development of an attack on mercantilism and state interference generally and the rise of *laissez-faire*; in so far as these developments became embedded in laws and policies, this meant the institution of free, unregulated competition, also cited by Mill as a *sine qua non* for a science of economics.

These trends were themselves caused by multiple and complex historical causes, including the emerging ideological side of classical and neo-classical economics themselves. Be that as it may, these economists identified such tendencies of institutional change, generalized them as typical if not universal in manifestation, froze them into general parameters, and on the basis of that creative simplification, were able to work out solutions, even 'laws' of various sorts, in a context of those parameters. This is the special significance and accomplishment of these theoretical traditions; in this sense they were elegantly-expressed Utopian views of an institutional system of market capitalism which never quite arrived historically but were thought to represent a kind of reality of the system if it were only allowed to become perfect and unfettered.

This model of creative simplification, followed by the elaboration of solutions, has proved to be something of a general model in the social sciences. Certainly it is found in other species of economic theory (Marxian and Keynesian, even though the parameters, variables, and solutions find different expression in each). Other kinds of theoretical traditions in the social sciences assume similar form, though they are seldom so elegant or elaborated. The study of intergenerational social mobility, for example, generally makes use of some kind of postulate of status-striving, and a motive to maximize that; such study also typically makes some kinds of parametric assumptions about the kind of stratification system within which such mobility takes place, and about the structural conditions that facilitate or discourage upward mobility.

Once consolidated as a more or less coherent theoretical system of the special Utopian form we have described, classical and neo-classical economic theory became an instrument for so-inclined intellectuals, politicians, merchants and manufacturers to criticize contemporary economic and political arrangements and to recommend policies to change them, *because these arrangements did not seem to measure up to the standards set up in the theoretical system* (existing poor laws un-motivate workers to find employment, and should be replaced by laws and arrangements that motivate them; tariffs inhibit the working of a free international market, and should be removed). The contrapuntal interplay between the development of an intellectual system or theory and its application to social criticism and policy should be underscored. There are no first causes to be discovered in this interplay. But surely the dynamics must be much as described.

THE PROBLEM OF ACKNOWLEDGING THAT THE WORLD IS NEITHER SIMPLE NOR PERFECT

At the basis of the conceptual paradigm of economics, both in the classical and in the neo-classical versions, lies the postulate of *Homo economicus*: a simplified set of assumptions about human action, seen as the result of the behaviour of isolated individuals, each pursuing his own interests and making free and rational choices after having calculated prospective costs and benefits. The economic actor is an 'exceptional statistician' as Arrow (1978) ironically defined him.

This creative simplification of the complexities of human nature and social relations was developed for very good methodological and sociological reasons. It was a model in a double sense: on the one hand, it was a theoretical simplification of empirical reality as any model of scientific inquiry; on the other, it portrayed a desired course of action and provided a criterion for judging economic behaviour and state economic policies.

But this simplification also involved a price. Cultural values were reduced to tastes and preferences; collective action was seen as an aggregate of individual rational actions; all types of social relations were reduced to monetary exchange relations; and government policy was seen as the result of the will of the people rather than the result of political conflict and negotiation among different ethnic groups.

The very function of economics as the first social science – through a process which expressed at the scientific level the social differentiation of relations of production and distribution from family and community relations – also raised the question of the relationships among the different social science disciplines.

As a matter of historical fact, the complexity of human nature and social reality, which for good reasons had been neglected by economic models, had to be either reintroduced little by little into those models in order to make theory more adequate empirically, or become the specialized object of other disciplinary lines of inquiry. These other disciplines – sociology, political science, psychology, anthropology – developed through other types of creative simplification, worked out different 'models of man' as their basic postulates, referred to different types of action – affective instead of instrumental, for instance – and focused on collective rather than individual behaviour.

The development of other social sciences, contiguous to economics, could throw light on those aspects of social reality which were less likely to be analysed by economic models (such as Pareto's *derivazioni* 1964). These contributed to the analysis of forms of economic behaviour historically different from those of capitalist industrial societies, such as the relations of reciprocity and redistribution in the primitive societies and in the early empires studied by Polanyi *et al.* (1957), and focused on those factors which are treated as exogenous variables in economic models (such as cultural values affecting attitudes toward work and consumption patterns).

In the best instances of the scientific division of labour, the postulates of economic theory can be transformed into research questions, for contiguous disciplines and the findings of the latter can modify the postulates in a direction closer to the changing empirical reality. Put another way, it is not the methodological soundness of the basic assumptions of classical and neo-classical economics that is put into question, but their claim to present economic theory as an exhaustive account of the structure of functioning of modern society and to consider economic laws as natural laws applicable to any historical epoch.

To be sure, economists of different schools and epochs differ according to the scope of applicability of their models. In Adam Smith (1937), social reality is governed by natural laws, and every interference with the free functioning of those laws has to be reduced to a minimum. The specific form of industrial capitalism in the making was transformed into universal laws. In this immanent natural order, prior to any social order, relations between social and economic structures and between individuals and classes, preferences and values are not problematic. Everything social which is different from the economic is either confused with the latter or excluded from scientific explanation.

But in later representatives of the classical school, like John Stuart Mill, and in neo-classical economists like Pareto, there is a much greater awareness of the limited scope of economics. Mill (1899), although striving to present his central theoretical propositions about value and production as unchangeable natural laws, sees political economy as one branch of a general theory of wealth, distinguished from other social disciplines by well-defined behavioural assumptions and by the predominating influence of a set of causes closer to the phenomena studied and recurring in fixed combinations.

Pareto (1964) criticizes the very common error which consists in denying the truth of a theory because it does not explain every part of a concrete fact, and the related attempt to formulate one single general theory, and points out that the only correct conclusion to be drawn from the complexity of social phenomena is *not to substitute* economic theory with other theories explaining the non-economic parts, but *to add* the latter to the former.

The nineteenth-century economists, however wedded they were to their logic, were at the same time keenly aware that their assumptions were special ones, that their parameters were not always 'given', that their empirical world did not bend itself to their theories. That kind of awareness, with varying degrees of articulateness and/or repression, has continued among economists and others up to the present. Such an awareness, moreover, constitutes a pressure on the perceiver of the less-than-perfect aspects of the world to confront them, to come to terms with them, and to make them compatible in some way with the kind of theory that one has developed and works with as his or her daily occupation. Basing our observations on illustrations contained in the papers of Professors Hartley and Hollander, we would like to identify a number of strategies that economists and others have used in dealing with this range of problems. We mention the following strategies:

1 To acknowledge the importance of non-economic phenomena of economic transactions in some sense, but more or less deliberately to leave them aside from consideration as falling sufficiently outside the essential assumptions of economic analysis as to constitute analytically foreign material. This would seem to be the case with Mill's transactions 'effected by force' or 'modified by voluntary gift'. Such types of exchange, while they have an economic aspect, appear to involve very different kinds of 'maximization' than traditionally envisioned by economic theory. Thus the *theoretical* significance of various kinds of theft and taxation, both coercive forms, has escaped economists' theoretical attention, even though the impacts of various types and policies of taxation have found their way into some theoretical discussions and many policy discussions. So has the theoretical significance of the other economic process of gift-giving, though some anthropologists have attended to reciprocal gift-giving in societies other than our own, and a few economists have written about the 'grants economy'.

2 To acknowledge the importance of non-economic phenomena, but to dismiss them as less important, mainly on grounds of logical considerations, in the face of more powerful forces incorporated into the main theory. This seems to be the main strategy used by Malthus with respect to the variables of 'moral restraints' on population growth and on technology, both of which came before his version, but for both of which he developed separate reasons for considering them relatively less important than the factor of the limitations on agriculture in relation to population supply.

3 To acknowledge non-economic phenomena as important determinants of economic factors, but to fail to incorporate them on grounds of difficulty of assimilation, difficulty of measurement, and/or degeneration of theory into descriptions of empirical variation. This kind of strategy is illustrated by Professor Hartley's citation of family variables that influence consumer tastes and preferences: 'social class of parents, education, marriage . . . family size . . . age and sex, as well as by laws and conventions'. More determinants could be added, if one took the entire life cycle of families as units into consideration. While various of these phenomena have entered into empirical studies (for example, race and ethnic membership of families in relation to savings behaviour), the systematic, quantitative inclusion of this multiplicity of determinants into theoretical models has proved to be formidable, and very general amalgamations of a number of them, imprecisely specified, into general models (for example, the 'permanent income theory of consumer behaviour') have been preferred. A second illustration is Mill's citation

of 'new wants and desires' as a factor in stimulating economic development. Mill mentioned these, Veblen (1934) stressed them, Nurkse referred to international demonstration effects (1962), and Duesenberry (1949) attempted to incorporate them into a modification of Keynesian consumption theory. Yet difficulties seem to have persisted in bringing such a phenomenon into the formal corpus of economic theory.

4 To incorporate traditionally difficult-to-incorporate types of non-economic phenomena by applying an economic or economic-like analysis to them. This is illustrated by the efforts to impose a mode of calculation on potential marriage partners, spouses, potential parents and parents' spouses, and seeking to separate them from one another. Professor Hartley has underscored some of the empirical difficulties involved in this kind of extension, and, from a broader point of view, serious criticisms about the feasibility of importing such rationality and calculation into such intimate relations can be raised. We agree with his assessment.

5 To acknowledge non-economic phenomena that constitute modifications or exceptions to traditional maximization models and to incorporate them into equally formal models of economic behaviour with different results. An example is to be found in the formal incorporation of market imperfections, early recognized in classical economic theory but only formally incorporated theoretically in models developed in the twentieth century. Other examples are those cited by Professor Hartley: the challenges to perfect information and knowledge; the alternatives to profit-maximization on the part of firms. One might add the recent preoccupations and models dealing with risk and uncertainty on the part of psychologists and economists alike, which can be regarded as a refinement of the concern with imperfect information and knowledge. In all these cases earlier traditions of economic theory have been creatively modified and extended. The other side of that positive aspect has been the tendency to fragment economics into a less unified form, with competing approaches identified on the basis of their primary informing assumptions and standing side by side with other competing approaches; the cited difficulties of putting any one of these approaches to a definitive empirical test adds to the 'babble-of-voices' effect that characterizes many branches of the social and behavioural sciences. One other observation about this strategy: those aiming to modify the *psychological* givens of classical and neo-classical theory (perfect information, maximization theory, and so on) have been more active and visible theoretically than those aiming to modify the *institutional* givens (the analysts of imperfect competition and the economic significance of government constituting the major exceptions).

6 To acknowledge the importance of non-economic phenomena that may have relevance for economic analysis, but to assign them the status of

more or less independent 'utility functions' or 'rationalities', subject to separate analyses which may or may not resemble formal economic analyses. Examples are Mill's mention of 'prudence' or 'social affections' that limit family size on grounds of maintaining one's status in life; a utility function of responding to the 'will of the electorate' and maximizing 'welfare of the community' on the part of governments; some kind of 'distributive' rationality constituting communal groups such as the family; or some kind of 'bureaucratic rationality', mentioned toward the end of Professor Hartley's paper (chapter 4), which yields propositions producing very different kinds of assumptions and outcomes envisioned by or incorporated into traditional economic models. The implications of these alternatives have not been very extensively spelled out or developed technically, except in some parts of the public choice literature, which employs a more political model of the rationality of actors.

The strategies differ in terms of their degree of methodological sophistication and in terms of the opportunities they offer for building useful relations with the social sciences. The first three strategies try, in different ways, to preserve the boundaries of economic theory by leaving outside all those factors which could blur the simplicity of the model. Everything which is difficult to incorporate into formal models or which appears to have only an indirect effect on economic processes, or which does not conform to the basic assumptions of economic theory is treated as a 'random disturbing cause', in Ricardo's sense. The risk is to widen the gap between the conceptual model and changing empirical realities.

The fourth type of strategy reacts to the increasing complexity of human behaviour and social relations by widening the boundaries of economic theory. It can be seen as an instance of 'scientific imperialism'. Confident in the explanatory potential of economic theory, as it appears in the analysis of the typical economic processes of production, distribution, and exchange, economists try to apply the same rational model to other areas of collective action – such as family decisions, voting behaviour, crime, and so on. Ironically, this attempt to widen the scope of economics has backfired in at least one sense, and has helped to bring into question some of the basic assumptions of rational models.

The fifth type of strategy takes into acount factors which modify the traditional assumptions and maximization models and incorporates them into new theoretical models. This strategy tries to save the core of the theory by updating it, at the cost of a fragmentation of economics into conflicting paradigms.

The final strategy, while apparently sensible, also yields a kind of pluralistic view of theory, admitting whatever separate kind of rationality might qualify; there seems to be no end of the road. It seems to us that the implied 'separate but equal' status suggested might be otherwise formulated. One of the implications of this brief commentary is that theories – including economic theory – are ultimately located in organizations and social structures that institutionalize that rationality, and that theory in the social sciences consists in part in systematizing the rationality of institutional complexes. Thus the possibility of numerous utility functions and numerous associated rationalities seems to be confirmed. Thus when the pursuit is fused with the goal and when there is a quest for collective identity, the actor behaves 'rationally' according to a different rationality from that of the *Homo economicus*. The more important observation, however, is that multiple institutional demands (and 'rationalities') come to impinge on individuals who are necessarily involved in many different institutional complexes simultaneously and during the course of their lives; furthermore, in so far as these 'rationalities' take a collective form, that is, become the ideological basis of protecting or advancing the 'interests' of that institution and its representative groups, they become publicly and politically significant and competitive with other institutionally-derived interests and points of view. By virtue of this circumstance, the problem of analysing the outlooks and behaviours of *individuals* becomes not so much one of how closely the outlooks and behaviour conform to the dictates of a single 'rationality' or set of expectations, but rather how the individual struggles to balance off and in some way come to terms with a multiplicity of bases for priority-making, decision, and action. This envisions a kind of meta-rationality, not involving preferences within con-sistently-formulated utility functions, but decisions involving the relative priorities among ranges of types of utility. For the *collectivity* the contest among rationalities also poses a priority question, and converts the process into a political and economic one, in which the relative merits of different value-positions, interests, and definitions of the situation become the order of the day, rather than the taking of decisions on the basis of a clearly-perceived and consistent set of preferences. We believe that a modification of our ways of theoretical thinking along these lines will ultimately prove to be more realistic and interdisciplinary than our present ways of thinking.

BIBLIOGRAPHY

Arrow, Kenneth (1978) 'The future and the present in economic life', *Economic Inquiry* 16; 157–69.
Duesenberry, James (1949) *Income, Savings, and the Theory of Consumer Behavior*, Cambridge, Mass., Harvard University Press.
Mill, John Stuart (1899) *Principles of Political Economy*, New York, The Colonial Press.
Nurkse, Ragnar (1962) *Problems of Capital Formation in Underdeveloped Areas*, New York, Oxford University Press.
Pareto, Vilfredo (1964) *Trattato di Sociologia generale*, Milano, Communita.

186 Alberto Martinelli and Neil Smelser

Polanyi, Karl, Arensberg, Conrad and Pearson, Harry W. (eds) (1957) *Trade and Market in the Early Empires*, New York, The Free Press.
Smith, Adam (1937) *An Inquiry into the Nature and Causes of the Wealth of Nations*, New York, The Modern Library.
Veblen, Thorstein (1934) *Theory of the Leisure Class*, New York, Modern Library.
Weber, Max (1968) *Economy and Society: An Outline of Interpretive Sociology*, in Guenther Roth and Claus Wittich (eds) New York, Bedminster Press.

Chapter 13

Law as an exogenous factor in economic analysis

Britt-Mari Blegvad and Finn Collin

INTRODUCTION

This paper offers some reflections upon the prospects for an endogeniz-ation of legal phenomena into economics. The framework of the investi-gation is that laid out by Ulf Himmelstrand in Project IDEA. The guiding objective of that project is to bridge the gap between economics and bordering social disciplines to effect an interdisciplinary approach to econ-omic reality. In so doing, Project IDEA is concerned to avoid the dangers of 'economic imperialism', that is, the attempt to subject those bordering disciplines to the rigours of economic methodology. Instead, the method envisaged is that of 'plugging' variables and parameters from the formulae of the neighbouring disciplines into the equations of economics. These items normally occur as exogenous factors in economic processes, influ-encing the latter but not themselves explicable in terms of economic theorizing.

We start out by commenting upon Professor Hartley's presentation of neo-classical economics and the role of exogenous factors in this discipline. Professor Hartley touches upon a number of attempts to apply economic conceptions to non-economic fields, such as public choice theory – conceptions which all too easily invite imperialistic overextension. We want to use his presentation as a foil to show the weaknesses of such approaches in the realm of law, when used in an imperialistic fashion. We go on to show in a more abstract way the fundamental heterogeneity of economic and legal thinking which resides in the normative nature of the latter, making it resistant to a purely economic approach. In the final section of the essay, we go on to suggest that there may be a third option between 'economic imperialism' and a mere 'plugging-in' of non-economic factors into the equations of economics; an interdisciplinary integration which is theoretical while not subjecting any of the participating disciplines to the methods of the others.

A few words are needed, at this stage, to clarify the normativity we attributed to legal thinking above. What we have in mind is the normativity inherent in the law *per se*, the fact that (some) legal provisions impose normative claims upon social agents, claims which are (often) accepted by the agents in question and determine their conduct accordingly. Normativity, or normatively binding power, is here a feature which social agents attribute to certain items in the reality in which they live, and which must be taken account of in explaining their reasonings and actions. This is to be carefully distinguished from the normativity which, according to certain legal theorists, characterizes *legal science* itself, being inherent in its task of specifying the contents of valid law in a given society. It is the difficulties for theoretical integration created by the former normativity, not the latter, which we shall examine in this article.

To round out the picture, we might add that certain parts of economics are normative, too, that is, they prescribe how economic transactions, or economic policies, ought to be conducted. An example is welfare economics, which endeavours to formulate principles for the distribution of the fruits of economic activities in society. But this is not the branch of economics which concerns us here: We are concerned with *positive* economics, the part of economics which seeks to describe how economies actually work, and to develop theoretical principles to explain those workings.

It is a moot question whether legal science embodies a normativity of its own, in addition to that inherent in its object of study. Clearly, such a normativity would create additional problems for the interdisciplinary integration we pursue. Fortunately, we need not enter that discussion here. For at any rate, the discipline with which economics is to be married in the present context is not legal science, but rather the field of *law and society studies*. Law and society studies pursue the same goals of description and explanation which (positive) economics pursues within the economic sphere. More concretely, its primary task is to determine the interaction between the legal system and the rest of social reality. As part of their overall project, law and society studies examine the way in which the legal system shapes other societal spheres as well as the way in which these spheres impinge upon the legal system.

From one point of view, it is possible to construe law and society studies as an auxiliary to legal science, supporting the latter or collecting data used in generating new laws. But they might also be regarded as a subdiscipline of sociology in a broad sense, comprehending not only sociology proper but also legal anthropology, social psychology and parts of political science. In this sense, it even includes some economics (Aubert 1972).

It has been argued that this conception of law and society studies is too broad, since it comprises the larger part of social science. But this objection misses its mark. Law and society studies rather represent a *cross-section* of the social sciences, made in the light of certain specific interests and problems. One might characterize the subject field of law and society studies as the legal system with its actors, processes, structure and institutions and its interaction with its surroundings.

Thus, to the extent that economics is to be reinforced with plug-ins dealing with legal matters, it receives those plugs-in from law and society studies. And as a matter of fact, a currently highly vigorous subdiscipline of law and society studies deals precisely with the interaction between the legal and the economic system, *sensu largissimo*. It is sometimes referred to as Law and Economics. Law and Economics has dealt with both major aspects of law and society studies, that is, with law as a dependent and as an independent factor in the social process. Economics may present a strong theory to study and discuss man's economically measured 'self-interest' (see Posner 1977).

This paper, however, does not regard economic activities in the light of an exclusive rationality, but rather as activities which not only contain economic, but also social elements as is seen in that fuller model of the social agent (or class or category of agents) which will emerge from the strategy of IDEA, if that strategy proves successful. (Of course, not all models generated by this methodology will be *agent* models.) The model is borrowed from Boudon (Boudon 1981), with a minor change in the order of items, introduced to make clearer the relationship between this model and the neo-classical model of the economic agent.

1 A set of options O_1, O_2 ... O_n available to the agent or to the category of agents A.
2 A's information I about O, which can depend upon A's social position P.
3 The set of values V_1, V_2 ... V_n attached by A to each of these options.
4 The influence upon O of the environment E.
5 The influence upon V of the environment E.
6 The influence upon V of the resources Q and, more generally, of the social position P of A.
7 The influence upon V of A's mental dispositions, expectations, habits, modes of existence and beliefs H.

Here, items 1–3 are basically identical to those which define the neo-classical economist's model agent, *Homo economicus*. Items 4–7 comprise those additional aspects which concern the other social sciences, those points where exogenous factors may be plugged into *Homo economicus* and turn him into a truly social being, *Homo sociologicus*.

EXOGENOUS FACTORS IN NEO-CLASSICAL ECONOMICS

In his paper, Professor Hartley makes a broad distinction of exogenous factors into the three categories of preferences, technology, and government, stressing that this tripartition is a traditional one in neo-classical economics. In this classical tripartition, legal concerns cut across the three headings; although most of the topics which concern the legal scholar will no doubt be encompassed under the heading of government. Hence it will come as no surprise that we shall focus on this one below. But legal influences make themselves felt in the two other fields as well. We may note in passing that one and the same legal prescription may appear under the heading of government and that of preferences, a fact revealing a certain overlap among the three categories: whereas technology and government are societal regions in which exogenous influences upon the economy originate, preferences constitute the point of impact on the economy of these influences.

Professor Hartley does not restrict himself to merely classifying the exogenous factors: he also hints at a way in which they can be endogen-ized. At least he does so in the category of government, where he seems to advocate a version of 'economic imperialism', although admittedly a rather benign version. He presents an outline of public choice theory, apparently with endorsement. This is not the place to criticize that pro-posal; let us merely state that we agree with the overall conclusion reached by Professor Lindberg in his contribution to this volume, namely, that public choice theory cannot deliver an all-encompassing 'economic' theory of government (and legislation). On the other hand, we are inclined to grant that the explanatory model devised by public choice theory may offer local insights into the political process, insights that will stand even when the 'imperialistic' uses to which that model is sometimes put are abandoned. Moreover, such an admission opens up the possibility that there may be similar local successes for other versions of 'the economic method' in political science.

LAW AND ECONOMICS

Below, we want to present such an alternative way to theorize about political (or legislative) matters in economic terms. This approach has largely been adopted by scholars working in the specialty known as 'law and economics, which is a subdiscipline of law and society studies. Let us emphasize that we are not suggesting that this approach will deliver that all-embracing 'economic' theory of government (or legislation) which public choice theory aspires to; this was indeed never the ambition of that approach. We just want to point out that it contains interesting findings that will be a part of any future theory of the interrelation between the legal and economic spheres, and that its achievements in this regard may be more impressive than those of Public Choice theory.

A central concern of law and economics has been the attempt to devise economic explanations of lawmaking. The idea is that the emergence of certain kinds of legal instruments, as well as details of legal provisions, can be understood as adaptations to economic necessities. More precisely, they are to be understood as adjustments serving to move the economy closer to productive and allocative effectiveness.

In this formulation, much hinges on the words 'adaptation' and 'adjustment'. It is hardly news that legislation is sometimes introduced with the conscious and express purpose of making the economy operate more efficiently, in the economists' narrow interpretation of this concept. Evidently, law and economics sets its sights higher than presenting such commonplaces. Instead, law and economics directs our attention to law-generating processes in which the attainment of efficiency is not an explicit policy goal on the part of the creators of those laws, but could rather be a 'latent function' of their efforts. It describes instances in which new legal instruments and provisions were instituted by people who did not have the restoration of the economy as their objective.

THE MONTAGNES'S FUR TRADE

Let us illustrate the mode of analysis just suggested by an example presented by Harold Demsetz, deriving from legal anthropology (Demsetz 1967). We shall afterwards point to some weaknesses in the functionalist stance which Demsetz's approach embodies, and discuss the general prospects for an 'economic imperialism' of the kind adopted by law and economics.

Anthropologists studying certain Canadian Indian tribes – among these the Montagnes of the Quebec area – were struck by the fact that these tribes had an institution of property in land. This set them apart from the Plains Indians, where such an institution was unknown, and raised a problem calling for explanation. Moreover, the ownership institution was apparently a fairly recent thing – records from the beginning of the seventeenth century make no mention of a system of landholdings among these tribes.

Now the explanation suggested by Demsetz goes as follows: the Montagnes and the other Canadian tribes examined are primarily hunters, and originally practised hunting only to provide food and clothing. This hunting was beset by an externality: each hunter's efforts had an adverse effect upon the luck of other hunters, without this being taken into account in determining the extent of hunting. This effect was simply so insignificant that it did not pay for anyone to consider it. There did not exist an institution of ownership in land at this stage (Leacock 1954).

However, the situation changed with the advent of commercial fur trading. The value of furs to the Indians increased, leading to a sharp rise in the scale of hunting. It was at this point that an institution of property rights emerged. The first stage in the process was an arrangement of territorial hunting and trapping by individual families, followed next by a seasonal allotment of hunting grounds. By the middle of the seventeenth century the hunting territories were already fairly well stabilized.

Now the economic explanation has it that these property rights arose as an adaptation to the new economic order: with the more intensive hunting, the externalities were no longer negligible; indeed, the game animals were threatened by extinction. The system of individual territories served to internalize those externalities, since such a system makes it advantageous for the hunter to husband the game, in the interest of his future hunt. With every territory owner thinking along the same lines, the aggregate effect was to secure the survival of the game animals, while simultaneously safeguarding the economic effectiveness of the fur production. But this outcome could only be secured if the individual had the right to prevent other hunters from exploiting his restraint by hunting on the same ground, that is, it could only be secured if it became legitimate to keep other tribe members from hunting on one's territory. This legitimation then developed into a property right.

Thus, according to Demsetz, the emergence of what might be termed individual property rights permit the owner to economize on the use of his resources. On the other hand, this exclusive system means that he has no right to the parcel of another owner and thus no *direct* incentive to utilize his parcel in a way which takes into account the effects upon other owners. For instance, if he builds a dam on his land, it is not in his direct interest to consider the effects upon the water level on his neighbour's land. But, as Demsetz points out, the property system provides him with an *indirect* incentive to consider other owners' welfare, since those affected by his activities may be willing to compensate him for abstaining from such harmful activities. (We return to this theme below when we discuss Coase's contribution.)

Let us note in passing that Demsetz's explanation, although exhaustive at the macro-level, needs supplementation at the micro-level. We would like to know precisely what happened at the level of the individual Indian hunter to bring about the change. Was this a case of the most powerful individuals eventually deciding to keep others away from a certain part of the common territory in order to protect their own hunt, with others then quickly following suit? What was the micro-sociological mechanism at play? More investigation is needed at this point to add sociological depth to the economists' explanation.

Before we go on to show how the above example of interaction between law and economics can be analysed in terms of Himmelstrand's method of successive dissection, we would like to present a more recent case showing how property rights have been extended under the weight of economic interests. This process introduces new types of dynamics between externalities and what is construed as property rights, dynamics the micro-sociological nature of which are in this case evident.

THE CHEMINOVA CASE

There are many examples to illustrate the process in question. We have chosen a recent, still ongoing conflict, which has been treated both by the political and by the legal system. Here we will summarize the legal treatment.

The case concerns a pollution lawsuit brought against the Danish chemical company, Cheminova. The company produces insecticides, using a strong poison termed dimethoate as an ingredient. Because of leaks from drainage pipes, the wastes discharged from the plant contained dimethoate.

In court, the company pleaded not guilty to the charge. Implicitly, its defence amounted to the position that the pollution was an accidental and unintended consequence of an activity which in its turn was warranted by the property right to the land on which the factory was built – however damaging that activity might potentially be to the environment. Apparently, this basic position met with a favourable reception in court. It was only because the courts found some proof of negligence that fines were imposed at all – a mere 40,000 D.kr. (approximately £3000) according to the High Court's decision – despite the fact that the leakage had caused extensive damage to fishing and wildlife.

Public opinion and parliamentary debate have adopted an entirely different stance, however, condemning the company's activities as morally negligent in the extreme, and criticizing the courts for being far too lenient.

In the Cheminova case, the externalities are environmental damages. The case is theoretically interesting in showing those societal forces at work which we lacked in the previous example. We see how a company tries to define or extend its property right in such a way as to maximize its own gain. We see, on the other side, those forces which condemn such a policy as immoral and which try to pressure the legislature to delimit the right in question. Thus, in the present case, the social mechanisms at work are not the micro-sociological processes – of an undisclosed nature – which we presumed to be involved in the previous example, but rather the macro-sociological formation which first gained theoretical recognition in Habermas's treatise *Strukturwandel der öffentlichkeit* (Habermas 1962). This is 'public opinion' or the 'public sphere', theoretically conceived as a forum in which private persons reason about public issues, thus exercising a mediating function between civil society and the state.

The causal tie between the economic activity and its external effects is not as visible in the present case as in the first one, due to the complicated nature of modern technology. Still, what we have here is clearly another case illustrating the relationship between property rights and externalities.

Moreover, the two cases point to relationships between the legal and the economic spheres which, when captured in theory, might bring about an endogenization of the relevant parts of law. We shall look more closely into this in the next section.

THE ENDOGENIZATION OF LAW

If we describe the above cases and similar ones presented by law and economics in terms of Himmelstrand's method of successive dissection, their congruity with certain characteristic traits of economic processes will strike us. We are clearly dealing with a feedback process, starting out within the economic sphere (in the fact of large-scale externalities), leading through the legal system (the generation of property rights) and back to the economic system, where it effects a change (the internalization of externalities) pushing the economy closer to productive efficiency. This is what Himmelstrand calls a NE-mediated feedback loop, that is, one mediated by non-economic processes.

This feedback loop should be characterized more carefully. It belongs to the kind in which cybernetics has taken a special interest, that is, feedback processes in which part of a system's outputs are directed back to it in such a fashion that some overall property of that system is maintained. Such feedback systems are *self-corrective* systems.

Now the neo-classical model of the economy is clearly that of a self-corrective feedback system. (We are here talking about the very theoretical core of that model, which represents an extreme degree of idealization. Evidently, present-day neo-classical theory goes far beyond this core conception.) The market-place is the general term for the mechanism whereby the correction is effected. When not interfered with, the market oscillates around an equilibrium, in which it is cleared in the sense that all goods are purchased at the asking price. Every disturbance of that equilibrium is met by compensatory movement. And with this equilibrium comes productive and allocative efficiency, as we know from a famous theorem of Arrow and Debreu (Arrow and Debreu 1954).

One way of stating the observation made by the law-and-economics scholars is to say that the economy is capable of extending this control by feedback even beyond the confines of the market-place, operating through other mechanisms than price signals. The economic system does to some extent generate and shape the non-economic institutions which surround and support it in such a way that a state of equilibrium is realized. To express the matter another way, we might say that the borders of the self-corrective economic system extend beyond the sphere of exchange transactions, by also including parts of the legal sphere and probably other institutions as well.

Evidently, in the present day and age, the 'control' exercised by the economic system over legislation is no longer one which merely operates 'behind the backs' of individual agents: the concern to make the economy work to its full potential of efficiency in production and allocation has long been the topic of explicit policy-making. Central to this endeavour has been the problem of externalities, the phenomenon illustrated by our two cases above. *Externalities are effects of the economic process which fail to feed back into that process in the favoured self-corrective manner.* Still they are economic effects in the sense that they are costs, that is, negative consequences that people would be willing to pay to be rid of or demand pay to endure. This will sometimes take the form of compensations distributed by the legal system and sometimes that of a special payment offered for the licence to go on producing the externality as, for example, in hunting or polluting (see our examples above). For the hunter or polluter, it will sometimes be economically rational to go on with his activities, even after such payment is exacted.

As shown, there are several ways to fight externalities, one of them being through legislation. Let us take our pollution example again. A way which has so far been favoured by the legislature is by simply placing a ceiling on the amount of pollution permitted. However, this solution is opposed by economists since there is no guarantee that allocative and productive efficiency for the individual polluting firm will be served in this way. *The method favoured by economists is one that will internalize the externalities*, that is, establish the feedback loops that do not arise naturally. One way to do this recapitulates the solution to the overhunting of game animals among the Canadian Indians. It consists in the institution of suitably-defined property rights to clean air, water, and so on, for the victims of the externalities. These property rights entitle them to compensation from the polluting agent. According to Ronald Coase, such a system of compensations will prompt the producer to run his production at the level which realizes the overall goal of productive and allocative efficiency (Coase 1960).

INTERNALIZATION VERSUS ENDOGENIZATION

The developments described in our two examples served to internalize external effects into the economy, to the satisfaction of practically working economists. But does the process of internalization also serve to *endogenize* the lawmaking process, that is, to draw it into the compass of *economic theory*, and hence count as yet another explanatory success for law and economics? Does the power of certain legal instruments to move the economy towards effectiveness show that, at least in this area, legislation can be understood solely as an adjustment to economic realities?

The theory under examination is a species of legal functionalism and thus has to contend with the problem often besetting functional explanations, namely, the existence of *functional equivalents*. For a functional explanation to be adequate, it must be shown that the actual outcome uniquely satisfies the functional requirements (Hempel 1965). And hence we may refer to another famous result of Ronald Coase's to show that the legal solution to the economic problem lacks uniqueness as a matter of principle: there will always be several different ways in which the equilibrium mechanism can be established through the distribution of property rights (Coase 1960). Coase shows, for instance, that it does not matter if we grant those who suffer from pollution the right to clean air or water, or whether we grant the producer the legal right to produce as he sees fit, regardless of the suffering he brings upon others. In the latter case, the victims will be willing to pay the producer for cutting down on pollution; and Coase showed in his model that the level of production and pollution emerging from these negotiations will be exactly the same as that resulting if the rights are bestowed upon the sufferer, and hence will be equally economically optimal.

As Coase himself stresses, however, these results hold only for an idealized case in which transaction costs are neglected. The inclusion of transaction costs will often tip the scales in favour of one particular solution, since one distribution of legal rights may allow less costly legal transactions than the other. Hence the ultimate conclusion to be drawn from Coase's work, as applied to our present explanatory concerns, is not that legal functionalism is unsound, but rather that functionalist conclusions cannot be established on the basis of the simple idealized economic models we have been offered so far – Demsetz's argument not excluded. The argument must always be conducted in terms of a model involving transaction costs, since, without such costs, two or more equally good solutions will always be available. These are requirements which very few legal-economic studies have honoured so far.

However, these complications in the methodology of legal functionalism will seem only a minor problem when we turn to reflect upon the large gap between functionalist theory and actual empirical fact in this realm. A glance at actual legislative practice shows that legal solutions often fall entirely outside the range of those economically optimal solutions which are equivalent prior to the consideration of transaction costs. Lawmaking designed to fight pollution, curb overexploitation of resources, and so on, has often chosen legal instruments which are not guaranteed to enhance economic efficiency such as emission ceilings, fishing quotas, and so on. These topics, especially that of pollution, are frequently viewed from a heavily moralistic point of view in which such coercive measures appear as appropriate instruments. The hypothesized drift of legislation towards the goal of economic efficiency, if real, is thus clearly at war with autonomous societal forces against which it is not strong enough to assert itself. This fact, of course, is no news to law and economics, which is precisely concerned with criticizing this kind of legislation in the interest of economic efficiency. Thus, imperialistic dreams on the part of economic functionalism are alien to the spirit of law and economics, and anyway utterly unrealistic.

PREFERENCES

Let us next make a brief comment upon the topic of preferences, the first item on Professor Hartley's list of exogenous factors. Here, too, he mentions the impact of the law. Preferences change as new legal prescriptions are introduced to either hinder or enhance the activities towards which those preferences are aimed. If they did not so change, legal control of human conduct would not be possible.

This means that to the extent that the contents of lawmaking themselves can be endogenized, so can the preferences that spring from that lawmaking, in so far as they are in accordance with the legal prescriptions. Hence they are no longer purely exogenous. For instance, legislation enhancing economic efficiency through a suitable assignment of property rights must be assumed to work through the motivation and preferences of individual economic agents. A person who prior to the introduction of a property right was willing to put up with a certain amount of pollution may afterwards insist upon a monetary compensation for relinquishing his right to clean air or potable water.

The above claims are contentious as viewed through the eyes of standard neo-classical theory. That theory will construe such facts not as changes in preferences, but in the costs, monetary or otherwise, of the available actions. For instance, the changes in behaviour brought about in A by bestowing a property right to clean water upon B is taken to be due to the increased 'cost' to A of polluting, which will now include the payment of damages to B or even the risk of imprisonment for A. However, as we shall argue below, it is not possible to construe agents' reactions to legislative measures as solely motivated by prudential reasons. We have to include a notion of 'respect for the law' as well, which cannot be reduced to a concern for utility maximation (as we shall argue at length below). This means that the introduction of a legal norm results in genuinely changed preferences, not merely in a different distribution of prices.

Be this as it may, it follows from our reflections in the preceding section that an economic, efficiency-based explanation of preferences via the legal measures that shape them could never serve as the methodological instrument for 'economic imperialism'. We possess a rich store of empirical findings demonstrating that legislation is heavily determined by various ideological and moral ideals which cannot themselves be reduced to economic rationality in any simple way, and which often are contrary to economic rationality. Nobody is more aware of these facts than law and economics scholars, who, in their normative capacity, are much concerned to criticize such legislation.

THE INTEGRATION OF ECONOMICS AND LAW: THEORETICAL OBSTACLES

Our examination of the findings of law and economics above brought out the same difficulties that were found with the public choice model, when used in an 'imperialistic' fashion: There may be local successes for one or another variety of economic theorizing in the field of lawmaking and preferences, that is, instances in which these fields can be shown to be amenable to explanation in economic terms. But such successes are never global ones. Hence, the endogenization of legal concerns into economics will not take place on terms dictated by economics, but must respect the methodological characteristics of the other science. There is no hope for a general strategy of 'economic imperialism'.

It is possible to strengthen this conclusion with reflections of a more theoretical kind. There are well-known obstacles to harmonizing legal concepts and principles with the fundamental methodological ideas of economics. To economic thinking, legal prescriptions appear as mere *filters*, eliminating certain actions from the feasible set but not interacting with economic calculations or economic rationality as such (Elster 1979, 1984; Blegvad 1985).

The methodological problems referred to strike at a different point in the interrelationship between economics and legal matters than the ones we have dealt with so far: they pertain to the possibility of legal concerns to serve as the *input* to economic considerations, whereas the ones we analysed above had to do with the possibility of deriving legal prescriptions as the *output* from economic rationality. In other words, while we have so far looked at problems for the attempt to derive the contents of laws from economic considerations as a *dependent* factor, thereby explaining those contents, our present problems pertain to the role of law as an *independent* factor feeding into economic considerations. Note that both aspects are necessary for a true endogenization of any exogenous factor into economics, in the standard technical sense. For exogenous factors are defined as those which determine economic processes, that is, serve as input to such processes while being themselves not explicable in economic terms, that is, derivable from economic considerations (cf. Bannock, Baxter and Rees 1972). Hence an exogenous factor can only be genuinely endogenized if there are no obstacles to its serving both as the input to economic equations and as the output from the same. Another way of expressing this is by saying that any endogenous factor, in the *strict* sense of the word, must be a *feedback* in the terminology of Project IDEA.

We may approach the opposition between the legal and the economic

realm by following a lead given by Professor Himmelstrand in the introductory article upon Project IDEA (Cf. pp. 8–11). If we conceive of neo-
classical economics as the theory of the perfect market, it is true that we
shall have left the domain of that theory when legal restrictions are introduced. Take the textbook favourite, rent control, and compare the effects
which it typically produces – in the short and long term – with those of
a naturally occurring event, for example, a shortage of oil. In the latter
case, the short-term effect will be an increase in the price of oil, caused
by the excess demand; this will reduce demand, and the market will be
cleared at the higher prices which the scarcer oil will fetch. In the long
run, the higher prices will attract capital to the oil sector; prospecting for
new oil resources will accelerate, causing an increased supply which will
tend to drive prices down from their short-term high. In the case of rent
control, on the other hand, the scarcity of housing will not be allowed to
lead to any short-term rent increase; the aim of the provision is precisely
to prevent such increases. Hence there will exist people who would be
willing to rent lodgings at the price demanded in the market, but who fail
to find any: in brief, the market will not be cleared. Second, there will
be no long-term effects easing the problem by entrepreneurs moving into
the market to erect new housing; for housebuilding is not profitable at
the permitted level of rents.

But while such restrictive legislation thus puts the economy – that is,
the market – out of action, it does not put economic science out of action:
indeed, the developments outlined above follow as plausible predictions
from market theory. So does the prediction – equally amply confirmed
by experience – that a thriving black market will tend to emerge beside
the official economy. In other words, while the imposition of legal constraints makes the economy diverge from the idealized situation of equilibrium in a perfectly competitive market, it does not render economic science
incapable of understanding and predicting what will happen.

However, there is a kernel of truth in the feeling that the introduction of
legislation is somehow incompatible with economic thinking. The reasons
become apparent once we move from the level of description and prediction down to the theoretical foundations of neo-classical thinking. Those
foundations, we know, construe economic action as springing from the
rational calculations of that idealized agent, *Homo economicus*. And it
would seem that, for all his computational powers, legal thinking and
action is beyond this creature, as he is normally conceived. This is so for
two reasons, which, however, are not altogether independent: we can
surmount one of these obstacles to an integration of legal and economic
thinking only at the cost of running into the other. Thus we are faced
with a dilemma.

Our reflections on these problems would be fairly uninteresting if they
were purely negative: if they did not point to conditions under which an

integration of legal and economic thinking can take place after all. Fortunately, our reflections do suggest such conditions, although, inevitably, the integration achieved will be less intimate than that which 'economic imperialists' dreamed of effecting.

The virtues of such an integrative model are obvious: it can achieve greater realism, a closer mapping of the empirical world than a traditional economic model, which has to construe normative concerns as mere extrinsic limiting factors, mere 'filters'. There is a corresponding gain in the realism of legal thinking, by the way, which is just as sorely needed as the softening-up of economic thinking. The model is especially well suited to describe what goes on at the interface where economic and normative-legal rationalities interact. Such issues are almost invisible in the absence of a conceptual framework powerful enough to describe them.

EGOISM AND LEGAL NORMS

A feature of the economic approach which has often been thought to clash with the normative character of law is the assumption that the economic agent is motivated solely by *egoistical* preferences. The predilection for explanation in terms of egoistical motives has its historical roots in politico-ideological concerns which were salient at the time when economics emerged as a science, but which we find much less compelling today. Still, it is possible to provide it with a sound methodological rationale which is independent of the historical roots of the discipline.

Let us assume that we operate with non-egoistic preferences in the mechanics of microeconomics, for example, attributing to economic actors a tendency to take pleasure in the well-being of other persons. We assume, that is, that the very experience of other people's flourishing gives a man a certain satisfaction and thus figures on his scale of preferences. Now this assumption is likely to violate a standard presupposition of the notion of an economic actor, namely the preference functions are *independently specifiable*. The rationale of this assumption is clearly demonstrated by a look at the consequences of violating it in favour of an altruistic conception of the kind suggested above: a circle of feedback is generated between the satisfaction of the economic agents involved in a particular economic transaction which makes it difficult to assess the utility of the distribution of goods which results from that interaction. A's recognition of the satisfaction which B derives from the resulting distribution of goods will produce a certain derivative satisfaction in A, which has to be added to the utility of that particular distribution of goods; and the same thing holds for A's knowledge of any other agents $C, D, E, \ldots N$ who take part in the transaction. But that is not all: each of $C, D, E \ldots N$ must be assumed to be altruistic, too, in such a way that they derive a certain satisfaction from observing each others' satisfaction. Finally, each one of them derives a certain satisfaction from their recognition that *A* derives a parasitic satisfaction from pondering their satisfaction; this recognition generates still further satisfactions in *A*, which again give rise to further satisfactions in *B*, *C*, *D*, *E* . . . *N* and so on without end.

Thus the assessment of the satisfaction which a single economic agent *A* derives from a particular distribution of goods turns out to be a highly complicated matter, requiring a computation of the satisfactions of all the other agents about whom *A* has information. Indeed, there is a threat that eventually we are debarred from attributing any determinate satisfaction to *A* at all – at least none that can be derived from a prior knowledge of his preference structure – because his satisfaction is tied up with that of other agents in a circular fashion. True, it is possible to show mathematically that the infinite sequence of accretions to *A*'s satisfaction which is engendered by this feedback process will sometimes converge towards a determinate value (Frohlich 1974). But such convergence will not always be found; and even under the most favourable circumstances, the altruistic assumption brings with it an enormous complication of the apparatus needed to describe even simple economic transactions. Thus, the independence of preferences is needed to safeguard the application of a crucial component of the theoretical apparatus of microeconomics.

Now the clash between the egoism presupposition and legal thinking arises because the latter will typically embody a non-egoistic attitude. After all, laws essentially exist to curb and restrict the perniciously egoistical tendencies of man: this is their societal rationale and the explanation of their existence. Hence they are typically at odds with those egoistical tendencies. This means that the motivational principles of neo-classical economics simply cannot be made to mesh with the logic of legal thinking. Since man is depicted as an egoistic utility maximizer in neo-classical thinking, it is not possible to encompass law-governed action within its conceptual framework.

It might seem that the economist has an obvious rejoinder to this, namely, that the threat of fines and other sanctions provides the motivational power of law-abiding action, one that is in perfect accord with egoism. Against this, we want to insist that although most people may obey the law out of prudential (=egoistical) considerations most of the time, and some people may do so all of the time, still not all people do so all of the time. That is, not all of us always obey the law only because we take the cost of transgression in terms of fines, and so on, to exceed the gains. And the occasional existence of such non-prudential action is all that is needed for this to constitute a theoretical problem for the integration of legal and economic conceptions.

Let us repeat that the clash pointed out here does not simply reflect the survival in economics of a naïve and unsophisticated definition of egoism, a relic from the century which gave birth to economics. Our problem cannot be solved by simply substituting a more sophisticated definition of egoism which admits that methodological egoism does not preclude that a man may set as much stake on other people's well-being as his own. It is precisely those people who derive pleasure from the observation of each other's pleasure, and who perform benevolent actions for this reason, who bring about that infinite regress. We seem to be forced to adopt a traditional, narrow conception of egoism to circumvent this methodological obstacle. And this conception places norm-guided action beyond the pale of the rational calculation of action that is central to the economic method.

Fortunately, closer inspection shows that we have more alternatives than narrow egoism and an infinite regress to choose between. We can avoid that unpleasant dilemma precisely by enriching the economic vocabulary with normative terms. Pure norm-following conduct does not lead to the regress problem that altruistic actions engender. This is because pure norm-abiding conduct is not motivated by the prospect of pleasure for the agent subsequent on seeing others being happy as a result of his actions, but is instead motivated by pure respect for the rule. Hence the feedback circle does not get started at all. If it be objected that this 'respect for the rule' is nothing but the prospect of enjoying a clean conscience – that is, a utility – we may respond, first, that there is a famous argument in philosophy, due to Bishop Butler, showing that this could not be the basic motivational mechanism in normative action, since an agent will only be rewarded with a clean conscience if he views the action performed as normatively right, and hence as independently motivated, in the first place (Butler 1726). If the critic points out that agents performing normative acts do as a matter of fact enjoy the feeling of a clean conscience, although this may not be the motive force behind their act, we may grant that this is the case, but add that this does not generate a regress problem. For this 'bonus' subsequent upon performing normative acts is paid in one lump sum, as it were, and draws no interest from the pleasure felt by others.

Note, finally, that there is such a thing as 'economic norms' too, that is, rules specifying the proper strategy to adopt in economic matters. These have their origin, not in empirical observation or scientific studies of how norms are supported by sanctions and thereby strengthened or weakened – like in law – but derive from an analysis of the control mechanisms inherent in economic systems and the models made thereof (Blegvad 1990).

UTILITY AND NORMATIVITY

However, the way we disposed of the above problem for the integration of norms brings us face to face with the second and more serious one; the two are actually the legs of a dilemma. It has just been argued that normative action is not motivated by the prospect of utility. But utility remains the fundamental conceptual tool of neo-classical microeconomics; hence its inapplicability to some region of human conduct means that the basic axioms of neo-classical thinking become inapplicable too. It is no use objecting that the notion of utility as used in modern economics is tautologically true of any object of choice, since it is nothing but a vacuous label for such objects and carries no substantial psychological meaning. For although we may accept the economist's terminological proposal, and agree to call even the thing aimed at in normative action a 'utility', the fact remains that utility must satisfy a crucial condition in order to serve the economist's theoretical purposes, as we shall argue below; and the satisfaction of this condition is not guaranteed by definition. The point is that utility as construed by the economist is essentially a *homogeneous* thing, which is necessary for it to serve as a general numeraire of the value of consumer goods.

The assumption of homogeneity is clearly made in the basic axiom of household demand theory, namely, that households will allocate their expenditure among available commodities in such a way that the utility of the last penny spent on each is equal. This clearly presupposes that the utilities derived from different, and alternative, expenditures are commensurable. Without this assumption, the notion of equality of marginal utility becomes meaningless.

The point is even clearer in terms of the alternative way to represent consumer behaviour, namely, in terms of *indifference curves*. An indifference curve specifies those combinations of two goods which the consumer considers to have equal utility, that is, between which he will choose indifferently. The curve allows us to see how a loss in one commodity can be compensated by an increase in the other commodity. (A generalized curve can be set up in which an identified good is compared with all other goods, represented by their monetary value.)

Now economists run into trouble with norms in both ways of representing preferences. It is easiest to see in the case of indifference curves. For most people, some normatively governed actions are such that no monetary reward could induce them to perform them. Thus, for instance, no amount of money could persuade them to kill another human being; no payment could make them desecrate the holy places of their religion. But this means that the option of avoiding such actions possesses a 'utility' of such a special kind that a loss in that utility – suffered through the actual performance of such an act – could not be made good by any monetary compensation. Performing the reprehensible act represents, as it were, a 'disutility' which no amount of money can outbalance.

The situation cannot be handled with the resources available to utility theory by simply attributing an *infinite* utility to such forbidden acts. For, as we shall see in an example below, the privileged actions (or goods) constitute an entire sphere within which exchange relations are possible, and within which we may thus attribute a 'price' to one action (or good) relative to another. The ascription of such determinate and differential prices is incompatible with the assumption that all actions (or goods) of the privileged kind possess infinite value.

The same problem besets the analysis of consumer behaviour in terms of marginal utility gain. If it is true that the 'utility' gained by avoiding the performance of some immoral or sacrilegious act cannot be equalled by any amount of utility gained by the consumption of ordinary goods, then the former utility is of a generically different kind than the latter, and it will make no sense to claim that the 'consumption' of one gives the same marginal utility as the other. The situation simply cannot be conceptualized with the resources available to consumer theory.

The relevance of this to our current question is, of course, that many legal provisions are theoretically construed as norms of precisely that coercive form which interests us here (others are not: see below). In many cases, the coercive, prescriptive nature of a legal rule is apparent from its very form: the rule which says that you are not allowed to pass through an intersection against a red light, places an unconditional ban on this manoeuvre. It is true that the prohibition is backed by the threat of fines if you disobey (with the risk of collision as an additional deterrent). Still the rule is not to be taken as giving you a choice between obedience and payment: it does not say that it is OK for you to run a red light as long as you remember to pay. It states unconditionally that you are not allowed to run a red light – transgressors to be punished with fines. The same thing holds of course for many legal rules which are not explicitly formulated as prescriptions. It is no objection against the point made here that many legal ordinances are of intricately conditional form, specifying circumstances under which the conduct prescribed for the standard case need not be displayed: the claim made here is that payment of a fine is *not* another such condition.

No doubt the reader will want to object here that this concern with the way legal rules present themselves is irrelevant in the present context: what matters to economics as an empirical science is how people actually conceive of legal prescriptions. And here the suggestion might be that most people do as a matter of fact adopt a purely 'economic' attitude, that is, they conceive of such prescriptions as mere obstacles that can be circumvented at a certain cost, monetary or otherwise. But here we may invoke Durkheim's criticism of Spencer's account of social order and similar accounts in the broad Hobbesian tradition: as long as we ascribe only utility-maximizing concerns to human agents, social order will remain inexplicable. We have to postulate some form of normative commitment, not only as an exception but on a scale large enough to shape macro-sociological processes.

To give a balanced picture of the function of law, we must add that not all legal norms have the property of coerciveness described above; others are *constitutive* rules, generating legal instruments which individuals can use as tools in their transactions (contracts, wills, and so on) (cf. Hart 1961). It should also be noted that a law does not mean the same thing to all members of society. A law which is a resource for one group, might to another group represent a threat or warrant the preferential treatment of another group at the first group's expense. Examples are laws concerning the distribution of social benefits (Aubert 1976).

Aubert also mentions the fact of laws changing character by, for example, starting out as coercive and then turning into an indirect resource. Consider legislation-threatening sanctions when a deal is not properly carried out. This is a coercive function, but at the same time one which guarantees stability in business dealings and the chance to foresee the future in relevant respects. Under such a regimen, agents operate in 'the shadow of the law' (Mnookin and Kornhauser 1979).

But the relation *between the parties* may also change and call for other than legal governance structures. One might, for example, develop 'a different contracting relation that preserves trading but provides for *additional* governance structure' (Williamson 1985: 75).

Even such an adjustment process may be regarded as insufficient – especially in *long-term contractual relationships*. These types of contracts are associated with recurring transactions supported by investments of mixed and highly specific kinds. So-called 'relational contract situations' develop, where exchange of goods is involved but the situation is rather based on economic and/or social norms.

These are found in *bilateral structures* where the autonomy of the parties is maintained, allowing other adjustments than legal ones. Examples of quantity adjustments are found (Blegvad 1990; Macaulay 1963, 1985), not only within a national market, but also in the international trade in natural resources (Daintith 1986, 1988). Such adjustments have much better incentive-compatibility properties than do price adjustments. Price adjustments, like legally based adjustments, often possess an unfortunate zero-sum quality.

This development is certainly also based on a need expressed by new actors in the market, such as franchisers. These actors call for solutions based on *social* rather than *legal* rationality. As a result, more and more problems come to be discussed in a 'mixed' way. Neither legal nor classical economic contracting is efficient from an economic point of view. The relations between the parties have become the core rather than societal needs for regulations and possibilities of calculating predictable effects. Equity will be given pride of place and compromises are the result (Blegvad 1990).

A COMMON CONCEPTUAL PLATFORM FOR SOCIAL SCIENCE

The above observations should sound the death knell to any ambitions of conducting a successful campaign of economic imperialism in social science – that is, the programme of subjecting all other social sciences under the sway of economic methods. Thus they vindicate the reservations about such methods which inspired Project IDEA.

On the other hand, there might be a feeling that the goal set in Project IDEA is too modest. In producing more elaborate models in which exogenous factors are 'plugged-into' the formulae of economics, we only manage to map the purely causal dependencies between the parameters in question. We do not effect a *theoretical explanation* of those interdependencies, for want of a common conceptual framework in which to express it. But might it not be possible to define a common theoretical platform on which economics and the other social sciences could meet, on terms not dictated by either?

What economics would contribute to the suggested methodology is its individualistic approach and its concentration on the crucial role of rationality. What would have to be relinquished is the identification of rational action with utility-maximizing action, thereby making room for a broader notion of rationality encompassing norm-guided action. This notion is the contribution of legal science – or better, of the rest of social science. For of course the notion of normativity is not unique to legal science. On the contrary, it is a dominant conception in the non-economic social sciences. For instance, a traditional way of defining sociology is that it is the science of social roles and the conduct they dictate. And roles are defined as the normative expectations to which a social agent is subject by virtue of his particular status. Law and society studies, which we previously introduced as a possible superordinate discipline in relation to law and economics, construes law as another, more formalized type of norms. Hence the proposed 'fusion of scientific horizons' will not only provide common ground between legal science and economics, but between the latter and large segments of social science in general.

In hammering out the broader notion of rationality, we might take our cue from a famous article by Amartya Sen (Sen 1979). Sen wants to get beyond *Homo economicus*, whom he regards as a social moron precisely because of his insensitivity to normative reasoning of the kind we encounter in ethics and in law. Sen introduces the term 'commitment' to refer to the kind of respect which is the distinctive attitude *vis-à-vis* norms, and sketches out a formal decision model in which this attitude can be captured. This involves the notion of *meta-ranking of preferences*. Take a set of action outcomes X and consider three different ways of ranking these outcomes, A, B and C. Evidently, these divergent rankings may themselves be arranged in a preference ordering, the preferences in question being at a meta-level *vis-à-vis* the preferences they organize. For instance, one might prefer the preference ordering A to B because A ranks a concern for the well-being of other people higher than does B.

Sen's suggestion is that moral (and other) rules may be viewed as meta-preferences ranging over preferences. Specific moral rules – or 'commitments' – should then be ascribed to agents in order to explain those economic, political and social phenomena which cannot be understood in purely egoistic, utility-maximizing terms. Among the norms invoked might for instance be the *Golden Rule* and *Pacta sunt servanda*. (M. Blegvad 1985). Such an examination would show how norm structures vary from one subject field to another. For instance, firms operate on the basis of mutual trust rather than legal instruments or (short-term) economic gain (Macaulay 1963); in wage negotiations the sense of solidarity on each side will have well-defined limits which cannot be accounted for in terms of utility-maximization. One might call such norm systems *multicentric moral systems* with a structure similar to the multicentric economic systems treated below.

However, to map the actual structure of normative preferences, we have to develop the idea of meta-preferences beyond Sen's sketch. For that structure has complexities which Sen's model fails to capture. Sen proposes a ranking of preference rankings of different combinations of all of the actions available to an agent. But what we need is, first, a *partition* of the agent's available set into mutually exclusive subsets, each with its own internal preference ordering, and with the meta-preferences ranging over these *subsets* instead of over preferences pertaining to the whole domain of available actions. (This very condensed description will be made intelligible in terms of a concrete example below.)

Next, we interpret the higher ranking of one such subset N over another subset M in the meta-preference function to mean that the satisfaction of a preference n in N has priority over the satisfaction of any preference m in M: the higher-ranking preference must be satisfied, if possible, before the satisfaction of the lower-ranking one is contemplated. Only such a structure is powerful enough to express the fact that people act on the basis of preferences that are sometimes *incommensurable*, in the sense exemplified above – namely, that a loss in the satisfaction of one preference cannot be compensated by a gain in the satisfaction of another, lower one. ('Non-equalizability' might be preferable, but for its clumsinesses, to 'incommensurability' as a name for the phenomenon, since the suggested stepwise preference structure *is* of course a comparison of sorts.)

As it happens, the preference structure we have sketched out is one whose formal properties have already been described and studied by economists (Georgescu-Roegen 1954; Chipman 1960; see also Elster 1984). It is known as a *lexicographic preference function*. According to such a preference ordering, the various dimensions $d_1, d_2, d_3 \ldots d_n$ in which we assess a certain good are ranked in such a manner that if good α surpasses good β in a certain dimension d_j, but is not surpassed by β in any higher ranking dimension d_i, then α is to be preferred to β even though β may surpass α in every lower ranking dimension. (This is parallel to the way that a word α is listed before another word β in a lexicon if α has an earlier letter in the alphabet than β at the first place at which they differ, regardless of whether β has earlier letters at all subsequent places).

Evidently, such a conception is perfectly suited to capture the relationship between legal concerns and purely 'economic', utility-maximizing ones. The fact that the former take precedence over the latter will be expressed in their higher ranking in the lexicographic ordering. Moreover, lexicographic preference functions may have as many levels as you like. Hence, they are powerful enough to express the fact that in our society, legal concerns are not the only ones that take precedence over utility-maximization. Moral concerns have a similar standing, and are, moreover, in many situations superordinate to legal concerns: It is generally accepted in our culture that, in the end, a man must decide in terms of his morality whether a certain legal rule is binding on him. He may, for example, decide that a certain prescription concerning race segregation is obnoxious and does not deserve his observance.

Thus lexicographic preference functions are ideally suited to express the insight which Professors Martinelli and Smelser urge in their article in this volume, namely, that we need to supplement the economists' uniform utility-maximizing rationality with a kind of meta-rationality, determining how the individual should navigate between a multitude of conflicting, socially institutionalized rationalities which impinge upon him. Enquiring how individuals come to master such navigation, Mogens Blegvad (Blegvad 1985) points to the early integration of norms as part of socialization and education. One might also examine why educators pick particular norms rather than others. One answer might be that they are *thematized* in the reference groups that agents turn to for social support. Society can only exist on the basis of such integration but, with increased complexity and diversity, the integration can no longer always be secured through the mechanism of actual bodily presence. Function and structure then become relevant, and the interaction moves into the legal system, among others. According to Luhmann (1981), *thematization* entails 'a decision about the status or location of the ongoing interaction within the total societal system'.

It is important to appreciate that a lexicographic ordering does not mean that certain things are absolutely beyond reach of the exchange relation, but only that the exchange takes place within certain different systems. For instance, although most people in our culture will not commit homicide at any monetary price, they may well be willing to kill under conditions, such as war, where other lives are saved: lives are traded against lives. And when the choice is forced upon us, it is *ceteris paribus* preferable to perform the action which will cost fewest lives. In other words, an economic mode of thinking is found to exist even in the region of normative values. This is why it will not do simply to attribute infinite utility to all such values, as we observed above.

In this feature, normative thinking in our culture shows an interesting similarity with certain aspects of economic action which are most clearly exhibited by tribal societies but are found in our own as well. These so-called *multicentric economies* consist in the fact that exchange is divided into a number of zones such that only specific goods are valid payment in each zone, with no or only restricted possibility of exchange across zones. A good example is provided by the Tiv of Nigeria, as described by Bohannan (Bohannan 1955).

The Tiv recognize (or recognized earlier, prior to becoming exposed to western civilization) three different economic spheres. In the first, the commodities exchanged included everyday goods such as foodstuffs, utensils and tools, and most raw materials. These goods were distributed either by gift-giving or through barter, which was organized into a highly developed market system. In the second sphere of Tiv economy, markets did not exist. Instead, goods were exchanged during ritualized ceremonies. Among those goods were slaves, cattle, medicines, and certain fabrics and metals. In the third economic sphere, the objects exchanged were women; this was simply the institutional framework for marriage in Tiv society. The three spheres were ranked in ascending order from the first to the last mentioned, and under normal circumstances, commodities from one sphere could not be exchanged for one from the others. However, such exchanges were possible under certain specified conditions. But the exchange of a good from a superior category for one from a lower category bore considerable social stigma. Thus, the different institutions of exchange among the Tiv were closely interwoven with normative evaluations.

The fact that the technical device of lexicographic preference functions will accommodate the multicentric economy of the Tiv, as well as the structure of western moral and legal thinking, testifies to the power of the idea of using law and society studies as the superordinate field. It is a truly interdisciplinary conception, capable of expressing findings from such divergent disciplines as economics, sociology, legal science and anthropology.

CONCLUDING REMARKS

Let us finally return to the kind of concrete cases of endogenization with which we started out in the beginning of this article, that is, concrete examples of 'plugging' legal factors into the formulae of neo-classical

economics. Does the above result mean that such plugs are only legitimate
if we expand the conceptual basis of neo-classical economics in the indicated direction, since such an expanded basis is apparently needed to
accommodate the complex conceptualization involved?

The answer depends upon which theoretical depth we want to operate
at. The problems for interdisciplinary integration we outlined above per-
tained to the methodological foundations of neo-classical economics, and
arise when we analyse economic processes as the aggregate effects of the
activities of individual, utility-maximizing agents, while at the same time
trying to do justice to the normative considerations involved. Now there
is no absolute need to penetrate to these theoretical depths in every
economic investigation; useful results can be obtained at a more superficial
level. Take the example of rent control once more. It is only when we
want a *rational* micro-explanation of the activities of landlords faced with
a rent-ceiling that we are forced to employ the wider rationality model
outlined above: such a model permits us to see how the landlord's 'respect
for the law' interacts *rationally* with his mundane preference for a higher
income and directs him to abide by the ceiling or to move into the black
market, as the case may be. But we might adopt a more extrinsic stance
instead and content ourselves with recording that the introduction of the
rent ceiling *caused* the landlord to find new normative solutions which
again brought about a change in his preference structure, making him
unwilling to offer a house for rent at prices which he was previously
happy to accept (namely such prices as are now banned by law). The
introduction of a rent ceiling may thus be plugged into the economic
formulae as a purely *causal* factor, with no attempt to accommodate it
within the *rational calculations* of the agents involved.

But while such a scientific stance is perfectly legitimate, we are convinced that the full potential of the programme of integrating economics
and neighbouring disciplines will only come to fruition if pursued at the
most basic level of theoretical explanation. This is why we have been at
pains, in this article, to point out that the methodological and ontological
framework for such an integration is actually available, a framework which
permits economics and its sister disciplines to meet on terms that are not
set by either.

BIBLIOGRAPHY

Arrow, K. J. and Debreu, G. (1954) 'Existence of an equilibrium for a competitive
    economy', *Econometrica* 22, 265–90.
Aubert, Vilhelm (1972) *Retssociologi*, Universitetsforlaget, Oslo.
Aubert, Vilhelm (1976) *Rettens sosiale funksjon*, Universitetsforlaget, Oslo.
Bannock, G., Baxter, R. E. and Rees, R. (1972) *The Penguin Dictionary of Econ-
    omics*, Penguin, Harmondsworth.
Blegvad, Britt-Mari (1990) 'Commercial relations, contract and court in Denmark

– a discussion of Macaulay's contracting theory', *Law and Society Review* 24, 2, 397–409.

Blegvad, Mogens (1985) 'Rationalitet, moral og samfund', *Filosofiske Studier* 7, 7–34.

Bohannan, P. (1955) 'Some principles of exchange and investment among the Tiv', *American Anthropologist* n.s. 57, 50–60.

Boudon, Raymond, (1981) *The Logic of Social Action*, Routledge & Kegan Paul, London.

Butler, Joseph (1726) *Fifteen Sermons and Dissertations on Virtue*, London.

Chipman, J. S. (1960) 'The foundations of utility', *Econometrica* 28, 193–224.

Coase, Ronald (1960) 'The problem of social cost', *Journal of Law and Economics* 3, 1–44.

Daintith, Terence C. (1986) 'The design and performance of long-term contracts', in Daintith and Teubner's *Legal Analysis in the Light of Economic Theory*, Berlin, De Gruyter.

Daintith, Terence (1988) 'Contract design and practice in the national resources sector', B.-M. Blegvad, D. Kalagoropoulos and A. Febbrajo (eds) in *European Yearbook in the Sociology of Law*, Berlin, De Gruyter, 173–93, see also ibidem (1988) 'Law as a policy instrument. Comparative perspective', in T. Daintith (ed.) *Law as an Instrument of Economic Polity, Comparative and Critical Approaches*, Berlin, De Gruyter.

Demsetz, Harold (1967) 'Toward a theory of property rights', *American Economic Review Proceedings*, 347.

Elster, Jon (1979) *Forklaring og dialektikk*, Oslo, Pax.

Elster, Jon (1984) *Ulysses and the Sirens*, (revised edn), Cambridge and New York, CUP.

Frohlich, Norman (1974) 'Self-interest or altruism, what difference?', *Journal of Conflict Resolution* 18, 55–73.

Georgescu-Roegen, N. (1954) 'Choice, expectations and measurability', *Quarterly Journal of Economics* 68, 503–34.

Habermas, Jürgen, (1962) *Strukturwandel der Öffentlichkeit*, Neuwied, Luchterhand.

Hart, H. L. A. (1961) *The Concept of Law*, Oxford, The Clarendon Press.

Hempel, C. G. (1965) 'The logic of functional analysis', *Aspects of Scientific Explanation*, New York, The Free Press.

Leacock, Eleanor, (1954) 'The Montagnes "hunting terrritory" and the fur trade', *American Anthropologist* (American Anthropological Association) 56 (5), part 2, memoir no. 78.

Luhmann, Niklas (1981) 'Communication about law in interaction', in K. Knorr-Cetina and A. W. Cicourel (eds) *Advances in Social Theory and Methodology*, London, Routledge & Kegan Paul.

Macaulay, Stewart (1963) 'Non-contractual relations in business: a preliminary study', 28 *American Sociological Review*, 55.

Macaulay, Stewart (1985) 'An empirical view of contract', *Wisconsin Law Review* 28, 55–69.

Mnookin, Robert H. and Kornhauser, Lewis (1979) 'Bargaining in the shadow of the law: the case of divorce', *The Yale Law Journal*, 88, 950.

Posner, Richard A. (1977) *Economic Analysis of Law*, (2nd edn), Boston, Little Brown.

Posner, Richard A. (1981) *The Economics of Justice*, Cambridge, Mass., Harvard University Press.

Sen, Amartya (1979) 'Rational fools: a critique of the behavioural foundations of

economic theory', in Frank Hahn and Martin Hollis (eds) *Philosophy and Economic Theory*, Oxford University Press.
Williamson, Oliver (1985) *The Economic Institutions of Capitalism: Firms, Markets, Relational Contracting*, London, Macmillan.

Chapter 14

Towards a lexicographic preference-actor-structure theory

Ulf Himmelstrand

INTRODUCTION

In a previous chapter by Martinelli and Smelser the contests of multiple rationalities, often collective in nature, were contrasted with the aggregation of individual preferences which dominates the thinking of economists. This chapter of mine intends to follow up on these ideas of Martinelli and Smelser, and to explore further how we can analyse multiple, collective rationalities in a manner which simultaneously may satisfy at least some amended versions of economic theory, and the basic assumptions of other social sciences than economics.

The notion of 'multiple rationalities' can fruitfully be explicated and made more precise by combining it with the notion of lexicographic preference rankings mentioned in previous chapters by Alan Lewis, and by Britt-Mari Blegvad and Finn Collin. As Blegvad and Collin have pointed out, these ideas have also been taken into account by a most respected economist, Amartya Sen.

If you find a vehicle which is able to traverse the distance between the territories of many different disciplines, a vehicle which furthermore is viewed as quite natural in several of those domains, then you can be pretty certain of having found a way to launch a new multi-disciplinary dialogue and with it a new interdisciplinary creativity. Lexicographic preference theory is such a vehicle.

Mathematical language is another vehicle which might serve such a multi-disciplinary dialogue. Within the natural sciences it has indeed done exactly that, but in the social sciences it would seem that mathematics on the contrary has contributed to lock the discipline of mainstream economics into defensive fortresses of formalism, thus separating economics from other social sciences, but also making those other social science disciplines reluctant to venture into the borderland domains toward economics. In the IDEA Project we have made an attempt to use certain properties of simple mathematical language to open a dialogue with economists, within the so-called 'method of dissection'. Being responsible for these attempts, the present author can only verify that it was relatively easy to address economists in mathematical language, and to make them communicate with the rest of us in such terms, and to make many of us understand different types of exogenous impacts on economic processes with the help of simple mathematics. However, the vehicle of mathematical language did not perform quite as great wonders on the other side of the divide between economics and non-economic social sciences.

Perhaps the vehicle we should be looking for is a language conveying certain *substantive* notions basic to several social science disciplines rather than the common but *formal* language of mathematics. Such substantive notions are the notions of *normative rules*, of *preferences*, of *rationality* and of *exchange*. Can these notions, used as they are in several different disciplines, be made to serve our understanding of the 'contests of collective rationalities' which Martinelli and Smelser in their chapter contrast with the ways in which economists aggregate individual preferences?

As long as the notion of preferences can figure prominently in a certain discipline, that discipline should be able to make use of *lexicographic preference theory*. The lexicographic aspect makes it possible to salvage basic and unique characteristics of different disciplines, and to maintain their limits, while still being able to make the best possible use of the interdisciplinary notions of norms, preferences, and even of exchange.

However, the notions of 'preferences' and of 'exchange' belong basically to an individualistic train of thought. This is the case in economics. As a sociologist with interdisciplinary inclinations I could make use of these notions, with their lexicographic ramifications, only if lexicographic preference functions could be linked to different kinds of *actors*, some of which would be collectivities, and to *structures* even beyond what must be defined in methodologically individualist terms. In this chapter I will attempt to build an interdisciplinary kind of theoretical approach on the basis of a combination of (1) concepts from lexicographic preference theory, (2) concepts pertaining to different kinds of actors, individual or collective, and (3) concepts pertaining to structural characteristics of societies, and sets of societies in which those actors are embedded. The intention is to explore the possibilities of relating economic theory, with its foci on preferences, rationality and exchange, to the 'exogenous' domains of other social science disciplines, and to do this within the framework of an interdisciplinary lexicographic preference-actor-structure approach.

SOME BASIC DEFINITIONS AND RELATIONSHIPS

1 A lexicographic preference function

A *lexicographic preference function* has the following characteristics, as indicated already by Blegvad and Collin:

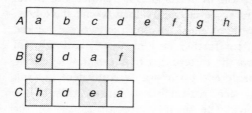

Figure 14.1 Diagram of lexicographic choice

(a) there exists a *partition* of the agent's preferences into mutually exclusive subsets;
(b) there exist *meta-preferences* ranging over such partitioned subsets ranking them from superordinate to subordinate subsets;
(c) the higher rank of one such subset *N* over another subset *M* in the meta-preference function implies that the satisfaction of a preference *n* in *N has priority* over the satisfaction of any preference *m* in *M*. The higher-ranking preference must be satisfied, if possible, before the satisfaction of the lower-ranking one is contemplated.

This is parallel to the way in which a word is listed before another word in a lexicon. If the first letter of a certain word, say 'oxygen', appears earlier in the alphabet than the first letter of a second word 'palace', then 'oxygen' will appear first in the lexicon regardless of whether that second word, 'palace' has earlier letters in all subsequent places.

In a simple diagrammatic form the lexicographic decision-making process, as described above, can be illustrated in Figure 14.1. *A* and *B* and *C* represent three different, incommensurable preference functions, *A* being the highest-ranked, and *C* the lowest-ranked preference dimension involved. The letters *a, b, c* and so on, in the figure represent various objects being ranked within each preference dimension. The 'shadowed' cells represent objects which are rejected or considered completely inadmissible in a given meta-rank – 'bad' objects.

Lexicographic choice always starts with a ranking of objects according to the highest meta-rank of preference dimensions (*A*). It then moves to the next meta-rank (*B*). Those ranked highest in the highest meta-rank (*A*) are ranked again with respect to the second meta-rank (*B*). To make the exercise a little more interesting and realistic I have on this level also included some of the objects considered inadmissible in (*A*) – namely *g* and *f*. Then we move to meta-rank (*C*) where also some of the *A*-inadmissible objects are included. In the figure the objects admissible according to meta-rank (*A*) are similarly ranked in (*B*) and (*C*). Object *d* is the object finally chosen – the lowest ranked among the objects considered admissible in (A). In this illustration of lexicographic choice less strict rules have been applied with regard to admissibility than would have been possible. It would have been possible to consider only the two top-ranked objects *a* and *b* in meta-rank (A) for further ranking in (B) and (C). Of course this will depend greatly on the differences between *a – d* among the *A*-admissible. If they are considered very close or equivalent in rank among the *A*-admissible it would seem reasonable to include them all in the ranking on the next level (B). The most important aspect of the lexicographic choice illustrated in Figure 14.1 is that objects considered completely inadmissible according to a higher meta-rank thereby are ruled out from choice in the final decision. Choice on lower meta-rank levels must be made among those singled out as admissible on higher meta-rank levels.

Only such a lexicographic preference function is powerful enough to express the fact that people can act on the basis of preferences that are sometimes incommensurable. Incommensurable preferences can guide action in a relatively unambiguous way when preference subsets are subject to a meta-preferential rank order as described above.

2 Varieties of preference subsets

In addition to the *economic* preferences dealt with by economists there exist in every society preferences which are not commensurable with economic preferences – for instance, *ethical* preferences dealing with personal and interpersonal morality, *religious and ritual* preferences, *legal* preferences, and in more recent times preferences relating to long-term *ecological conditions* which cannot be measured exclusively with current economic measures, or several other current measures for that matter. I have also mentioned *æsthetic* preferences. The wish to maintain your actually existing position of *power* could in some cases be a preference with a higher priority, or meta-rank than any specifically economic, or even legal preferences. Later on I will make a reference to such cases.

It might be argued that legal rule-following, as well as the following of a religious creed, cannot be reduced to preferences. According to this view there exists no subset of ordered preferences with regard to, say, legal rules; rather there is a binary action-set in that a rule is either followed or not followed. However, in actual fact we may rather find a 'grey zone' of activities conforming more or less with a given rule where an individual can make a choice according to legal preferences. This is even more obvious in rule-making where several alternatives can be contemplated, and one of them chosen on the basis of a legal preference function. Furthermore it has obvious advantages for lexicographic preference theory to be able to include the legal and religious systems within the logic of this theory.

3 Meta-rankings of preference subsets may vary

Most stable societies have a distinct lexicographic meta-ranking of mutually exclusive subsets of preference. In some societies the ethical subset ranks highest followed by the legal subset and the economic subset. In other societies the economic subset would seem to rank highest. In some societies the religious subset is virtually missing as distinct from the ethical subset; in other societies it is ranked highest. In some societies like in certain North-American Indian tribes, and among Australian aborigines, some kind of ecological subset would seem to rank very high whereas it has been insignificant and low-ranking in western industrial societies until recently.

Socio-cultural change can often be described either in terms of a reordering of lexicographic preference subsets, or in terms of the emergence of some new subset, or in terms of a breakdown and disruption of lexicographic ordering and the fusion of previously distinct subsets, or in an emerging dissensus between classes or groups within the given society as regards lexicographic preference ordering.

In reviewing possible causes of such socio-cultural changes of lexicographic preference ordering it would seem to be of particular interest to note the impact of breakdowns of national boundaries, the emergence of international exchange, trade and dependency (see below).

4 Trade-offs between preference subsets stigmatized

The existence of a lexicographic meta-ordering of preferences is indicated when a *stigma* is attached to exchange or trade-offs *between* elements of lexicographically different preference subsets. Such exchange or trade-offs constitute transgressions of lexicographic order. If such transgressions are frequent and occur in a concealed form to avoid the stigma, that is an early symptom of a breakdown of consensus regarding lexicographic meta-ordering of preferences. If such transgressions can be made openly by influential people, without a stigma attached to it, this indicates a complete breakdown of consensus regarding lexicographic meta-ordering of the preference subsets involved.

However, lexicographic ordering does not mean that certain elements are absolutely beyond reach of the exchange, but only that such exchange must take place within a subset of a lexicographic preference order.

5 Adjustments between preference subsets

The fact that one lexicographic subset of preferences is considered more high-ranking than another, does not necessarily mean that it *determines* or *influences* the preferences in the lower-ranking lexicographic subset. It only means that it has a higher priority in the decisions of a given actor; its preferences must be satisfied first before the more low-ranking preferences are satisfied, as indicated above.

However, in the long run choices relating to one lexicographic preference subset may be *adjusted* with respect to the preferences in another, higher or lower, lexicographic subset simply because one subset of preferences is placing constraints on the other subset. I prefer the expression adjustment 'with respect to' rather than adjustment 'to'. By definition, adjustments *to* another lower-ranking lexicographic preference subset is not possible without a breakdown of the lexicographic meta-ranking of preference subsets. Adjustments *with respect to* another lower-ranking subset can take place by settling for less satisfying but still admissible choices within the given higher-ranking subset, as indicated in Figure 14.1.

Let us assume that in a given society the legal subset is ranking higher than the economy subset. In such a case, when legislated house-rent control is preferred in the legal set, this could be met by marginal utility-maximizing rational choices of normally less-preferred alternatives in the economy-set – for instance, by changing over from production of new houses to illegal rent increases in the black market among already existing houses. But in such a case we may also, over time, find adjustments within the legal set with respect to such emerging illegal distortions in the economy, thereby preserving the legal order by making it more realistic. Legislated rent control can be removed and replaced by more market-conforming legislation but with aims similar to those motivating rent control, as a rectifying and realistic adjustment to the actual performance of the market.

6 Actors and structures associated with lexicographic preferences

However, from a sociological point of view any *preference* theory is incomplete without specifying the actors and institutions associated with various preference subsets. Each lexicographic preference subset is thus seen associated with a set of typical actors/agents and institutional structures which are more or less specialized 'bearers'[1] of the relevant preferences. Actors and institutions may thus specialize in certain lexicographic preference subsets, but can also be bearers of several different-ranked lexicographic subsets. For instance, legislators, law adjudicators and law enforcers are typical agents associated with the legal set, while shareholders, managing directors and consumers specialize in the economic set.[2]

Citizens can be considered non-specialists who span over several different subsets in the lexicographic meta-ranking of such sets; they are expected to take all or most of the various subsets into account in their decisions as citizens.

7 Transactions and adjustments between or within preference actors-bearers

The more pronounced the lexicographic preference *specialization* among actor-bearers, the more frequently we find that emerging constraints and conflicts occur *between* the relevant actors with consequent transaction costs for settling of conflicts; the *less specialized* the actor-bearers are, the more frequently we find that emerging constraints and conflicts occur *within* the relevant actors who must arrive at a solution internally, with less transaction costs.

8 Actor involvement in lexicographic constraints

Constraints are normally handled by adjustments with respect to the constraining lexicographic preference subset, as stated above. *Conflicts between* actors-bearers are normally dealt with either through rule-adjudication and compliance with the more high-ranking preference subset – particularly when the legal subset is involved – or through negotiations between actor/ agents representing the preference subsets involved or, in difficult cases, through mediation by agents of a more high-ranking preference set not directly involved in the conflict – usually the legal set, perhaps with the support of citizens obliged to span all or most such preference sets. If such conflicts are left unresolved they could lead to various kinds of actions aimed at undermining the strength of the other side, and intended to force resumption of negotiations or mediation on the basis of these new premises of strength or weakness. Continued failure to arrive at a settlement could eventually lead to a breakdown of the lexicographic ranking of preference subsets, and of social order.

9 Typical resources and outputs associated with preference actors-bearers

Each lexicographic preference subset is also associated with the use of *typical resources*, and with the production, distribution and use of *typical outputs* – goods and services in the economic context; environmental effects in the ecological context; laws and other legal acts in the context of legislation; moral principles in the ethical context; knowledge in the scientific context; metaphysical beliefs in the religious context; children and childrearing in contexts of social reproduction, and so on.

10 Normative, rational, technological and natural orders, and lexicographic orders

While the lexicographic meta-ranking of subsets, their internal rankings and their associated sets of actor-bearers, resources and outputs are part of a historically-grown *normative order*, and while adjustments *within* each subset are determined largely by an *order of rational choice* given typical sets of actors, resources and outputs, the constraints and conflicts that may emerge between such subsets and their actor-bearers are often manifestations of a historically-grown underlying *economic, technological and natural order* characterized by a mixture of economic and technological causal determination, with stochastic variation. The economic, technological and natural orders of seventeenth century European feudalism thus gave rise to other constraints and conflicts between actors and agencies than the periods of early or late industrial capitalism, or the period of centralistic command economies of Eastern Europe. In a historical study of changes in lexicographic preference structures, or even in a study of contemporary preference structures aimed at producing a historically-based understanding of these preferences, we cannot avoid taking the natural order of endowments and constraints, and the technological order into account. The natural and technological orders are often the main factors introducing contradictions between differently-ranked preference subsets, and conflicts between the agents specializing in these different preferences.

11 Between the clock and the cloud – organized lexicographic orders

In the *natural order* of things there are elements and processes which simply are causally incompatible within one and the same concatenated space-and-time unit – for instance, fire and water. In the *economic* order there are elements or processes which cannot be maximized simultaneously within such a unit as a result of a scarcity of resources which is due partly to the natural order and partly to institutional constraints. Such elements and processes may still be brought together for limited periods of time. In *technological* construction it is usually the order of things that elements and processes are artfully combined to prevent incompatible or perhaps stochastic relations, and to maximize harmonious deterministic relations between the components of those artefacts. But technological artefacts such as mechanical machinery and industrial processing of chemicals may exhibit *external effects* as a result of their less than harmonious relations with the surrounding natural and economic orders of compatibilities and scarcities.

Between technological orders and natural, partly stochastic orders – between the clock and the cloud (Popper 1979) – we can distinguish a domain combining elements of both as a result of deliberate but not always perfectly efficient attempts at organization. In such a domain actors can normatively and/or rationally adjust themselves and predict outcomes rather well but not with the same accuracy as in a pure normatively regulated system, or in a mechanical machinery. The capitalist mode of production, competitive markets, parliamentary multiparty democracy and centrally controlled one-party states are examples of such a *mixtum compositum* – neither clock nor cloud, but a mixture of normative, economic, technological and natural orders with stochastic variation. To distinguish them from such orders, we introduce the term *organized orders*, which are made up of lexicographically meta-ranked preferences, their associated actor-bearers, resources and outputs, and some underlying economic, technological and natural orders, as subjected to stochastically-occurring events or 'shocks'.

12 Incompatibilities in organized lexicographic orders, and their possible resolution

More or less incompatibilities, and their correlates – constraints and conflicts – may emerge in organized orders since, at some point, such orders are rooted in a natural order, or in a combination of economic, technological and natural orders which contain elements and processes which are more or less incompatible within the organized concatenating unit bringing these elements and processes together.

However, an organized order – an industrial firm, a trade union, a bureaucracy trying to implement environmentalist legislation, a mode of production, or a society as a whole – can be structured in different ways, given the same basis of economic, technological and natural orders. These different structures may involve more or less incompatibilities, and bring about more or less conflict internally within the actor-bearers, or externally between the actor-bearers in the given organizational nexus. This also means that organized orders can be restructured to minimize constraints and conflicts, and to make remaining conflicts internal to its main actor-bearers, thereby also minimizing costly and possibly disruptive conflicts between actor-bearers. However, this restructuration process itself may necessitate articulation of conflict and struggle. The historical materialism of Marx and his followers has a lot to say about these matters, and its relevance, in some respects, has not been affected, in my view, by the fall of the Eastern European regimes which borrowed the label of Marxism.

While many findings and analytical results among the social sciences can be reinterpreted and followed up within the theoretical framework suggested by the notion of lexicographic preference functions, and related notions of actor-bearers and their associated resources and outputs, it remains to carry out research specifically oriented to illuminating, supporting and refuting the assumptions and conjectures implicit in this kind of framework. Some research questions with this specific focus, and of particular concern in the context of our inquiry into exogenous factors in economic processes, will now be listed with numbers corresponding to the twelve different points made above.

RESEARCH TASKS IN LEXICOGRAPHIC PREFERENCE-ACTOR-STRUCTURE THEORY

1 The mathematization of lexicographic choices

This is a highly complex affair as pointed out by Alan Lewis with reference to Fishburn (1974), but is a necessity for most mainstream economists, and should therefore be pursued to help build a much needed bridge between economics and the 'exogenous domains' of other social sciences. In fact lexicographic choice is applicable even *within* the domain of economics since many commodities on the market – for instance, the motor car mentioned by Alan Lewis in his account of models of choice (p. 168) – may have characteristics which are so important to the consumer that they cannot under any circumstances be traded-off even for other particularly excellent characteristics. Lewis suggests that such lexicographic preferences – even when they are seen as manifesting themselves strictly within the economic domain – are an anathema to some or perhaps most neoclassical economists since 'indifference surfaces cannot be drawn and choice cannot satisfy the axiom of continuity'. Hopefully this kind of resistance can be overcome with mathematization of lexicographic choice and with some necessary further developments of neo-classical theory in such a manner that even non-economic preferences can be taken into account lexicographically, as exogenous constraints on economic rational choice. Amartya Sen (1977) has already suggested that moral and other rules – or 'commitments' – may be viewed as meta-preferences ranging over preferences, more precisely over hypothetical permutations of all of an agent's ground-level preferences. Blegvad and Collin in their chapter of this book (pp. 206–7) have understood Sen's suggestions as an opening in the wall of resistance with which many economists have surrounded themselves to avert the introduction of lexicographic choice in economic theory.

Empirical research methods to establish the existence of a lexicographic structure among different preferences have not yet been extensively tried out and tested. At an individual level, and among aggregates of individuals, this is a task for psycho-metricians (Kelly 1963). They are hereby challenged to undertake this kind of innovative psychometric research. But we can also assume that lexicographic structures of preferences will be reflected in ethical treatises, and legal documents – particularly as they apply to dilemmas and conflicts at the intersection of moral, legal and economic interests. In such cases methods of content analysis of relevant treatises and documents could be developed to establish the existence of lexicographically-ordered subsets of different kinds of preferences. Whether psychometric methods, or methods of content analysis are developed to establish the existence of a lexicographic order of preference subsets, such methods will not be complete unless they are complemented by methods to establish actual behavioural choice in lexicographically-ordered choice situations. It is of course possible that a verbalized lexicographic preference structure is nothing more than a set of dissociated symbol acts with an 'independent emotive meaning' (Stevenson 1944: 72; Himmelstrand 1960: 43–9). In such cases actual behavioural choice is likely to exhibit a structure different from the structure of verbalized preferences. Methods for measuring the extent of 'independent emotive meaning' of verbalized preferences have been developed by Himmelstrand (1960: 72ff, 126ff, 162ff, 193f, 401f).

2, 3 and 4 Varieties of lexicographic preferences. Breakdowns and effects of lexicographic orders

2, 3 and 4. There is a need for further development of research methods to establish which lexicographically-ordered subsets of preference exist in addition to the obvious subset of economic preferences, and to find out where the economy subset is placed in the meta-ranking of preference subsets in given societies. Comparative research on economic systems can probably be further stimulated by incorporating notions of lexicographic meta-preferences. One particularly important circumstance on this point is that the modern economy, being international in character, stretches beyond the national context. While in the national context the economic preferences subset is likely to rank lower than the legal subset of the lexicographic order, they are likely to be ranked higher than the legal set in the international economy where legal rules are non-existent or weak and difficult to enforce. Nationally-based businessmen involved in both domestic and international trade must therefore act on the basis of two conflicting lexicographic orders unless, as loyal national citizens, they give priority to the national order thereby possibly sacrificing part of their potential advantages in responding to competition in the international setting.

For sociologists and political scientists it would be interesting to start investigating the repercussions for a social system as a whole of a meta-ranking of lexicographic preference subsets placing economic preferences at the top, as would seem to be the case in the international system. Such studies could be pursued with particular reference to adjustments in lower-ranking preferences subsets, conflicts among subset actor-bearers, the role of the citizenry in the ensuing conflicts, and consequences for the society as a whole of such conflicts (see Chapter 9 by Leon Lindberg in this book).

The methods to be developed and applied in establishing the relative position of economic preference subsets in lexicographic meta-preferences will come mainly from sociology, social psychology and political science, and perhaps focus on the stigma attached to what we have labelled lexicographic transgressions, and on the stigmatization process through which this can be observed (see point 4, p. 217). Alan Lewis has mentioned some methods of cognitive construct psychology which can be married with lexicographic choice theory and thereby contribute to the empirical exploration of existing lexicographic meta-preference structures at the micro-level (Kelly 1963; Earl 1983).

However, even a macro social science like economic history can be expected to render interesting results on the emergence, maintenance and change of different varieties of lexicographic preference ordering, and the place of the economy in such orders, once it recognizes the usefulness of this approach and develops methods to tackle the research problems involved.

4 Exchange and rational choice within lexicographic preference subsets

We have pointed out that lexicographic choice, far from placing every choice in non-economic domains beyond the reach of exchange relationships such as those explicated by economic theory, only requires that such exchange is seen as taking place within single subsets of the lexicographic preference order. This means that a soft version of, say, public-choice theory may be applicable *within* non-economic domains such as those where its critics have rejected its validity – that is, as long as public-choice theory does not pretend to explain fully the relationships *between* lexicographic preference subsets. While public-choice theorists would be welcomed by non-economic social scientists to pursue the limited kind of explorations in non-economic domains indicated above, there is still every reason to point out that public-choice theory on its own can provide, at best, what Blegvad and Collin (p. 190) characterize as 'local insights' in the field of legal science, and what Samuel Preston (p. 159) highlights as the limited, short-term, cross-sectional validity of public-choice and related neo-classical theory in the field of demography (see also Lars Udéhn's chapter in this book).

5 Adjustments between preference subsets and welfare state 'schlerosis'

Problems of more or less mutual adjustments between preferences in differently-ranked lexicographic subsets is a fascinating and intriguing field of research. Keynesians, neo-Keynesians, post-Keynesians and monetarists have already contributed a great deal to this field without making any references to lexicographic preference functions, but sometimes in a way which, to a non-economist, seems more ideological than scientific – particularly in the axiomatic downgrading, found among monetarists, of the potentially positive role of state interventions. Much of this can be reinterpreted or criticized from the point of view of lexicographic theory.

However, the problem of ideological imposition on scientific analysis is not limited to certain schools of economic theory – monetarism among them – but involves lexicographic theory as well. Unless actually existing, and harmoniously operating, lexicographic preference functions are established independently on the basis of cumbersome empirical research, and taken as exogenously given on empirical grounds, the lexicographic preference order may be stipulated on ideological or normative grounds: the legal order *ought to* take precedence over the economic order, and so on. The best one can ask for in this case is that such normative conceptions are arrived at on the basis of the best available historical and comparative knowledge of how different lexicographic meta-rankings of economic and non-economic domains have functioned in different societies at different times. Simply to deduce from some brand of neo-classical theory, with its limited conceptual horizon, that *optimal* relationships between economic and non-economic domains are this or that, is not good enough, since it converts neo-classical theory into ideology and the economist into a true believer, or what Samuel Bowles in his chapter typifies as a priest.

The kind of theoretically-guided reinterpretations of already available empirical research, and the new research which is needed to illuminate the more or less mutual adjustments made between lexicographically ordered choices certainly requires the involvement of empirically inclined economists, but also calls for the participation of economic sociologists, political scientists and economic historians. Case studies with considerable historical depth would seem particularly suited to enlighten us on how such adjustments are made, what their consequences are, and under what conditions the historical process of adjustments involves a social learning process leading to more consistent and harmonious lexicographic preference functions, or otherwise (see 8 below).

Comparative research on the political economy of societies exhibiting somewhat differently operating lexicographic preference functions is also needed. Mancur Olson's (1982) well-known comparative study, *The Rise and Decline of Nations*, with its focus on 'social rigidities' and 'sklerosis', shows that an empirically-minded economist, in spite of what some may consider to be ideological blinkers, has a lot to contribute to our understanding of some problems illuminated by lexicographic theory. Of particular interest is his finding that Sweden, counter to theoretically/ideologically derived expectations – that is, in spite of its extensive use of state interventions and its emphasis on extensive collective contracts in the labour market – exhibits rather few symptoms of sklerosis and rigidities (Olson 1982: 89–92). Olson's explanation of the deviant Swedish case comes rather close to the points which I will make next on the role of citizenship as a bridge cutting across emerging conflicts between actor-bearers representing different preference subsets in the lexicographic order. Olson points out that Swedish trade unions, in spite of articulating special interests, have moved far beyond the narrow and often stifling focus often associated with trade unions, and with employer's unions in many other countries. Swedish trade unions are 'encompassing organizations' which, because of their extensive and inclusive memberships, and their great power, must show a broader responsibility for the wide-ranging interests of citizens, including economic growth, as well as equity and welfare. In our terminology this could perhaps be explained in terms of a lesser degree of actor-specialization of different lexicographic preference subsets within 'encompassing organizations', and therefore also lesser transaction costs, and less of rigid and 'sklerotic' stalemates in handling conflicts of interests.

One can only hope that more than one economist will embark upon the cumbersome road of comparative economic research in a way that does not imply a biassed selection of countries 'proving' what mainstream economists already profess. However, if economists are marginal utility-maximizing creatures, as Keith Hartley (p. 71) suggests – perhaps with tongue in cheek – and if they allow their rational choice of research topics to reflect only economic preferences, and preferences for applause from like-minded formalistic peers in the community of economists, then there is little hope, of course, that economists will contribute much to the research needed in the problem area indicated above.

6–8 Actors, structures and transactions in various lexicographic orders

It is a macro-sociological task of enormous proportions to study comprehensively the typical actor-bearers and institutional structures associated with different lexicographic preference subsets, their degree of specialization, the 'non-specialized' case of the citizen, the handling of emerging conflicts under conditions of varying degrees of actor-bearer specialization, the historical antecedents and the historical effects on the development of society as a whole of such various conditions. The magnitude of this task can only be compared with Adam Smith's magnum opus *The Wealth of Nations*, or *Das Kapital* by Karl Marx. While we wait for the geniuses capable of responding to this challenge we must move ahead with research on bits and pieces of this complex problem area. Such a limited field of research of particular interest for our work with exogenous factors in economic processes concerns the relationships between citizenship and economic behaviour.

Current changes in Eastern Europe at the beginning of the 1990s will probably provide us both with food for thought, and occasions for analytical reasoning and empirical research on these grand macro-sociological questions. The handling of economic, environmental, legislative, constitutional and moral questions in the newly-emerging societies of Eastern Europe once they find ways of relinquishing command economies to face the challenges of economic growth as well as the threats of unemployment, inflation and social insecurity generated by more or less unregulated market economies, also raises a number of significant analytical and empirical research questions which require the use of a lexicographic preference-actor-structure approach.

Among already available research findings, a comparative study on the past and current operation of the Nordic welfare states, such as the brilliant, and empirically well-grounded book by Alan Wolfe (1989) on the moral fabric of welfare state politics, and its limits, helps to illuminate the problem of what actors and institutions are typically associated with different lexicographic preferences subsets – particularly those involving moral as distinct from legal obligations. Wolfe also addresses the problem which actors/institutions are most suited to be the main bearers of a moral obligation – obviously not the market, and its typical actors. But he also expresses some scepticism about the enduring capability of the welfare state to be a moral agent, and turns to more or less informal agents in 'society', perhaps to the spirit of the citizen and citizen groups, to find the most suitable moral agents in a world dominated by markets, commodified relationships, and formal state interventions.

The legitimacy and workability of the contemporary welfare state with its corollary – a sizeable, largely tax-financed public sector – depends largely on the extent to which citizens are actor-bearers associated with more than just the economic preferences subset in the lexicographic order. In the ideal-typical case the citizen supports an order which ranks ethical and legal subsets higher than economic subsets; she also actively makes choices at all levels according to general rules of priority laid down in lexicographic ranking of preference subsets. A social system structured in this way acts as a set of exogenous parameters, a given condition under which economic processes must be analysed and to which economic agents must lexicographically adjust. But will they in fact do so?

Formally speaking, most economic agents in a country, with the exception of certain Third-World countries where expatriate economic agents abound, are citizens of the country in which they live and work. But more relevant than this formal, administrative definition of citizenship is the sociological ideal-typical definition suggested above. If economic agents are citizens in a sense approximating this ideal type – and this is an empirical question – then they may in fact operate just as we suggested above, namely by adjusting their choices lexicographically, that is by allowing higher-ranking preferences to be satisfied first and then make their rational choices in the economic context within the constraints imposed by the moral and legal order. In countries and in times when the bourgeoisie was the ruling class, and legislators the representatives of this class, those constraints were probably easier to accept for the bourgeoisie than in societies where other social classes have had a major impact on ethics and legislation. The empirical question here is how far economic agents as citizens accept, and in their economic behaviour adjust to, the exogenously-given lexicographic order even in this second case.

Empirical research in this sensitive area is lacking. Much of it can be done by indirect empirical indicators. Three exogenous conditions would seem to be of particular significance in this context, and should therefore be studied with special care. *One* condition is the degree of internationalization of the national business class. In my remarks to points 2, 3 and 4, I have already suggested that the internationalization of national economies may bring about changes in the meta-ranking of preference subsets among economic agents, and perhaps in governments over-sensitive to their demands, so as to place the economic subset higher than the nationally grown legal and ethical sets. This obviously will reduce the weight of citizenship.

However, this process could be partly counteracted by a *second* condition – the frequency and depth of dialogue between agents associated with internationalized economic preference subsets and national agents representing legal and ethical subsets. The extent of such dialogue can, of course, be stimulated and encouraged at a time when economic agents already are 'giving up' the sociological aspects of their citizenship, but then it is usually too late since the economic agents already have the upper hand and are likely to promote a monologue of demands rather than a dialogue. A historically-grown dialogue with roots back in times of much less internationalization is a more favourable condition. That such a dialogue can be historically rooted even in societies where the working class have had a great impact on politics – perhaps particularly in such national contexts, as suggested by the findings of Mancur Olson – was shown, until recently, by the case of Sweden.

A *third* condition could relate to the international experiences of nationally or transnationally based international businessmen. Some of them at least may find that the relative anarchy of international trade, and the vagaries of a transnational existence involves transaction costs and personal costs too high to be neglected in business-like cost-benefit analyses. As a result of such experiences a new understanding of the role of legal and ethical rules may emerge; a greater appreciation of the role of national or regional legislation, and of binding international conventions such as the Bretton-Woods agreement may also arise. Moreover, the kind of lexicographic ordering of preferences implied by national citizenship, sociologically defined, may thus again be favoured but now with a broader base than the single nation. However, this revival and transformation of such an order probably requires that an early dialogue is initiated between actor-bearers associated with different levels of the emerging regional system so that a consistent and legitimate lexicographical order of preferences can be attained in this new and broader context. This conjecture would seem quite relevant in contemplating current and possible future changes within the EEC. The European Common Market during the 1990s offers a great number of significant research topics relating to the emergence and destruction of lexicographic rankings, and their associated rules, actors and institutions.

Some businessmen involved in capitalist international trade can probably be counted out in the process outlined above. These are the businessmen investing most of their time and money on moving money around electronically among the fluctuating currencies and different interest rates of the world today in order to make the most of it. The economist Howard Wachtel (1986) has baptized this category with the telling name *The Money Mandarins*. Their role in amplifying the ups and downs of the international economy and in magnifying the anarchic elements of this economy could be debated – but here what counts is their lack of interest in establishing the kind of consistent and institutionalized lexicographic preference functions indicated above, and suggested in the final chapter of Wachtel's popularly written book – without any reference by Wachtel to lexicographic theory, of course.

9 Are attributes of all outputs suitable for lexicographically unregulated market mechanisms?

The attributes of the typical resources and the typical outputs associated with different kinds of domains and preferences, whether or not they are ordered lexicographically, would seem to be a neglected area theoretically as well as empirically. In my concluding chapter in Part IV (pp. 290–1) of this book I have hinted at the fact that certain attributes of goods and services such as their involvement in rare vs. frequently repeated purchases or use, the time it takes for a trial-and-error process to establish their use value, the degree of irreversibility of effects of their use by consumers, and the extent to which their availability to consumers depend on collective and solidaristic solutions, are extremely important from the point of view of consumer choice. These are the kind of attributes associated with several public goods in health and education. Nevertheless economists who claim to have a theory focusing on marginal utility for consumers seem to be completely uninterested in such attributes of consumer goods and services, perhaps because they are difficult to incorporate in highly-formalized economic theory.

One of the research challenges on this point concerns the possibly comparative advantages from a consumer point of view of supplying goods and services exhibiting certain problematic attributes in a non-commodified or decommodified form through the public sector, where such goods and services have been ethically and scientifically approved, and where legally-prescribed professional competence and responsibility in producing and supplying such goods and services can be given a wider scope.

Expanding this kind of research to include types of resources and output usually not associated with the consumer market would not seem to be immediately relevant for studies on exogenous factors and non-economic preferences in relation to economic processes. But in view of the claims, not only of public-choice theory, but also of neo-liberal politicians that a number of such non-economic resources and outputs can be handled beautifully by market mechanisms, there is obviously a need to pursue research on the attributes of various kinds of non-economic resources and outputs in order to meet the challenge of public-choice theory and neo-liberal politics. Are the attributes of those resources and outputs such that they can be made part of a competitive market without their meaning and their normal use to their users being negatively affected – and then leaving users without a non-market alternative?

10–11 The interplay of normative, technological and natural orders

The points raised regarding the normative order, the order of rational choice, the economic, technological order and organized orders, and their interplay with each other and with their attendant stochastic circumstances, are topics which should be addressed within the macro-sociological research context 6–8 indicated above. The degree of preference subset specialization of actor-bearers mentioned in 6–8, and the constraints and contradictions involved in structures with more or less specialization of this kind is determined to a considerable extent, or as a Marxist would put it, is determined 'in the last instance' by economic and technological orders. Therefore the research problems indicated in section 6–8 must also be dealt with in the context of research problems 10–11.

12–13 Structural incompatibilities, and their resolution, in organized lexicographic orders

To study structural incompatibilities emerging in organized orders, and the related contradictions and constraints within a lexicographic order, and to explore ways of restructuring the organization so as to minimize the contradictions, and the conflicts between agents, is of course much easier in theory (Himmelstrand 1986) than empirically. Such studies necessitate taking the whole historically-grown 'system' of interlocking, and partly contradictory normative-social, economic, technological and natural orders into account. This comes very close to what Samuel Bowles outlines as 'an integrated totality of reproductive and contradictory structures none of which can claim monopoly on economic affairs'. Furthermore, none of these structures are sufficient as explanatory concepts without the insertion of the *practice* of relevant agencies. Still, after having taken an overall synoptic view of this macrocosm, it is possible to single out even in this case some more limited problems regarding incompatibilities, 'contradictions', constraints and inefficiences manifested within some microcosm reflecting the problems exhibited by the larger system.

Kelvin Lancaster's analysis of the 'dynamic inefficiency of capitalism' (1973), rarely quoted by main-stream economists in spite of Lancaster's excellent reputation in such quarters, but quoted the more frequently by Marxist or Marxisizing social scientists, is a good example of this kind of 'microcosmic' analysis which has ramifications much beyond the microcosm under scrutiny. In a highly-formalized and mathematical way Lancaster derives what he calls the dynamic inefficiency of capitalism from the structural fact that capitalists and workers make their decisions separately in a situation where, in the long term, these two categories of actors have incompatible interests in consumption terms. Or to be more precise: workers control their own consumption, within the constraints of the situation, but do not control investment and capital accumulation, whereas capitalists control the allocation of the remainder of output between their own consumption and investment, thereby potentially generating constraints both on investments and workers' consumption. There are no irredeemable pledges about the division of output in the future. This creates a kind of iterated game instability which contributes to suboptimal efficiency, or 'dynamic inefficiency' in the capitalist firm. In this brief summary I have left out the details of Lancaster's formal derivation[3] and I have emphasized only some of the structural contradictions which, according to him, generates this suboptimality.

I have also left out references to some remarks made to me by one reader of an earlier draft of this chapter, namely, that the downfall of the economic systems of Eastern Europe has proved that capitalism is the most efficient of all economic systems. Perhaps capitalism is. But that is not the point at which Lancaster's analysis becomes relevant. Even 'the most efficient' of all actually existing economic systems could be suboptimal. Furthermore, what is interesting in Lancaster's analysis, as read by an economic sociologist, is that he focuses attention on dynamic effects of structural arrangements of different categories of actors – structural arrangements which can be changed to eliminate that sub-optimality while retaining essential features of a capitalist market economy.

Thus even a neo-classically-trained economist can provide a basis for an analysis of capital-labour relationships which conceives workers, not as objects, but in terms of the 'practice' of workers, as Bowles insists. Workers here emerge as actor-bearers of specific preferences which in the capitalist firm are subject to constraints produced by the predominant capitalist economic preference subset. In an ideal-typical capitalist firm, this capitalist economic preference subset is more high-ranking, by definition, than other competing preferences. However, a post-Marxist economist like Samuel Bowles (1985) has asserted that capitalists, and their managers 'will generally select methods of production which forego improvements in productive efficiency in favour of maintaining their power over workers'. In the language of lexicographic preference theory, this implies that there is a preference subset among capitalists with an even higher priority, and meta-rank than the economic preference subset which mostly is considered the highest in a capitalist economic system, namely, the preference for maintaining power over the workers, even if sharing this power with workers might have contributed to lower transaction costs, and to increasing economic benefits, as Lancaster's analysis suggests. Bowles is thus taking exception to Paul Samuelsson's assertion (1957:894) that 'in the competitive model it makes no difference whether capital hires labor or the other way around'. To capitalists it does seem to make a difference, but this is, of course, an empirical question.

It is within the Marxist and post-Marxian theoretical tradition that analyses of structural incompatibilities or 'contradictions' and their ramifications have been most elaborate. In view of the fact that this tradition has occupied a rather peripheral not to say despised position in western academic contexts until recently, and still does to some extent, it is unfortunate that academically more respectable schools of thought have neglected this whole area of research and analysis. If this challenge can be met also within non-Marxist circles of social scientists, it may become easier to link the results of such studies to more respectable analyses of socioeconomic systems. Lancaster's type of analysis needs following up with a wider angle including more than the economic preference subset, and with the use of lexicographic theory.

From the above systematic listing of research tasks which flow from a lexicographic preference-actor-structure approach when analysing exogenously embedded economic systems and processes, it is quite obvious that much research remains to be done in this area. But a lot of the research already carried out in economic history, economic sociology, economic aspects of demography, economic aspects of government and legislation, can also be re-analysed and re-interpreted within a lexicographic preference-actor-structure approach. This is obvious not only when reading Blegvad's and Collin's excellent treatise in this book. When Martinelli and Smelser in their chapter elaborated the contrast between the general economist practice of aggregating individual preferences, and the sociologist's and political scientist's interest in 'contests of collective rationalities', this contrast helps to bring out the need for notions which conceptualize ways of ranking these 'collective rationalities' either in processes of contest and deliberation, or in processes of slow adjustment and historical development. This is where the lexicographic approach can make its greatest contribution, it seems to me. The lexicographic approach provides a framework which permits economics and other social science and disciplines to meet on terms that are not set by either, but is of an overarching interdisciplinary nature, as emphasized by Blegvad and Collin in their chapter.

NOTES

1 My concept of 'bearers' is not conceptually equivalent to Althusser's notion of actor-bearers. An actor-bearer is not an 'abstract instance of abstract processes' but a concrete actor-agent. I have adopted this term from an attempt of mine (Himmelstrand 1986) to design a formalized method of 'actor-process-matrix analysis' (APM-analysis). This method has guided my discussion in the following, without reference to any of the formal paraphernalia involved. At this point a question could be raised about the relationship between my actor-process matrix and the 'social fabric matrix' suggested by Gregory Hayden (1985). It would seem that his matrix is rather too close to what I have called a process matrix. In APM-analysis such a process-matrix is introduced to explore degrees of compatibility or contradiction of processes, and the degree of process concatenation before actors are introduced in the analysis to generate actor-process matrices. Actors are not explicitly entered into Hayden's social fabric matrix, however, but are implicit. This makes it impossible to use the so-called social fabric matrix to account for varying degrees of actor-process differentiation and polarization.

2 For quite particular reasons I have not included workers among specialized actor-bearers associated with the economy subset. In my sociological perspective the worker in democratic 'industrial society' could be seen as the archetypical and ideal-typical *citizen*. His preferences span the whole gamut of the lexicographic order, and are not limited to economic preferences alone. His beliefs about justice in capital-labour relations, and his resentment against 'maltreatment' from management are ethical in character, and may in some countries even be legally based, and involve a conception of what is a fair and just society. Consequently his preference and incentive structure is multi-dimensional (Himmelstrand *et al* 1981: 133–4) and cannot be reduced to the purely economic preferences which occupy a particularly high rank among other agents associated with the economy preference subset. These contentions of mine are in accord with Samuel Bowles assertion in this book (p. 104) that the capitalist firm is basically a political entity. An interesting and provocative theoretical analysis of this problematic can also be found in a paper by Offe and Wiesenthal (1980) on 'Two logics of collective action'. The notion of citizenship is dealt with briefly in the main text at the top of p. 219.

3 A rather detailed summary of Lancaster's derivation can be found in Himmelstrand and Horvat (1987) which also discusses some consequences of his theory for workers' self-management, and some weaknesses of so-called Illyrian theory. However, some mathematically inclined but critical economists have pointed out to me that the mathematical part of Lancaster's argument could have

produced rather different results, in spite of his tests of the robustness of his conclusions – with some slight changes in assumptions about parameters and exogenous conditions. According to these critics, this lack of robustness is a feature of a considerable number of mathematical models in economics. It is usually possible to arrive mathematically at the conclusions you favour, or those favoured among established economists, after some appropriate and usually not verifiable adjustments of your basic assumptions. Of course, this potential weakness of some types of theorizing are inherent also in non-mathematical, say, sociological derivation. Still, what is most convincing to the present author in Lancaster's argument are the non-mathematical and structural or even sociological aspects of his paper.

BIBLIOGRAPHY

Bowles, Samuel (1985) 'The production process in a competitive economy: Walrasian, Neo-Hobbesian and Marxian models', *American Economic Review*, 75, (1), 16–36.

Earl, Peter E. (1983) *The Economic Imagination. Towards a Behavioral Analysis of Choice*, New York, Wheatsheaf-Sharpe.

Fishburn, P. (1974), 'Lexicographic orders, utilities and decision rules: a survey', *Management Science*, 20, 1442–71.

Hayden, F. Gregory (1985) 'A transdisciplinary integration matrix for economics and policy analysis', *Social Science Information* 24 (4), 869–904.

Himmelstrand, Ulf (1960) *Social Pressures, Attitudes and Democratic Processes*, Stockholm, Almqvist & Wiksell.

Himmelstrand, Ulf (1986) 'Formalized historical materialism as a research tool', *International Sociology* 1(2), pp. 113–36.

Himmelstrand, Ulf and Horvat, Branko (1987) 'The socio-economics of workers' self-management" published in a special IDEA issue of *International Social Science Journal*, no. 113, 353–64.

Himmelstrand, Ulf, Ahrne, Göran and Lundberg, Leif (1981) *Beyond Welfare Capitalism, Issues, Actors and Forces in Societal Change*, London, Heinemann.

Kelly, G. (1963) *A Theory of Personality*, New York, Norton.

Lancaster, Kelvin (1973) 'The dynamic inefficiency of capitalism', *Journal of Political Economy*, 81, 1091–109.

Offe, C. and Wiesenthal, H. (1980) 'Two logics of collective action: theoretical notes on social class and organizational form', in M. Zeitlin (ed) *Political Power and Social Theory*, Connecticut, JAI Press, republished in Claus Offe (1985) *Disorganized Capitalism*, Cambridge, Polity Press.

Olson, Mancur (1982) *The Rise and Decline of Nations. Economic Growth, Stagflation and Social Rigidities*, New Haven and London Yale University Press.

Popper, Karl (1979) 'Of clocks and clouds: an approach to the problem of rationality and the freedom of man', in Karl Popper *Objective Knowledge. An Evolutionary Approach*, 2nd edn. Oxford University Press, 206–55.

Samuelson, Paul (1957) 'Wage and interest: a modern dissection of Marxian economic models' *American Economic Review* 47, 884–912.

Sen, Amartya (1977) 'Rational fools: a critique of the behavioural foundations of economic theory,' *Philosophy and Public Affairs* 6, 317–44.

Stevenson, Charles L. (1944) *Ethics and Language*, New Haven, Yale University Press.

Wachtel, Howard (1986), *The Money Mandarins*, New York, Pantheon Books.

Wolfe, Alan (1989) *Whose Keeper? Social Science and Moral Obligation*, Berkeley, University of California Press.

Part IV

Bridging the gap

Chapter 15

The limits of economic imperialism

Lars Udéhn

According to an often quoted definition, 'Economics is what economists do' (Boulding 1955: 3). On this definition, there has been, in the last three decades, a vast expansion of economics into territory previously occupied by political scientists, anthropologists, sociologists and legal scientists (see Hartley, pp. 57ff in this book). This phenomenon has been referred to as 'economic imperialism' (Tullock 1972; Brenner 1980; Stigler 1984; Radnitzky and Bernholz 1987).[1] There seem to be two slightly different forms of economic imperialism. There is, first, Gordon Tullock's more modest version, which recognizes the limitations of economic analysis (Tullock 1972; Tullock and McKenzie 1985: viii) and opts for peaceful coexistence between economics and the other social sciences.[2] But there is also Gary Becker's more aggressive version (1976), which aims at conquering the territory of neighbouring disciplines. This form of economic imperialism launches economics as a general approach to human behaviour that is superior to competing approaches and should, therefore, reign supreme.[3]

The basic intuition behind Project IDEA is altogether different. While recognizing economics as the most developed of the social scientific disciplines – in certain respects, at least – it assumes that the other social sciences also contribute to an understanding of social life, economic life included. The strategy of Project IDEA is to look for interconnections between economics and the other social sciences in the exogenous factors of economic theory (See Himmelstrand, Chapter 1, 'Introduction'). The purpose is to arrive at a better understanding of social phenomena through co-operation and, if possible, to arrive at a more comprehensive theory of economic phenomena.

Given this fundamental difference of approach and strategy, the topic of economic imperialism falls outside the proper scope of Project IDEA. But it is an alternative approach that cannot be ignored. To the extent that economic imperialism is right, Project IDEA is wrong. Considering also the general significance and present popularity of the economic approach to human behaviour, an assessment of its claims seems imperative.[4]

As a challenge to traditional approaches in the other social sciences, the economic approach is, of course, most welcome. Competition between theories and approaches is the key to scientific progress. To the extent that economic imperialism awakens sociologists and others from their dogmatic slumbers and stimulates social scientific debate, it is all to the good. Unfortunately, dogmatism seems evenly distributed between the disciplines. Economics is no exception. The potentially wholesome effects of economic imperialism, therefore, have largely failed to appear. We have seen very little of dialogue, but much more of territorial disputes.

Given the apparent superiority of economics over the other social sciences, one might be led to believe that the latter have something to learn, namely, the economic approach to social phenomena, but nothing to offer in return. This is the view of those advocating economic imperialism (see, for example, Brenner 1980; Lindenberg 1985: 254; see, however, Becker 1990: 43–5). There is no denying that the other social sciences have much to learn from economics, but I would like to believe that the opposite is also the case. It has also been suggested that economic imperialism may be interpreted as an attempt to divert attention from internal difficulties (Schanz 1979: 257). Be that as it may, it is the thesis of this article that economics is of limited fertility outside the traditional boundaries of economics. More specifically, I am going to argue that turning economics into a general theory of human behaviour, by *logical necessity*, also makes it increasingly empty and trivial in content. This argument is *a priori* and not likely to impress those who are already convinced of the relative superiority of economics over rival approaches, such as sociology. A second line of argument, therefore, is to show that economics has failed to give conclusive, or acceptable, explanations of phenomena outside the realm of the market. Since an exhaustive account is impossible, I have singled out for special attention the field of politics. This is because politics is, without compare, that part of social reality most subjected to economic imperialism. The conclusion of my investigation is that there seems to be nothing in politics that economic theory can fully explain and much that it cannot explain at all.

The burden of my argument is not that economics is inapplicable to phenomena outside the market. But I do wish to argue that economic *imperialism*, at least in its strong version, is a mistake. The economic approach can only give a partial explanation of social life. I also believe that this conclusion is supported by recent developments in the social sciences. What we witness today is the decline of the economic empire.

THE DIMINISHING RETURNS OF THE ECONOMIC APPROACH

'The combined assumptions of maximizing behaviour, market equilibrium and stable preferences, used relentlessly and unflinchingly, form the heart of the economic approach as I see it'. These are the words of Gary Becker (1976: 5), who goes on to argue that:

> the economic approach is a comprehensive one that is applicable to all human behavior, be it behavior involving money prices or imputed shadow prices, repeated or infrequent decisions, large or minor decisions, emotional or mechanical ends, rich or poor persons, men or women, adults or children, brilliant or stupid persons, patients or therapists, businessmen or politicians, teachers or students.
>
> (Becker 1976: 8)

I will have nothing to say about the assumption of market equilibrium and little to say about that of stable preferences. My main concern is the fundamental assumption of maximization applied to *all* behaviour; the assumption that all human behaviour is maximizing behaviour. This assumption re-establishes the close link between economics and Benthamite utilitarianism, the difference being that the economic approach does not conceive of utility as a psychic magnitude. The emphasis is upon *maximization*, not upon utility, and maximization is closely akin to rationality. 'By "behaving rationally," I mean "maximizing" consistent behavior that looks forward and tries to anticipate as far as possible what the future will bring' (Becker 1990: 40; see also Arrow 1986: 204–6).

The assumption of rationality is one of the most discussed parts of economics. I will not try to contribute to this discussion, merely comment upon a recent development in the economic theory of 'rational choice'. Most economists admit the obvious: that there is also irrational and non-rational behaviour; that people often commit errors; that they act on impulse, out of habit or tradition, and that they follow rules. Faced with this undeniable fact, economists typically react in one of two ways (cf. Hirschleifer 1985: 59): (1) They admit that the assumption of rationality is often false, or unrealistic, but defend its use as a simplifying assumption, or as a heuristic device. (2) They redefine all human action as rational. I have no quarrel with the first. The second is more of a problem.

But is economics necessarily a theory of rational choice? Kenneth Arrow has argued that economics might equally well be based upon some other behavioural assumption. One plausible candidate would be that people act out of habit (Arrow 1986: 202). This would not be a threat to the identity of economics, if defined by its problems and subject matter, but it would put an end to the economic *approach* within economics.

The question of the identity and distinctiveness of the economic approach is also raised by the theories of *as if* rationality and natural selection (see, for example, Alchian (1950) and Becker (1976: 153–68). According to Milton Friedman (1955: 21f), 'firms behave as if they were seeking rationally to maximize their expected returns . . .'. Only those firms behaving as if they were rationally seeking to maximize returns survive. Rational choice is replaced by natural selection. Economics appears as a branch of biology; alternatively, natural economy and political economy appear as two subdivisions of general economy (Hirschleifer 1977; 1985: 62–6). The question arises why we should choose to call this approach 'economic', rather than 'anthropological', or 'sociological'. It might not be a very interesting question, but it is at least relevant, since biological models and analogies have been much more common in anthropology and sociology than in economics. It becomes even more relevant against Hirschleifer's ideas on cultural evolution and adaptation (1977: 45–9; 1985: 62).

The assumptiom of stable preferences plays an important part in Becker's economic approach to human behaviour:

> Since economists generally have had little to contribute, especially in recent times, to the understanding of how preferences are formed, preferences are assumed not to change substantially over time, nor to be very different between wealthy and poor persons, or even between persons in different societies and cultures.
>
> (Becker 1976: 5; see also Stigler and Becker 1977: 76)

The reason Becker adduces for assuming stable preferences is methodological, not substantive. Explanations in terms of changing preferences are frequently *ad hoc* and used to explain away failures of prediction (Becker 1976: 5). It is, of course, altogether commendable to try avoiding *ad hoc* explanations, but nevertheless I find it a bit odd when Becker suggests that the assumption of stable preferences makes the following of that sound methodological rule easier – as if this consequence were a good enough reason for making that unrealistic assumption. Preferences do change. We all know that and Becker admits that they do (1976: 13f). Is it really reasonable scientific practice to rule out of court hypotheses known to be true?

In fact, Becker's whole economic approach to human behaviour is no less *ad hoc* than what he is trying to avoid by assuming stable preferences. On the contrary, the impression you get from reading Becker, himself, is that of excessive *ad hocery* (see Rosenberg 1979: 513ff; Blaug 1980: 242f; Farmer 1982: 194–6). Any number of auxiliary assumptions seem permitted in order to make the model fit the facts and enhance its *prima facie* explanatory power (see, for example, Simon 1986: 28–8). In addition to more familiar things, such as human capital and information and transaction costs, there are even more elusive entities, such as 'shadow prices', 'psychic costs' and time as a 'scarce resource'. There are such things as a 'taste for discrimination', children as 'durable consumer goods', 'the preference for risk' among offenders and 'utility of separation'. But, as Jon Elster (1979: 156) has argued:

> To postulate costs of information, costs of transaction, psychic costs or different time perspectives just to make the behaviour fit the theory is an unacceptable way out. Some independent evidence for these additional variables should always be given; the *ad hoc* hypotheses should have some independent predictive power.

The assumption of stable preferences, then, is no guarantee against *ad hoc* explanations. The main problem with the economic approach to human behaviour is the vacuity of the assumption of utility-maximization; that it leaves people's utility functions unspecified.[5] The large number of possible arguments in a utility function, leaves the economist with an equally large number of possible explanations of a particular piece of human behaviour. The number of conceivable arguments in people's utility functions becomes unlimited as the economic approach is turned from a specific theory of market behaviour into a general theory of human behaviour. When we turn to non-market behaviour, there is the additional problem of empirical specification, or operationalization. Shadow prices simply lack the reality of money prices that we actually pay. Psychic benefits and costs, although real enough, are difficult to quantify and to measure. The meaning of expressions referring to various psychic costs and benefits, therefore, tends to be metaphorical, or mere guesswork. The result is models flexible enough to 'explain' every fact and finding only because they lack empirical content (see Barry 1970/1978: 31, 33; Rosenberg 1979: 518–22; Blaug 1980: 244–7; Hannan 1982: 71; Etzioni 1988: 30f).

Economic imperialism, then, leads to models with low *empirical content*. This is because of the difficulty to operationalize concepts denoting psychic entities. Opportunities to invoke various psychic costs and benefits *ad hoc* and *post hoc* become unlimited. But this is not all. Economic imperialism leads to low *informative content* as well. Empirical content depends, to some extent, upon informative content, but not *vice versa*. Informative content is *logical* content (Popper 1934/1972: 120). The low informative content of the economic approach to human behaviour is due to its extreme generality.[6]

It is probably the example of the natural sciences which have deluded many social scientists into believing that generality is necessarily and always a good thing. Stigler (1984: 312f) refers, approvingly, to Heinrich Gossen, who compared the scope of utility theory to that of Copernicus's theory of the movements of planets. But this is misleading. Generality increases the informative content and explanatory power of a theory only if its specificity and precision remain constant (Popper 1934/1972: 121ff;

1963: 217ff, 385ff). This seems, indeed, to be the case with some theories in the natural sciences. But if generality can only be increased at the expense of precision and specificity, then there will be a decrease of informative content and, ultimately, of explanatory power. This, I suggest, is the case in the social sciences. The reason is that human beings and social phenomena are dissimilar to a high degree. Therefore, if you wish to say something about all human beings, or all social phenomena, there is very little you can say.

> As a first step, social scientists must recognize that all science is not physics. Physics has obtained equations that apply to all electrons because all electrons are, in the relevant sense, alike. All voters or consumers are not alike. When phenomena are heterogenous, generality can only be gained at the price of content. One is forced to say less and less about each case in order to include all possible cases.
>
> (Roberts 1974: 58)

This simple fact of logic is known as 'the principle of the inverse variation of extension with intension' (Nagel 1961: 575). In the social sciences, it leads to a trade-off between generality and informative content, which sets limits to the fertility of universal laws and assumptions. Unfortunately, this principle is little understood among social scientists. The economic approach to human behaviour is a case in point. One who did understand it was Max Weber. Writing specifically about 'economic laws', he concludes:

> Laws are important and valuable in the exact natural sciences, in the measure that those sciences are *universally valid*. For the knowledge of historical phenomena in their concreteness, the most general laws, because they are most devoid of content are also the least valuable. The more comprehensive the validity, – or scope – of a term, the more it leads away from the richness of reality since in order to include the common elements of the largest possible number of phenomena, it must necessarily be as abstract as possible and hence *devoid* of content. In the cultural sciences, the knowledge of the universal or general is never valuable in itself.
>
> (Weber 1904/1949: 80)

It is easy to see that Weber's argument applies to the economic approach. Stigler and Becker (1977: 89) admit, as a weakness of their approach, that it does not explain 'why some people become addicted to alcohol and others to Mozart'. Nor does it explain why some turn to theft and robbery, while others go to work, or why some pray to God and others to Allah. What the economic approach cannot explain, are differences between people; between religions, cultures, nations, the sexes, ethnic groups, classes, peasants and city-dwellers, superiors and subordinates. In the wonderful world of Becker and company, we are all equal and alike: the mother at home, the manager of the firm, the Buddhist monk, the criminal; the girl who wants to marry, the woman who wants divorce and the man committing suicide; the general who commands and the soldier who obeys, the woman brushing her teeth and the man going to sleep;[7] all of them have this much in common: they are all incessantly engaged in the maximization of their utility, subject, of course, to the constraints of their respective budgets. But as Karl Popper (1957: 154) has remarked, 'we can conceive of very few events which could not be plausibly explained by an appeal to certain propensities of "human nature". But a method that can explain everything that might happen explains nothing'. This is exactly the case with the economic approach to human behaviour.

Economic imperialists may believe that they will emerge victorious. I don't think so, but if they do, theirs will be a Pyrrhic victory, won at the price of an almost complete loss of substance.

THE RISE AND DECLINE OF PUBLIC CHOICE

Outside its traditional domain, the economic approach has proved most useful as applied to politics. In the last thirty years there has been an invasion of economists into political territory. Many political scientists too have surrendered to the apparent power of this novel approach to their field. Being a discipline with a topic, but no particular approach, political science is easily subjected to the influence of neighbouring disciplines.

Before economics became the model, political science received a strong impetus from sociology. There were, in the main, two sources: the movement known as 'behaviouralism' in political science was to a considerable extent an importation from sociology, or its empiricist branch. The main instrument of research, the survey, came from sociology, as did some of the classic investigations.[8]

But political scientists were also much influenced by sociology's theoretical branch; the structural-functionalism of Talcott Parsons. There was, first, a widespread interest in political culture and an emphasis upon the importance of social values for democracy. There was, second, a short upheaval for systems theory, which may have had something to do with Parsons's adoption of this perspective in 1951.

In the 1960s, however, there was a shift in hegemony. Economics replaced sociology as the main external source of inspiration for political scientists (see, for example, Mitchell 1969). Great hopes were placed upon the economic approach (as before upon the sociological approach, or method) as a means of making political theory more scientific or, at least, more explanatory. Behind these hopes lay an important development of the economic approach itself. In the 1940s and 1950s it had become enriched by game theory, dealing with strategic behaviour – a phenomenon of some importance in political life.

In his influential *Sociologists, Economists and Democracy* (1970), Brian Barry set out to compare the sociological and the economic approaches to politics and to democracy in particular. He came to the conclusion that the economic approach is superior to the sociological (Parsonian) approach in rigour and fertility (Barry 1978: 84, 165–83). Unlike many other proponents of the economic approach, however, Barry was aware of its limitations. If the economic approach is superior, this is not because it is terribly good, but because the sociological approach is even worse. This may very well be the case. I am not going to argue the reverse – that the sociological approach is superior to, or even as good as, the economic approach. I believe that a comparison is difficult to the point of being entirely devoid of meaning. In what follows, I am going to argue that there are definite limits to the economic approach to politics; that there are certain phenomena it is not well equipped to deal with, and some phenomena it cannot handle at all. Those political phenomena not amenable to economic analysis have to be treated, however imperfectly, by alternative approaches, whether sociological, anthropological, legal, psychological or belonging to the traditional arsenal of political science.

The economic approach to politics is, in a wide sense of that term, identical with 'public choice'. In a more narrow sense, 'public choice' refers to the Virginia school, headed by James M. Buchanan. In my account of the theory of public choice I am going to concentrate on the latter and on James Buchanan in particular. This may be regarded as an undue limitation of the subject, but I think it can be defended. First, but least important, Buchanan and his early collaborators, especially Gordon Tullock, have a special right to the name 'public choice'. Second, James Buchanan is generally recognized as the head of this school (in 1984 he was awarded the Nobel prize for his role as a founder of 'public choice'). Third, James Buchanan has done more than most proponents of the economic approach to clarify its meaning and proper use in the analysis of political life.

It is common to make a distinction between *positive* and *normative* public choice (Mueller 1976: 23f; 1979: 2–4, 263–70). My interest is in 'positive' public choice, as advanced by people like Anthony Downs, James Buchanan, Gordon Tullock, Mancur Olson and William Niskanen, and not with the more explicitly normative theory of welfare economics and the normative version of the theory of the social contract. This does not mean that I uncritically accept the distinction between positive and normative theory as made by public choice theorists, nor that I fail to see the strong, if largely implicit, normative element in most public choice writing and that of Buchanan in particular. It should be mentioned that Buchanan, himself, has become increasingly aware of the normative

character of his own theory of constitution and also turned it in a normative direction.

According to Buchanan, the theory of public choice is the application
and extension of economic theory and economic tools to politics, or
governmental choice (Buchanan 1978: 3; 1979a: 13; 1986: 13, 19; Brennan
and Buchanan 1984: 185). Alternative names are 'the economic theory of
politics' or 'the new political economy' (Buchanan 1979a: 11). Politics is
the activity having to do with the collective provision of collective, or
public, goods; with public choice. Collective, or public choice, in its turn,
is occasionally equated with non-market choice, but is more often limited
to government, or state activity.

> In my vision of social order, individual persons are the basic component
> units, and 'government' is simply that complex of institutions through
> which individuals make collective decisions, and through which they
> carry out collective as opposed to private activities. 'Politics' is the
> activity of persons in the context of such institutions
>
> (Buchanan 1979b: 144)

A preliminary distinction, then, is between traditional economics as the
science of the private choice of private goods on the market and the new
political economy as the science of the public choice of public goods
through government (see Buchanan 1972: 14–16; Brennan and Buchanan
1985: 34–7).

Having followed Buchanan in his characterization of 'public choice' as
'the economic theory of politics', my next query concerns his definition
of economics. In his view of economics proper, Buchanan is very much
of an Austrian and a follower of his teacher Frank H. Knight. Economics
is seen as a theory of exchange – as *catallactics* (Buchanan 1979b: 19ff;
1986: 19ff; 1989a: 14ff). Buchanan is opposed to seeing economics as a
'logic of choice', because logic is empty and 'objective'. It says nothing
about the choices and exchanges of actual human beings. In particular,
Buchanan is averse to Lord Robbins's famous definition of economics as
'the science which studies human behaviour as a relationship between ends
and scarce means which have alternative uses' (Robbins 1935/1972: 16).
An undesirable effect of this definition, according to Buchanan, is that it
opens the way for turning the economic problem into a mathematical-
technical problem to be solved by some objective utility function, but
with no basis in the subjective evaluations and preferences of individual
human beings. Buchanan's main target of attack is, of course, welfare
economics, which aims at maximizing an objective utility function for the
community as a whole. Lacking any connection with the subjective utility
of individuals, these social utility functions can only reflect the preferences
of economists themselves. The only way to 'solve' a social utility function

is by exchange on the market, or, in politics, by the market analogue of unanimous consent.

When Buchanan turns to public choice, however, it is not exchange, but self-interest, which appears to be the most important constitutive element in the science of economics. The main task of public choice is to replace *homo politicus* by *homo economicus*. According to Buchanan, it is an unacceptable inconsistency to work with different conceptions of man in the spheres of economics and politics; to assume that, on the market, man is moved solely by self-interest and in politics solely by the public interest (Buchanan 1972: 12ff; 1986: 36–8; 1989b: 29, 64f; Buchanan and Tullock 1962: 19ff; see also Stigler 1982: 136ff). This inconsistency is all the more serious when it appears, not between the two sciences of economics and politics, but within the discipline of economics itself. In welfare economics, it is assumed, as a matter of course, that the rational egoist appearing on the market will suddenly turn into a benevolent despot when acquiring political power (Buchanan 1973: 165, 169; 1975b: 177; Brennan and Buchanan 1981: 386f). In opposition to this unhappy state of affairs, Buchanan urges economists to 'close the behavioural system' (1972).[9]

Behind Buchanan, you can trace the influence of his teacher Frank H. Knight, the Austrians and, perhaps most important, the political economy of Adam Smith. Economics, according to this tradition, is essentially the science of self-interested individuals exchanging private goods (and services) on the market. Public choice, then, is the science of self-interested individuals trading public goods in political institutions analogous to the market. What makes public choice an 'economic' science, then, is the reliance upon two assumptions: (1) the *self-interest* of individuals and (2) the *market analogy* of political institutions.[10]

Self-interest in politics

The most important and most controversial contribution of public choice, to a science of politics, has been to challenge the presumption that political man acts in the public, rather than in his own, interest. This assumption, implicit in most political theory, is not only wrong, but dangerous. It makes us unable both to understand political life and to guard against its dangers. If, on the other hand, we assume that political man pursues his own selfish ends, we are able to explain the growth of government and of bureaucracy and to defend ourselves against the new Leviathan.

As we have seen, Buchanan finds it inconsistent to operate with two different conceptions of man. If economics is correct to assume that man is, first of all a selfish creature, then he must be so, not only on the market, but in politics too. The task of public choice, then, is to close the behavioural system (Buchanan 1972: 11ff). The attempt to do so has resulted in a set of new behavioural and, especially, motivational assumptions concerning people in their varying political roles. In this section I will take a look at the most important behavioural assumptions used by public choice theorists and some of the evidence against them. I conclude that, in the light of that evidence, the assumption of egoistic political man cannot be sustained.

Public choice

The first important contribution to a theory of public choice was Anthony Downs's *An Economic Theory of Democracy* (1957). The main novelty of this pioneering work was to populate our political institutions with *homo economicus*; a man who acts rationally (ibid.: 4ff) and for his own selfish ends (ibid.: 27ff, 282ff). For members of political parties, this means that 'they act solely in order to attain the income, prestige, and power which come from being in office'. Politics is reduced to a means for the politicians' private ends. 'Upon this reasoning rests the fundamental hypothesis of our model: parties formulate policies in order to win elections, rather than win elections in order to formulate policies' (ibid.: 28). This hypothesis is operationalized as the assumption that politicians in democratic countries seek to maximize votes (ibid.: 11, 31). Voters act so as to maximize their own utility; the benefits they expect to receive from voting in one way rather than the other; their so-called 'party differential' (ibid.: 36ff, 274). Surprisingly, Downs suggests that his 'model leaves room for altruism in spite of its basic reliance upon the self-interest axiom' (ibid.: 37).

One of the most well-known hypotheses, derived by Downs from his self-interest axiom, concerns competition in a two-party system. Borrowing an idea, originally used by Harold Hotelling in another context, Downs suggests that parties in a two-party system tend to converge ideologically upon the centre (ibid.: 115–17). Ideologies are reduced, by Downs, to mere instruments in the competitive struggle for votes. The function of ideologies is to reduce uncertainty and information costs. Ideologies serve parties mainly by decreasing the need to inform voters about policy and the latter by saving them the trouble of collecting more detailed information about party programmes (Ch. 7).

The assumption that voters maximize their own expected utility has turned out to be the Achilles heel of public choice (see pp. 252–7). Despite the fact that it gives rise to some seriously disturbing questions, however, this assumption has remained an important part of orthodox public choice (see, for example, Tullock 1976: 5; Mueller 1976: 40; 1979: 97).

Politicians and voters are not the only figures in political life. A personage steadily growing in number and importance is the much despised bureaucrat. Having exploded the myth of the benevolent politician, seeking nothing but the common good, public choice theorists shifted their attention to the bureaucrat; this loyal and self-denying servant of politicians and citizens bent on nothing but doing his/her duty. Against this idealized picture of a political eunuch, commonly ascribed to Max Weber, it is argued that bureaucrats, no less than other people, look after their own interests first and, only after that, the interests of others.

The most consistent use of an economic approach to bureaucracy is Niskanen's *Bureaucracy and Representative Government* (1971). Niskanen assumes that bureaucrats are selfish and maximize their personal utility (Niskanen 1971: 36f; 1973: 20f). His interest is in the output of bureaux. Treating them as production units on a par with firms, Niskanen asks what, instead of profit, do bureaux maximize? His answer is: their budgets:

> Among the several variables that may enter the bureaucrat's utility function are the following: salary, perquisites of the office, public reputation, power, patronage, output of the bureau, ease of making changes, and ease of managing. All of these variables except the last two, I contend, are a positive monotonic function of the total *budget* of the bureau during the bureaucrat's tenure of office.
>
> (Niskanen 1971: 38; cf. 1973: 22)

But this is not the whole story. Unlike profits, budgets include costs, which must somehow be introduced as constraints upon budget maximization. The relation between supply and cost may be opaque in the activity of a bureau, but it is not entirely absent. At least, bureaux have to keep their promises and produce what is expected of them. A full statement of the motivational assumption for bureaucrats, therefore, reads like this: 'Bureaucrats maximize the total budget of their tenure, subject to the constraint that the budget must be equal to or greater than the minimum total costs of supplying the output expected by the bureau's sponsor' (Niskanen 1971: 42; cf. 1973: 27; 1978: 164).

I have mentioned politicians, voters and bureaucrats. But there is, in our western democracies, at least, a fourth important political force: interest groups.[11] The classic in this field is, of course, Mancur Olson's *The Logic of Collective Action* (1965/1971). In this work Olson challenges conventional wisdom (including political science, sociology and Marxism) by arguing that 'unless the number of individuals in a group is quite small, or unless there is coercion or some other special device to make individuals act in their common interest, *rational, self-interested individuals will not act to achieve their common or group interest*' (p. 2). The reason is that interest groups trade in collective, or public, goods, which are characterized by non-excludability (p. 14). Public goods, if provided at all, have to be, or are best, supplied to all members of the group. But if this is so, the most rational course of action for a self-interested individual is to take a free ride: to enjoy the benefits of the collective good without contributing to the cost. This is no problem if the group is small, or 'privileged', which means that 'each of its members, or at least some one of them, has an incentive to see that the collective good is provided, even if he has to bear the full burden of providing it himself' (p. 50). But, as the size of the group increases, there is a decrease both in the relative importance of each individual's contribution to collective action and in each individual's share of the collective good. Large, or latent groups, therefore, have to rely on selective incentives, such as journals or insurances, or on coercion, in order to secure support (p. 44). This conclusion leads Olson to advance the so-called 'by-product theory' of pressure groups (pp. 132ff). If the provision of a public good is not enough to motivate people to join an organization, then they must also be organized for some other purpose. Lobbying for collective goods is a by-product of organizations that receive their strength from selective incentives. Olson's logic of collective action calls for a leader, or political entrepreneur, to explain the emergence and existence of interest groups (pp. 174ff).

The main ingredient in the economic approach to politics, then, is the assumption of self-interest. Political man, no less than economic man, acts in his own interest. This view is in line with a long tradition of 'realism' in political theory represented, in varying degrees, by people like Machiavelli, Hobbes, Smith, Tocqueville, Marx, Weber and Schumpeter. It is opposed to another tradition, based upon the assumption that political man acts in the public interest. Which view is the more correct? Probably both are incorrect, if universalized. The most reasonable assumption seems to be that political man is moved both by his own *and* by the public interest. Of course, the extent to which one of them dominates the other varies between persons, institutions and cultures. In what follows, my concern is to argue that political man is not the selfish creature suggested by public choice. I am not foolish enough to deny that he is, generally, much more selfish than we would like him to be.

In his contribution to this book, Leon Lindberg argues that the assumption of selfish political man lacks empirical support. In a recent book by the Swedish political scientist Leif Lewin (1988), we find what comes close to a definitive refutation of public choice. Invoking a massive body of empirical research, Lewin argues that the most common motivational assumptions used by public choice theorists cannot be sustained. Available evidence tends to suggest that political man is motivated by the public, no less than by his private, interest.

Politicians, generally, do not maximize votes. They do not even seek election, or re-election, at all costs. In particular, there is little to support the hypothesis that politicians, by their vote-maximizing behaviour, contribute to the creation of political business cycles (Lewin 1988: chapter 3). 'The emphasis in recent political science contributions seems increasingly to be to point to the lack of empirical evidence for the existence of systematic electorally motivated political business cycles implying sub-optimal economic outcomes' (Lindberg, p. 144 in this book). It might be added that Anthony Downs's hypothesis about a convergence around the centre in a two-party system becomes problematic in the light of the recent rise of a Liberal party in between the Labour and Tory parties in British politics (Heath 1987). Maybe ideology matters to some extent, at least. In any case, Downs's fundamental hypothesis is empirically wrong. But even if politicians were maximizing votes, this would not imply that they were pursuing their own selfish interests. 'Whether a politician is motivated by self-interest or group-interest or any compromise between them, he must win votes to carry out his purpose' (Margolis 1982: 97).

Nor do bureaucrats, generally, maximize the budget of their bureau. Not even those top bureaucrats who are in a position to do so (the vast majority of officials, of course, have no direct influence on the size of the budget). It is not even obvious that budget-maximization is always the best way, for a bureaucrat, to further his, or her, own selfish ends. Sometimes, the way to make a career might be to reduce the budget or at least to save money. A first problem with the budget-maximization hypothesis, then, is that there are many ways for a bureaucrat to act in his/her own interest.

A second problem with the budget-maximization hypothesis is that self-interest is not the only plausible reason for a bureaucrat wishing to increase the budget of his bureau. Also a bureaucrat motivated entirely by a wish to serve the common good and convinced that the public goods supplied by his bureau contribute to this goal, would wish to increase the budget. These complexities make it extremely difficult to test the budget-maximization hypothesis and, especially, the assumption of self-interest. In his article 'Bureaucrats and politicians' (1975), Niskanen cites some empirical studies that support his theory of bureaucracy and representative government. None of these studies, however, has a direct bearing upon the assumption of self-interest. Niskanen finds support for his hypotheses about overspending, inefficiency, oversupply and overcapitalization and the hypothesis that bureaucratic structure matters. But there is no need to invoke self-interest in order to explain these results. They are equally compatible with the assumption that bureaucrats are altruists, or that they are simply trying to do their duty.

The most problematic assumption of public choice is that voters maximize their utility. Already Downs had problems explaining why, on this assumption, people bother to vote at all. The expected benefit of voting in one way, rather than the other, is often small and always surrounded by uncertainty. Why do people take the time and trouble to go to the polls? In the end, Downs had to resort to people's long-term interest in maintaining a democratic political system in order to explain the act of voting (Downs 1957: 265–74). But as Barry (1970/1978: 23) points out, this doesn't help matters, since even this is irrational, given the infinitesimal effect of each vote. Barry concludes, correctly, that the economic approach cannot, except at the cost of emptiness, be modified so as to account for the fact that people do vote. Other factors, such as habit, self-expression and duty must be invoked.

Probably the most effective refutation of the economic interpretation of voting came from the philosopher Paul Meehl (1977). Demonstrating the ultimate 'irrationality' of voting from a utilitarian point of view, he argues, convincingly, that voting can only be explained by using some quasi-Kantian perspective, in terms of duty or obligation.

The fact that people do vote – despite the often negligible and uncertain gains from doing so and despite the infinitesimal probability that their vote will have an effect upon the outcome of an election – is the first conspicuous anomaly confronting an economic theory of politics. We have still to see whether it is enough, to threaten seriously the theory of public choice.

But even if the anomaly of voting does not lead to its overthrow, public choice is in serious trouble and a crisis is to be expected. A sign of this is that Buchanan, himself, takes the matter seriously, indeed. In a remarkable article written with Brennan (Brennan and Buchanan 1984), he abandons most of positive public choice and, especially, the theory of voting. As with Meehl, both the act of voting itself and the choice among alternatives is deemed 'irrational' from a utilitarian point of view. The reason is the absence of any clear connection between the act of voting and the outcome of an election when the electorate is large.

Voters do, in fact, participate in electoral processes, and they care about political outcomes. But there is no logical connection between these two facts, and the absence of this logical connection is crucial. It arises from the fact that the relation between how any individual voter votes and the outcome of the election is virtually negligible. We cannot, therefore, explain voter behavior in terms of preferences over outcomes: Voter behavior must be explained on its own terms. People vote because they want to – period. And neither the act of voting nor the direction of the vote cast can be explained as a means to achieving a particular political outcome, any more than spectators attend a game as a means of securing the victory of their team.

(Brennan and Buchanan 1984: 187)

But if voting does not make sense in a utilitarian framework, how can it be explained. Brennan and Buchanan believe that much voting is 'habitual' (ibid.: 191). They also suggest that it is 'symbolic', or 'liturgical' (ibid.: 196).

Brennan's and Buchanan's critique of public choice is *a priori*, not empirical. They leave open the possibility that people do in fact vote in their own presumed interest and in order to maximize their utility – even if it is not rational – but ask for more evidence (ibid.: 200). I believe that sufficient evidence (if evidence can ever be sufficient) on this point has been provided by Leif Lewin (1988, chapter 2; see also Lindberg, pp. 145f, in this book): it shows that people vote in, what they believe to be, the 'public interest'. It may be added that most people conceive of the public interest in macroeconomic terms as having to do with the overall performance of the economy and, especially, with regard to unemployment and inflation.

It should also be pointed out that Brennan's and Buchanan's rejection of public choice is not wholesale. It concerns only the positive, predictive, branch, but not their own normative, comparative, theory of constitutions (see p. 264). They also wish to save part of the positive theory, especially the part which deals with lobbying (Brennan and Buchanan 1984: 197). This seems reasonable enough. Lobbying is often easy to understand in terms of narrow self-interest, especially in the case of business associations and corporations working upon government in order to obtain competitive advantages. In this case, if the group is small, or 'privileged', lobbying may take the form of a straightforward economic transaction. Nevertheless, it has been argued by Mancur Olson that, when groups are large, the gains from lobbying are insufficient to motivate people to support a lobby. Thus we are led to consider the vexed issue of collective action.

Collective action

Mancur Olson's theory of collective action is, in important respects, analagous to Downs's theory of voting. The important difference is that, whereas Downs leans upon self-interest in his explanation of voting, Olson makes sure at the outset that self-interest is not enough for collective action. Therefore, considering the amount and importance of collective action in the world, Olson's theory does not lend unambiguous support to an economic theory of politics. Howard Margolis has remarked, appositely, that Olson's theory 'overkills the issue' (Margolis 1982: 6).

While acknowledging the free-rider problem as 'absolutely crucial', Margolis correctly observes that it is a problem, not only for collective action, but for economic theory as well:

> The conventional economic model not only predicts (correctly) the existence of problems with free riders but also predicts (incorrectly) such severe problems that no society we know could function if its members actually behaved as the conventional model implies they would.
>
> (Margolis 1982: 6)

After all, people do co-operate. The fact that people vote – the so-called 'paradox of voting' – is the first serious anomaly of an economic theory of politics (see p. 253). The fact that they co-operate, is the second. Voting may, of course, be seen as an instance of collective action, or co-operation.

The most comprehensive discussion of the logic of *Collective Action*, to date, is by Russell Hardin (1982). He argues tht the problem of collective action is identical with that of an N-person prisoner's dilemma. For each person, defection dominates co-operation, irrespective of the choice of the others. But if all players defect, they will all be worse off than if they all co-operate. Universal defection is Pareto-inferior to universal co-operation. The problem of collective action, then, is the prospect of an outcome that is the reverse of Adam Smith's invisible hand. A situation when individual rationality leads to collective irrationality, instead of to the common good (Hardin 1982: chapters 1–2; Barry and Hardin 1982: 23–6).

Hardin argues that the selective incentives, mentioned by Olson, fail to explain all collective action. In particular, Olson's by-product theory does not explain the *origin* of interest groups. Nor does reference to political entrepreneurs. At least, not if they are narrowly self-interested (Hardin 1982: 31–7). Jimmy Hoffa may have been a rational egoist, but hardly Joe Hill. 'Under the logic of collective action, we should expect to see very little large-scale collective action motivated by narrow self-interest . . . Yet we know that many large-scale interests are organized' (Hardin, 1982: 101). This fact can only be explained by assuming 'extra-rational' (read: extra-economic=non-egoistic) motivations, such as morality, the desire for self-development through participation and ignorance about the relation between costs and benefits (Hardin, 82: 102ff).

A fourth extra-economic 'motivation' is contract. A contractarian is a person who plays fair if other people do (Hardin 1982: 90). Contractarianism does not work in a static analysis of a one-shot prisoner's dilemma, where people meet only once, but in a dynamic analysis of an iterated game, contract may suffice to ensure co-operation. In a dynamic context, it is even possible to achieve co-operation on strictly utilitarian grounds (Hardin, 1982, Chapter 10). In this case we may speak of a conventional norm of fairness. But in many cases co-operation is also based upon an ethical *norm of fairness*. What is morality and what is merely convention may in many cases be difficult to tell (Hardin, 1982: 216–19). It is a major shortcoming of Olson's analysis that it is static. The insight that in real life people meet again, and often remember what happened last, has proved to be of paramount importance for an understanding of the logic of collective action. Hardin's theory of iterated games is only one of several attempts to make more realistic use of game theory for this purpose.

An already famous attempt in this direction is Robert Axelrod's computer tournament in an iterated prisoner's dilemma game, reported in *The*

Evolution of Cooperation (1984). Axelrod invited a number of philosophers and social scientists to participate in the tournament, each using a strategy of his own choosing. The tournament consisted of an indefinite number of two-person prisoner's dilemma games, where all participants played against one another. To Axelrod's surprise, the strategy that emerged victorious was the simple 'tit-for-tat', suggested by the well-known game-theorist Anatol Rapoport. Tit-for-tat is the strategy of always co-operating in the first round and to defect only when the other player defects. What this result suggests, is that, in the long run, it is rational even for the egoist to co-operate. The implication for social life – to the extent that it resembles an iterated two-person prisoner's dilemma – would be that co-operation, or social order, is possible even in the absence of government authority.

Axelrod's argument is that co-operation *could* occur even in a world of pure egoists. There are two conditions: 'that the co-operation be based on reciprocity and that the shadow of the future is important enough to make this reciprocity stable' (Axelrod 1984: 173). The second condition is no problem. Under certain, not too unlikely, circumstances, egoists are also likely to meet again. But can reciprocity become established in a world of egoists? As I understand Axelrod, a positive answer to this question hinges upon the possibility that a small cluster of individuals hit upon the strategy of reciprocity by mere chance, learn that it is advantageous and defend it against invasion by other strategies. This is, of course, nothing but a story (cf. Elster 1986b: 24–8). It tells us how co-operation *could* have emerged, given some specified conditions. But did it emerge this way? This is an entirely different matter. One thing is certain: the prospects of co-operation are much greater in a world of altruists and with a morality to defend it. I interpret Axelrod as maintaining that co-operation could emerge in a world of egoists, but can only be maintained by morality. This interpretation presupposes that the norm of reciprocity is a moral rule or, at least, a social norm rather than a mere convention. Axelrod does not discuss this matter explicitly, but it seems to me that he implies that the norm of reciprocity emerges as a convention and develops into a social norm or moral code. In any case, I submit, that norms do not belong in the hard core of economics. If, as in Axelrod's theory, a norm of reciprocity is needed for co-operation to be possible, this is a concession to the sociological perspective. The importance of social norms, for social life and, *a fortiori*, for social science explanations, is brought out more clearly in Axelrod's article 'An Evolutionary Approach to Social Norms' (1986). In addition, we find an emphasis on the fact that real games are played in the context of, indeed, are constituted by, social institutions and social structure (Axelrod 1984: 145ff; Axelrod and Keohane, 1985).

I will end my discussion of collective action with a brief mention of

Jon Elster's latest view on this subject. Most important, for my purpose, is his new-born insight that *homo sociologicus* has a role to play in the explanation of human action, collective action included.

It is Elster's contention that collective action can only be explained by assuming *mixed motivations* (1985: 141ff; 1986b: 16ff; 1989a: 187ff). Besides self-interest, there are altruism, morality and social norms. Altruism is a psychological motive directed at particular persons, whereas morality consists of general principles (Elster 1985: 148; 1989a: 47). Elster also makes a distinction between moral and social norms; the former being consequentialist, the latter non-consequentialist (1985: 145; 1986b: 8f; 1989a: 100f). What this means, is that morality is concerned with the outcome of actions, while social norms tell us to act, or not to act, in certain ways, irrespective of the result. An alternative way of looking at this distinction would be to treat moral norms as a subclass of social norms – those social norms that are justified in terms of the *good*, whether it is freedom, justice, equality or some other moral value. In addition, there are other social norms, such as technical norms and mere conventions. The distinctions between altruism, morality and social norms are not sharp. Though different types of motivation, they shade off into each other. One reason for this is that they have a common basis in emotions (cf. Elster 1989a; 99f; 1989b: Ch. 7).

Elster does not attach much importance to altruism in explaining collective action. The reason is that altruism is limited to a close circle of family and friends (1986b: 25). There remain two categories of non-selfish motivations: morality and social norms. Within these two categories Elster (1989a: 187ff; see also 1985: 148ff and 1986b: 8ff) recognizes three specific types of special importance for collective action: utilitarianism, everyday Kantianism and the norm of fairness. Utilitarianism is a morality oriented wholly to outcome. It motivates people to participate in collective action if it leads to increasing average benefit. Everyday Kantianism is a blend of morality and social norms, but more of the latter. It tells people to co-operate unconditionally, because it is their duty to do so. The norm of fairness, finally, is conditional upon the co-operation of others. It is a norm against free riding.

Elster's idea is that these motivations interact and reinforce one another, so that the result is more than the sum of their isolated effects. They do so, in part, by being effective at different stages in the cumulative development of collective action. The explanation of collective action, therefore, requires a sequential model (Elster 1989a: 204–6; 1989b: 132–4): in the beginning only everyday Kantians co-operate, because they, alone, do so unconditionally and irrespective of outcome. Everyday Kantians, therefore, are necessary to trigger off collective action. If there are enough Kantians, the utilitarians might find it worthwhile to join, thereby creating the conditions necessary for the norm of fairness to come into play. The norm of fairness, by its very 'logic', functions as a multiplier leading to universal co-operation. This sequential model lacks the simplicity and elegance of most economic models, but, according to Elster, something like it is the best we can hope for, in terms of simplicity, at least (1989a: 205).

My discussion of collective action has led progressively away from the theory of public choice. With the possible exception of Mancur Olson, none of the authors discussed could be, or would like to be, associated with the theory of public choice and certainly not with the Virginia school. I suspect that, on both theoretical and ideological grounds, those concerned with the problem of collective action would prefer not to appear under the rubric of 'public choice'. It seems, however, as if the theory of collective action has had an impact on the theory of 'public choice', in a wider sense. In a recent introduction to *Public Choice* (1987), by Iain McLean, the former is incorporated as an important part of the latter. More important, for my purposes, McLean (1987: 3), drops the assumption of self-interest, arguing that economics assumes rationality, but not necessarily self-interest. Rationality is equally consistent with altruism. This is correct. But McLean forgets that many economists consider the assumption of self-interest equally constitutive of economics as that of rationality. More surprisingly, he forgets that this is the case with the founders and most adherents of public choice (see pp. 248–51).

McLean's revised version of 'public choice' is based upon Howard Margolis's influential 'new model of rational choice'. Margolis's objective is to provide the basis for 'an empirically tenable theory of public choice, . . . a model of individual choice that does not fail catastrophically in the presence of public goods'. The presupposition is that 'the conventional model of choice does so fail, the most familiar illustration being its inability to account for the elementary fact that people vote' (Margolis 1982: 1). Margolis's 'new model of rational choice', then, is primarily a theory of social, or public, choice. The theory of private choice appears as a special case, applicable, especially, to behaviour on the market.

Margolis's main idea is to split up the individual in two (or three) – one private man, motivated solely by self-interest (S-Smith), and one public man, motivated only by group-interest (G-Smith). Both are utility-maximizers, but their utility functions are separate and do not intermesh. Thus, there is no way of arriving at a single utility function for both selves, as in Becker's economic approach to human behaviour. Instead, the choices of S-Smith and G-Smith are mediated by an arbiter, or referee (U-Smith), that allocates resources between them according to a rule of 'fair share':

> The larger the share of my resources I have spent unselfishly, the more weight I give to my selfish interests in allocating marginal resources. On the other hand, the larger benefit I can confer on the group com-

pared with the benefit from spending marginal resources on myself, the more I will tend to act unselfishly.

(Margolis, 1982: 19)

Since Smith is, himself, a member of the group, resources allocated to G-Smith are, usually, also in the interest of S-Smith. G-utility includes some S-utility. As a consequence, group-interest and self-interest go a long way together, without clashing.

Margolis's model has the great advantage, over the conventional model of rational choice, of being able to account for the simple fact that people do give and help. Not only as a means to more ultimate selfish ends and not only as an exception, but regularly and for 'higher' ends. Altruism is as much a part of human nature as is egoism.

Of special importance, for my argument, is Margolis's answer to Buchanan's and Tullock's plea for consistency. With Margolis's model, there is no inconsistency in assuming that man pursues his self-interest on the market and the public interest in politics. It is simply a matter of the most efficient – given his/her beliefs – allocation of resources. There is no rational outlet for group-interest on the market. The way it works would give rise to an entirely haphazard use of resources allocated to G-Smith. Also, on a perfectly competitive market, there is an irresoluble conflict between group-interest and self-interest. You cannot allow altruism to affect your choices without causing your own ruin. These are the rules of the game. However, if you wish to contribute to the common good, politics, in a broad sense, is the obvious way to do it.

Throughout his writings, Buchanan upholds the thesis that morality is a scarce resource. In an often quoted article (see, for example, Samuelson 1970: 777; Phelps 1975: 1; Kristol 1981: 203) Dennis Robertson asked 'What does the Economist economize?' His answer was 'love', having in mind Christian love, that is altruism and morality:

There exists in every human breast an inevitable state of tension between aggressive and acquisitive instincts and the instincts of benevolence and self-sacrifice. It is for the preacher, lay or clerical, to inculcate the ultimate duty of subordinating the former to the latter. It is the humbler, and often the invidious, role of the economist to help, so far as he can, in reducing the preacher's task to manageable dimensions.

(Robertson 1956: 148)

But is 'love' a scarce resource? Margolis's model, discussed above, seems to be based on this assumption. But is the assumption warranted? I don't think so. Love is not a scarce resource. We all know that those who have received much love have more to give. But what about morality, strictly speaking? I suggest that it is the same. The idea that we go about with a fixed amount of good deeds that can somehow ebb, like certain natural resources, is absurd. As Albert Hirschman has argued (1984: 93; 1985: 17), morality is an *ability*, not a resource, and like all abilities, it may atrophy if we don't practise. Therefore, we should beware of demolishing those institutions that depend upon morality and civic duty for their proper functioning.

This leads to a reversal of Brennan's and Buchanan's argument for assuming self-interest. Rather than minimizing our dependence upon morality, we should extend its scope. The market is the only place where self-interest meets with social approval or, at least, acceptance. We do not expect good deeds from businessmen, at least not in their ordinary business transactions. Brennan and Buchanan (1985: 60–3) suggest that there is a sort of Gresham's law in politics such that bad behaviour drives out good behaviour.[12] I don't wish to deny the existence of such a mechanism, but I certainly wish to argue that it is more effective on the market. Because of competition, good deeds are virtually impossible on the market. Buchanan seems to argue that standards of morality are higher on the market than in politics (Buchanan 1986: 89).[13] It may be that there is more honesty in business than in politics, though I very much doubt that it is. But if it is, that is because trust is so very important for market exchange (McKean 1975; Stigler 1982: 22). Without honesty, people couldn't trust their business partners and the all-important institution of contract would cease to function and, ultimately, to exist. But honesty, however important, is far from all there is to morality. Business morality is a minimal morality. Therefore, if we wish more social morality, we should minimize market relations, relying instead upon institutions more conducive to good deeds.

Dennis Robertson suggested that it is for the preacher to teach morality. But if the economist is a preacher, teaching egoism? George Stigler (1982) admits that economists have increasingly assumed the role of preacher – equating preaching with policy recommendations – but denies that they have had much influence upon policy (also cf. Bowles, this book, p. 107, where he mentions the role of economists as 'priests'). According to Stigler, this is due mainly to their limited knowledge about the effects of different economic policies. He, therefore, impels his fellow economists to engage in more empirical research, aimed at providing a more secure base for policy proposals. But the economists' preaching is certainly not confined to recommending this or that economic policy. It is the conviction of many economists – perhaps a majority, including, most obviously, the members of the Austrian, Chicago and Virginia schools of economics – that economics, like the other social sciences, teaches a morality (cf. Wolfe 1989: 222–6). Following Knight (1935), Stigler calls it the 'ethics of competition' (1982: chapters 1–2). Self-interest is the central pillar of this economic ethic, preached with much confidence by economists, and especially those from Chicago and Virginia, during the last decades.[14]

Politics as exchange

The economic, or public choice, approach to politics consists, as we have seen, of two elements: the assumptions of self-interest and of exchange. I have dealt with the former, and it remains to take a look at the market analogy. As before, I will concentrate on the work of James Buchanan. And now I am entirely justified to do so. Buchanan, more than any other public choice theorist, sees economics as catallactics and an economic theory of politics as based upon the assumption of politics as exchange.

In this section I am going to argue that there is little actual exchange in political life and that the market analogy, therefore, is of limited value for a theory of politics. The real force of the market analogy is normative, rather than positive.

Following Charles E. Lindblom (1977), I recognize three principal mechanisms of social organization (ibid.: 4), or methods of social control (ibid.: 11–13): exchange, authority and persuasion – all important in politics, but exchange probably the least important.[15] A theory of politics, based upon the politics-as-exchange paradigm, therefore, fails to account for the most important aspects of political life.

Exchange

There is little direct exchange *quid pro quo* in the sphere of politics. The relations between the principal political actors in our western parliamentary democracies – politicians proper, bureaucrats, voters, interest groups and the press – are not relations of exchange, or not predominantly so. To the extent that an element of exchange enters the interaction between political actors at all, this is beside, or within, more basic relations of power and representation. Political exchange, therefore, when it takes place, is rarely between free and equal parts, as on a competitive market.

The relation between politicians and voters, or citizens, is not that of exchange at all. Politicians represent voters and voters 'authorize' politicians to govern the country. I don't deny that you might conceive of the relation between voters and politicians as involving some kind of quasi-contract, but it is very different from contracts between parties to market exchange and not amenable to the same kind of analysis. There is no trade taking place between voters and politicians and, therefore, no possibility of specifying the terms of trade (cf. Brennan and Buchanan 1984: 194f.) Talk about exchange between voters and politicians is metaphorical and, at best, of some heuristic value. Probably the most important contribution of public choice to a theory of voting is Anthony Downs's use of a spatial analogy to explain the distribution of parties over the ideological spectrum. But the important part of this analysis is, exactly, the spatial analogy, not the market analogy.

The relation between politicians and bureaucrats, also, is not that of exchange. What, exactly, do they exchange? Politicians have the power to decide about the budget of bureaux, but what have bureaucrats to offer politicians? According to William Niskanen (1971: 25; 1973: 14), 'A bureau offers a promised set of activities and the expected output(s) of these activities for a budget'. A problem with this suggestion is that these activities and these outputs are public goods for the benefit of the citizens of the state, not just its politicians. What the politician may possibly gain from an exchange with bureaucrats is re-election (cf. Niskanen 1971: 137; 1973: 16; 1978: 164). The gain to politicians from the activities and outputs of bureaux are indirect. An efficient bureaucracy is a good support for elected politicians at the polls. It may be noted that bureaucrats are directly related only to politicians in power, or office. Niskanen has analysed this relation as one of bilateral monopoly. But this is to forget something important: the government has the power, the legal right, or authority (see below), to order bureaux to do the things it wants to see done. Niskanen models the bureau as offering the sponsoring government a package of activities and outputs and the government as a passive recipient of these goods. I don't know to what extent this is an accurate description of reality, but I suppose that politicians sometimes interfere with the working of bureaux (cf. Margolis 1975: 652ff; Peacock 1978: 120ff). At least, they set the goals of the activity. In any case, the fact that governments have, not only the monopoly power, but the legal right, to control the activity of bureaux, makes the relation between them qualitatively different from that of market exchange.

The relation between officials (politicians *and* bureaucrats) and citizens; between the state (and other authorities) and its subjects, again, is that of legal authority, not voluntary exchange. The fiction of a social contract does nothing to alter this fact. According to Hobbes, what the citizen pays in exchange for some order and security is submission to the authority of the sovereign.

The relation between politicians and interest-groups is usually captured by the term 'lobbying'. Included under this rubric is, undoubtedly, a great deal of activity, adequately described as 'exchange'. Interest-groups sometimes (or usually?) buy policies in exchange for their support, financial or other (cf. Brennan and Buchanan 1984: 197). But they are also engaged in an activity better described as persuasion (see pp. 268–72). They work upon the preferences of politicians, directly and indirectly through public opinion.

The relation between interest groups and their members has been modelled, by Mancur Olson (1965: 25–7), as a case of oligopoly. As we have already seen, Olson maintains that it is not in the self-interest of members of large groups to contribute to the provision of collective goods. One reason is that collective goods are characterized by non-excludability, which turns free riding into the obvious option for the rational egoist. But there is another reason: with increasing group-size, the personal gain to each member will normally be less than his/her contribution. One way out of this dilemma is for the interest group to offer some selective incentive. But, usually, this is not enough. Interest groups, or their leaders, have to resort to extra-economic means, that is, *coercion*, to secure membership. According to Olson, then, the relation between interest groups and their members is not that of voluntary exchange.

Public choice has nothing at all to say about the press and other media. There are several reasons for this neglect (see pp. 268–72). One reason is that the mass media are not engaged in exchange, except, of course, in so far as they are involved in business. The political function of the mass media is to provide information and to further the *exchange of ideas*, which is something entirely different from the economic exchange of goods.

There is one obvious form of exchange in politics: log-rolling, or vote-trading, between parties or politicians. This explains the prominent place occupied by vote-trading, including vote-selling, in the theory of public choice.[16] Not only is this phenomenon subjected to much scrutiny, it is defended as an important part of an ideally working democracy. The argument is that vote-trading makes it possible also for minorities to exert some influence and, so, to alleviate the tyranny of majorities. It also opens a possibility for the *intensity* of preferences to matter in political decision-making, something which is impossible with the voting-rule 'one man, one vote'. Vote-trading brings us closer to the ideal of Pareto efficiency. This is the key to Buchanan's analysis of politics-as-exchange (see Buchanan and Tullock, 1962: chapter 18; Reisman 1990: 45–53).

The basic intuition behind Buchanan's analysis of politics-as-exchange is that politics ought to approximate the working of a perfectly competitive market. On the market, resource allocation is Pareto efficient, reflecting the tastes, or revealed preferences, of individuals. There is no special problem of distribution as distinct from allocation. The distribution of economic goods over individuals is a function of the allocation of resources to different uses.

In politics, things are different. As we have seen, there is little *simple* exchange between two parties. In politics, exchange is indirect, or *complex* (Buchanan 1975a: 43–8; 1986: 90; 1989a: 14f; Brennan and Buchanan, 1985: 25). It takes the form of agreement, or consent. But if it is easy for two parties to exchange private goods, to their mutual benefit, on the market, it is impossible for millions of people to agree on the provision of public goods by the state or some other collective agency. Even in a democracy, policy does not reflect the preferences of all voters, but, at best, of a majority of them. As Kenneth Arrow (1951/1963) has shown, no voting rule can transform the preferences of individuals into a consistent set of preferences for the community as a whole.

Buchanan's 'solution' to this problem is to pick up an idea of the Swedish (socialist) economist Knut Wicksell, who argued that the political analogue of economic (Pareto) efficiency is unanimous consent (see Buchanan 1975a: 6–8, 149–51; 1986: 23; 1989b: 62f; Buchanan and Tullock 1962: 8; Brennan and Buchanan 1985: 135–7). The idea is simple and, in itself, unobjectionable: unanimous consent concerning public goods is the only obvious condition in which a change is possible without making someone worse off. But, of course, it is no solution, since it does away with the problem. The problem of social choice occurs only because people have different preferences, making unanimity impossible. Buchanan's 'solution' consists in avoiding the problem by minimizing public choice to those issues, if any, where unanimous consent is possible.

Confronted with the impossibility of everyone agreeing on the production of particular public goods and of accepting his/her share of private goods, Buchanan shifts attention from goods proper to the rules of the economic and political games, namely, the constitution.[17] If people do not agree upon the distribution of wealth, maybe they can be made to agree upon the rules governing its acquisition. If only the game is fair, people may accept the result. The precondition for accepting a particular distribution of wealth, or allocation of resources, is that individuals, when entering the game (the social contract), are uncertain about their future position in the social order. They do not know in advance whether they will eventually turn out to be winners or losers.[18]

Buchanan's analysis, once again, is far removed from anything we observe in reality. No state and no constitution is, or was, the result of an actual social contract and unanimity is impossible in constitutional, as in other, matters. All constitutions are imposed; in most cases by a minority, nowadays more often by a majority. In some countries, the passing of a constitution even requires something more than a simple majority, but unanimity – never. Buchanan, of course, knows this. His intention is not to provide an historical account of what actually happened or, in the words of Ranke, 'Wie Es eigentlich gewesen war'. His purpose is to provide a 'conceptual', or 'logical', explanation of the origin of constitutions (Buchanan 1962: 317–20; 1975a: 6, 54; Brennan and Buchanan 1985: 19ff).

In the end, constitutional economics turns out to be a normative enterprise, like welfare economics (Brennan and Buchanan 1985: 54–6, 65f). The difference is that constitutional economics shifts 'the domain of normative inquiry from the set of imaginable *income distributions* to the set of feasible *institutional arrangements* from which income distributions will emerge' (ibid.: 117). There is irony in this development. Public choice, we recall, started as a movement against welfare economics. The latter was accused of being normative and, above all, of lacking in realism. Public choice, on the contrary, was launched as uncompromising realism, depicting man as the selfish creature he really is. Today public choice, itself, appears no less 'idealistic', both descriptively and normatively.

Authority

The predominant relation between individuals in politics is authority, not exchange (see, for example, Lively 1976; Lindblom 1977: 17–32, 119ff). But authority is in no way confined to the political sphere. It pervades every corner of our society and especially organizations. Authority is important also in the economic sphere. If relations between firms take the form of exchange, those within firms are, largely, in the form of authority. We find authority also outside organizations. Elders used to have authority over younger people. Parents still have some authority over their own children.

Authority is often seen as distinct from power. The difference being that people comply with authority out of their own free will, but bow down to power only against their own will (see, for example, De Jouvenal 1957: 32; 1958: 161). This distinction is inadequate as it stands, since it equates power with coercion, or the capacity to issue credible threats. But we certainly wish to call those people powerful, who get their way mainly by positive sanctions, or inducements. A better distinction is between methods operating upon peoples' preferences and beliefs and those operating upon their situation (cf. Parsons 1963/1986: 104f). Authority, like persuasion, operates upon the preferences and beliefs of people, while power operates upon their opportunity set. Parents offering their children sweets, toys, or money in exchange for their compliance rely upon economic power rather than authority. As methods of control, authority depends either upon personal qualifications, or upon the activation of commitment to rules, whereas power is the capacity to affect the incentives of other people. If authority is exercised through advice or command, power is exercised by means of threats, offers and their combination: 'throffers' (see Barry 1976: 69ff and Taylor 1982: 11ff).

I prefer to see authority as one particular form or, perhaps, basis of power, but will not defend this view here. I see two important sources of power in society: resources, especially property, and rights, or authority. It may be tempting to locate economic power exclusively in the market and authority in the state, but things are a bit more complex, because each of the two forms of power is, to some extent, convertible to the other.

As I have already pointed out, relations within firms, or corporations, are those of authority. Even if there has been, recently, a tendency to the contrary, most firms are still hierarchical structures of command and obedience. But authority within firms is based upon economic power.

Employers buy the right to command their employees, and to organize their firms as authority structures, in much the same way as citizens, according to Hobbes, submit to the authority of the sovereign in exchange for order and security. In the contract between capitalist and worker, the former buys the labour-power of the latter in exchange for a wage. This contract gives capitalists the right to order their workers about while at work. But the analysis could be taken one step further, because economic power, in its turn depends upon property rights, established in the constitution. We could, if we wish, talk about authority over resources, in addition to authority over people. The constitution might seem to be rock bottom. But the rights it defines lend authority only to the extent that it is legitimate. Constitutions may be only *de jure* and defended, ultimately, by naked power.

The state and other authorities, in their turn, do not rule by authority alone. The economic basis of their activity is the right to tax. But this means that the state has vast economic resources, or economic power, in addition to authority. Also, much legislation aims at affecting the incentives of people and is, to that extent, different from authority. Pure authority is limited to the rule of law. But since law is general, it does not dictate what to do in each particular case. Because of this, officials are given discretionary powers, which, in themselves, are part of authority, but which give plenty of scope for exercising power that goes beyond the authority of their office. As the authorities take an increasing interest in the life of citizens, there opens up a new *vista* for the exercise of power on the part of officials.

Power, then, is usually a mixed bag of authority and resources. The main locus and source of power based on property is, of course, economic life. The main seat of authority is, equally obviously, the state. Property gives power to private man. Authority is the form of power proper to public man. While dispersed over society, we find a tremendous concentration of authority in the state. No wonder that the problem of authority has been at the heart of political theory in all times.

According to Talcott Parsons, authority, or 'power', is the proper subject matter of political science. This is not the place to dig deeply into Parsons's complex theory of the social system. Suffice to say that he assigns, to political science, the task of analysing the polity; one of four subsystems of the total social system, or society. The others being the economy, the social and the cultural systems. The polity, or political system, is organized around the specific functional requisite of collective goal-attainment.

Economists, generally, do not pay much attention to the phenomenon of power, especially not economic power. The reason is that they tend to see exchange on the market as voluntary and to the mutual benefit of all parts. To the extent that economists see any power at all, they tend to locate it in the state, but as exogenous to economic life, proper. This tendency, of course, is most pronounced in those of a libertarian persuasion, including those belonging to the Chicago and Virginia schools of economics, and Buchanan is no exception. In a recent article, 'Man and the state', Buchanan argues that 'within the limits of the authority so assigned to the state, we are necessarily subjects, or, more dramatically, slaves, to the state, as master' (Buchanan 1989b: 54). But how, then, is a theory of politics-as-exchange at all possible? There seems to be an irreconcilable conflict between Buchanan, the libertarian ideologist and Buchanan, the political economist.

Buchanan was not first among public choice economists to recognize the phenomenon of authority. In his book *The Politics of Bureaucracy* (1965), Gordon Tullock is perfectly clear about the decisive difference between politics and economics:

> *Generally speaking, 'politics' describes social situations in which the dominant or primary relations are those between superior and subordinate ...* This general meaning can perhaps best be clarified by comparison and contrast with 'economics.' The latter as a discipline describes social situations in which persons deal with one another as freely contracting equals.

(Tullock 1965/1987: 11)

Summarizing, we can say that economic theory is based on the assumption that the central behavioral relationship to be analysed is that among freely contracting individuals. This relationship is recognized to be an approximation to reality rather than an accurate description in all but a few limiting cases. Economic theory abstracts from the other aspects of the human relationship, and studies its own limited part of reality. There are important areas for which the economist's assumptions are clearly inapplicable, notably the government bureaucracy.

(ibid.: 13f)

According to Tullock, then, there can be no economic theory of the state. And yet he advocates the economic approach to politics (Tullock 1976: 1–6; Buchanan and Tullock 1962: Ch. 3) and to all human behaviour (Tullock and McKenzie 1985: Ch. 1). The solution to this seeming puzzle is that Tullock conceives of the economic approach as being confined to the assumption of self-interest (see Buchanan 1986: 26).

But what of Buchanan, himself, who identifies economics with exchange more than with self-interest? In his 'Foreword' to Tullock's book on bureaucracy, he suggests that it is 'economic' in approach only, but not in content. This is not an objection, however. Buchanan admits that the political relationship is different from the economic. Rather than looking upon it as a relation of authority, however, Buchanan sees the political relation as a form of slavery (Tullock 1965/1987: 5). Buchanan is, thus, aware of the limits to an economic theory of politics at an early stage (1965) in his intellectual development (see also Buchanan, 1963/1979b: 33ff). But this does not prevent him from propagating an economic theory of politics-as-exchange, while remaining silent (to my knowledge) upon the subject of the political relationship of authority (which is surprising, indeed, for a follower of Hobbes). Until recently, that is. In the 1980s, Buchanan introduces the distinction between 'economics as catallaxy' and 'political science' or simply 'politics', the former being concerned with exchange and the latter with authority, or power. He observes that it 'is the same distinction as that proposed by some political scientists and sociologists (for example, Talcott Parsons)' (Buchanan 1986: 21; see also 1989a: 15). As a consequence of this recognition of a science of politics that is not economic, Buchanan now explicitly repudiates economic imperialism. Together with the sociologist Viktor Vanberg, Buchanan makes the categorial distinction between 'the economy' and 'organizations', such as clubs, associations, unions, firms and states. 'The essence of organizational membership is subjection to the authority system . . .' (in Buchanan 1989b: 330)

The obvious implication of this argument is that the scope of public choice is severely restricted. It is limited, in its scope, to the play of self-interest and exchange within (and between) relations of authority. What this means, in quantitative terms, is impossible to say. But this much is safe to say: there are definite limits to economic imperialism.

Persuasion

Authority does not make up the only limitation there is to an economic theory of politics. Standard economic theory assumes certain things as given to analysis. These things include technology, institutions and preferences. My present concern is with preferences, and I wish to add: beliefs. This exogenization of preferences gives rise to another serious shortcoming of the economic approach to human behaviour. We certainly want to know, not only how people with certain preferences and beliefs choose, but how they acquired those preferences and beliefs in the first place, and why they differ between individuals, classes and cultures. Despite some attempts to explain preferences endogenously, it has been the concern of the other social sciences to explain the formation of preferences and beliefs. Now, this is not exactly news. It is precisely what Gordon Tullock suggested in his article 'Economic imperialism'.

Economists in general have been relatively little interested in the preferences that individuals have. They assume the preferences and then deduce what the outcome is but do not pay such attention to investigation of these preferences. Traditionally, an economist will tell you that this is a problem for the psychologist rather than the economist. In practice, however, it is not only the problem of the pscyhologist, it has to a very large extent been the problem of the sociologist and of the behavioralist political scientist. A great deal of the research of the sociologists, behavioralists, and political scientists concerns the type of person who is apt to be involved in some particular activity. This can be thought of as an effort to determine which people have certain sets of tastes and preferences.

(Tullock 1972: 323)

Tullock does not only register a traditional division of labour between the different social sciences, he goes on to argue that it is a proper and desirable division. '(M)y proposal for the future organization of social sciences is that they be divided into two grand domains, the sciences of choice and the sciences of preferences' (ibid.: 324). I do not accept this division, at least not as stated by Tullock. As I have already indicated, preferences must be supplemented by beliefs. But, more important, I do not accept it because norms cannot be reduced to 'preferences', as conceived by a theory of rational choice, and much behaviour is governed by norms. What matters here, however, is preferences and beliefs.

But why argue something that public choice theorists already know and admit? First, because I am not certain that all public choice theorists are aware of the implications of this limitation for public choice as a theory of politics. Second, because I do not believe that many social scientists, who are not economists, know that this is a limitation of economic theory. Third, because, the matter has not been given much attention, neither by public choice theorists, nor by others. The argument of this subsection is that public choice, by working with fixed preferences and beliefs, leaves out much of what is generally considered essential to political life (cf. March and Olsen 1984: 739; Wildavsky 1987: 5).

One exception to the rule that economists assume fixed preferences, is the dissenting voice of Albert Hirschman. While sometimes seen as a contributor to public choice (see, for example, Mueller 1979: 125), Hirschman is critical of its scientific imperialism (Hirschman 1970: 19f; 1981: 267ff, 298ff) and his view of politics is fundamentally different. Public choice delimits the political domain to the provision of public goods. Others suggest the more inclusive category of collective action (Taylor 1987: 20). As opposed to both these views, Hirschman derives his view of politics from his now famous distinction between *exit* and *voice*. As different ways of influencing the behaviour of an organization, exit belongs to the economic and voice to the political realm.

The customer who, dissatisfied with the product of one firm, shifts to that of another, uses the market to defend his welfare or to improve his position; and he also sets in motion market forces which may induce recovery on the part of the firm that has declined in comparative performance. This is the sort of mechanism economics thrives on. It is neat – one either exits or one does not; it is impersonal – any face-to-face confrontation between customer and firm with its imponderable and unpredictable elements is avoided and success and failure of the organization are communicated to it by a set of statistics; and it is indirect – any recovery on the part of the declining firm comes by courtesy of the Invisible Hand, as an unintended by-product of the customer's decision to shift. In all these respects, voice is just the opposite of exit. It is a far more 'messy' concept because it can be graduated, all the way from faint grumbling to violent protest; it implies articulation of one's critical opinions rather than a private, 'secret' vote in the anonymity of a supermarket; and finally, it is direct and straight-forward rather than roundabout. Voice is political action par excellence.

(Hirschman 1970: 15f)

I agree that voice is political action par excellence, but it is not the only type of political action. I have already discussed the exercise of authority, which is something else. Nevertheless, Hirschman points to something important, and even though he does not address the issue of preferences at this point, the implication is clear: one, obvious, aim of raising one's voice is to change the preferences and beliefs of those in authority.

In a later work, *Shifting Involvements* (1982), Hirschman takes explicit issue with the economists' habit of working with fixed preferences (1982: 5, 9ff). His specific purpose, in this book, is to argue that there is a recurrent shift, or cycle, between the pursuit of private and public interest. Periods of withdrawal from public life and an exclusive concern with private happiness are followed by outbursts of collective action aimed at the transformation of society, or parts of it. The key to an understanding of preference change is disappointment; with political activity in the first case and consumer goods in the second case. A serious deficit with the standard economic analysis of political activity, according to Hirschman (ibid.: 85), is the failure to understand that such activities 'carry their own reward'. Participation in collective action is not in all circumstances a cost we must pay. In many cases people receive a benefit, not only from the results of such activity, but from the activity itself (see also Hirschman 1981: 290–3 and 1985: 11–15). *Activism*, might be a value, or 'good'.

Still later (1984: 89f; 1985: 8–11), Hirschman makes the distinction between two kinds of preference change: (1) the usually unreflective change in tastes and (2) the reflective change in values. Behind this distinction, is a theory of tastes and values as two types of preferences related to each other as first-order preferences and second-order meta-preferences. In addition to our preferences for consumer goods and services, we have meta-preferences for our preferences. We reflect upon our first-order preferences and change them in accordance with the kind of person we want to be and with our values.[19]

The disregard of preference formation and change in the theory of public choice, reflects orthodox economic methodology. It is possible, however, to surmise a libertarian blessing of this neglect in the case of Buchanan and a majority of his public choice fellows. Libertarians are those liberals who see economic, or market, freedom as the 'essence' or basis, of a free society. They see the need for a state, as a 'nightwatchman', but wish to minimize its activity, as, indeed, all political activity, to a small number of public goods. Preferences are revealed and satisfied on the market and, in the case of public goods, with the vote. But there is another liberal tradition, which is equally concerned about freedom of mind, conscience, speech and the press. Part of the *Utopia* of this tradition, is the creation of a public sphere (see Habermas 1962/1989) where public man (see Sennett 1978) participates in the shaping of public opinion (see, for example, Lippman 1922).

The recent work of Jürgen Habermas (1984; 1987), can be seen as a continuation and radicalization of this, second, liberal tradition. The foundation of Habermas's critical theory is a pragmatic theory of communicative competence. In order for communication, mutual understanding, to be possible, certain conditions must be fulfilled. Habermas recognizes five validity claims raised in communication: (1) Truth of propositions and efficacy of teleological actions, (2) rightness of norms of action, (3) adequacy of standards of value, (4) truthfulness or sincerity of expression and (5) comprehensibility or well-formedness of symbolic constructs (Habermas 1984: 305ff). To the extent that these validity claims are satisfied, we approach an ideal speech situation, which is also a precondition for an optimally functioning democracy. This is the least controversial part of Habermas's theory of communicative action. More difficult to accept is his suggestion that history actually leads in the direction of this ideal speech situation. Habermas argues that historical development is a collective learning process with an inbuilt tendency towards mutual understanding. Be that as it may, the attempt is certainly heroic. Of immediate interest, however, is the fact that James Buchanan and Viktor Vanberg recently distinguished two interpretations of the role of agreement in politics: 'the *social contract notion* and the *dialogue notion* of agreement' (Vanberg and Buchanan 1989: 46). Buchanan's constitutional economics, of course, belongs in the first category, while Habermas's theory of communicative action equally obviously belongs in the second category. The main difference between them is that, while constitutional economics starts from given preferences and beliefs and seeks the preconditions for a compromise, the theory of communicative action assumes that it is possible to change people's preferences and beliefs so that they agree. 'Stated differently, *agreement* is viewed as a *discovery* process, a process by which persons [do] not simply reach a compromise but 'discover' what – in some objective sense – *is* fair or just' (ibid.: 57).

Habermas's ideal speech situation represents the bright side of persuasion. But there is another, dark, or 'irrational', side of the coin. Post-modernism is the fashion of the day and its primary aim is the deconstruction of rationalism, or 'logocentrism'. Post-modernism is not at all impressed by the power of rational argument, but much more so by the power of rhetoric. The term 'persuasion' is sometimes used, in a more narrow sense, to denote rhetoric, rather than dialectic, or rational argument. I use the term to signify both.

We have seen, over the past century, a bureaucratization and technocratization of politics. This development, by itself, diminishes the scope for persuasion, especially as rhetoric. But we have also seen, over the past decades, a revolution of the mass media. We do not know the exact effects of this technological development, but we know that the consequences for politics are tremendous. One thing that we do know, is that the mass media may be used, and are used, for persuasion. There is also reason to believe that the mass media favour the art of rhetoric, at the expense of the more noble art of dialectic.

To conclude: there are many forms of persuasion, including rational argument, rhetoric, education, indoctrination, propaganda, brainwashing. They are all used in politics and form an important part of it. We may not know very much about the different ways of persuasion, but it is of the utmost importance that we keep them constantly before our eyes. Lack of vigilance may prove fatal: Hitler, for one, knew how to use persuasion. Unfortunately, an economic theory of politics is of no help, whatsoever, in the understanding of this important, and potentially dangerous, phenomenon. It lacks the theoretical and methodological equipment necessary even to address the issue.

CONCLUSION

The aim of this article has been negative, namely, to criticize economic imperialism by pointing to some obvious and other less obvious limitations of the economic approach. A positive approach might have been preferable, but is more difficult to accomplish. Much has happened in the other social sciences in the last thirty years, but it has not led to a clearly-developed alternative to the economic approach. To reject economic imperialism entirely, therefore, is tantamount to suggesting a return to a state of social science before economists began to show imperialist ambitions. Or perhaps worse, since the main alternative, sociology, has moved in the direction of increasing disarray. A wholesale rejection of economic imperialism is not what I suggest. Clearly, models based on rational choice have much to contribute to our understanding of behaviour outside the market. The point is to see the limits.

There are clear signs that the economic empire is on decline, especially in political science. The number of critical voices increases steadily and fast. A growing number of defenders of the economic approach, or, more generally, of rational choice, also begin to see its limitations. This increasing awareness of the limits to economic imperialism has led to various attempts to revise the economic approach and even to combine it with other approaches, such as the sociological. Most of these attempts focus on the model of man. Instead of one-dimensional economic man, we hear of mixed motivations and multiple selves.[20] Closely akin to these models of man is the suggestion by Blegvad and Collins and Himmelstrand, in this book, that peoples' preferences are lexicographically ordered. To the extent that different social scientific disciplines deal with different and 'incommensurable' sets of preferences, we have a basis both for division of labour and co-operation.

Instead of focusing on man, we might direct our attention to institutions and, *a fortiori*, to organizations. This is, very much, the traditional approach of anthropology, sociology and political science. We may see a return to traditional institutionalism, in the wake of economic imperialism as suggested by Geoffrey Hodgson in his contribution to this book, and in his own book, *Economics and Institutions* (1989).[21] But there is also the possibility of combining institutionalism with rational choice. Traditional institutionalism ignored the individual. Traditional economics ignored institutions. Much of contemporary rational choice, including some versions of the 'new institutional economics', seems intent upon doing justice both to the individual agent and to social institutions. Maybe these combined approaches represent a step forward in the development of the social sciences?

NOTES

1 Richard Swedberg (1990: 14) has traced the term 'economic imperialism' to R. W. Souter (1933) *Prolegomena to Relativity Economics: An Elementary Study in the Mechanics of an Expanding Economic Universe*, pp. 94f.

2 It may be mentioned that R. B. McKenzie eventually lost faith in the omnipotence of economics. See his 'The Non-Rational Domain and the Limits of Economic Analysis' (1979), where he complains that economists have lost sight of the limitations of their methods. As a consequence, McKenzie did not paticipate in the fourth edition of Tullock and McKenzie (1985).

3 See, however, Becker (1976: 14) where he admits that 'many noneconomic variables are necessary for human behavior' and also denies 'trying to downgrade the contributions of other social scientists'. See aso Becker (1990) where he tries to soften down his economic imperialism. I don't know how to interpret Becker's ambiguous position. If non-economic variables make a difference, then the economic approach must be complemented by other

approaches. In the end, however, Becker seems to believe that rational choice is enough. Having conceded that sociologists are concerned with the big problems, he ends by suggesting that their solution depends upon adopting rational choice.

4 Economic imperialism is discussed and criticized also in several other contributions to this book, but especially in that of B. M. Blegvad and F. Collins, which deals with the economic theory of law and the property rights paradigm, in particular.

5 A highly problematic feature of utility-maximization, which I am not going to discuss, is the dubious assumption of homogeneity, or substitutability of all goods. Attempts to overcome this difficulty usually involve the idea of lexicographic preferences (see, for example, G. W. Nutter (1976), A. K. Sen (1979) and, in this volume, B. M. Blegvad and F. Collins, pp. 206–9 and U. Himmelstrand, ch. 14).

6 An argument, similar to the one advanced here, can be found in A. Etzioni (1988: 27ff).

7 Cf. A. S. Blinder, 'The Economics of Brushing Teeth' (1974); D. S. Hammermesh and N. M. Soss, 'An Economic Theory of Suicide' (1974) and T. C. Bergstrom, 'Towards a Deeper Economics of Sleeping' (1976). Is it a joke, or not?

8 I think especially of Lazarsfeld, Berelson and Gaudet (1944) and Berelson, Lazarsfeld and McPhee (1954).

9 In a similar vein, Assar Lindbeck (1976) calls for an economic analysis with 'endogenous politicians'. It should be pointed out, however, that Lindbeck is more macro-oriented and less willing to accept *homo economicus* wholesale. Politicians are both selfish and benevolent, but increasingly selfish as they approach election day.

10 This conclusion receives strong support from Buchanan himself (1989a: Ch. 21). The public choice perspective, he says, is a combination of two elements: (1) The *homo economicus* postulate and (2) the politics-as-exchange paradigm. While the first element has dominated the public choice theory of bureaucracy, Buchanan's constitutional analysis relies heavily upon the second.

11 There is, in addition, the press as an important political power, but public choice has nothing at all to say about it. Probably that is because the mass media have no place in a theory which assumes stable preferences.

12 A similar argument can be found in Friedrich von Hayek's *The Road to Serfdom* (1944/1991), Routledge Chapter 10, with the title: 'Why the worst get on top'.

13 See, however, Brennan and Buchanan 1981: 387ff., where they seem to admit that political man is a better or, at least, less egoistic man than is economic man. For a history of the defence of commerce, relative to politics, see Hirschman (1977).

14 For a powerful attack upon the assumption of self-interest in politics, see Mansbridge (1990).

15 Lindblom makes no claim to having achieved a classification that exhausts possible alternatives. A similar classification of 'ways of getting people to do things' can be found in Michael Taylor, 'I shall subdivide them into power (treating coercion as a subclass of the ways in which power can be exercised), force or physical constraint, persuasion, the activation of commitments, and authority' (1982: 2).

16 The sociologist James Coleman (1964: 170ff; 1966: 621ff; 1972: 145ff; 1973:

60, 75ff) has developed a theory of social exchange that seems to be a generalization of the phenomenon log-rolling.

17 Of vital importance for an understanding of Buchanan's constitutional economics is his distinction between decision-making within a framework of rules and decisions about the rules themselves (1975a: x; 1989b: 57f; Brennan and Buchanan 1985: 5–7). A more complete analysis reveals, at least, three levels: (1) Decisions within a legal framework, (2) Decisions about laws and regulations, but within a constitution, and (3) Decisions about the constitution, which are necessarily also within the constitution, or we end in an infinite regress (cf. Buchanan and Tullock 1962: 6, 15). The legal framework, then, is a two-layered structure (cf. Buchanan 1981: 440ff). The constitution has a special status, since it comprises laws about legislation. The implication for public choice is this: while private market transactions take place within the constitutions *and* other laws and regulations, decisions about public goods by the state are regulated only by the constitution (cf. Buchanan 1975a: 35ff).

18 Buchanan's approach has a certain similarity to that of John Rawls in *A Theory of Justice*. Buchanan accepts Rawl's analysis of justice as *fairness* and sees in his own (and Tullock's) use of uncertainty about future position in constitutional choice an analogue to Rawl's 'veil of ignorance' (Buchanan 1975a: 70f, 175–7, 181 n. 4; 1979b: 196 n. 5; 1986: 126ff, 168, 243ff; 1989a: 27f, 65f).

19 Cf. Sen (1979: 102ff). Hirschman's analysis also connects with the idea of lexicographic preferences as used by Blegvad and Collins and Himmelstrand in this book.

20 See, e.g. Elster (ed.) (1986a).

21 See also March and Olsen (1984, 1989).

BIBLIOGRAPHY

Alchian, A. A. (1950) 'Uncertainty, evolution, and economic theory', *Journal of Political Economy*, 58, 211–21.

Arrow, K. J. (1951/1963) *Social Choice and Individual Values*, New Haven, Yale University Press.

Arrow, K. J. (1986) 'Rationality of self and others in an economic system', in Hogarth and Reder (eds) (1986).

Axelrod, R. (1984) *The Evolution of Cooperation*, New York, Basic Books.

Axelrod, R. (1986) 'An evolutionary approach to norms', *American Political Science Review*, 80, 1095–111.

Axelrod, R. and Keohane, R. O. (1985) 'Achieving cooperation: strategies and institutions', *World Politics* 38, 226–54.

Barry, B. (1970/1978) *Sociologists, Economists and Democracy*, Chicago, University of Chicago Press.

Barry, B. (1976) 'Power: an economic analysis', in Barry (ed.) (1976).

Barry, B. (ed.) (1976) *Power and Political Theory. Some European Perspectives*, London, John Wiley.

Barry B. and Hardin, R. (1982) *Rational Man and Irrational Society?* Beverly Hills, Sage Publications.

Becker, G. S. (1976) *The Economic Approach to Human Behavior*, Chicago, University of Chicago Press.

Becker, G. S. (1990) 'Interview', in Swedberg (1990).

Berelson, B., Lazarsfeld, P. F. and McPhee, W. (1954) *Voting: A Study of Opinion Formation in a Presidential Campaign*, Chicago, University of Chicago Press.

Bergstrom, T. C. (1976) 'Toward a deeper economics of sleeping', *Journal of Political Economy* 84, 411–12.

Blaug, M. (1980) *The Methodology of Economics*, Cambridge, Cambridge University Press.

Blinder, A. S. (1974) 'The economics of brushing teeth', *Journal of Political Economy* 82.

Boulding, K. E. (1955), *Economic Analysis* New York, Harper & Brothers.

Brennan, G. and Buchanan, J. M. (1981) 'The normative purpose of economic "science": rediscovery of an eighteenth-century method', in Buchanan and Tollison (eds) (1984).

Brennan, G. and Buchanan, J. M. (1983) 'Predictive power and the choice among regimes', in Buchanan (ed.) (1989b).

Brennan, G. and Buchanan, J. M. (1984) 'Voter choice. Evaluating political alternatives', *American Behavioral Scientist* 28, 185–201.

Brennan, G. and Buchanan, J. M. (1985) *The Reason of Rules. Constitutional Political Economy*, Cambridge, Cambridge University Press.

Brenner, R. (1980) 'Economics – an imperialist science', *Journal of Legal Studies* 9, 179–88.

Buchanan, J. M. (1962) 'Marginal notes on reading political philosophy', in Buchanan and Tullock (1962).

Buchanan, J. M. (1972) 'Toward analysis of closed behavioral systems', in Buchanan and Tollison (eds) (1972).

Buchanan, J. M. (1973) 'The Coase theorem and the theory of the state', in Buchanan and Tollison (eds) (1984).

Buchanan, J. M. (1975a) *The Limits of Liberty. Between Anarchy and Leviathan*, Chicago, University of Chicago Press.

Buchanan, J. M. (1975b) 'The political economy of the welfare state', in Buchanan and Tollison (eds) (1984).

Buchanan, J. M. (1978) 'From private preferences to public philosophy: the development of public choice', in Buchanan, *et al.* (1978).

Buchanan, J. M. (1979a) 'Politics without romance: a sketch of a positive public choice theory and its normative implications', in Buchanan and Tollison (eds) (1984).

Buchanan, J. M. (1979b) *What Should Economists Do?* Indianapolis, Liberty Press.

Buchanan, J. M. (1981) 'Constitutional restrictions on the power of government', in Buchanan and Tollison (eds) (1984).

Buchanan, J. M. (1986) *Liberty, Market and State*, Brighton, Wheatsheaf Books.

Buchanan, J. M. (1989a) *Essays on the Political Economy*, Honolulu, University of Hawaii Press.

Buchanan, J. M. (1989b) *Explorations into Constitutional Economics*, Texas A & M University Press.

Buchanan, J. M. and Tollison, R. D. (eds) (1972) *Theory of Public Choice. Political Applications of Economics*, Ann Arbor, University of Michigan Press, 317–29.

Buchanan, J. M. and Tollison, R. D. (eds) (1984) *The Theory of Public Choice – II*, Ann Arbor, University of Michigan Press.

Buchanan, J. M. and Tullock, G. (1962) *The Calculus of Consent. Logical Foundations of Constitutional Democracy*, Ann Arbor, University of Michigan Press.

Buchanan, J. M. and Vanberg, V. (1989) 'Organization theory and fiscal economics: society, state and public debt', in Buchanan (1989b).

Buchanan, J. M., *et al.* (1978) *The Economics of Politics*, London, The Institute of Economic Affairs.

Coleman, J. (1964) 'Collective decisions', *Sociological Inquiry* (Spring), 166–81.

Coleman, J. (1966) 'Foundations for a theory of collective decisions', *American Journal of Sociology* 71, 615–27.

Coleman, J. (1972) 'Systems of social exchange', *Journal of Mathematical Sociology* 2, 145–63.

Coleman, J. (1973) *The Mathematics of Collective Action*, London, Heinemann.

De Jouvenal, B. (1957) *Sovereignty. An Inquiry into the Political Good*, Chicago, University of Chicago Press.

Downs, A. (1957) *An Economic Theory of Democracy*, New York, Harper & Row.

Elster, J. (1979) *Ulysses and the Sirens: Studies in Rationality and Irrationality*, New York, Cambridge University Press.

Elster, J. (1985) 'Rationality, morality, and collective action', *Ethics* 96.

Elster, J. (ed.) (1986a) *The Multiple Self*, Cambridge University Press.

Elster, J. (1986b) 'The norm of fairness', paper prepared for the conference 'Rationality and Social Norms', Paris, 31 May – 1 June 1986.

Elster, J. (1989a) *The Cement of Society. A Study of Social Order*, Cambridge University Press.

Elster, J. (1989b) *Nuts and Bolts for the Social Sciences*, Cambridge University Press.

Etzioni, A. (1988) *The Moral Dimension: Toward a New Economics*, New York, The Free Press.

Farmer, M. K. (1982) 'Rational action in economic and social theory: some misunderstandings', *Archives Européennes de Sociologie* 23, 179–97.

Friedman, M. (1955) *Essays in Positive Economics*, Chicago, University of Chicago Press.

Habermas, J. (1984) *The Theory of Communicative Action*, vol. 1, *Reason and the Rationalization of Society*, Boston, Beacon Press.

Habermas, J. (1987) *The Theory of Communicative Action*, vol. 2, *Lifeworld and System: A Critique of Functionalist Reason*, Boston, Beacon Press.

Habermas, J. (1962/1989) *The Structural Transformation of the Public Sphere*, Cambridge, Polity Press.

Hammermesh, D. S. and Soss, N. M. (1974) 'An economic theory of suicide', *Journal of Political Economy* 82, 83–89.

Hannan, M. T. (1982) 'Families, markets, and social structures: an essay on Becker's *A Treatise on the Family*', *Journal of Economic Literature* 20, 65–72.

Hardin, R. (1982) *Collective Action*, Baltimore, Johns Hopkins University Press.

Hayek, F. A. (1944/1991) *The Road to Serfdom*, Routledge.

Heath, A. F. (1987) 'The economic theory of democracy: the rise of the liberals in Britain', in G. Radnitzky and P. Bernholz (eds) (1987).

Hirschleifer, J. (1977) 'Economics from a biological viewpoint', *Journal of Law and Economics*, 1–52.

Hirschleifer, J. (1985) 'The expanding domain of economics', *American Economic Review* 75, 53–68.

Hirschman, A. O. (1970) *Exit, Voice, and Loyalty. Responses to Decline in Firms, Organizations and States*, Cambridge, Mass., Harvard University Press.

Hirschman, A. O. (1977) *The Passions and the Interests. Political Arguments for Capitalism before Its Triumph*, New Jersey, Princeton University Press.

Hirschman, A. O. (1981) *Essays in Trespassing. Economics to Politics and Beyond*, Cambridge, Cambridge University Press.

Hirschman, A. O. (1982) *Shifting Involvements. Private Interest and Public Action*, Oxford, Basil Blackwell.

Hirschman, A. O. (1984) 'Against parsimony: three ways of complicating some categories of economic discourse', *American Economic Review* 74, 89–96.

Hirschman, A. O. (1985) 'Against parsimony: three easy ways of complicating some categories of economic discourse', *Economics and Philosophy* 1 (expanded version of Hirschman, 1984), 7–21.

Hogarth, R. M. and Reder, M. W. (eds) (1986) *Rational Choice. The Contrast between Economics and Psychology*, Chicago, University of Chicago Press.

Knight, F. H. (1935) *The Ethics of Competition and Other Essays*, London, George Allen & Unwin.

Kristol, I. (1981) 'Rationalism in economics', in D. Bell and I. Kristol (eds) *The Crisis in Economic Theory*, New York, Basic Books.

Lazarsfeld, P. F., Berelson, B. and Gaudet, H. (1944) *The People's Choice*, New York, Columbia University Press.

Lewin, L. (1988) *Det gemensamma bästa. Om egenintresset och allmänintresset i västerländsk politik*, Borås, Carlssons Bokförlag.

Lindbeck, A. (1976) 'Stabilization policy in open economies with endogenous politicians', *American Economic Review* 66, 1–19.

Lindblom, C. E. (1977) *Politics and Markets. The World's Political-Economic Systems*, New York, Basic Books.

Lindenberg, S. (1985a) 'An assessment of the new political economy', *Sociological Theory* 3, 99–114.

Lindenberg, S. (1985) 'Rational choice and sociological theory: new pressures on economics as a social science', *Zeitschrift für die gesamte Staatswissenschaft* 14, 244–55.

Lippmann, W. (1922/1946) *Public Opinion*, New York, Penguin.

Lipset, S. M. (ed.) (1969) *Politics and the Social Sciences*, New York, Oxford University Press.

Lively, J. (1976) 'The limits of exchange theory', in Barry (1976).

McKean, R. N. (1975) 'Economics of trust, altruism and corporate responsibility', in Phelps (ed.) (1975).

Mckenzie, R. B. (1979) 'The non-rational domain and the limits of economic analysis', *Southern Economic Journal* 46, 145–57.

McLean, I. (1987) *Public Choice. An Introduction*, Oxford, Basil Blackwell.

Mansbridge, J. J. (ed.) (1990) *Beyond Self-Interest*, Chicago, University of Chicago Press.

March, J. G. and Olsen, J. P. (1984) 'The new institutionalism: organizational factors in political life', *American Political Science Review*, 734–49.

March, J. G. and Olsen, J. P. (1989) *Rediscovering Institutions. The Organizational Basis of Politics*, New York, The Free Press.

Margolis, H. (1982) *Selfishness, Altruism and Rationality. A Theory of Social Choice*, Chicago, University of Chicago Press.

Margolis, J. (1975) ' "Comment" on Niskanen', *Journal of Law and Economics* 18, 645–59.

Meehl, P. (1977) 'The selfish voter paradox and the thrown-away vote argument', *American Political Science Review* 71, 11–30.

Mitchell, W. C. (1969) 'The shape of political theory to come: from sociology to political economy', in Lipset (ed.) (1969).

Mueller, D. C. (1976) 'Public choice: A survey', in Buchanan and Tollison (eds) (1984).

Mueller, D. C. (1979) *Public Choice*, Cambridge, Cambridge University Press.

Nagel, E. (1961) *The Structure of Science*, London, Routledge & Kegan Paul.

Niskanen, W. A. (1971) *Bureaucracy and Representative Government*, Chicago, Aldine – Atherton.

Niskanen, W. A. (1973) *Bureaucracy: Servant or Master?* London, The Institute of Economic Affairs.

Niskanen, W. A. (1975) 'Bureaucrats and politicians', *Journal of Law and Economics* 18, 617–43.

Niskanen, W. A. (1978) 'Competition among government bureaus', in Buchanan, *et al.* (1978).

Nutter, G. W. (1976) 'On economism', *Journal of Law and Economics* 19, 263–8.

Olson, M. (1965/1971) *The Logic of Collective Action. Public Goods and the Theory of Groups*, Cambridge, Mass., Harvard University Press.

Parsons, T. (1963/1986) 'Power and the social system', in S. Lukes (ed.) *Power*, Oxford, Basil Blackwell.

Peacock, A. (1978) 'The economics of bureaucracy: an inside view', in Buchanan, *et al.* (1978).

Phelps, E. S. (ed.) (1975) *Altruism, Morality and Economic Theory*, New York, Russell Sage.

Popper, K. R. (1934/1972) *The Logic of Scientific Discovery*, London, Hutchinson.

Popper, K. (1975) *The Poverty of Historicism*, (second edition) London, Routledge & Kegan Paul.

Popper, K. R. (1963) *Conjectures and Refutations: The Growth of Scientific Knowledge*, New York, Harper & Row.

Radnitzky, G. and Bernholz, P. (eds) (1987) *Economic Imperialism. The Economic Method Applied Outside the Field of Economics*, New York, Paragon House Publishers.

Reisman, D. (1990) *The Political Economy of James Buchanan*, London, Macmillan.

Robbins, L. (1935/1972) *An Essay on the Nature and Significance of Economic Science*, London, Macmillan.

Roberts, M. J. (1974) 'On the nature and conditions of social science', *Daedalus*, 47–64.

Robertson, D. H. (1956) *Economic Commentaries*, London, Staples Press Limited.

Rosenberg, A. (1979) 'Can economic theory explain everything?' *Philosophy of the Social Sciences* 9, 509–29.

Samuelsson, P. A. (1970) *Economics*, 8th edn., New York, McGraw-Hill.

Schanz, G. (1979) 'Ökonomische theorie als sozialwissenschaftliches paradigma?', *Soziale Welt* 30, 257–74.

Sen, A. K. (1979) 'Rational fools: a critique of the behavioural foundations of economic theory', in F. Hahn and M. Hollis (eds) *Philosophy and Economic Theory*, Oxford, Oxford University Press.

Sennett, R. (1978) *The Fall of Public Man*, New York, Vintage Books.

Simon, H. A. (1986) 'Rationality in psychology and economics', in Hogarth and Reder (eds) (1986).

Stigler, G. J. (1982) *The Economist as Preacher*, Oxford, Basil Blackwell.

Stigler, G J. (1984) 'Economics – the imperial science?', *Scandinavian Journal of Economics* 86, 301–13.

Stigler, G. J. and Becker, G. S. (1977), 'De Gustibus Non Est Disputandum', *American Economic Review* 67, 76–90.

Swedberg, R. (1990), *Economics and Sociology*, Princeton, NJ: Princeton University Press.

Taylor, M. (1982) *Community, Anarchy and Liberty*, Cambridge, Cambridge University Press.

Taylor, M. (1987) *The Possibility of Cooperation*, Cambridge, Cambridge University Press.

Tullock, G. (1965/1987) *The Politics of Bureaucracy*, New York, University Press of America.

Tullock, G. (1972) 'Economic imperialism', in Buchanan and Tollison (eds) (1972).

Tullock, G. (1976) *The Vote Motive*, London, The Institute of Economic Affairs.

Tullock, G. and McKenzie, R. B. (1985) *The New World of Economics. Explorations into the Human Experience*, Homewood, Ill., Richard D. Irwin.

Vanberg, V. and Buchanan, J. M. (1989) 'Interests and theories in constitutional choice', *Journal of Theoretical Politics* 1, 49–62.

Weber, M. (1949) *The Methodology of the Social Sciences*, New York, The Free Press.

Wildavsky, A. (1987) 'Choosing preferences by constructing institutions: a cultural theory of preference formation', *American Political Science Review* 81, 3–21.

Wolfe, A. (1989) 'Market, state and society as codes of moral obligation', *Acta Sociologica* 32, 221–35.

Chapter 16

In search of an interdisciplinary approach for economic and social analysis

Ulf Himmelstrand

Let us recall the main reasons for launching an interdisciplinary, or at least multi-disciplinary approach to economic processes and events.

Historically there have been an increasing number of factors and actors entering the arena of economic processes and events which contribute to the *complexity* of contemporary societies. At the same time economic theory has undergone a process of successive theoretical *simplification*, from classical to neo-classical economic theory. As a result of these two simultaneous and divergent, not to say contradictory trends, we are now faced with an increasing discrepancy between an increasingly complex global reality and an increasingly simplified theory which would seem to be unable to account for what goes on economically in the real world.

One of the strategies proposed to overcome this discrepancy is the strategy of 'scientific imperialism' which was assessed in the previous chapter, and found wanting. In this chapter we will focus more of our attention on an interdisciplinary approach. But initially we will briefly illustrate the possible usefulness of a purely *heuristic*, and in that sense not substantively imperialist, application of economic theory in under-standing non-economic events and processes.[1] Some of the papers pro-duced for the IDEA Project by specialists in non-economic disciplines have made use of economic theory in this manner, to assess its limits and to discover 'missing factors' not usually recognized by economists in understanding or changing the world.

In the following I will first deal briefly with some heuristic applications of economistic imperialism as reflected in papers written for this project, and then proceed in the remaining sections to summarize and extract those points in previous chapters which are suggestive of a multi-disciplinary or even interdisciplinary approach to the analysis of economic processes and events.

SOME HEURISTIC APPLICATIONS OF ECONOMISTIC IMPERIALISM

If a marginalist rational-choice approach produces hypotheses which rather frequently are falsified, or predictions that fail, and if these negative instances are taken seriously rather than as 'exceptions' to be disregarded, then they can turn out to be powerful instruments in the discovery of new facts or possibilities. But such instances can be seen as interesting deviant or negative cases, only if there is a reasonably firm and precise hypothesis or prediction to be disconfirmed. A few illustrations of predictions which failed will be called to our attention from the papers included in Part III of this book, with the purpose of indicating the fruitfulness, as well as the limitations, of marginalistic scientific imperialism.

Cyril Belshaw, eminent social anthropologist, but perhaps not typical of this multifarious discipline,[2] in a paper not included in this volume, was the only one of our non-economic project participants who explicitly supported a heuristic and perhaps even a weak version of substantive marginalist imperialism (Belshaw 1986). He asserted that the explanatory power of Gary Becker's rational-choice model is 'considerable'. Provided that 'measurement is possible – testable hypotheses abound'. But he was also aware in that paper that predictions derived even from such a powerful model may fail. 'The model then enjoins the search for "missing factors" or the factors which were not appropriately weighted in the original schema'. In this way we can discover that Gary Becker and rational-choice economists 'need to adjust the schedule of preferences accordingly' (Belshaw 1986), or that they must be prepared to 'add elements into the preference schedule' that may seem 'non-rational', such as search for prestige, altruism, asceticism, and so on.

Obviously Cyril Belshaw was convinced, in that paper, that social anthropology and ethnology can contribute to the clarification of the role of such superficially non-rational elements in a manner which can be brought to bear on our understanding of exogenous factors in economic analysis; but ultimately he prefers incorporating, that is, endogenizing such exogenous variables into the basic models of marginalistic rational choice offered by neo-classical and public choice economic theorists.

There are obvious risks of circular reasoning in this kind of position, as Lars Udéhn has shown in the previous chapter. If human action typically is considered rational by definition, then you only need a certain mix of anthropological knowledge and imagination to explain any kind of outcome by reference to 'needed adjustments of the schedule of preference'. But Belshaw concurs with 'the special meaning of rationality in classical economics, where the concept is truly tautological' (Belshaw 1986), and he seems to find the tautological character of this concept in order, as a necessary axiomatic foundation of this imperial theory. However, it may turn out to explain nothing at all by claiming to explain too much.

Other writers, while not endorsing such a marginalist imperialism, but taking a more or less critical stance to it, still provide many interesting examples of marginalistic predictions that fail and thus may help to trigger that search for 'the missing factors'.

Samuel Preston, in his chapter on linkages between demography and economy, while admitting that there is 'no more powerful analytic framework available' than the neo-classical models for explaining *cross-sectional* variation in demographic behaviour, still asks whether the exogenous variables on which these models focus 'are where the action is'. With regard to *trends* in fertility and mortality 'it seems that much of the action lies outside the core of the neo-classical framework', Preston contends. Technical improvements in methods of disease control, the diffusion of knowledge, however rudimentary, of the germ theory, and its application in the spread of sanitary practices have turned out to be much more important than any economic circumstances; and such technical and sanitary improvements and their implementation in their turn cannot be successfully predicted over time with the help of neo-classical models. Large comparative social science projects have found that predictions by neo-classical theory on fertility decline have failed. These projects highlight the importance of 'culture' as represented by linguistic group, religious and political practice in conditioning the decline of European fertility in the past century. Once begun, this culturally determined fertility decline spreads quickly irrespective of levels and changes of economic conditions. However, in addition to the narrow, cross-sectional and local validity of some neo-classical predictions, Preston finds a small niche for a possibly successful application of neo-classical theory also among innovative elites whose behaviour perhaps can be seen 'as a straightforward neo-classical response to changes in endowments and prices (including family planning programs)', and whose innovative adoption of family planning then in a second step may spread to the rest of the population, where cultural factors allow this to happen.

As a political scientist, Leon Lindberg asserts that there is no evidence of electorally motivated political business cycles such as those predicted by public choice theorists – that is, booms fabricated by politicians before elections for vote-maximizing purposes, and demand-propelled inflation or other crisis symptoms after elections. Neither is there any empirical evidence of any general tendency toward budget-maximizing bureaucracies, according to Lindberg.

Around the turn of the century about 60 per cent of the Swedish state budget was allocated to military defence.[3] Today that percentage is devoted to covering welfare costs, including cash transfers, while defence exhibits about the same percentage figure today as the social welfare expenditures of *anno dazumal*. Of course no public choice theorist would say that these changes in budgetary allocations are due to a diminishing budget-maximizing inclination in the military bureaucracy, and an increasing budget-maximizing tendency of welfare bureaucrats. The budget-maximizing propensity must be constant, since it is axiomatic. Variations in budgetary allocations such as those mentioned above can only be due to variations in exogenous constraints, opportunities, challenges and institutional factors which counteract, prompt or amplify the 'budget-maximizing propensity'. If that is the case, however, would it not be correct to say that these exogenous factors are the really significant ones in determining the budgetary allocation process while the 'budget-maximizing propensity' as such is only the medium through which these factors operate? Perhaps the 'missing factors' are the main determining factors?

Some of the 'missing' exogenous factors that public choice theorists may have failed to take into account in making their predictions of electorally motivated political business cycles, and which can be 'discovered' by extending the area of application of marginalist theory, as suggested by Cyril Belshaw, are the inability of politicians to fabricate booms when needed, and the fact that marginal voters are far from completely myopic and amnesiac, and that parties and politicians are interested, not only in short-term vote-maximizing and re-election, but also may have a concern for the long-term effects of political decision-making on the economy and on the party (cf. Lindberg in this volume). *The question is, however, whether we could not discover these matters without empirically pursuing the kind of marginalist imperialism which finds an expression in rational or public choice theory.*

In all fairness, however, it must be admitted that the 'missing factors' may not always be possible to identify with the same clarity when we try to discover them without the helping hand of neo-classical or public choice theory. We should also remember what Samuel Preston emphasized; that neo-classical theory, in its own kingdom or in its imperial territories, may be more powerful as a predictor in cross-sectional studies within one cultural context, that is when the *ceteris paribus* clause is not only arbitrarily stipulated but reasonably realistic. Blegvad and Collin also emphasized, in their chapter, that neo-classical may have some limited empirical validity *locally* where conditions and circumstances are relatively constant.

There are other neo-classical predictions than the ones we have covered so far which seem more plausible simply because they are derived from an *economic* analysis of government *economic* policies rather than from an 'imperialistic' application of economic theory in the domain of politics generally. For instance, high public spending and taxing are predicted to generate poor performance with regard to economic stabilization and growth. But even here there is no empirical evidence convincingly supporting such a prediction; if anything there is a weak association in the opposite direction, according to Lindberg (p. 148). The so-called *crowding-out* effect has not been generally confirmed – except analytically, under special circumstances rarely prevailing. Perhaps the direction of causality is opposite from the one assumed: good economic performance in a democratic society allows and generates high public spending and taxing? Another possible explanation of the lack of confirmation of the crowding-out effect is poor book-keeping on the part of economists who have maintained the existence of this effect. They seem to have forgotten that a large portion of the percentage of GNP which they attribute to the public sector consists of money transfers to citizens, for instance, in the form of retirement pensions – money which to a very large extent goes to private consumption of commodities produced in the private sector which thereby is boosted rather than crowded-out. Furthermore, a significant portion of public expenditure goes to the creation and maintenance of public infrastructure utilized by the private sector which it may not itself be able to produce at a lower cost and at the level of quality required. Again, the private sector is not crowded-out by these public expenditures but rather relieved of costs that otherwise could be much higher.[4]

A more politico-sociological interpretation of the lack of unambiguous evidence for a crowding-out effect in countries like Sweden with a large public sector is that high public spending and taxing usually has gone together with a strong and responsible labour movement – what Mancur Olson (1982: 89 ff) has called 'encompassing organizations' – which at the same time has caused public sector expenses to be considered legitimate among a majority of the electorate, *and* helped to promote an accord between capital and labour which operates as a kind of comparative economic advantage for the country, thus promoting reasonably competitive economic growth.[5]

The causal structure implied by the kind of politico-sociological interpretation suggested above is represented in Figure 16.1.

The lower and upper parts of the diagram represent feedback loops involving exogenous social and political factors mediating the feedback. This is an exogenous impact of type IV in our method of dissection.

A related mechanism is hinted at in Lindberg's conjecture that 'non-interventionist strategies without compensation tend to create continuous political conflicts that disrupt the functioning of the market-place. A stable settlement of the distributional gains and pains of economic change is a political prerequisite for a smoothly running economy', according to Lindberg. To the extent that this conjecture could be shown to receive empirical support in comparative, cross-national studies, it would constitute a failure of predictions made by monetarists but also by some neo-classical economists. Conflict or accord among political and economic actors would appear to be an intervening non-economic variable in vicious or beneficial feedback circles affecting the operation of the economy. Amitai Etzioni's

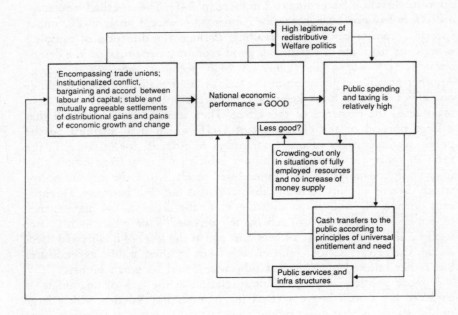

Figure 16.1 An Alternative to 'crowding out'. A possible causal structure.

(1985) conjecture about 'encapsulated competition' is also highly relevant on this point. Etzioni argues that competition on the market may easily destroy or undermine market mechanisms themselves in a self-destructive manner, unless protected against itself by a 'capsule' of institutional arrangements. On this point the reader is also referred to Geoff Hodgson's chapter in this book.

The causal structure of the exogenous explanations suggested above for predictions that failed should not be difficult to understand among economists. Still they may have objections. First of all they can reject the validity of those studies which seem to disconfirm predictions by economists. Second, they may admit the existence of the kind of exogenous impacts suggested, but look at them as 'causes only in a secondary degree'. Obviously a settlement of such disputes between economists and other social scientists require more empirical comparative studies, preferably of a quantitative, multivariate nature, which allows an assessment of the relative importance of different kinds of variables. Still, economists confronted with such empirical data may remain unconvinced unless the results happen to coincide with their own predictions.[6]

In the following sections I will now proceed to take account of the lessons obtained from previous chapters by Alan Lewis, Alberto Marinelli and Neil Smelser, and by Britt-Mari Blegvad and Finn Collin.

ECONOMIC PREFERENCES AND LEARNING PROCESSES: PSYCHOLOGICAL ASPECTS

The vote-maximizing and budget-maximizing propensities postulated by public choice economists could be conceived as psychological constructs – even though many economists themselves cautiously refuse to admit that they are making genuinely psychological assumptions. Public choice economists seem to treat these maximizing propensities axiomatically, that is, as constants, or at least as powerful, randomly-fluctuating variables with a steady central tendency uncorrelated with other independent, explanatory variables. Social psychologists would find it difficult to accept such an axiomatic proposition, and would instead assume that this propensity is a variable related to many other explanatory variables.

Those economists who refuse to admit that their axiomatic assumptions are basically *psychological* in nature, must consequently consider any psychological argument on this point as a misunderstanding of economic theory, and therefore as completely irrelevant. What matters to 'positive economics' is not the empirical relevance and validity of axiomatic assumptions themselves, but the empirical validity of the conclusions logically deduced from such assumptions. For instance, Milton Friedman (1953) has argued that the underlying assumptions of economics are more or less convenient instruments for prediction, even if obviously false in themselves. Their falsity, moreover, in no way diminishes their scientific value, according to Friedman. The philosophical untenability of such an 'instrumentalist' stance will not be discussed here; it has been treated at length elsewhere.[7] To whisk away the need for empirical verification of basic assumptions like the one on vote- and budget-maximizing propensities, and even refusing to consider it meaningful to discuss empirical aspects of the problem, is hardly scientific. Ideological self-defence manifests itself in similar ways.

In fact empirical attempts to assess the strength, distributions and correlations of these kinds of motivational variables do not support the existence of constant or stochastically varying vote- and budget-maximizing propensities uncorrelated with other social and psychological variables.[8] Such empirical studies could help to forge a strong interdisciplinary link between psychology, economics and political science.

Alan Lewis, in his chapter in this book, distinguishes 'economic psychology' which emphasizes *dependent* variables of a psychological nature such as economic attitudes, preferences and behaviour, on the one hand, and, on the other hand, 'psychological economics' which rather focuses on the measurement of psychological variables treated as *independent*, explanatory variables contributing to improve economic predictions and economic comprehension.

By combining 'economic psychology' with 'psychological economics' it would seem possible to endogenize a considerable portion of relevant psychological variables in economic theory and econometric research: 'economic psychology' could show how certain attitudinal, cognitive and behavioural variables *depend* on economic factors; and 'psychological economics' would then demonstrate how such dependent variables of a psychological nature can be considered as *independent* psychological variables which, in a feedback loop, again influencing economic processes and events. By combining the study of this kind of psychological feedback with studies on sociological, ecological, political and technological factors which prevent or facilitate such psychological feedback, one could further expand the interdisciplinary understanding of economic processes. In terms of the typology of exogenous relations conceived in our so-called method of dissection, this can be classified as a relation of type IV – a feedback mediated by non-economic factors.

A well-known example of such a feedback loop involving social-psychological processes was discussed by Daniel Bell (1976) in his *The Cultural Contradictions of Capitalism*. He described how the capitalist system, founded as it was on the 'protestant ethic', undermined itself by replacing that ethic with the ethic of uninhibited consumption. Both a vehicle and a symbol of this change was the credit card – a most profitable invention of capitalism itself. With the help of this invention it became easier and more tempting to indulge in instant gratification. 'Unrestrained appetite' was spilling over, not only into the public sector with increasing demands for welfare services, but also into youth culture. A telling rubric in Bell's book refers to the development 'from protestant ethic to psychedelic bazaar'. Psychedelic experiences may not be as fashionable today as they were when Bell wrote his book, but on the other hand youth now is supposed to have become 'narcissistic' – again quite probably in response to life in a capitalist society. So a type IV feedback loop involving the creation of a mentality alien to the kind of self-discipline, delayed gratification and rational innovativeness which, supposedly, was a cornerstone of capitalism, has been generated by capitalism itself, according to Bell. These conjectures are longitudinal and historical in nature; in such contexts the analysis of exogenous factors in economic processes cannot avoid taking feedback loops into account.

It could be argued that these new attitudes of youth, far from being contradictory to capitalism, are perfectly well attuned to so-called post-industrial capitalism which needs less of hard work and self-discipline, and more of an ability to establish values outside working life. Whatever the argument, these are clear-cut examples of how mental states can be linked in a feedback loop to economic processes both as dependent and independent, explanatory variables – combining the perspectives of what Alan Lewis has called 'economic psychology' and 'psychological economics'. Similar feedback loops are described in a book by Tibor Scitovsky (1976) on *The Joyless Economy*.

Learning psychology is another branch of psychology which might be able to contribute to an understanding of exogenous factors such as tastes and preferences. With or without consumer education, consumers do learn from their experience in buying and using commodities and services. And, as Alan Lewis reminds us, learning theory is perhaps the most developed of psychologists' theories. So-called 'socialization' of roles, for instance, the roles of women and men, are instances of learning processes which inevitably have an impact on consumer behaviour and other economic activities.

Alan Lewis also mentions the more complex learning experiences generated by the implementation of political legislation. The reduction of taxes in California, in the spate of fiscal referenda, would seem to have led to a learning process by which voters have become more aware of the fiscal connection between taxation and benefits, whereas previously taxation was viewed narrowly as an unfair imposition.

However, most of this remains anecdotal. One of the difficulties of making more systematic use of psychological variables in *expanding* the reach of economic analysis, is that learning theories come so very close to economic theory itself. Both theories are branches of a tradition with deep roots in hedonistic social philosophy. The rewards and punishments that reinforce and extinguish activities, according to psychological learning theory, have conceptual properties very similar to the notions of utility and disutility in economic theory – similar also in the sense that they invite tautological formalism.

Faced with this problem of tautological formalism, learning psychologists usually look for some biographical or historical explanation, to avoid the formalistic predicament, while economists are satisfied with a less 'dynamic' approach, namely, the approach of 'comparative statics'. But while this may help psychologists to avoid tautological formalism, their search for a history of previous conditioning of so-called secondary needs and rewards may imply an infinite regress. Therefore it seems that psychological learning theory can contribute to expanding the reach of economic analysis only if it can overcome its own limitations, perhaps by becoming more explicit about relationships with its own exogenous factors, as is the case of *social* psychology.

On this point Kurt Lewin's notion of 'ecological psychology' becomes useful (Lewin 1951). This term refers to a psychologist's concern for the boundary conditions which mediate non-psychological, external and, in that sense, 'ecological' impacts on human beings. This psychological approach becomes quite useful in understanding the impact of external non-psychological factors on the psychological processes of learning in the type of information system found in competitive markets.

According to market theory, one of the main advantages of the market economy is that it provides the consumer with competing alternatives, the marginal utilities of which are determined by the consumer through a trial-and-error, that is, a learning process, which at the same time generates aggregate figures of demand on which producers of commodities and services can base decisions on supply and prices.

But for such utilitarian comparisons of competing alternatives to make sense, a number of conditions must be fulfilled. Usually these conditions are summarized in a phrase on the availability of information on the given alternatives. For a large number of goods and services such information is generated through repeated use and comparison of several alternatives, that is, through a trial-and-error type of learning process. Repeated alternating use, then, is a main 'ecological' prerequisite for such a learning process to take place, or rather *repeated use with repeated alternative purchases*. Otherwise you cannot change your mind and buy another make or brand next time, if you wish. Another prerequisite can best be defined in terms of *how quickly the effective properties and the use value of the service or commodity make themselves felt for the consumer*. Even frequently-repeated purchases do not contribute to a trial-and-error learning process, if the properties and potential 'errors' of the commodity or service purchased reveal themselves only very slowly in the trial-and-error process, for instance, after several years of use. Even worse are cases when such *effects of the use of goods or services are both negative, delayed and irreversible*, as is the case with certain pollutants and chemicals. Then the availability of alternatives is purely academic from the point of view of the consumer. The consumer may have died, or suffered irreparable physical damage before he can make his next purchase in this truncated trial-and-error process.

Repeated everyday use with repeated alternative purchases, prompt display and experience of the effective properties of goods and services, absence of effects which are at the same time negative and irreversible – these are some of the 'ecological' preconditions, in Kurt Lewin's sense, that must be fulfilled for market forces to function in the manner theory assumes. This argument is particularly pertinent in understanding the shortcomings of the so-called neo-liberal advocacy for privatization and commodification of public health services in welfare societies of the Scandinavian type. Health services simply do not fulfil the 'ecological' conditions of frequently repeated use and purchases, prompt display of the effects of using these services, and the absence of possibly negative and irreversible effects. These 'ecological' conditions are required to allow the kind of trial-and-error processes associated with a competitive market system assumed to benefit consumers. There are other conditions which could be added for certain types of public goods such as health services whose availability for mass consumption depend on collective and solidaristic solutions of an institutionalized kind (Persson 1980, 1986).

The absence or presence of the 'ecological' and institutionalized conditions just mentioned obviously are most important exogenous factors in economic processes. They constitute *external parameter plug-ins*, their impact focuses on the parameters of the information processing which is a prerequisite in a market economy, and they may generate market imperfections which cannot be eliminated. To the best of my knowledge there is very little systematic research on the extent to which such exogenous preconditions actually exist for different categories of goods and services, as assumed for the operation of utilitarian comparisons in competitive markets. In all fairness such research must deal, not only with the irreparable kind of market imperfections just mentioned, but also with the administrative imperfections associated with the delivery of politically-institutionalized public services outside the market. Politically speaking, however, such administrative imperfections must be dealt with as such, through administrative reform; they should not be replaced by market mechanisms which cannot safely deliver the services demanded by all consumers, due to the absence of the 'ecological' and institutional conditions which I have pointed out.

Another field of psychology, which may need more attention when we look for exogenous factors plugging into endogenous economic processes, is the psychology of the 'subconscious' which is concerned with the libidinal, aggressive or otherwise self-assertive or self-defensive emotional complexes which may manifest themselves in the tastes and preferences of the market-place. But even though the psychology of the 'subconscious' may appear to emphasize aspects very different from the adaptive learning and concept formation which attracts most of the attention in Alan Lewis's paper, the relationships of these two psychologies to economics would seem to be very similar in one respect: Both of them plug into the preferences, tastes and expectations of consumers, and thus constitute *independent variable plug-ins*.

It is conceivable, however, that the psychology of the 'subconscious', by its emphasis on seemingly more irrational aspects of mental states and overt behaviour, may help us to identify exogenous *parameter plug-ins* as well. The psycho-dynamics of the 'subconscious' may act to nullify parameters of elasticity in econometric equations, for instance, by making people completely insensitive to certain market appeals of price and quality, while making them more sensitive to brand names and brand symbols. But obviously this kind of psycho-dynamic mechanism would be interesting from the point of view of economics only if it is shared by a larger group of people such as a generation or a subculture.

In his chapter, Alan Lewis mentions 'lexicographic' cognitive construct theory as a more promising alternative than learning theory. But just like learning theory and, indeed, neo-classical economic theory, it seems that cognitive construct theory needs to be firmly anchored in external realities in order not to become formal and simplistic. In previous chapters Blegvad and Collin, and myself, have elaborated upon the usefulness of lexico-graphic theory in bridging the gap between economics and other social sciences, including social psychology.

Apart from the deviant or deviously subconscious mechanisms mentioned earlier, and apart from some of the information constraints indicated in ecological psychology, most psychological variables seem to relate to economic processes in the shape of exogenous independent variable plug-ins, sometimes also in the form of psychologically mediated feedbacks from economic processes to independent economic variables, as the references to Daniel Bell's book suggested.

While psychological theory would seem to plug-in rather easily into economic theory – at least in terms of content, if not always in style and form – there is another subject matter of social science which by its very nature would seem to resist any 'plugging' into the equations of economics, namely, legislation. Legislation offers an alternative to the flexible adjustments of the market-place – an alternative seemingly incompatible with the kind of processes represented in the models of economics. Yet I will indicate one or two ways in which legal science might help to specify extremely important plug-ins in econometric equations.

ECONOMIC LEGISLATION: NULLIFICATION AND EMERGENCE OF ECONOMIC PARAMETERS

Legislation can determine certain quantitative parameters of economic activities such as interest rates, taxes and tariffs. The state with its monopoly on printing money determines money supply. These are clear cases of exogenous variable plug-ins.

But these kinds of plug-ins are not yet clear illustrations of the incompatibility hinted at above between certain types of legislation and a free market economy. Less ambiguous is the case of price control where prices are fixed by government statutory order, for instance, by freezing prices at a certain level. In this case legislation intervenes by eliminating the core mechanism of a free market economy – namely, price determination by demand and supply – replacing it with a completely different and incompatible price-fixing mechanism. How can this possibly be represented as an exogenous plug-in into economic processes if the core of the economy is being destroyed or nullified? Plugging into a non-existent entity would seem meaningless.

The nullification of economic *parameters* is the key word here. A parameter attaining the value of zero is not meaningless. Consider an extreme case: an elasticity coefficient b_i is set at zero. When multiplied with the variable x_i the product becomes zero, and the additive shift parameter a will then determine a greater part of the dependent variable y. Considering the oversimplified case of only one independent variable x, the nullification of b implies that the econometric equation $y = a + b \cdot x$ is converted into $y = a$, a 'legislative' equation.[9]

Lexicographic preference theory, to the extent that it implies that moral and legal preferences occupy higher-ranking preference subsets when compared with economic preferences, would certainly imply such nullification of elasticity, and similar slope parameters of demand for *certain* goods, and services relating to the lower-ranked economic preferences, that is, for goods and services which are not morally or legally allowed. But empirically, the situation may be complicated by substitution effects.

As most economists can tell you, drastic price-fixing legislation will not have straightforward effects, and simply produce any value $y = a$ which legislators intended. Various substitution effects may emerge. Producers may create shortages in the regular market, and instead sell their products at a higher price than a in the so-called black market. The informal sector of the economy will swell at the cost of the formal economy. But how can this latter conclusion be expressed econometrically?

If I may be allowed to try myself as an amateur econometrician, my hint is the following: parameters in econometric equations are interlinked so that the nullification of one parameter b_i pertaining to the 'formal' economy affects another parameter b_k referring to processes in the 'informal' economy. This parameter b_k which previously had been zero, or close to zero, now 'emerges' as a significant parameter in its own right. The coupling of nullified and emerging parameters can be written in its most general form as: $b_k = f(b_i)$. This general form allows us to consider more than one kind of outcome in the coupling of legislative and economic effects.

Economists quite naturally tend to emphasize the deleterious effects of legislative interventions or collective agreements by pointing out the emergence of informal and less effective substitutes for the regular economy. However, since predictability and convertibility are desirable premises for economic decision-making in certain cases such as international trade, collective agreements have occasionally met with the approval of economists, at least for some limited time, and explained endogenously as a rational choice. The so-called Bretton Woods System with its fixed exchange rates is a case in point. In this and similar cases where predictability would seem to be a prerequisite for maintaining the flexibility of the market in other respects, the coupling of nullified and emerging parameters seem to be of a different order than in the case of the emergence of an informal economy as a result of legislative interventions.

However, in the long run the nullification of economic parameters such as elasticity coefficients, by legislative or equivalent mechanisms, seems to generate unacceptable consequences; and at some point the system may collapse, as indeed the Bretton Woods System eventually did, only in order to be succeeded by a less predictable system of floating currencies.

It is a challenging task in a dialogue between legal and economic science, to determine when the predictability and constancy introduced by legislation can be seen as an asset, and when it becomes a burden inducing a breaking up of legal rules, and a return to the more flexible adjustments of the market – or perhaps to the flexibility of recurrent negotiations, a negotiated order being more flexible than a legislated order but less flexible than the market. Expressed in the terminology suggested in my earlier chapter on a lexicographic preference-actor-structure approach, the question now emerges how, when and why adjustments are made 'with respect to' what is actually preferred in a higher or lower preference subset, taking the assets or burdens of legislation, or of economic 'rational choice' into account (see p. 218).

In confronting such theoretical challenges one often forgets asking the questions: Assets for whom? Burdens for whom? Who are the *actors* for whom certain legislation is a burden, or an asset?

In economic theory actors are usually invisible, and represented by variables; in legislation and legal theory the definition of an actor or a person is often crucial. The 'legal person' is a matter of legal definition. By legislation a sociologically-existing collective agent can be acknowledged as a legal person or fail to receive such legal acknowledgement, thereby being made into a non-entity, legally speaking. Such a sociologically-existing legal non-entity may find it more difficult than a legal person to respond to the assets or burdens of economic legislation. Their entry on the stage, to become fully visible and legalized, perhaps at some later time, often takes place in the context of disruptive historical events.

Here we encounter another, and perhaps more severe difficulty in establishing links between exogenous legislation, or institutionalization in an extended sense, and endogenous economic processes. In order to find ways to resolve this difficulty I will now turn to some relevant remarks in the paper by Martinelli and Smelser.

THE AGGREGATION OF INDIVIDUAL PREFERENCES, OR CONTESTS OF COLLECTIVE INSTITUTIONALIZED RATIONALITIES?

Martinelli and Smelser in their chapter have called to our attention that one of the strategies of economic theorists for coping with the increasing complexity of human behaviour and social relations – the attempt to apply the rational choice model of economics to non-economic areas of collective action – is yielding a kind of pluralism, 'admitting whatever separate kind of rationality that might qualify; there seems to be no end of the road'.

Paradoxically, this kind of 'scientific imperialism' may help to generate theories very different from classical and neo-classical economic theory. But, as Martinelli and Smelser suggest, this 'pluralist' attempt at widening the scope of economic theory may also, ironically, help to throw doubts on some of the basic assumptions of rational models.

Martinelli and Smelser are not satisfied with the 'babble-of-voices' effect that this pluralism creates. One of the conclusions they draw from their thoughtful commentary on various ways of expanding the reach of economic theory is that the rationality postulated is

> ultimately located in organizations and social structures that institutionalize that rationality, and that theory in the social sciences consists in part in systematizing the rationality of institutional complexes. . . . Thus when the pursuit is fused with the goal and when there is a quest for collective identity, the actor behaves 'rationally' according to a different rationality from that of the *homo economicus* (p. 185).

Geoff Hodgson also emphasizes the institutionalizing of rationality in his contribution to this book.

This emphasis on the institutional and organizational structures which constitute the boundary conditions of rational choice also helps to illuminate the multiple institutional demands and rationalities which often impinge on individual actors who are involved in several institutional complexes at the same time, or consecutively in the course of their lives.

Depending on the degree of crystallization *or* cross-cutting of opposing organizational and institutional loyalties and 'interests', the actors involved must attempt to 'balance off and come to terms with a multiplicity of bases for priority-making, decision, and action' between themselves *or* within themselves, respectively. It is significant theoretically that the extent of external *versus* internal struggles and trade-offs are due partly to legal definitions of the actors involved. In a system of workers' self-management, for instance, the contradiction between capital and labour is situated *within* a legally-defined actor, the workers' council, while in capitalist economies the contradiction, and possibly emerging compromises and trade-offs, are enacted *between* opposing actors (see Himmelstrand and Horvat 1987). Organizational realities reflected in legal definitions (or vice versa) may thus crucially influence the kind of contests of collective rationalities emerging in a given society.

When we consider the significance of such organizationally and perhaps legally-defined conflicting or interlocking 'multiple rationalities', we can no longer be content to aggregate individual rationalities involving preferences within consistently formulated utility functions. Instead we must envision a kind of meta-rationality, according to Martinelli and Smelser (p. 185), which concerns decisions involving the relative priorities among ranges of types of utility. For the *collectivity* the contest among rationalities also poses a priority question, and converts the process into a political and economic one, in which the relative merits of different value-positions, interests, and definitions of the situation become the order of the day rather than the taking of decisions on the basis of a clearly-perceived and consistent set of preferences.

Martinelli and Smelser believe that a modification of our thinking along these theoretical lines will 'prove to be more realistic and interdisciplinary than our present ways of thinking'. In a previous chapter of mine I have suggested a way to 'modify our thinking' – so-called lexicographic theory – which has also been suggested by Blegvad and Collin in their chapter, and which hopefully could fit at least some of the formal requirements of neo-classical economic theory at the same time as it responds to the obvious need to take into account both organizational and legal definitions of relevant actors, and the contest among collective rationalities, within or between collectivities.

THE EXOGENOUS DOMAIN: 'PLUGGING-IN' AND LOOKING OUT

Two equally important and potentially cross-fertilizing approaches and areas of research emerge from our attempts at deriving lessons from different social-science disciplines in building an interdisciplinary framework for the analysis of economic systems and processes: (a) the techniques of 'plugging-in' exogenous factors such as lexicographic preference orders and their associated actor-bearer structures into economic analyses, and (b) providing economists with better maps of the 'exogenous territory' so that they will be encouraged to look out at that outside world for the benefit of their own understanding, if not for the building of their models.

Plugging into the endogenous

First of all there are the kind of plug-ins suggested by the so-called method of dissection. Among these the *exogenous variable plug-ins* can usually be handled without difficulty within the neo-classical paradigm as long as they can be treated as cardinal variables. In the appendix to this chapter I have listed a number of the exogenous factors of this and other types mentioned in the papers by our economist participants (Hollander, Mandel, Hartley and Bowles). However, the kind of constraints emanating from exogenous lexicographic preference subsets cannot be expressed in cardinal numbers; they rather exhibit a binary on-off character; they could therefore be handled crudely but effectively in the shape of so-called dummy variables (see below). The constraints emanating from lexico-graphic preferences structures may also appear as some kind of *exogenous parameter plug-ins*. Such parameter plug-ins can easily if somewhat crudely be handled with the help of dummy-variables, so called shift or slope dummies, which are made to affect the parameters a and b in econometric equations, as I have hinted in my brief discussion of legal impacts on economic processes above.

So-called shift dummies specifying the value of the parameter a in an econometric equation are sometimes used by economists to account for seasonal influences on econometric data. A shift dummy can be specified to take on the value of unity for one season, and the value zero at other times, and will thus indicate the degree to which a relationship shifts between different seasons by augmenting the constant a of the equation.

Dummy variables affecting the shift as well as slope parameters of econometric equations, and thus constituting so-called exogenous par-ameter plug-ins, can also be used to take account of other qualitative exogenous factors in quantitative economic analysis – for instance, the onset or discontinuation of some particular state intervention or policy, or the imposition of some particular lexicographic meta-ranking of preference subsets.[10]

Very often dummy variables are introduced rather arbitrarily with a minimum of theory that could account for the 'plug-in' effect of such a variable. For this and similar reasons theoretically-minded economists with a 'commitment to formalism' often frown on the use of dummy variables in economic analysis. This negative attitude would seem less justified when dummy variables are derived theoretically, say, from lexicographic preference-actor-structure theory. However, a negative attitude to the plugging-in of lexicographic meta-preferences in economic analysis by way of dummy variables may still persist among economists unless lexico-graphic preference theory can attain a degree of formalization that econom-ists can accept.

The 'commitment to formalism' which prevails among several different 'schools' of mainstream economics might be a main hindrance for relating theories such as lexicographic theory to the neo-classical models. Given that commitment it must seem very complicated to try to include, that is, to endogenize 'all kinds of variables' in economic models. References to psychological states such as expectations and shifting perceptions strike the formalist as vague and seem impossible to formalize. Therefore such variables must remain exogenous. Unless, of course, they can be endogen-ized under the umbrella of so-called imperialist public choice theory.

At this juncture some of the points made in the introductory chapter of this book should be reiterated. As I have emphasised in Chapter 1, the so-called IDEA Project has not been aiming at the endogenization of 'all kinds of variables' in formalist economic models. Quite the contrary. To endogenize an exogenous variable, for instance, a given lexicographic meta-ranking of preferences subsets, or the behaviour of politicians, and of legislative and administrative bodies, implies that such exogenous variables are made subject to explanations in terms of economic theory, as indeed is the case in public choice theory (see Keith Hartley's chapter in this book). But as far as the philosophy of the IDEA Project is concerned, there are extremely good reasons for allowing certain variables, extricated as they are from the exogenous terrain, to remain exogenous in the sense that they remain unexplained by economic theory but are explained by other social science theories. Once that is reasonably achieved we must look for ways in which the interlocking of exogenous and endogenous domains of economics can be attained in more precise and formally satis-factory ways.

By way of summary we thus have the following five tasks to accomplish:

1 First there are a number of non-preference type of exogenous variables which economists regularly take into account – such as budgetary con-straints, money supply, available technology, and so on – which should be systematically listed and conceptualized to facilitate plugging them into economic equations. This is already, to a considerable extent, achieved in economic analysis.

2 The preference-type of exogenous variables should be made subject to lexicographic analysis, and the mathematization and formalization of lexicographic preference theory should be further developed. With suc-cessive and successful mathematization and operationalization of lexico-graphic theory the resistance among some economists to such theory may be minimized, and allow the 'plugging-in' of lexicographic prefer-ence subsets into neo-classical and related economic theory, after some necessary and potentially fruitful amendments of economic as well as lexicographic theory.

3 In order to make it possible effectively and realistically to incorporate lexicographic preference theory in economic analysis, methods should be developed and applied for empirically establishing the existence of relative consensus or dissensus among classes and strata of a given population with regard to various kinds of lexicographic meta-rankings of preferences subsets.

4 Concepts and techniques for the study of normative as well as causal-theoretical and empirical linkages between lexicographic preference rank-ings and economic processes – for instance, with the help of theoretically derived shift and slope dummies, or functionally equivalent but more sophisticated plugging-in techniques – should be developed and applied.

5 Other targets which lie a bit further into that enigmatic 'exogenous terrain' must be dealt with later on, within the broader range of prob-lems indicated by lexicographic-preference-actor-structure theory. They

require us to look out for the historical growth and degree of structural specialization and polarization of the actor-bearers associated with different lexicographic preferences subsets, and the underlying structures of more or less constraining or contradictory normative, economic, technological, organized and natural orders, the breakdown or growth of lexicographic preference orders, and so on.

With regard to points (3) and (4) above – the plugging-in of lexicographically ranked preferences into economic equations – I would like to make a few additional remarks. A lexicographic ordering which ranks legislated requirements higher than economic preferences, can be plugged into economic equations by setting a fixed and forbiddingly high 'price' on legally-proscribed activities, goods or services, thus making them completely unattractive in a rational choice situation. If this 'price' is a legal fiction only, without any other reward than compliance itself, that is, with a self-conscious assertion of doing the right thing, then that kind of situation would closely conform with the idea of a lexicographic ordering which ranks legal requirements higher than any economic preferences. However, in real life and given the fallibility even of socialized human nature, the forbidding 'price' may have to be more than an imperative legal fiction, and make a demand for substantial real payment whenever the given rule is broken. But the setting of a real, material 'price' in the shape of a large fine is, of course, an indication that we distrust the realism of lexicographic preference theory.

   Yes, perhaps the realism of such a lexicographic preference theory can be called into question, if monetary punishments and rewards turn out to be necessary to make more high-ranking preferences or requirements maintain their higher rank. Blegvad and Collin have discussed this particular case, and maintain that 'although most people may obey the law out of prudential (=egoistical) considerations most of the time, and some people may do so all the time, still not all people do so all of the time'. And these authors continue to assert that the very existence 'of such non-prudential action is all that is needed for this to constitute a theoretical problem for the integration of legal and economic conceptions' (p. 201). And this theoretical problem cannot be evaded in a reductionist manner by saying that 'the prospect of enjoying a clean conscience' is nothing but a 'utility' of the kind identified in public choice theory. An agent cannot be rewarded with 'a clean conscience' unless he views 'the action performed as normatively right, and hence as independently motivated, in the first place' (p. 202). But still it is obvious that lexicographic preference theory is far from 100 per cent realistic.

   In the case of economic theory proper, its own lack of realism sometimes makes its adherents shift their appreciation of the nature of economic theory. It is no longer considered as a manifestation of a realistic, 'positive' science, but as an exhibit of a normative approach defining what kind of requirements *should* be fulfilled to qualify us to talk of rational, economic choice. Similarly, a proponent of a lexicographic preference theory could retreat into appreciating such a theory as a normative theory only. But in both cases – both in the case of economic theory, and in the case of lexicographic preference theory – we should keep an avenue open to make these theories into empirically reasonably valid 'positive' theories. This can be done by asking and empirically answering the query under what empirically documented conditions that these theories become empirically valid. My own attempt in a previous chapter to sketch a number of theoretical and empirical research tasks within a so-called lexicographic preference-actor-structure approach did attempt to specify how we could move in such a direction.

Once the research programme indicated from (1) to (5) above has been reasonably well accomplished, it would be much easier to conceptualize the operation of all kinds of feedback loops, or forward and backward linkages within one and the same composite multi-disciplinary or even interdisciplinary theoretical framework for economic analysis. At that stage it would not be incorrect to speak of *the endogenization of economic theory into a broader interdisciplinary framework* which takes into account the 'embeddedness' of the economy in a larger context of normative, technological, organized and natural orders (cf, Swedberg, Himmelstrand and Brulin 1987). This amounts to nothing less than turning public choice theory upside down, since this theory proclaims to have achieved the endogenization of non-economic exogenous variables into economic theory, while we are considering the possible endogenization of economic theory into the broader theoretical nexus of lexicographic preference-actor-structure theory. But as yet this is only a challenging possibility which remains to be realized.

The IDEA Project has certainly not achieved, and never aimed at attaining, such a level of interdisciplinary theoretical integration in one or a few steps. However, we have outlined a path in five steps along which such achievements could be sought.

Such an undertaking may not only improve the scientific quality of so-called *positive* economics, without sacrificing much of its formalistic elegance. It may also help to make the *normative* or perhaps 'ideological' applications of economic theory more adequate and relevant to the normative and ideological problems debated in contemporary society. A larger number of preference subsets could be taken into account without imposing on them the attributes of economic preferences. If economists are at all concerned with their standing and their reputation in wider circles than the community of established economists – and their reputation in those wider circles is no longer what it used to be, as admitted even by many economists themselves[11] – then it is imperative to reassess the simplistic and oftentimes unrealistic normative advice rendered by economists to decision-makers in the 'exogenous domain'. Lexicographic preference-actor-structure theory, even in a tentative and unfinished stage, or a lexicographic preference theory pure and simple, would seem to provide useful vehicles for such a reassessment.

Furthermore, such theoretical and normative reassessments would enhance relations between economists and other social scientists, and could possibly provide non-economist social scientists with impulses for improving their own disciplines that are more fitting than those provided by present-day public choice theory. In fact lexicographic preference theory, or the broader-based lexicographic preference-actor-structure theory as I have come to understand them, and to apply them tentatively in this paper, do not belong to any particular social science discipline but lend themselves to applications in most such disciplines. Their application with the help of insights from the various social science disciplines is therefore not simply a vehicle for multi-disciplinary research and analysis, but a truly interdisciplinary venture.

Looking out at the 'exogenous terrain'

Research on the 'exogenous terrain' obviously must be carried out, not by economists, but by economic historians, sociologists, political scientists, legal scientists, demographers – and human geographers, who were invited to participate in our project but unfortunately did not deliver. Of course it might be said that such research has been pursued for quite some time by economic sociologists and other social scientists specializing on the interface between their disciplines and economics (see Swedberg 1986). But what is required now is a much more concerted and systematic effort guided by an adequate theory and with methods that makes it easier to compare and cumulate research findings, and to relate them to the kind of 'plug-ins' into economic theory suggested above under (a), and in Chapter 1.

From the various papers submitted to our project, and the way in which Blegvad and Collin and myself have been able to integrate crucial arguments from these papers within lexicographic theory, I conclude that this kind of theory, supplemented with notions of actor-bearers, their degree of specialization, and so on, could be an effective vehicle for such a concerted and systematic effort. This is a conclusion, a finding on my part. I had no particular stake in lexicographic theory when this project started, but I have become convinced of its fruitfulness as a result of our work within the project. It remains to be seen what the fruit is going to be like.

But while lexicographic preference theory, pure and simple or formalized, might be plugged into economic theory in ways acceptable to many economists today, what is there to be gained by economists in the much more broad-ranging, unfinished and informal lexicographic preference-actor-structure kind of theory suggested in chapter 14, in view of the fact that this 'exogenous terrain' as such cannot easily be 'plugged into' economic theory in the shape of single exogenous variables? One obvious answer is that the new brand of economists that we are expecting need to be enlightened by 'exogenous' experts on actually existing lexicographic preference structures, and their associated structures of actors, institutions, technological and ecological orders, to be able to set some of the exogenous parameters of economic analysis, not by arbitrary stipulation, but with reasonable realism. This is not a question of developing and applying formally stringent plugging-in techniques, as under (a), but rather a question of improving the *intuitive* element no doubt involved already now when economists, implicitly or explicitly, stipulate assumptions underlying their formal analyses, and offer advice to decision-makers in industry or government. Even if it takes a decade or two for non-economic social scientists to render satisfactory information of the kind required, it may also take some time before that new brand of economists emerge in sufficient numbers. Meanwhile even tentative findings and groping attempts to build this bridge between the disciplines would seem to be better than sheer guesswork.

Second, some economists, constrained by their necessary concentration on rather limited and theoretically stringent models of economic processes, may feel a thirst for *Bildung*, and for a historical awareness which cannot be fully satisfied within their own discipline, and which unfortunately has been lacking also in several other social science disciplines – except for some rather nebulous versions produced by temporarily fashionable social philosophers. The kind of explorations into the 'exogenous terrain' suggested above, if carried out with sufficient coherence, historical depth and comparative cultural scope, could help to end this poverty, this lack of *Bildung* among both economists and other social scientists, for the benefit of intellectual discourse, and an understanding of the human predicament, as seen in relationship not only to the subject matter of economic analyses.

NOTES

1 Substantive scientific imperialism implies not only the application of the methodology of a particular discipline like economics in a number of other disciplines but also the application of its ontology. This is the case when marginalistic rational choice is assumed to constitute the very nature and reality of human action in a number of disciplinary domains beyond economics proper, and when deviations from such rationality are seen as insignificant cases, or as a result of exceptional circumstances. Blegvad and Collin have discussed the tenability of this ontological assumption in their chapter in this book. A purely tentative and heuristic application of economic theory, without accepting its

implicit or explicit ontology, is possible, however. This heuristic use of economic theory in explaining non-economic events comes close to what Max
Weber called the ideal-type approach. Another much more controversial
approach implying a methodological use of economic theory without necessarily accepting the underlying ontology is the instrumentalist approach of
Milton Friedman (see note 7).

2 In addition to the so-called formalist school of economic anthropology, with
its roots in neo-classical economic theory, there are two other orientations –
substantivism and Marxism – which have questioned the adequacy of formalist
theory when applied to primitive economies. For an insight into substantivist
theory see, for instance, Polanyi, Arensberg and Pearson (eds) (1957) *Trade
and Market in the Early Empires* and Sahlins (1972) *Stone Age Economics*. For
Marxist economic anthropology see, for instance, Godelier (1972) *Rationality
and Irrationality in Economics*, and Meillasoux (1981) *Maidens, Meal and
Money*.

3 I owe this telling example to Bo Rothstein, a Swedish political scientist.

4 'Crowding-out' is defined in *The Dictionary of Modern Economics* (Pearce (ed.)
1981) as 'A fall in either private *consumption* or *investment* as a result of a rise
in government expenditure'. This is because increased government expenditure
'reduces the real money supply which in turn reduces the amount of money
for speculative purposes', and this leads to a fall in investments. Obviously this
seemingly authoritative statement does not take into account that considerable
portions of government expenditures cover present or future costs which otherwise would have to be covered by private, non-governmental agencies or
companies, perhaps sometimes at lower price and quality levels. For studies of
crowding-out effects see, for instance, Buiter (1977), Barker (1980) and Taylor
(1979). A textbook treatment of different types of 'crowding-out' can be found
in Lipsey (1983: 680 f and 766 f).

5 A side-remark on the political economy of the so-called crowding-out effect
is justified on this point. Just as working classes in some advanced industrial
countries are told that complaints about the lack of relative improvements of
their position in comparison with other classes are beside the point, since
absolute improvement is what counts in terms of Pareto optimality, the same
argument could be advanced in the other direction. So-called 'crowding-out'
does not necessarily imply a deterioration in absolute terms of the resources
available for investments, production and profits in the private sector. They
can continue to grow in absolute terms in periods of normal economic growth
in spite of the 'crowding-out effect'. The predicted weakening of international
competitiveness as a result of the smaller magnitude of absolute improvements
of the position of private capital in countries with large public sectors is another
matter, which brings us back to our politico-sociological argument about comparative advantages. A slack or recession in the international economy is also
another matter, and could be due to other causes than crowding-out.

6 The tendency for economists to favour theoretical conclusions (often based on
ideologically-selected premises), rather than conclusions based on thorough
empirical research, was illustrated in a debate in a leading Swedish news-
paper (*Dagens Nyheter* 85–03–30 and 80–04–20) between the economist Assar
Lindbeck and the sociologist Walter Korpi. The economist tended to emphasize
the methodological difficulties in empirical research while completely neglecting
the difficulties of drawing valid political and practical conclusions from simplified theoretical models. Compare Samuel Hollander on John Stuart Mill in this
book!

7 Friedman was heavily attacked by Paul A. Samuelsson (1963) who coined the term 'F-twist' to designate Friedman's instrumentalist position. For a critique of Friedman's instrumentalism, see also Nagel (1963: 211–19), Rosenberg (1976: 155 ff) and Blaug (1980: 103 ff).

8 The Swedish political scientist Leif Lewin (1988), in a well-documented book, *The Common Good. On Self-interest and Common Interest in the Politics of Western Countries* (in Swedish), has summarized and commented on most of the literature and available research findings on so-called vote- and budget-maximizing tendencies. See also Leon Lindberg's chapter in this volume!

9 In empirical fact we can expect deviations from the legislated '*a*' – probably in the shape of Floyd Allport's (1934) classical J-curve.

10 Dummy variables are also in common use in comparative sociological or political science studies where different nations can be introduced as dummies.

11 See Thurow (1983).

BIBLIOGRAPHY

References to other chapters in this book have not been included in this bibliography.

Allport, Floyd H. (1934) 'The J-curve hypothesis of conforming behavior', *Journal of Social Psychology* 5, 141–83.

Barker, T. (1980) 'The economic consequences of monetarism: a Keynesian view of the British economy 1980–1990', *Cambridge Journal of Economics* 4.

Bell, Daniel (1976) *The Cultural Contradictions of Capitalism*, New York, Basic Books.

Belshaw, Cyril (1986) 'Culture, holism and the limits of the exogenous', unpublished paper written for the *Second IDEA Symposium*, Maison des Sciences de l'Homme, Paris.

Blaug, Mark (1980) *The Methodology of Economics*, Cambridge, Cambridge University Press.

Buiter, W. H. (1977) ' "Crowding out" and the effectiveness of fiscal policy', *Journal of Public Economics* 7.

Etzioni, Amitai (1985) 'Encapsulated competition', *Journal of Post-Keynesian Economics* 7 (3), 287–301.

Friedman, Milton (1953) 'The methodology of positive economics', in M. Friedman (ed.) *Essays in Positive Economics*, Chicago, Chicago University Press.

Godelier, Maurice (1972) *Rationality and Irrationality in Economics*, London, New Left Books.

Himmelstrand, Ulf and Horvat, Branko (1987) 'The Socio-economics of Workers' self-management', published in a special IDEA issue of *International Social Science Journal*, no. 113, 353–64.

Lewin, Kurt (1951) *Field Theory in Social Science*, New York, Harper & Row.

Lewin, Leif (1988) *Det gemensamma bästa. Om egenintresset och allmänintresset i västerländsk politik* (The Common Good. On Self-interest and Common Interest in the Politics of Western Countries), in Swedish, Stockholm, Carlssons Bokförlag.

Lipsey, Richard G. (1983) *An Introduction to Positive Economics*, 6th edn, London, Weidenfeld & Nicolson.

Meillasoux, Claude (1981) *Maidens, Meal and Money*, Cambridge, Cambridge University Press.

Nagel, Ernest (1963) 'Assumptions in economic theory', *American Economic Review* 53, 211–19.

Olson, M. (1982) *The Rise and Decline of Nations. Economic Growth, Stagflation and Social Rigidities*, New Haven and London, Yale University Press.

Pearce, David, (ed.) (1981) *The Dictionary of Modern Economics*, revised edn, London, Macmillan Press.

Persson, Gunnar (1980) 'Skall sjukvården privatiseras?' ('Should health services be privatized?), in Swedish, *Ekonomisk Debatt* 4, 284–7.

Persson, Gunnar (1986) *The Scandinavian Welfare State: Anatomy, Logic and Some Problems*, London, Sticerd London School of Economics Welfare and State Programme Publications, no. 7.

Polanyi, Karl, Arensberg, Conrad and Pearson, Harry W., (eds) (1957) *Trade and Market in the Early Empires*, New York, The Free Press.

Rosenberg, A. (1976) *Microeconomic Laws. A Philsophical Analysis*, Pittsburg, University of Pittsburg Press.

Sahlins, Marshall (1972) *Stone Age Economics*, Chicago: Aldine Atherton.

Samuelson, Paul A. (1963) 'Problems of methodology – discussion', *American Economic Review* 53, 231–6.

Scitovsky, Tibor (1976) *The Joyless Economy*, New York and Oxford, Oxford University Press.

Swedberg, Richard (1986) *Economic Sociology: Past and Present, Current Sociology* 35 (1), 1–221, London, Sage Publications.

Swedberg, R., Himmelstrand, U. and Brulin, G. (1987) 'The paradigm of economic sociology. Premises and promises', *Theory and Society* 16, 169–213.

Taylor, C. T. (1979) ' "Crowding out": its meaning and significance', in Cook and Jackson, (eds.) *Current Issues in Fiscal Policies*.

Thurow, Lester (1983) *Dangerous Currents. The State of Economics*, New York, Random House.

A synopsis of statements on exogenous factors (in chapters by Hollander, Mandel, Hartley and Bowles)

EXOGENEITY – GENERAL STATEMENTS

Hollander on J. S. Mill

According to John Stuart Mill a *general* theory of political economy would, ideally, combine a variety of specialist scientific treatments each taking into account motives other than wealth maximization – for instance, 'aversion to labour' and 'the desire for the present enjoyment of costly indulgences' – these other motives generating 'disturbing causes' within a more restricted field of economics. This notion of 'disturbing causes' might be considered as referring to a certain type of 'exogenous factors'.

Mandel on classical Marxist economy

Exogenous factors (= partially independent variables) can determine the speed, direction, degree of homogeneity/heterogeneity of capitalist development but not overturn the general historical trends of the capitalist system; furthermore they are 'partially independent' since they also to a significant extent are dependent on the 'endogenous' capitalist mode of production, and they reach the limit of their 'exogenous', independent impact when they threaten to eliminate basic mechanisms (parameters) of capitalist society. Therefore 'the impact of the extra-economic variables upon the economic process is seen in turn as being at least partially determined by the logic of the economic system itself'.

Hartley on neo-classical theory

Exogenous factors subdivided into: preference functions, technology, government, population and natural resources; their effects on demand and on supply incorporated into equations; a distinction is made between exogenous factors within the system, that is those which in principle can be endogenized, and exogenous-endogenous factors outside the system (weather . . .) which cannot be endogenized. Exogenous factors are the explanatory variables; but there are also explanatory parameters which are endogenous to economic theory. Furthermore there may exist 'exogenous-exogenous' variables that explain preferences, technology, etc; for instance social class, education etc.

Bowles on post-Marxist theory

Exogenous factors are, in addition to consumer tastes and technologies, the non-reproducible inputs of land etc, and the distribution of ownership, or initial property claims, as historically determined. 'For most analytical tasks it is useful and not misleading to consider some aspects of a problem as exogenous . . .' But usually the couplet exogenous/endogenous is replaced in post-Marxian theory by the couplet structure/practice. Seen in a sociology-of knowledge perspective the exogenous-endogenous distinction appears as follows: the *priests* of neo-classical theory find this distinction useful in deflecting the criticism of economic injustice, insecurity, the dictatorship of the workplace etc. to an exogenous domain of government and voters' preferences; the *engineers* of neo-classical theory seeing the exogenous variables rather as means for manipulating the economy; the *critical scientist* asserting that the distinction 'has little value except as a scholarly simplification'; the *militant*, applying the practice-structure distinction rather than the exogenous-endogenous distinction, is looking for interventions within a given structure which are able to enhance the possibilities for structural change by taking the structural parameters not as a datum, as in neo-classical theory, but as objects of analysis and militant mobilization (exogenous parameter plug-in?).

BIOLOGICAL AND NATURAL CONSTRAINTS AND ADVANTAGES

Hollander on J. S. Mill

Biological constraints; food demand relatively inelastic = exogenous parameter plug-in. Natural advantages; soil, climate etc. affect shift parameters exogenously.

STRUCTURE AND LEVEL OF PRODUCTION, TECHNOLOGY, ECONOMY AND SOCIETY

Hollander on J. S. Mill

Division of labour, and specialization has 'a debilitating effect upon – the individual – but not on collective intelligence.' 'What is lost in the separate efficiency of each, is far more than made up by the greater capacity of united action' (Mill). Division of labour is therefore a social structure

endogenously chosen for economic reasons, and feeding back on efficiency.
– Social structure: the relationship between the lending and borrowing
classes; distribution of activities between manufacturing, agricultural and
mining with their different amenability to improvement vs. diminishing
returns; distribution of work force between unproductive and productive
classes – all of these exogenously affect variables and parameters in the
equations of economics.

Technological change increases productivity of labour = exogenous
parameter plug-in affecting shift parameters; but technological change also
emerges as an economically (endogenously) determined variable 'in the
prospect of a remuneration from the produce'. Technology of retailing:
the 'transport revolution' eliminates market imperfections that cause price
differentiation by location if not by product.

Hartley on neo-classical theory

Technical change is a classic case of an exogenous factor which embraces
all types of plug-ins, spill-overs and feed-back effects (types I to VI
according to the method of dissection); information technology offered as
an illustration, and its impacts on competitiveness of firms, environmental
spill-overs, employment and unemployment, family and leisure, government, and on Society as a whole (*Type VI effects*).

MARKET IMPERFECTIONS: BLACK MARKETS

Hartley on neo-classical theory

'If left to themselves private markets might fail to work properly'...
monopoly, oligopoly, entry barriers, restrictive practices may emerge;
externalities – neo-classical economics recognizes that there is a role for
Government in 'correcting' such market failures. – However, through
prohibitive legislation (for instance laws banning or restricting the consumption of alcohol, cigarettes and drugs; type I and II plug-ins) black
markets may be created which feed back on supplies and prices (Type IV
feed-backs).

LABOUR AND INDUSTRIAL RELATIONS: CLASS STRUGGLE

Hollander on J. S. Mill

'Trustworthiness of labour, and friendly industrial relations – which themselves have sociological sources' – exogenously affect labour quality. –
Manpower quality which is partly culturally determined is an exogenous
independent variable plug-in (Type I).

Mandel on classical Marxist economics

Class culture and consciousness, historically derived; the specific political traditions of bourgeoisie, petty-bourgeoisie and working class; differences in 'modern revolutionary tradition' influences present-day development of capitalist economy. Class Struggle, intensity of, as a dependent variable (feeding back on the economic process) 'is much more a function of the relative militancy of the working class accumulated as a result of the *previous* phases of the business cycle, than a straight function of *current* levels of employment (could be interpreted as a historical, lagged exogeneity). – In what rhythm a historical process will 'radicalize' the employers, or the workers or both will depend on a variety of 'other circumstances' which therefore can be considered at least partially as 'exogenous' to the current economic process itself.

Hartley on neo-classical theory

Subject to the costs paid for policing and supervision, and given a certain employment contract, employees will seek to obtain additional utility from their working situation, for instance, through on-the-job-leisure which will be reflected in organizational slack and X-inefficiency. This may seem to be an exogenous effect of labour psychology, but could as well be deduced endogenously, given the structure of management-labour relations, and assumptions about individual self-interest which are endogenous to economic theory.

Bowles on post-Marxist economics

Labour as (1) object (input), and (2) as agency. Aspect (1) is emphasized both by classical Marxian theory and by neo-classical economic theory in their treatment of the combination of labour, and non-labour inputs; (2) is emphasized by post-Marxian theory which rather emphasizes the Labour extraction relationship, that is the combination of labour power with whatever inputs the owner allocates to *induce* a specific level of work intensity. This inducement takes the form of authority (hierarchy), surveillance and control, threats of firing in combination with maintaining job scarcity which makes it costly for labour going slow, or challenging authority, due to the risk of being fired. Effects are not only resentment but also a lowering of efficiency which is a cost that the capitalist is willing to accept in order to maintain the basic authority and exploitation which is fundamental for the capitalist system. – The Labour extraction relationship is endogenous to capitalism in post-Marxian theory, but appears in neo-classical theory as a variable exogenous cost of surveillance and control depending on the quality of management-labour relationship.

INFORMATION AND EXPERIENCE

Hartley on neo-classical theory

Information: ignorance and uncertainty (exogenous variable or parameter?) prompts continuous equilibrating tendencies rather equilibrium (cf. Austrian school on moving equilibrium); it also leads entrepreneurs in the private sector to respond to ignorance and uncertainty by seeking to make money before anybody else and to protect this monopolistic profit by establishing property rights over the profitable ideas involved. – Learning-by-doing and experience are partly exogenous (culture, opportunity structures etc), partly endogenous (subjective utility assessments; investments in human capital); they determine buying, job search and acceptance.

PSYCHOLOGICAL FACTORS; MOTIVATION, STANDARDS AND EDUCATION

Hollander on J. S. Mill

Three types of motivation according to J. S. Mill: desire for wealth, aversion to labour, and enjoyment of costly indulgences. Even other incentives may be at work in 'theoretical science', education and health. From a national or universal point of view theoretical discoveries must be considered 'part of production'; but they are therefore not a cost on production; in the individual perspective of the theoretician it could still be considered a gain. – 'Prudence' may be an exogenous parameter plug-in, affected by education.

Note that neo-classical theory, except for the assumption of utility maximization, has little to say about motivation.

GOVERNMENT, LEGISLATION, RULES, CONTRACTS; NATIONAL vs. INDIVIDUAL CONSIDERATIONS

Hollander on J. S. Mill

'National' as distinct from an 'individual' point of view, while very important to distinguish particularly in contexts referring to education, and health expenditures, could be legated to 'some other social science'. This 'indicates strikingly that economics, narrowly defined as based on purely economic rationality was not a predictive science'.

Mandel on classical Marxist economics

The shape of the State apparatus, as historically given, depends on the extent to which the native capitalist classes have been able to use it as an instrument of 'primitive capital accumulation'; furthermore its 'historically specific' relations to pre-capitalist ruling classes etc. have an impact on present-day capitalist economies. – Military power and weight are partially independent exogenous variables, but they also partly depend on the economic strength and relationships between different 'national' fractions of the international capitalist class'. . . .

Hartley on neo-classical theory

Government (exogenous) analysed in terms of characteristics of the governing party, elected politicians, bureaucracies, pressure groups, industries subject to government interventions (for instance alcohol and tobacco industries) and linkages between all these – an analysis aimed at making these elements amenable to public choice interpretations.

Government Controls on product and factor prizes will result in shortages or surpluses, and should therefore be eliminated.

Government should play a significant role only in correcting market failures through competition policy, taxes and subsidies for correcting externalities, and through preference for marginal cost pricing etc. The policy issues of choosing most appropriate policy solution should be preceded by dealing with the technical issue of identifying the causes of Market failure, and with a cost-benefit analysis appraising public sector decisions 'from society's viewpoint' which requires an inter-disciplinary approach.

Index

Note: n after page number indicates material in notes.